UNSTOPPABLE

How One Person with Autism
Is Never Giving Up on His Lifelong Dream
To Become a Teacher and Worldwide Influencer

Matthew Kenslow

RIVER BIRCH PRESS

Mesa, Arizona

ISBN 978-1-956365-58-0 (print)
ISBN 978-1-956365-59-7 (e-book)

For Worldwide Distribution
Printed in the U.S.A.

River Birch Press
P.O. Box 7341, Mesa, AZ 85216

Table of Contents

Introduction

Who Am I?

First of all, who am I?

My name is Matthew Kenslow, and back around 2001, I was formally diagnosed with Asperger's Syndrome. Up until 2013, when the Diagnostic and Statistical Manual of Mental Illness (DSM-5) came out, people were given this former diagnosis to describe a mild form of Autism. As of this writing, people are just diagnosed with Autism Spectrum Disorder.

I therefore have Autism, which came with limitations and a quarter century of trials. In 2018, I began to voice my firsthand perspective about living with Autism on my YouTube channel, which, as of the publishing of this book, has surpassed 80,000 subscribers. In the years since, I continued to upload a myriad of videos that educate the world about Autism (the pros and the cons), the multiple things that interest me (such as piano playing, juggling, photography, survival skills, aviation, emergency vehicles, and so much more that I want to share with others), and chronicling my journey through life to those who are interested. The latter is connected to the purpose of this book.

Prior to uploading those Autism Awareness and Acceptance videos, however, I began writing about my firsthand perspective on living with Autism. In 2016 I hired a literary agent who significantly helped me along this journey. Long story short (no pun intended), when I was twenty-three years old, my first book was royalty-published. It's called *Juggling the Issues: Living with Asperger's Syndrome* (2019, 2020), and it has since earned two awards.

While going through my credential program, student teaching, and during breaks, I was featured and interviewed in various podcasts, blogs, magazines (including *Newsweek*), radio shows (broadcasted on iHeart, Sirius XM, and NPR), and television news, such as *ABC7 Los Angeles*, *Scripps News*, *Spectrum News*, and *Afternoon Live*.

Whether speaking locally, nationally, or internationally, I gladly and proudly explain who we are as people with Autism. I dispel the common myths about Autism. I express how we are human beings and not aliens from some exoplanet out in the cosmos somewhere, which we are sometimes perceived to be. I impart my encouragement to those on the spectrum and their families, caregivers, and teachers. I encourage the nondisabled person to get to know us for who we are, since everyone is unique, and help us feel included.

- I never allowed Autism to have the prerogative to slow me down, which makes me ascribe the befitting adjectives *unstoppable* and *ambitious* next to my name.
- Beginning in elementary school, I have played piano and juggled for thousands of people in my area for over fifteen years.
- I earned a medal that is equivalent to the rank of Eagle Scout through the Royal Rangers.
- I wrote an award-winning, royalty-published book that is read in every habitable continent on Earth.
- I earned two science degrees and now have a full math credential from the State of California.
- I became a social media influencer with my largest following currently being over one million people on my verified Instagram page.

The bottom line is this: if I can do all these things *with* a disability, then you can too! Plus more! Nobody has an excuse. I do not take pleasure in listing out all my accomplishments whatsoever. The purpose is to communicate to the current eight billion people on this planet that people with disabilities have a purpose. I am perpetually under the philosophy that *anybody* can do whatever they set their heart and mind to do, despite a so-called "disability."

To the neurodivergent, you have a purpose. Do not allow a label to define you. Set your standards on yourself and not on other people. You can do it if you *choose* to.

To the neurotypical who does not yet understand neurodiversity, please open your mind. Please learn what Autism is. Please learn what all the other disabilities are. Accept us as human beings in lieu of lost causes. Believe that there *is* purpose for us and that we should not be used as objects to poke fun of or to demotivate. Essentially, stop judging a book by its cover.

Regardless of already accepting neurodiversity, if you notice anybody around you at your school, work, or house of worship that may have a disability and are usually alone, then please go to that person and be a friend to them. Introduce them to your other friends. Find out what they are comfortable doing and help them feel included. If there are people walking around the neighborhood that might be perceived as strange or like a wild animal, they might just have a disability, so just smile and say hi as you pass by each other.

Readers of this book are eventually going to find out why I am so passionate about this and why I am making these points and calls to action now. The only reason I accomplished everything that I did in life thus far is not just living out my passions (what makes me feel valued and belonging), but to show the world that we can be unstoppable and reach our fullest potential, regardless of what the world tells us!

The sooner people accept this, the sooner this world will be at relative peace. Nothing will stop me from communicating that to every single person in the current population and the next generation.

My current goal is to teach mathematics at a middle school and maybe add science thereafter. In this book, I will articulate the steps of my journey from the beginning to the present day to become a teacher, disregarding all the demotivation that others (including my mind) endeavored to give me, overlooking all the discrimination that I faced in the interim, and overcoming all the limitations that come with Autism.

I will reveal things that might make me nervous to reveal, but if I am not honest, then I would be doing a great disservice to Autism. I would be no different than a bully. I will explain what I had to go through (especially socially and academically) just to get to where I am now. It might even shock people as to what was really going on behind the scenes throughout this adventurous journey.

Notwithstanding my limitations and being heavily discriminated against, I am not giving up on my lifelong dream of becoming a teacher. In the end, I hope that this book takes the reader on a thrilling adventure and above all, provides motivation to anybody who is considering doing what they love to do in life, especially those affected with a "disability."

~1~
THE EARLY DAYS
(How It All Got Started)

My passions of both writing and teaching started around the same age and has stayed with me all my life. My earliest recollection of wanting to become a teacher was about first grade. I made a lot of friends, but because I was shy and rarely spent time with any of them after school, I used my free time to do a diversity of things. Alone.

One of those things included playing school. I would pretend to be the teacher and do everything that my teacher would do, from taking attendance to teaching lessons to assigning homework. My mother gave me an unused checkbook register of hers and that was my "attendance sheet."

Who were my students? Let's just say that I had a lot of stuffed animals.

This continued throughout the rest of elementary school, but soon the stuffed animals morphed into invisible students. My lessons would parallel what I learned at school, such as teaching expanded notation versus standard notation in third grade. They would also reflect what I was interested in to teach, such as American history, geography, and mathematics.

Growing up, I was almost always excited for the first day of school. I would sometimes be excited to the point of sleeplessness the night before.

I was the one who always went back to my former teachers to say hi and give an update on how things were going, even after I left each school. All the teachers appreciated that and felt great that they made such an impact on one of their former students.

I was mainstreamed in third grade, which meant that I had proven I could handle a normal, large-sized class, unlike the smaller, special-day classes that I was in from kindergarten to second grade. This also meant that I had to go to a different school, Newport Heights Elementary of Newport-Mesa Unified School District.

Toward the latter third of the year, there was a fundraiser. Students would buy raffle tickets for one dollar each. After writing their names on them, students would drop them in a bag and whoever's name was drawn at the end of the fundraiser became "Teacher for a Day." My heart was set on it, so much so that if I did not win, I said that I would be very sad for a long time.

The day of the drawing finally arrived. Some of the students spent their birthday money for this, I overheard. I was one of the early birds at the flag deck.

One of my classmates told another, "I'm not going to win. I only put one ticket inside."

Eventually, my teacher came up to the microphone. He pulled the ticket, and it was the student who said that she was not going to win. Oh well.

I took it as a lesson of humility. A lot of us had dozens of tickets in there, but the winner only put in one. She said that she was not going to win, but she ended up winning anyway. She also did a great job being Teacher for a Day when the day arrived, bringing us candy as an incentive for correct answers and good behavior.

I tried again the next year, in fourth grade. One of my friends said that if he won, he would make me student teacher. I said likewise. Out of all the tickets I put in that year, I put this friend's name on one of them.

Early one morning, as the day of the drawing drew closer, my teacher, mother, and I sat down at the back of the classroom. My teacher heard that my heart was so set on becoming Teacher for a Day that if I did not win, then I would be very sad.

My teacher gave me a good pep talk, during which she drew a ticket out of the bag at random, just to simulate what might happen. The person whose name was drawn was my aforementioned friend; looking at it, it was my handwriting. However, I did not say anything. Her point was to show how there were chances of winning or not winning, and to have good sportsmanship.

The day finally arrived. I said good-bye to my mother and went to the flag deck. My teacher went up to the microphone and drew a ticket. My name was called and echoed around the entire property!

I was ecstatic on the inside. I looked out the school gate and noticed that my mother stayed the entire time. She had both of her hands over her mouth and was pacing back and forth. After school that day, I got a present and a balloon from her.

On April 20, 2005, I got to be Teacher for a Day, and it was one of the best days of my life. I wore a lanyard badge with my name on it. I also designed a makeshift word search with all the students' names to find, which my teacher said was very cute. That is what she told others during the party, which was held at lunchtime. These used to be held on Wednesdays, which are early-out days. School was over five minutes after lunch, so unfortunately, Teacher for a Day did not last a regular full day. Nevertheless, it was a fun experience.

Winning once did not stop me in subsequent years from trying again. In fifth grade, I competed with a classmate. She and I perhaps had the most tickets in the bag, roughly one hundred of them or more (to the best of my memory). She ended up winning that year, though.

My last opportunity was sixth grade. My teacher came up to the microphone at the flag deck and pulled out a ticket.

"I know he's going to die when I say this. It's Matthew!"

I jumped up in excitement and felt privileged for this second opportunity.

Leading up to the big day, I began to fill out a notebook of things I wanted to teach, which included American history and geography, neat trivia, and more. One day after school, I went over it with my teacher. She said that she would not ordinarily teach all of what I put down. However, she thought it was great that I was organizing and planning ahead of time, but other things needed to be covered.

The day arrived—May 30, 2007. My fellow classmates called me "Mr. Kenslow" for the day. It was, once again, one of the best days of my life.

During my two years at Ensign Intermediate School, however, my career plans had changed. I was ultimately set on becoming President of the United States . . . seriously. I enjoyed history, especially presidential history. I loved the idea of writing historical documents and giving speeches. Many students told me that they would vote for me.

As a freshman at Newport Harbor High School, during the Resource Specialist Program (R.S.P.), we took a test on the computer. After a litany of questions about our interests, my test results said that I would be good in finance. That got me wondering.

As a sophomore, I told my R.S.P. teacher, "Hey, I think I know who I want to be—an officer or a doctor."

She thought for a second and replied, "An officer? That's too dangerous. And a doctor? That's ten years of college, Matt!"

Ten years of college?! I thought. I never knew that.

In retrospect, I am a little perplexed that I actually considered being a doctor, due to the fact that I was struggling in Honors Biology that same year. In fact, I always hated science. My perspectives began to shift once again. It depressed me to see most of my classmates in Honors Biology understand the content. I was close to calling a conference requesting that I get transferred to a normal biology class, as if that would help.

But I chose to persevere! I do not know how, but I ended up getting a B in that class after my final in June 2011.

In the meantime, my mother, whom I expressed my struggles to, helped me out and referred me to a series of books that she found at Crean Mariners Branch Library in Newport Beach, which taught the building blocks of literacy, mathematics, science, and social studies. The series was made for teachers teaching kindergarten through sixth grade.

I not only taught myself out of those books over the next few years, but it also brought back my early desire to become a teacher. I would pretend to teach out of these books to my invisible students in my room. During free time at school, walking home from school, or walking around the neighborhood, I would mentally go over what I learned. This would continue for years to come.

At last, science became more and more understandable to me. Plus, I picked up on things I forgot in the other subjects. I took on the mission to make everything as concise and understandable as humanly possible, and to have an explanation for anything when asked, even if a person randomly asks me a question in the middle of nowhere.

—2—
SOLIDIFYING MY DECISION TO BECOME A TEACHER

In September 2011, a person from the Mentor Program came to speak in my English class. I was a junior, and surprisingly, I was not totally set on becoming a teacher. The person gave us a small packet that included a list of possible careers. When we chose one, a mentor in that field would come over and talk to us about it.

I thoroughly looked over it and raised my hand.

"I don't see President of the United States on here," I said, knowing how hopeless it would be anyway.

Thus, I looked over it again. And then I saw it. *Teaching.*

I therefore chose teaching to be my career pathway. This one instant in my life in English class had catastrophically eradicated most of my other passions. I was positively set on becoming a teacher.

I thought, *What is wrong with me?* I should have already known that I was destined to become a teacher since I began playing school all those years prior. I told several people in my life, including my teachers, past and present.

One morning soon after, I ran into my ninth grade art history teacher, who had been teaching there for over forty years at that point. I was trying hard to explain how I was feeling inside but could not describe it.

He interrupted me, saying, "Do you know what that's called?"

"No." I shook my head.

"That's *passion!*" he said with a big smile.

Right then and there, I knew my ultimate passion was to teach others in a manner where the content makes sense.

"Which grade?" my Multimedia International Business teacher asked me when I told her. She was so happy to see my excitement after deciding upon my career.

"I'm not sure yet, but I'm thinking early elementary."

For five years thereafter, I heavily considered teaching somewhere between first and third grade. The reason I was initially uneager to teach fourth, fifth, or sixth grade was because of the science projects that I always loathed. However, self-teaching myself science through those aforementioned library books made me less fearful.

Sometime later that academic year, I visited my third-grade teacher over at Newport Heights Elementary, who, at the time, was teaching second grade.

"Had you ever watched the movie *Front of the Class*?" he asked me.

"I haven't yet," I replied.

"Well, I think you should watch it. It's about a man who has Tourette's Syndrome. He never gave up and became a teacher. If I find it, I'll give it to you to watch."

"Okay, I would love to watch it. Have you ever watched *The Ron Clark Story*?"

"I have not."

"It's an inspirational film about a teacher who went to New York. He never gave up and found a teaching position, where he brought the troubled class up to reaching their full potential."

Later on, the teacher found the DVD of *Front of the Class* and gave it to me. I also gave him the DVD of *The Ron Clark Story*, which I had watched many times in the past.

"It might make you sad," he warned me, "because he has Tourette's, and nobody believed in him at first."

I understood and acknowledged it but was still excited to watch it anyway. As soon as I got home a few blocks away, I put in the DVD and watched the entire movie. The next day after school, I watched the whole movie again as I did many times throughout the summer. It became one of my favorite movies.

The fact that Brad Cohen never gave up, especially enduring all the hardships in his life, became an inspiration to me. Having Autism, I have endured similar ableism (the discrimination against people with disabilities). I was reassured that I, too, can land a teaching career. The scene where Mr. Cohen enters his classroom for the first time with that awestruck countenance gave me the feelings that he must have felt—excitement and passion. I knew that one day, that *would* happen to me too.

Unfortunately, something occurred that summer that made me feel torn about it for the next six years.

―3―
SIX YEARS OF CONFLICTION

"Do you want to be CPR certified?" I barely heard over the morning announcements.

I was in my eleventh-grade U.S. History and Geography class. I knew that I had to be CPR certified to earn the Gold Medal of Achievement at Royal Rangers. This is the equivalent to the rank of Eagle Scout, which was very important to me. After searching around the library and office, I finally found the place where I needed to go to sign up. This was because students tend to talk during the morning announcements, and I could not make out where to go.

It turned out to be the ROP class, Emergency Medical Responder (EMR), from June 25 to July 19. I signed up for it and, as my first book describes in detail, I barely made it in the class, due to being on the waitlist. This fifteen-day class played a pivotal role in my life. This was not just a first aid/CPR course; this was the precursor to taking an EMT class. We were trained in various medical procedures that a basic first aid course would never teach.

All of a sudden, I had an equal passion to help people in the medical field. I felt alive at the thought of saving lives. I sought to continue with the next steps of training!

At the last minute, I enrolled in Human Anatomy for twelfth-grade science, which significantly proliferated my knowledge of biology and chemistry. Alas, I had to drop out of Trigonometry/Precalculus in order to keep that class. (More details of that story are in my first book.)

All year round, I felt very motivated and privileged to be in that class. I *chose* to be in that class. I felt proud of myself for that, as well as all the knowledge that I learned.

In the middle of that academic year, I pursued taking EMT through ROP, but it did not work out, which upset me. I decided to try taking it during the summer, but it was too expensive because I was no longer a student since I had graduated.

I began taking classes at Orange Coast College on August 27, 2013. I went in with an undeclared major. I knew that I wanted to be both a teacher *and* a person in the medical field, such as a physician assistant.

On September 8, right after beginning my journey at Orange Coast College, I was awarded the prestigious Gold Medal of Achievement with a friend of mine. After thirteen years in the program, I reached the highest rank. The Court of Honor was held at Needham Chapel, which is on the campus of Vanguard University.

From 2013 to 2016, I took general education courses for an associate degree, as well as the IGETC certification, which is designed for students who want to transfer from a community college to a four-year university. Throughout my time there, I made it in three honor societies: AGS (3.0+ GPA), PTK (3.5+ GPA), and MAT (Mathematics). I looked into MDR (the medical honor society), but it did not work out due to my busy schedule.

Semester after semester went by.

My academic counselor told me that I must decide between the two career paths and *soon*. He knew that I had exactly the same amount of passion to teach as I had to become a physician assistant.

"Look," he told me, looking straight in my eyes, "anybody can teach, but not everybody has the mathematical and scientific mind like you have."

I took his suggestion and instantly decided to go into the medical field first. Then, after I get settled in the career, I would pursue teaching and hold both careers simultaneously.

I subsequently declared Biochemistry as my major in the middle of 2016, with the nearby Vanguard University of Southern California as my number-one choice to transfer to. For the next two years, I continued taking courses in science and mathematics. I continued taking various chemistry, biology, and physics courses, and went up to Calculus 2 in mathematics.

Suddenly, something happened. In the summer of 2016, I was pre-studying my general chemistry textbook, taking notes on what I read. I would study often, even all night long sometimes. It was around this time when I began to teach out of it as if I were teaching a class, just like all those years before with those library books. (I would do the same thing with my anatomy textbook in twelfth grade.)

What occurred was like a paradigm shift. I concluded that I wanted to teach mathematics and various science disciplines at a middle school. The first school that came to mind was Ensign Intermediate School where I attended for two years. I remembered a specific brick building at the edge of that school adjacent to Irvine Ave. The building is a huge science classroom, and I had been in it a few times. Ever since that night in the summer of 2016, I had always imagined myself teaching there. My heart became set on teaching math and science at Ensign Intermediate.

Toward the end of my Spring 2018 semester, I received math tutoring in the Disabled Students Programs and Services (DSPS) building. I remember sitting there and pondering about teaching. I felt that I made a grave mistake. For years, my medical and teaching passions were fifty-fifty, but then, my teaching passion had started to increase a smidgen. I began to lose sleep over the thought that I had just wasted valuable time.

In the summer of 2018, right before my final semester at Orange Coast College, I was working at the Orange County Fair as a carnival ticket seller. Somewhere in those weeks of working, I allowed the percentage gap between my passions to increase. My teaching passion became 75 percent and my medical passion 25 percent.

Boom! I nearly lost my entire medical passion. I became set on becoming a middle-school teacher. I felt *horrible*. If only I would have known that going in to Orange Coast College. If only I had known back then what I know now, then I believe I could have saved a couple of years. Darn it!

Before I conclude this chapter, I want to explain that *all* of my semesters at Orange Coast College were memorable, and I would not trade most of the memories, learning, or friendships for anything else. Additionally, if it were not for me barely getting in the EMR course, then I would not have enrolled in Human Anatomy, which also served as a catalyst to increase my chemistry knowledge as a bonus. If it were not for all of that, on top of having medical passions, I doubt that I would have chosen biochemistry as a major and would have probably ended up being an elementary school teacher as I originally planned.

One final note: One early morning in May 2021, a family member of mine had to be rushed to the hospital via ambulance concerning a medical condition. My mother and I went over there. Long story short, that was when I lost my medical passion. It may have been because the person was family, but I became queasy and deduced that I just could not handle it, especially since I did not keep up with medical courses or training for years. Plus, living in a worldwide pandemic for over a year, I felt drained to say the least. I determined that I was always built to teach and perhaps teach students who will ultimately save lives in the medical field themselves.

–4–
MY EARLY TEACHING OPPORTUNITIES IN THE FACE OF SETBACKS

I *always* wanted to teach and volunteer with children and teenagers. I wanted to encourage and motivate them. I also wanted to add my juggling, piano music, and "magic" tricks as well. (I put magic in quotation marks because as I always say, I never do real magic, nor will I ever; these are simply skills of illusion and sleight-of-hand that I practiced.)

I love putting smiles on their faces, discerning the wheels turning in their minds, witnessing those lightbulbs go off above their heads, seeing the sense of wonderment in their eyes, and hearing the laughter after I recount funny stories or tell jokes.

In tenth grade, my former third-grade teacher told me that I could stop by at any time to juggle for his class. From October 22, 2010, to the present day (barring the COVID years), I would enter his classroom many times throughout the year. I would juggle and do magic tricks with coins, rope, and playing cards. A couple of times, I taught them the parts of a rope and how to tie knots.

One day in my junior year, I shyly asked the teacher if I could teach a lesson.

"How about you teach about Abraham Lincoln?" he asked, smiling.

"Okay," I said.

After school one day in May, I went over to Newport Heights and taught about Abraham Lincoln for an hour. The students enjoyed it. It was quite an experience to teach something to a whole classroom of children.

Over at the nearby St. Andrew's Presbyterian Church, where I regularly ushered, I endeavored to get involved in their children's ministries. They happily allowed me to observe them a couple of times, but I hardly got to do anything. Again, my goal is to both help *and* teach, with the greater emphasis on *teaching*. Previously, I did get to help out a lot at the children's church of California Victory, back when I was fourteen.

A half week before the Gold Medal of Achievement Court of Honor, I was in an orientation meeting at St. Andrew's for the children's ministries. There I came up with a description of how it feels to not be involved in children's and youth ministries; I had hopeless feelings wondering if I will *ever* be accepted to volunteer anywhere for these age groups. I described it as "literally tearing my heart."

During this time, I had been trying hard to get involved in their music ministry and become one of the leaders for their high school youth group. I spent all four years of high school going to that youth group, but for some reason, I could not go back and volunteer. (This was in spite of spending four years there and knowing all the leaders with good rapport.) A similar thing happened with the music ministry, but I described what happened there in detail in my first book.

Everywhere I went, I stressed the word *volunteer* to them. I never need to be paid for doing what I believe I am called to do.

Recounting this story, I remember trying to get involved in the Boys & Girls Club of Costa Mesa during high school to get a feel for teaching and helping out with elementary school children. I walked in one day and saw two of my friends from school who were already involved there, unbeknownst to me. We were happy to see each other. I asked if there was a volunteer application.

"To get your community service hours?" one of my friends asked.

"No," I said, for I had already exceeded my forty hours minimum, which was required for high school graduation. "I just want to volunteer. I'm not looking for a job." Even though I did not have a job, I was silently making a point that I do not need to be paid to help teach and encourage children and teenagers!

After getting the information, I left, but unfortunately, this did not work out either. However, while I was there, I saw a boy walk up to my other friend to ask something. My friend answered him, told him where to go, and the boy left accordingly. I witnessed that in awe. The boy addressed my friend by his name, seeming to have a respect for him, and did what my friend told him to do.

Having Autism and a lifetime of being rejected a lot, as well as being made fun of by younger children, even later when I was in high school, I truly wondered deep down inside, *Will I ever gain that respect and trust?*

When I took on leadership roles throughout my life and authoritatively told others what they needed to do, sometimes the response was chuckles. Other times, people looked at each other, wondering if I was serious. *Yes,* I was serious, simply following the orders of the leaders above me. Usually, they respected my directions but not without exhibiting a strange look or chuckle first.

Just to conclude the part of my story about St. Andrew's children's ministries, I was never asked to help, nor have I been told what the next steps were. Same with their youth program.

Besides my former third-grade teacher and for a brief time, California Victory, the only other organization who really gave me a chance in working with children and teens was Royal Rangers. Just as I expressed to St. Andrew's youth group, I expressed to my commanders there that I always planned on coming back and becoming a volunteer commander.

On September 11, 2013, three days after earning the Gold Medal of Achievement, I put my uniform on and went over to Royal Rangers. It was the happiest day of my life, imbued with unrelenting excitement. I could not wait to arrive there that evening.

I was walking toward the front door, thankful for such an opportunity to mentor young men, when I noticed one of the boys looking at me from the bench. He continued to stare at me until I was out of sight, but right before I entered the door, he degradingly yelled out to me, "Overachiever!"

Despite the hurt that I still feel to this day, I chose not to let that bother me. Sure, his comment lingered like a dark cloud all night, but I can tell you that my first night being a commander was quite fun. Most of the other boys were accepting of me, marveling at my awards vest. Soon, I described myself being overwhelmed with passion. I knew that this was where I belonged. I felt elated to know that I could now begin motivating more children and teenagers so that they will grow up to be the men they are called to be.

Throughout my first year, I got to help and teach. On rare occasions, I had the opportunity to handle the entire Ranger Kids (the kindergarteners, first and second graders) by myself, since we were low on commanders. The senior commander would float around on those nights and check in from time to time, only to see all the boys quietly seated and listening to the story I was reading to them.

"Wow," he said a couple of times, laughing, amazed to see a group of Ranger Kids seated quietly and on good behavior under my watch.

I have continued to be a commander every year since and was able to utilize my first aid skills multiple times, making me finally feel useful and valued while fulfilling multiple passions.

I served in Ranger Kids my first two years. When I was told that I was going to be a commander for that age group, I had to accept it, but I always assumed that I would either be placed in Discovery Rangers (third to fifth grade) or Adventure Rangers (sixth to eighth grade). I had a couple of reasons. First, Ranger Kids is a new program. When I was their age, they had Straight Arrows and Buckaroos. Second, Discovery and Adventure Rangers had all the fun outdoor survival merits (among others) that I love and *really* wanted to teach.

There were blessings, however, in being placed in Rangers Kids. For one, I gained firsthand experience of how to effectively run the age group. Furthermore, remember my passion for playing piano? Well, I sincerely desired to play piano with children singing along. In my second year, I started the Ranger Kids' Christmas Choir, which grew to be the Royal Rangers Christmas Choir. Alas, it ended because of COVID, but hopefully it will revive someday. I dedicated an entire chapter in my first book to this, in case you want more detail. (Just to quickly add, *I* play piano, and *they* are the ones singing; I do not want to ruin a good performance.)

Something else happened during my second year as a commander. I was placed in charge of the entire second grade for the entire year. There were pros and cons, but one con that I saw was the low number of children participating. Throughout the year, only four second graders were part of the program, and almost every single week, only three showed up. I have always believed that I am called to teach a whole classroom of people, not just three.

I am thankful for those four (do not get me wrong), and I gladly served them as their commander. Still, I looked over to the Discovery Rangers side almost every week, longing to be one of the commanders there. They were a huge group. Likewise with Adventure Rangers.

Toward the end of my second year, I went to the senior commander and asked again if I could move up to Discovery Rangers starting in fall 2015. A year prior, he told me to stay one more year in Ranger Kids, but this time, he accepted my request and placed me in Discovery Rangers. Soon thereafter, I asked him if I could teach the Astronomy merit, for I had developed a substantial interest in astronomy earlier in February and felt as if I could adequately teach all the requirements.

"Sure," he said.

I was ecstatic. After eagerly waiting all summer long and getting extra prepared for it, the first night back finally arrived. I was to start teaching the merit the following week. I was so excited to be teaching this merit to a room *packed* with boys between third and fifth grade.

However, it was seven o'clock, and hardly any boys showed up. Same thing for the other age groups. *What was going on?* The classes had always been packed for several years prior.

Of all the years, there appeared to be a split in the church, and we lost most of the boys and their families, unbeknownst to me. For the next few months, I taught the merit every week to only five boys on average. Again, do not get me wrong. I would definitely do this again a million times over, but I got the same debilitating feelings of lonesomeness that I had the year before, due to the small number of boys.

Nevertheless, it was one of the greatest learning experiences of my life. I implemenated different teaching strategies as well. During the months of teaching the merit, I was taking Astronomy 100 at Orange Coast College. My professor just received a doctorate, and it was his first semester teaching. One of the strategies he always employed was having us students write down one thing we learned and one thing we still had a question about. Then, at the beginning of the subsequent lecture, he would answer our questions. I did the same thing for the boys I was teaching.

I went all-out for this merit, bringing in science demos and homemade visualizations, from meteorite impacts, to building a scale model of the solar system, to having the boys walk around the "moon" (Styrofoam ball) to get a simulation of how the lunar phases work, to bringing my telescope and having them see Saturn (including its rings) and the moon, to navigating around constellations one night, and so much more!

It did not come without feeling bruised, however. One time, I must have drawn the lunar phases too quickly, insofar as drawing the same phase on both sides. One boy laughed mockingly about him "correcting a teacher." I definitely want to be corrected, when necessary, but I was not prepared for that. I really felt bad because I should have paid attention to what I was putting on the board beforehand.

Multiple times, the boys would ask questions that I literally could not answer, but most of the time, they understood. I would usually inquire of my professor and then answer them the following week. Every time I taught this merit thereafter, I always denied having any degree in astronomy and applauded them for asking the most astronomically amazing questions. However, even though I could not answer every single question, I sometimes interjected some advanced knowledge of astronomy, typically what I was learning at Orange Coast College and through independent research due to my own curiosity.

Overall, I believe that the boys enjoyed it. The senior commander at the time still speaks about one of those boys hardly liking anything about Royal Rangers, but the one thing that he was totally engaged with and excited for was the Astronomy merit that I was teaching him. That was reassuring to me, even years afterward when he retold that to me.

Furthermore, a couple of months after completing the Astronomy merit, something extraordinary happened (or at least to me, that is). It was something I needed to hear, for I started to feel discouraged about myself again.

"Can you help me with a school project, Commander Matthew?" one of the fifth-grade boys asked me. He was one of the Discovery Rangers who took the Astronomy merit.

"Sure, I can," I replied.

During the Ranger meeting, I sat down with him one-on-one and helped him with his school project. He asked questions about astronomy for himself and his friend. They were both doing an astronomy project.

"What a coincidence that I taught you the Astronomy merit and here you are, assigned an astronomy project," I said.

However, I found out that the topic of astronomy was his *choice, not a given one*. The boy told me with a huge smile on his face, "You inspired me."

That moment just about changed my life, because it changed my entire mood as to what I had been feeling. I honestly did not think that I did the greatest job in the universe teaching the Astronomy merit, and likewise with any of the other things I taught thus far within my two and a half years as a commander. I even questioned if I were amounting to anything to anybody.

I never went on the record saying this before, but even though the boys at Royal Rangers seemed to like the merits I taught (most of the time), I still went home usually feeling like an utter failure. I expressed my concern to a couple of commanders over the years, but they said not to worry about it. They consoled me that I am, in fact, doing a great job.

I am my biggest critic, as the old adage goes. Every week, I cannot help but reflect on all the points that I felt I got wrong, despite them not being detected by the boys and other commanders. My brain always reminds me of things I forgot to say or ways I should have phrased things better. My brain replays all the times I stuttered, including times when I knew the answer or knew what I was saying. There were even times over the years when I blanked out on answering a question.

Anyway, it was about that same time when I determined that I would probably be best suited to teach fifth grade. However, that summer, as I revealed earlier in this book, I decided to teach middle school.

I dealt with the pros and cons. If I taught elementary school, then I would get to teach more subjects, but I would have to put a limit on what I could teach. (I cannot teach trigonometry to ten-year-olds.) If I taught middle or high school, then I would get to teach more advanced content, but I could only choose one subject, or so I thought. I looked up Ensign Intermediate School online. I saw one teacher who taught both science *and* history, which reassured me. That solidified my choice permanently, and I have been set on pursuing teaching middle school ever since.

—5—

SEEKING ADDITIONAL OPPORTUNITIES TO TEACH DESPITE OPPOSITION

Knowing that I will always be a commander brought me peace of mind (if all else fails in life, then I have at least one place to teach at), but Royal Rangers was only once a week for a couple of hours. I therefore sought every opportunity I could to help out in Rangers during special events. Events were usually offered one to two Saturdays a month, such as merit day camps at the church, barbequing or sing-alongs at a senior citizen facility, Pinewood Derby workshops, and the Pinewood Derby itself. I would also branch out and get myself involved in sectional and district events too, such as teaching leadership merits to boys from different outposts, which were incrementally larger. Most of the time, I got to either teach and/or train boys in a skill. I also took several days (total) in commander training and conferences as well.

Nevertheless, I was not 100 percent content in my heart. I still had a *lot* of lonesome days during the week and at least half of the Saturdays. I could have helped teach, tutor, or train others during that time. I knew that I could have done more.

By 2015 and 2016, I had both painstakingly memorized and self-taught myself a plethora of knowledge in a wide range of subjects. I read and studied various science books for fun. I did "fun" algebra practice problems from websites and my old textbooks to keep up with the practice, including textbooks that I bought at garage or rummage sales.

I watched hundreds of YouTube videos in mathematics, science, and history to solidify what I learned and did the same with other subjects and trivia. I tested my retention of what I learned by going over it in my head, as if I were either teaching a class or answering a question that a random person might ask me.

I had the order and spelling of the 118 elements of the periodic table memorized just for the heck of it, as well as all the countries of the world. By high school graduation, I had all the U.S. presidents' birthdates, death dates, and term dates memorized.

For years, I desired to teach what I knew for other people's benefit. What purpose is it for me to have all this knowledge and skill if I cannot help others? I did not do it to earn money on a trivia show! I did not study and memorize all that for myself! I did not earn two science degrees for myself! I did not learn all that I needed for the Gold Medal of Achievement for myself! I did not conscientiously (and sometimes stressfully) spend all those *thousands* of hours getting my first book written and published for myself! I did not become the highly followed social media influencer I am for myself!

I did it *all* for others! I did it *all* for billions of people and the next generations! I want everybody to understand things that they do not yet understand.

I love hiking around my neighborhood, as I often did all my life, but a bonus would be running into a person who might actually need help on a homework question, or who might be curious of how the lunar phases work, or what *matter* is in chemistry, or how to work a compass, or how to tie the bowline. Or if it is at night, I can help others navigate through the constellations, despite what season we are in, or how the planets got their names. Things like that.

I always weighed myself down carrying rope with me, a pocket first-aid kit in case somebody had an emergency, a compass, pens, slips of paper, etc. I was *always* ready, as is the motto of Royal Rangers, but 99.999 percent of the time, I never got to do *any* of that. It was too few and far between to pass by others who actually said hi to me, which is a treat in and of itself since a lot of people in my neighborhood had discriminated against me for my Autism. (I decided to say that now to foreshadow what is to come later in this book, adding to the purpose and *emphasis* of this book's title, *Unstoppable*).

In October 2015, after five years of ushering at St. Andrew's Presbyterian (where I rose to the rank of Usher Captain), I decided to attend Newport Mesa Church. I immediately plugged myself into their First Response Team (first aid, CPR/AED) and soon, the AV/Tech. The AV/Tech brought back memories of when I was thirteen and fourteen and a cameraman and director at California Victory Church. Also at California Victory from 2013 to 2017, I volunteered as the sound guy, working the lights, lyrics, and graphics from the computers at the same time. This was during a once-a-month afternoon service on a Sunday. I was sometimes asked to play the keyboard too, before running back up to the sound booth. I also worked for the main church as a sound editor for a couple of months on Mondays, until my classes at Orange Coast conflicted with the schedule.

Within that entire time at both churches, I always took mental notes on how I would *teach* and *train* others. Once again, to my dismay, it never happened. I got close to finally training a boy one time with the computers and audio mixer, but he did not show up to the service, deciding not to pursue it.

In late 2015, while now attending Newport Mesa Church, I went onto St. Andrew's Presbyterian's website and saw a job opening. It was to be an assistant teacher for their WATCH After School Program for students from the neighboring schools.

Perfect! I described more details in my first book, but I thoroughly and passionately filled out the application. I called up my fellow commanders, asking if they could be references. I submitted everything I needed to. I even submitted it all twice because they did not get my first submission.

My family, friends, and I all prayed diligently. Through this adventure, I was assertive, which is quite a leap for me, as a person with Autism. After a long time of waiting, in February 2016, I got the email. To my utter disappointment, it said that the position had already been filled. However, I went back to their website, and it still said they had an opening. Perhaps it was just a mistake this entire time.

Mistake or not, I was crushed! I questioned if I was destined (or even trusted) to do *anything* in my life for a *ton* of people and not just a couple. It seemed like every time I had the opportunity, 90 percent of them left before I had the chance. The person at St. Andrew's said they would keep my information on file, but I have never been contacted. However, in recent years, they did ask me to juggle at a few special events.

In May 2016, I became a member of Newport Mesa Church, and in June, after expressing interest, I once again observed children's ministries. A few of them were on Sundays, such as JBQ (Junior Bible Quiz), the ministry for children up to fourth grade and the ministry for the fifth to eighth graders. I observed all three over the course of a couple weeks. I stayed with JBQ and the fifth to eighth graders. For the next fourteen and a half months, I volunteered at JBQ for the first service. For the second service, I alternated between AV/Tech and the fifth to eighth graders. I also attended various after-church safety trainings and meetings.

Just like at St. Andrew's Presbyterian, my goal is to *teach*. I possessed a myriad of Bible knowledge and had memorized tons of Scripture verses. However, in the beginning, I usually sat or stood there as another person being taught. In JBQ, I sometimes got to read the questions, but that was it. One of the volunteers got concerned that I was being "underused."

One morning, I was talking with the JBQ teacher about something as he was getting stuff written on the whiteboard. All of a sudden, during our conversation, his eyes widened, and he looked me straight in the eyes. "Do you want to teach?" he asked me.

"Yes, please," I responded, nearly flabbergasted that he just happened to ask that. And that was not the last time when I had the pleasure of teaching in JBQ.

So what about the other side of things? I observed the fifth to eighth graders throughout the summer of 2016. I decided that I was willing to take up the volunteer position as I did with JBQ. I talked with the lead youth pastor of the fifth to eighth graders in his office one Tuesday in September. He accepted me, and I signed a contract to volunteer. I expressed interest in giving devotions and teaching some of the messages.

A week prior to this, I talked with the Family Ministries pastor in her office. I felt that it was placed in my heart to begin a tutoring ministry at the church. I told the pastor all of my ideas, and she jotted down a page full of notes by the time we were done. My idea was for me to be present in Fellowship Hall (along with anyone else willing to tutor) for a couple of hours in the late afternoon or evening. There, I would finally get the honor to tutor students. And of course, all for free. Students can walk in and walk out as they please.

I waited patiently. That same month, as Royal Rangers started back up, something immensely special happened. The Ranger Kids and Discovery Rangers grew quite huge, in fact. For one, the church converged all of its ministries on the same night. Second, a nearby church, Lighthouse Community, heard about Royal Rangers and brought all their boys over. I was exceedingly thankful to see a big outpost again.

From 2015 to 2018, even though I got the privilege of serving Discovery Rangers, I still retained the Christmas Choir program that I established in

2014 with the Ranger Kids. Within those years, I would initiate the Discovery Rangers with the opening pledges and announcements, hand it off to another commander, and go over to the Ranger Kids' side. We would walk upstairs to where a piano was and rehearse the Christmas songs. After that and after the Discovery's recreation time, I would head back to my side and teach Discovery.

At the start of the academic year of 2016, I was set to teach the First Aid Skills merit in Discovery. I waited and had prepared for a couple years to do this. However, every new ranger in Discovery was recommended to take a couple of other merits first. That left me with only *two* boys. Yes, that's right.

As I said before, I have always wished to teach a *classroom* of boys, especially merits like Compass, Rope Craft, Astronomy, and, among others, First Aid Skills. Alas, it did not end there.

Pretty soon, the attendance of those two boys seemed to alternate, and I only had one boy at a time. That got me nervous because each week is filled with important information, and the lessons typically build on top of each other. I decided to spend time reviewing so that it would be easier for the other boy to catch up and continue with the merit the following week.

After a few weeks, both boys stopped showing up indefinitely. For a few weeks thereafter, I once again had nothing to do but just sit around in the back, while the other commander taught his merits. (Serendipitously, it was the same person who taught JBQ.) However, I did get to help out.

As time went on, I talked to the aforementioned Family Ministries pastor about the tutoring ministry that I was eager to start. Unfortunately, my idea was not accepted; instead, she was looking into a science-based after-school club at the local elementary school, College Park. Coincidentally, I had gone to preschool there. Perhaps I could help in *that* manner, she thought. Alas, I was never told the details.

Earlier in June, during the time when I considered fifth-grade teaching, I started to kick myself. I realized that I could have looked into Discovery Cube Orange County the entire time, which is a children's science center in Santa Ana, California. After applying online and sending a couple of thorough emails to check up on things, I was never contacted by them once. All I received was an automated email saying that they received the application and resume. Nobody answered my follow-up emails.

I still believed nothing was going to stop me! I volunteered as an assistant leader at Newport Mesa's Vacation Bible School (VBS) in July 2016. For one week, I helped lead a patrol of second graders, culminating with my birthday that Friday, the twenty-second. The theme was Cave Quest, and it was a wonderful experience. I felt glad to be there. I felt as though I encouraged at least a couple of the children in my group, which I believe is the sole reason why I am living—to encourage, motivate, mentor, and teach, especially younger ones.

Unfortunately, however, I could not do much teaching. I was simply the assistant leader. The leaders and assistant leaders were only there to keep everybody in line, walk them to all the different stations, help them with the crafts, and reinforce the daily theme when applicable. It was the main person at each station, along with the pastors, who did all the teaching. Nevertheless, I am thankful that I got to do it. Furthermore, moments happened where we leaders got to engage with the children and build positive relationships.

Recounting this story, I am reminded about being asked to teach a camping class for their VBS the previous year, filled with Royal Rangers skills such as rope craft, compass, first aid, and basic tips and tricks of survival. It was to be held for three of the five days. Once again, I got tremendously excited and built high hopes up. I filled out a form and communicated back and forth with one of the coordinators for the next ten days. I put quite a lot of planning into this.

Then, three days before VBS began, I got an email saying that the camping class was cancelled because of low numbers. I was utterly disappointed. However, they still allowed me to help out a tiny bit at one of the stations. That is probably what made me inquire of 2016's VBS in the first place. The setup was slightly different, so again, I only got to be an assistant leader.

Just like responding back to St. Andrew's when they broke the news to me (that the assistant teacher position was already filled), I emailed Newport Mesa back in a positive way that gave the impression of optimism. Deep down in my heart, I *am* optimistic, and I *do* have hope for the future. However, on the surface, I hardly felt that in my mind and in my body. My mind thought that I was about to reach my end!

I sincerely said, "thank you," and interjected, "maybe next year," to Newport Mesa (and similarly to St. Andrew's) within my replies. Notwithstanding an optimistic and thankful tone, I was still broken on the inside and expressed my willingness to still come and serve instead of waiting, to which I never got replies. Perhaps they would write back and say that I could teach anyway.

Although I got heavily involved with JBQ, the ministry for the fifth to eighth graders was a completely different story. Again, I expressed how much I desired to teach, but to tell the honest truth, I was never asked. From September 2016 to August 2017, every time I was there, I might as well have been invisible.

As a person with Autism, it is hard for me to go up to people. Therefore, I always waited for people to come to me. Hardly knowing anybody there (except for a few Royal Rangers who rarely said hi to me), I relied on the other leaders to introduce me. They practically never did that, assuming that I was as extroverted as they were.

(Note: This is not admitting any incompetence of being a teacher, as this book will later prove. In fact, I already proved it, because I had been a commander for three years up to this point with testimonials and continual training, and I even earned the Outpost Leadership medal in 2015. I *can* manage and effectively teach a group of boys. I did not know everything about pedagogy (the art and science of teaching) as I do now, but I still impactfully taught merits, skills, and devotions up to this point. The problem here was that I am in a *new* ministry with *new* people, and I was under *other* leaders in charge, unlike Royal Rangers where I had a relatively higher position.)

Oh well. I just walked around, week after week. Everybody was in their own zone. Most of them did not seem to know that I was present in the room. One group was playing a video game. Another group was on the other side playing another video game. Others were talking and building a house of cards. Some were playing dodgeball in the other room. Not once do I recall that youth pastor introducing me to the group once everybody gathered around for the message. At least on the day I observed the first to fourth graders, the children's pastor pointed at me, giving me some introduction.

Why did I not go back to the younger ministry? Well, since I wanted to be a middle school teacher at this point, I felt that this was the best place to be. Furthermore, JBQ is filled with younger children, and at Royal Rangers, I mostly help out with boys from kindergarten to fifth grade. Thus, I am now in a ministry where I can serve the middle-school age range.

I had dozens of messages in my heart to share, but alas, I was never asked to deliver one. I was also never asked to perform for them, such as juggling or playing the keys in opening worship. Sometimes, the youth pastor said my name in front of everybody, which made me perk up, only to hear him tell me, "Can you please turn off the lights," or something. One morning, the youth pastor asked me to come up on stage.

I was like, *Can this be true?*

"Please take this, and put it back there," he said, handing me a vase of flowers, if I remember correctly.

"Okay, sure," I faked a smile. As I turned around to watch my next step off the stage, one of the students just looked up at me with a blank stare as if I just strangely appeared out of nowhere, as if she had never seen me before. I had been there for months at this point.

I got the sense (even in retrospect) that most people did not know that I could have helped them, like if they needed to talk about anything or ask academic questions for school. I am all ears. I was there as a *minister*. I was not some robot that just stands there in the back and knows nothing but how to work a light switch or close a door. A lot of my friends can tell you that I can hold great conversations and that they enjoy talking with me. Conversely, *I* personally desire to sit down and talk with others. Otherwise, not doing so just adds to the loneliness that I have almost always felt.

I am confident, however, that if the youth pastor would have just given me the opportunity to introduce myself, speak, and perform, then it would have been a different story all those months. He definitely knew who I was and what I said I wanted to do, but he put his higher priorities first, and I had to accept that.

This story reminds me of something eerily similar that occurred at St. Andrew's Presbyterian, sometime before I switched to Newport Mesa. I believe it was Mother's Day one year. Again, I ushered practically every week, but I came in a bit earlier than usual on this day.

"Matthew Kenslow!" the worship leader spoke in his mic for the entire building to hear. The band was up on the stage, rehearsing before the service, and I was all the way in the foyer. "Please come up here, buddy!"

Exhilarated, I entered the sanctuary and triumphantly walked down the main aisle. Band members were smiling at me, which confirmed my assumption. Admittingly, I built my hopes up greatly at this time of my life, especially at this moment.

For sure, I'm finally going to be asked to play piano in front of everybody again! I said to myself, assuming that there is no possible alternate conclusion. This is why I *always* carried sheet music with me almost everywhere I went—for over a *half a decade* at this point.

"Matthew, can you please take these flowers and put them in the usher's room for me?" The worship leader handed me a vase of flowers.

"Uh, sure." I faked a smile and left, leaving the vase of flowers exactly where he told me to. As of publishing this, I have never yet been asked to play piano at St. Andrew's in over a decade.

Let us go back to Newport Mesa. I was completely giving up on raising my hopes and optimism, because in the end—almost always—I kept being turned down, over and over again, without being given a chance to show the leaders, much less children and teens, who I truly am—a person who just wants to teach, tutor, talk to, motivate, encourage, and mentor the current generation and the next. I simply wanted to share what I could do too, such as piano playing and juggling.

I did get to juggle and play piano at an annual Autism benefit called HALO (Healing Autism through Learning and Opportunities) every year since their inception in 2012. Also, throughout every year, I have been getting the chance to juggle for my former third-grade teacher's class.

But what about elsewhere? Why can I not juggle and speak for *all* the other classes? Or why not entire schools, school clubs, community clubs, churches, and their children's and youth ministries? I have just as much tenacity to make a difference in that manner as I do in teaching.

One day in years past, one of the librarians at Crean Mariners Branch Library thought I would be great at juggling for the children during a summer program they had. However, unbeknownst to both the librarian and me, they could not accept me as a volunteer because I was not yet qualified. Because it dealt with minors, I needed to obtain special clearance, the process of which must have been out of my reach. I forget exactly what the problem was, but the answer was essentially no. I would simply juggle for about ten minutes one day, and that would be it. Heck, I have been juggling at Newport Heights Elementary since my high school days. And I have been a Royal Rangers commander since 2013, where I cleared a background check and the whole nine yards.

Oh well.

~6~
2017: A Year of Despair

You may have thought that I have described *everything*; anything that could possibly go wrong in a human life was happening to me, despite just wanting to serve and help people at my own expense. That was only half of it.

Before I continue, please note that I served at several places in the past. I am not forgetting those. I had a loving and supportive family, made wonderful friends, and influenced thousands of people of all ages in my community over the years. It is just that I passionately wanted to gain all the experience in teaching that I humanly could. I wanted to share my knowledge and skills with others and teach them those things in understandable ways. The most important thing to me was that others benefitted from what I had to teach them.

Time was not the issue. I *know* I had plenty of time due to all the lonesome hours I spent by myself, seven days a week, longing to volunteer or work somewhere to fulfill this passion of mine. However, nobody was communicating with me. Nobody was responding to my emails. Those that did denied me. I spent *thousands* of hours alone all those years, when I could have made an everlasting impact on tens of thousands of children/teens at the least. Nobody needs to pay me. I wanted to build trust and positive relationships with everybody.

I concluded the previous chapter with me being in the first half of 2017. At this season of my life, I was recuperating.

First, my grandfather lost his brother on February 12. His sadness that morning, while picking me up from church, upset me, and I empathized with him. I also wished to have met his brother in person after an entire lifetime of hearing about him. At the same exact time, one of my closest aunts, being eaten up by cancer, was being placed under hospice care at the age of fifty.

Second, in early March, I had to drop my entire semester at Orange Coast College. I suffered an "academic burnout," as I called it. (I had previously dropped Calculus 1 after the second day because I could not understand the professor one bit.) I was studying hard in General Chemistry B, which was spiraling downhill. I was laboring to absorb every detail of information so that I could give an explanation to anybody who asks me a question. My chemistry professor discerned this without me even telling her. She gave me a great, wise pep talk in her office, but I was simply too far behind. Just because I dropped General Chemistry B does not mean that I ignored it. I was still reading and studying out of the textbook for months and months on my own. That way, when I reenrolled, the course would be easier for me.

My family situation was another reason I was struggling since a ton of my family members were dying throughout this decade. Another was a depressing feeling I was having: would I ever amount to *anything* besides teaching Royal Rangers and JBQ?

There I was, trying hard to memorize everything (for years and years) in order to teach, tutor, and train others (especially those who are from kindergarten to twelfth grade), but none of them were asking me to do so. Leaders involved are hardly introducing who I fully am and what I can completely do. Multiple times in all these years, I offered to the boys at Royal Rangers that if they have homework questions, to bring them in; before or after the meeting, I could try to help. That rarely happens.

On top of this, my tutoring idea at the church was not accepted. College Park Elementary had not responded back. My applications to teach had been turned down, and my e-mails seemed to have been ignored. There seemed to be unreachable requirements.

A small VBS camping class was cancelled due to low numbers. Whenever I got full responsibility to teach a group at Royal Rangers, all of a sudden, the number of boys dropped due to various circumstances. Such was the case when I took over second grade during my second year as a commander in 2014, when I taught the Astronomy merit in fall of 2015, when I attempted to teach the First Aid Skills merit in fall of 2016, and when I taught the Weather merit in spring of 2018.

Third, later that March, I lost a friend from middle school due to a heart attack. It was the second friend my age who died. Another friend from middle school had died due to a disease in 2015.

Fourth, on top of everything, as I briefly foreshadowed earlier, I am typically the target of discrimination in my area. Up to this point in 2017, I have been stared at with the strangest looks, laughed at, teased, called "a weirdo" by a man who was talking to his son, and probably likened to a dangerous person. This is all because I am a person with Autism walking in the neighborhood.

I walk down a street at a leisurely pace, and people assume that I am a kidnapper. I am not even approaching their child and if I do, then it is just me walking past them. They stare me down to ensure that I do not jump back and grab one of their children, as if I am physically strong enough to even do so in the first place. Sometimes, back in my high school days, I saw parents draw their child closer to themselves upon seeing me, even if I was hundreds of feet away.

I have been teased throughout school (mostly in elementary school), starting in kindergarten when two fellow classmates shouted angrily at me, "Go away, Matthew! You're NOT our friend!" Another fellow kindergartener shouted to me one day, "You're not playing with us!" I never did *anything* but be who I am. And who I am is simply a person with Autism who has a different lens with which to view the world and a different ability to succeed in life.

I have an impediment and may look awkward at times. However, I just wanted to be a friend. I am not an alien from outer space who crash-landed on this planet. I did not deserve to be literally voted out of people's presence in elementary school, or to have a handball chucked at my face, or to never-endingly be called the r***** word if you know what I am referring to. (*Nobody does.*) Middle school was when the discrimination started to taper off significantly.

Now allow me to divulge two more harrowing experiences that occurred around this time in my life in 2017. On two different days, I was walking around, happening to pass by a couple of middle schoolers. (In both cases, they were different groups of middle schoolers, just to clarify.)

"Where's my animal!" one of them yelled aloud upon looking up at me. We both kept walking. *Okay? That was random*, I thought . . . and still do.

Another time was at Newport Mesa Plaza on East 17th Street. A middle schooler was leaving a group of friends, saying good-bye. The other one said good-bye too, saw me, then turned back to her friend and yelled out, "Don't get abducted!"

Nearly everything that I am explaining here, I kept to myself for years. I did not talk these things out with anybody, adding to my despair. And more and more acts of discrimination continued to pile up on top of each other, so much so that I could never forget them. This caused me to lose hundreds of hours of sleep and concentration time.

And now I am spending years where I truly feel underused, misunderstood at times, rejected at places where I *know* I belong at, and invisible.

Even while I am proofreading this, I cannot for the life of me get rid of several vivid, painful memories that are flashing before my eyes every second now. (No, I do not have a photographic memory.) These include harsh memories from before 2017, as well as memories after, especially those from 2021-2023.

And *fifth*, after a couple of months recuperating by going through family pictures, followed by proofreading and adding to my trilogy that I was writing, May 1, 2017 arrived. (To briefly explain, I had written a trilogy before my first book, but my literary agent recommended that I publish a non-fictional piece about myself first. As of now, I intend to publish the trilogy sometime later.)

What happened on May 1, 2017? It was only one of the most distressing evenings of my life. Again, I was recuperating for nearly two months at this point, but this threw me into a partial relapse.

It started with a phone call in the early evening. My aunt, who was dying of cancer, wanted my grandfather to come over. She lived about eighty miles away in Mira Mesa, San Diego. She wanted only him to come over and not my mother or me. We were told that she wanted my grandfather to help install something at her house.

I am unable to explain this to anybody, but as my mother and I were witnessing my grandfather drive off in his truck, I knew deep down in my spirit what was going to happen. And I was right.

I was writing a side story in book two of my trilogy. It was early in the night at this point, and an episode of *Emergency!* was playing on our DVD player. My main character in the book has Autism too, and I was writing a scene that takes place in his seventh grade science class. In the scene, he is being misunderstood and name-called by a classmate who would not let him have a word in edgewise. Through the life of my character and the words that he says, I get to articulate the crippling hurt in my mind and physical body when such bullying happens to me. It is a sense of closure to write these things out, but also serves to educate the readers about Autism and what we go through when we are not accepted as human beings.

As I was meticulously authoring this side story, my mother interrupted me and told me to pack. Just like I knew earlier that evening what was going to transpire, she must have gotten the same discerning feeling I did.

I paused the episode of *Emergency!* that was playing, and to this day, I still remember the exact spot. A few moments later, as we were starting to pack for San Diego, the phone rang for the first time since my grandfather left. It was not on the speakerphone, so I only heard one side of it. I assumed she was talking to my grandfather. I stood nearby.

For several minutes, I heard my mother talking to someone, and she became upset. She really wanted to come over right then and there but was told no. Deep down, I was hoping for the best, since I did not hear the other side of the phone call.

Eventually, however, my mother walked toward me and whispered, "No Facebook."

Bang! That was code word for me at that instant. My aunt was dead at the age of only fifty years young. Cancer. For over half of a decade (as of typing this), I never told the story of that night and still, there are a lot more details I will not disclose here. It had just been replaying in my head all these years.

The reason why "No Facebook" somewhat served as a code word for me is because we both knew not to post about the demise of a family member or friend until it is cleared by everyone. I am sure most people do not want to find something like that out via social media. My mother was kindly reminding me. In times like these, it is a struggle. Talking about it and receiving support is my catharsis during the grieving process. Otherwise, I just hold it in, and that depresses me. With Autism, those feelings are greatly enhanced.

That is what I thought was occurring on February 12. After my grandfather painfully and tearfully told me about his brother's passing in the parking lot that afternoon, I told him that I needed to talk to a pastor really quick.

In reality, I was overwhelmed with shock. I did not know what I would say or how I would say it once I found one of the pastors. I ran (nearly sprinting) toward the sanctuary. Literally limping inside, I ran into one of the pastors. She could tell that I was upset and asked if she could pray for me. I nodded and she did, for I was crippled with emotion and could not speak. I messaged her later that day on what it was about.

My aunt was very special to me. She was the aunt who was coaching my mother in the delivery room the moment I was born. The aunt whom I lived with as a toddler with my mother and cousins. The aunt who gave me tons of big presents and great advice over the years. The aunt who I saw remain extraordinarily strong in the face of cancer. The aunt who I had last seen in person nearly five weeks prior. The aunt who I talked with over the phone just a couple days before her death.

"Okie dokie, artichokie" were the last words I heard of her voice, weak as they were.

That night, we called a family member in Texas and a couple of friends from church. The morning after, we called Newport Mesa Church and a couple of other close friends to let them know. We received condolence messages from people thereafter.

Still, with all the grief and sorrow, with all the discrimination that I have endured (from kindergarten to May 2017), with all the many rejections I received in life to volunteer or work anywhere, with the assumption of being a failure many times (even though most of the time, I was just too hard on myself), with the suffering of an academic burnout, and with the feelings of being an invisible volunteer while serving the fifth to eighth graders, my mind did not allow me to feel the total peace and comfort from all the love, prayers, and condolences of others.

I was heading into deeper despair; I am amazed to this day that I hung onto what hope I had. I somehow continued, even though I did not feel appreciated all the time.

I will be an author one day soon, I kept telling myself for years.

Then all the people in this world will understand us who have Autism, treat us like human beings in lieu of subhuman aliens, and give us opportunity. *Then* all the people who have a disability will believe in themselves. *Then* everybody on earth will feel included.

That was my motivation. That was what drove me every single day and every single night. That was my light at the end of the world's longest and darkest tunnel.

"Sorry about your aunt," one of the commanders told me before the Royal Rangers' meeting on May 3, just two days after the harsh death of my aunt. At the time, I was training one of the boys in Discovery Rangers. I was catching him up on the Tool Craft merit that I was teaching and was having him practice how to properly hold, carry, and pass a long-handled axe.

I still went to serve with all my heart and teach at Royal Rangers. It is because I care more about those boys than my own life and that it was currently one of the only opportunities that I had to serve the younger ones. Heck, *all* boys and girls in the world, regardless of who would accept me at first and who would not yet accept me.

Weeks after my aunt's passing, I went to serve the fifth to eighth graders again. Everybody was playing an original version of dodgeball that they called "Dynamite." The youth pastor came over to me with his huge smile and asked how I was.

"It's hard!" I abruptly whispered to him without giving it a second thought. I had just been dropped off. My mother was taking the death of her sister hard, which really debilitated me mentally.

The youth pastor dropped his countenance, understood what I was referring to without me explaining, and with encouragement, he whispered back to me, "Be the man. Be the man," and walked off.

I received that advice and continued to serve that morning, as I intended to, regardless. After all, that is partly why I came to church in the first place—to serve. Still, as seemingly always, I did not do much, if anything. Nobody else there knew that my family was suffering a loss, and therefore, nobody else gave me any encouragement. I once again felt invisible with an even greater sense of loneliness.

I know I cannot just go to anybody (of any age) and say that my aunt died of cancer. I know that that would not be appropriate. However, it makes me feel worse when I *cannot* speak out my mind and heart. It just feels like a lose-lose situation.

The heart-shredding year of 2017 was not yet over. Yes, you read right. In June, I lost another friend who was only twenty-six, followed by some older friends over the subsequent months.

Notwithstanding, from June to mid-July, I had written the bulk of my book, *Juggling the Issues: Living with Asperger's Syndrome.* This followed the previous one and a half months of proofreading and editing my trilogy.

On June 12, I returned to school. I was a bit numb after the burnout, but it was actually a pleasant semester. I took English 101. Also, I got to juggle for my former fourth-grade teacher's class at Rea Elementary; she moved to that school after I completed fourth grade. That brought me momentary joy in the chaos that I was living in! Again, that is part of why I am living: to put such smiles and looks of amazement on people's faces, especially children and teens. I also did my magic tricks as well, and at the end, everybody asked for my autograph.

I was more antsy, however, in July and August. On July 17, I mailed the manuscripts of my four books to my literary agent in Pennsylvania. It meant so much to me to become a published author because I assumed that everybody will finally treat me like a human being, trust me, talk to me, stop discriminating against me, invite me to speak and juggle everywhere, and acknowledge that I actually know a lot of things and care so much for humanity!

That was what motivated me to live every day to the best of my ability instead of caving in and giving up on my dreams. I just believed that every school in Newport-Mesa Unified and beyond would quickly ask me to speak and juggle for all of their students in assemblies. Likewise with every church for their main congregation and children/youth ministries.

I unwaveringly believed that every local, national, and international radio program, newspaper, talk show, and news station, from Christian to secular, would interview me in a heartbeat, like everybody else who becomes an author. This is why I chose royalty publishing in lieu of self-publishing.

However, at the same time, when I mailed my package to Pennsylvania, in the middle of July, more discrimination began. On July 30, I went to downtown Los Angeles for a late birthday trip. It was my first time being there, and I had really wanted to go check it out for a long time. My mother and grandfather came too. As we were sitting on a bench at the base of the newly opened Wilshire Grand Center, enjoying a Starbucks drink, I noticed from afar a woman staring at me for several seconds. She was briskly walking down the sidewalk, not looking where she was going, and clutching her purse strap, just staring at me. She looked fearful and on guard. We were several yards from each other, but somehow, seeing a person with Autism simply seated on a bench, she must have equated to seeing an animal on the side of the road.

After attending two funerals for my two friends in early August, and eager to hear back from my literary agent, I entered perhaps the most roughest time in my life thus far. The date was August 18, 2017. I poured out so many details in a 2020 YouTube video like a waterfall deluging over the streets of Costa

Mesa. In short, I took a neighborhood hike around dusk, as I always loved to do, notwithstanding the time of day or night.

At this time of my life, I had been pre-studying calculus with the textbook that I bought ahead of time. Almost every night, I stayed up all night long, thereby sleeping most of the day. As some may have guessed, I have watched dozens of YouTube videos too. In my defense, that Calculus 1 class wherein I lasted two days had really terrified me. I waited for almost a decade to be in a calculus class (since 2007 when I first heard the word), but now, I thought that it was impossible. Two tutors could not even make me understand it, which further made me decide to drop it.

That is why I spent all that time in the summer of 2017 pre-studying, just like I did a year prior for General Chemistry A. Doing so on my own and at my own pace actually built my confidence. I was finally understanding the intuition behind limits and derivatives. I will go ahead and just say this now, since I will not be bringing it up again. I loved that class and got a 94.9 percent, scoring high on all my exams, including one where I got a 100 percent. The professor lowered my anxiety levels and thoroughly explained everything. I did not even see anything that my first professor tried to explain. All that pre-studying helped considerably as well.

Back to August 18, 2017, when I approached Heller Park. I saw from afar a man and his child on the bench, pointing up at the stars. As I walked closer, the child recognized me. I juggled in her class a few times at Newport Heights Elementary.

Her father, on the other hand, began staring down at me once I got in sight. He would not let it up. I explained why his daughter knew me and said neighborly, "Have a good night." The only things he uttered were just low, monotone, forceful, short answers. It sounded like he was being neighborly back only because somebody was twisting his arm. That is the best way I can concisely explain it. I walked away, crossed Knox Place, and tried to enjoy the rest of my hike.

This happened before, Matthew. Just don't think about it, I endeavored to tell myself, but it was no use. In fact, something eerily similar happened in June 2014 with two teenagers on the same bench, who both chuckled at my presence and stared me down until I was out of sight. I told the story as I opened up chapter 17 in my first book. As I always do, I tried giving that man the benefit of the doubt. Maybe that was just his personality.

Most of that night, I stayed up working out of my calculus textbook again, but as always, every couple of minutes, my mind kept on bringing up that man at the park, which brought up all the hundreds of other horrible memories that I had endured all my life, as well as the current situations of the day. I will not go into detail, but I highly recommend everybody to read chapter 17 of my first book regarding "soliloquies," or watch my YouTube video about it. That is precisely what goes on in times like these, but in short, when people are mean to me, my mind gets distracted for hours with countless painful memories, and I lose much sleep consequently.

The next evening, I was once again walking around the neighborhood. It was August 19, 2017. In retrospect, I began wondering why I should continue all this labor if most of the world is going to treat me like this, hating me on first sight.

If I even become a teacher, would I *really* be able to gain trust and be accepted? Will students, families, and colleagues take me seriously?

Will parents pull their child out of my class due to a lack of acceptance of a teacher with Autism, just like the parent who pulled his daughter from Brad Cohen's class in *Front of the Class* because of his Tourette's Syndrome?

I am extremely thankful that most of the boys at Royal Rangers, their parents, and fellow commanders accepted me. Royal Rangers is the organization that consistently gave me a chance to teach, as well as JBQ. But what about the other places?

I sometimes wondered if it was predetermined that I could volunteer as long as I do not teach. (And as long as they do not notify me of such predetermination, but rather pretend that I will have a bright future one day.) I know my mind is lying to me, but I just have to wonder why. Why else was I never asked or even given a formal introduction, thereby causing most of the students not to come up and talk to me or ask me something?

And I have, of course, communicated directly and indirectly that I wanted to teach, as well as perform juggling or music. The youth pastor did invite me to play Christmas carols on the keyboard at the Family Ministry's Christmas party in 2016, but that was the first time and also the last.

Now it is August 19, and my optimism was being quite precarious. I was questioning why I should push on. Why should I move forward with all of my studies that were going to get more and more challenging?

I was wondering, therefore, if it was a waste to have spent those tens of thousands of hours assiduously self-teaching myself if I cannot even seem to help others with it. Not only was I teaching myself calculus, but I was simultaneously teaching myself chemistry. Like I mentioned earlier, I was still reading and studying several chapters of my General Chemistry textbook throughout the first two-thirds of 2017.

Additionally, this was the day before starting a new volunteer position at a new church. Thus, I was about to find out where *this* would lead. The senior pastor at Newport Mesa introduced me to another pastor who was in desperate need for a pianist who could play hymns. From August 2017 until the declaration of a pandemic in March 2020, I was the piano player at Oasis Assembly, which was a small church for senior citizens. Excepting parts of 2017 and 2018, I was the sole instrumentalist, reviving the great hymns and Christmas carols.

So back to August 19. I decided to walk through Heller Park again. This time, it was early evening and there were a lot more people there, including that man and his daughter. The daughter, again, was happy to see me, but when the father turned and saw me, he *immediately* dropped his countenance and gave me a very mean look. They were just leaving. I had just seen the father smiling and saying his good-bye to another man, but he frowned just seconds later upon seeing me for the second day in a row at the same park.

This was the ultimate test to see if I correctly interpreted him the night before. Did he really hate me on first sight because I am an Autistic walking in public? Since we had to pass by each other, as we walked closer, neither of us stopped staring at each other.

Your move first, I determined in my head.

Finally, he spoke in a low, monotone voice, "Hi, how are you?"

I put on a smile, glad that he cared enough to ask me, and replied, "I'm doing good. How are you?"

That was when the father blew up, put on a cartoonish smile, and yelled at me, "Don't *worry* about it!"

"Da-a-ad!" the daughter said and gave a laugh of embarrassment.

The father muttered something in reply to his daughter that was unintelligible as they walked off. I walked off too in the other direction. I was paranoid for the rest of what I wanted to be a cathartic neighborhood walk. I was scared to run into him again.

He had no idea of all that I can do, the talents and the knowledge I have.

He had no idea that I wrote a manuscript for a future book about Autism and what it would become for the betterment of society. He had no idea about all the years I had spent volunteering, inspiring hundreds of children and teenagers. Et cetera, et cetera, et cetera! And that was only the beginning!

The next Monday, I was laughed at and discriminated against inside a Ralphs in Newport Beach because I have Autism. All I was doing was picking out cereal, saying nothing. However, I got the miraculous opportunity to let those two teenagers go ahead of me in line. That way, I got the pleasure to return their unjustified meanness with unmerited kindness. Anybody there could easily see the remorse on their faces. Still, those two teenagers bothered me for years by continually haunting my thoughts.

That Thursday, the 24th, I was at the lowest part of my life yet. For the first time, I disclosed that I have been struggling greatly, coming forward with it in a lengthy post on Facebook. I poured out everything that was bothering me—my life, mind, and spirit.

I said in my post, "I am experiencing a month-long tornado that I never experienced in my life before . . . It takes a deal of courage to admit this (even to myself) . . . I am spiraling at a million miles per hour, and it is seriously affecting my sleep, strength, diet, concentration, etc. I have had a near nightmarish past month and some change . . . In the interim, I am extremely thankful for three of my commanders at Royal Rangers who huddled with me on August 13th to pray; their love and passion warms my heart . . ."

That is merely a fraction of the post. The post was just under 700 words long, and at the end, I noted that it took a half hour to write. Facebook gives the option to choose how you are feeling. I chose "drained." In the post, I revealed that I have been working on a project for nearly four years up to that point. The project was becoming an author and getting an encouraging book about Autism published. However, I said that I will not "disclose what it is until it comes to fruition," but when it does, it "will go all around the world and be an encouragement and blessing to" others.

Why did I not disclose the exciting news? It is because I dreamed for years to *surprise* my friends *after* the fact. I stood my ground and withheld my soon-to-be authorship from most of my friends and parts of my family. Unbeknownst to me, I still had nearly two years of waiting, which came with ever-increasing hopelessness. I wholeheartedly believed that my book would be one step closer to relative world peace, where *everybody* can finally understand and accept one another, in lieu of ignoring one another or worse.

The next morning, on August 25, I woke up once again feeling hurt inside. Recent events haunted me for a length of time. My mind replayed the scenes like a reel of film. I felt more queasy than the queasiness that I had already been feeling for several years leading up to that point. Therein lies the reason of my thinness. *There.*

I now went on the record with it, which I was not intending to do in this book, but I now believe that it is extremely befitting to reveal it, since everybody reading should have the context by now. However, there are a couple more factors as to why I am thin and hardly have an appetite. Nevertheless, I would say a chunk of the reason is because of the harsh discrimination and rejection that I have *constantly* been battered with since kindergarten.

The perpetual, hopeless feeling that a ton of people view you as incompetent, a joke, or even subhuman is indeed nauseating, if I can say so, with over twenty years of experience. Not given the chance to tutor, teach, speak to, or perform in front of *several* people is like a railroad spike hammered into my gut. I literally *feel* that pain 24/7, due to the chain link knots that are tied within me. I *know* I can teach an entire room of boys in Royal Rangers or everybody who shows up in the fifth-to-eighth-grade ministry. Heck, I *know* I can speak to an entire school or church with thousands of people in it.

The only thing, the *one and only* thing, that motivated me to move forward in this life, in spite of this lifelong tribulation, was the fact that I *will* be an author someday, influencing *billions* of people around the world to finally accept each other and themselves for who they are. And that I *will* be a respected and influential teacher to thousands of students. I do not want to be famous, and I never will be. I simply want to be a benefactor to society. (There *is* a difference in my perspective.)

The day after that, on August 26, 2017, I was scrolling through "On This Day" memories on Facebook. At that time, Facebook was the only social media I had. I saw a piano playing video that I did one year prior at a friend's condominium. Somehow, someway, in some form, I felt that I should share it publicly on YouTube. That changed my life!

I subsequently uploaded the video onto YouTube. It was my second upload in my life; my first one was in May, but I ended up making that private. Thus, "officially," on August 26, 2017, I started a YouTube channel. One of my first thoughts was the unlikelihood of getting a huge following.

I thought, *Well, if I do end up getting a huge following on YouTube while I wait to become an author, then perhaps people would respect me sooner. Perhaps leaders would trust me with higher responsibilities or believe that I can do things; I'm not incompetent. Perhaps people would take me seriously. Perhaps people would want to talk to me. I can finally begin helping others, or just be there if they need someone to talk to, or to just listen to them. People will stop rushing to their preconceived notions and judgments against people with Autism or any disability.*

But what about in the meantime? Even though I hung onto that tiny, thin sewing thread for dear life, I was still far from being an author. I was farther still from getting my degrees and starting student teaching. And in this journey, I am still being discriminated against by both the younger and the older, which is becoming more and more prevalent as time goes on. I thought 2014 was the worst year of my life in terms of discrimination. Then it was 2017, not even mentioning the relatively light discrimination that I received all throughout 2015 and 2016.

So I ask again, what about in the meantime? How did I have the strength to continue my calling all those years? Well, for one, it was Royal Rangers. Therefore, I had a place to teach and to mentor. Two, it was getting to juggle for first graders at Newport Heights Elementary throughout each year. Three, it was the new hope that I would be asked again to juggle at Rea Elementary. Four, because I have been juggling at Newport Heights since 2010, I periodically hear, "Hey, Matthew!" from children around the neighborhood or at the market.

That is what brings me significant joy. In a neighborhood where I was constantly inundated with laughter and stares (and still am), children still remember me because I juggled for them. (Such was the case of that man's daughter on August 18 and 19.) They were courteous enough to say hi, and just hearing that from them changes my entire mood for the day (as long as nobody discriminated against me right afterward). And if they stopped what they were doing just to have a small conversation with me, then that gave me total serenity. It always brings me peace amid the storms I face. I accumulated them in my long-term memory. It proves to me that I *do* amount to something in this life.

One moment greatly helped me in the midst of the storm, and it occurred in early August 2017. It was my second year volunteering for Newport Mesa

Church's VBS, and I was the leader this time, as opposed to being an assistant. I had an older group of children. By the end of the week, everybody was signing each other's T-shirts.

"Did you read what I wrote on your shirt yet?" one of the girls asked me before I left for the day.

"Not yet, but I will," I said, smiling.

"You should read it," she said, nodding her head.

After I got home, I read what she had written. I must tell you; it completely changed my life. It gave me so much hope and is one of the things I hung onto as I was being tormented with discrimination later that month.

On my shirt, she had written, "You are the best teacher ever!"

I took a picture of it and posted it on Facebook with the description:

HERE IS THE EPITOME AND QUINTESSENTIAL CULMINATION OF THE REASON WHY I DO WHAT I AM SINCERELY PASSION-ATE TO DO! Such a benevolent compliment that makes my summer and is the paradigm which cordially tells me that I am on the right track.

From VBS 2017. Maker Fun Factory Vacation Bible School at Newport Mesa Church (NMC) July 30 - August 4, 2017.

As you can tell, I got so excited that I used all caps, as it meant a lot to me, especially as a person with Autism who is just trying his best to encourage everybody on the planet, starting locally with the people around me.

In conclusion, during the latter third of 2017, the tempest was easing up greatly. I experienced much less discrimination and hardships. I heard back from my agent on October 2. He told me to cut my manuscript down, for it would be a book of over three hundred pages. In mid-November, it was complete, and he submitted it to various publishing houses to review and consider.

Now I have to be patient . . . *some more.*

Simply put, for all those years past, I tried my best to be patient as my heart was being eaten alive. I would give my life to help mentor and teach students from elementary age to high school, and ultimately become a middle-school teacher. I would give my life to juggle for tens of thousands of students all over the county in assemblies.

Meanwhile, in spite of constant rejections for the most part, as well as difficulty to have people in my own neighborhood stop jumping to conclusions against me on first sight, I refused to be idle!

—7—
No Longer Being Idle, No Matter What

Readers might have been wondering why I did not just go to a tutoring place and ask for an application. I am getting to that part of the story right now. I *did* go to one along East 17th Street.

"Do you have any applications?" I asked a person who worked there.

"Yes," the person said with a smile and grabbed an application for me.

"Thanks." I smiled back.

"Um, but just to let you know, we're only hiring people with a *bachelor's* degree or higher," she notified me as she handed me the paper.

"Oh, well thanks. I'm close to an Associate of Science Degree in chemistry myself," I said and walked out of there, feeling hopeless. I foresaw at least three more years before earning a bachelor's in biochemistry. I filled out the application anyway and put it on the shelf until further notice.

Around this time, I had a couple of alternative ideas in mind. If I could not yet be a tutor because I was undereducated (despite scoring 99-100 percent on several math exams at OCC), if I cannot be an assistant teacher at St. Andrew's Presbyterian, if I cannot teach lessons to the fifth to eighth graders at Newport Mesa Church, if I cannot help out at College Park Elementary in science, if I cannot work at Discovery Cube Orange County and teach science to children because they won't open my emails and application, then I will have to find a way to still help students. That is partly why I am on earth, after all, and I almost always had mountains of lonesome free time amid skyscrapers of knowledge to share.

As I mentioned previously, I attended Ensign Intermediate School for two years; thus, I knew the bell schedule. I knew that Wednesdays were early-out days so they did not serve lunch (well, it was an option). Therefore, students usually went out to eat at fast food restaurants. A popular one (even when I was a student at Ensign) was a Wendy's on East 17th Street in Costa Mesa.

With this in mind, from 2017 to 2019, I would walk over to Wendy's to study almost every Wednesday, arriving between 12:40 and 1:00 in the afternoon (excepting semesters where I had Wednesday courses at that time of day). Within those years, I usually studied out of my General Chemistry, calculus, and physics textbooks.

However, I was *not* there to go up to students offering my free tutoring. I needed to wait for students to inquire what I was studying. From there, they could decide if I would be great at helping them with their homework or understanding concepts in math or science. I was sure it would be a success after *one* person asked for my help. He or she might come back the next week with more questions; he or she might tell their friends that there is a person at Wendy's who might help them with their homework. Essentially, I was relying on word of mouth.

In the beginning, none of the students typically said hi or asked what I was studying until the 2017-2018 academic year. In that year, the same sets of students would come in every week. Thus, they always saw me there. They usually smiled and waved at me; I smiled and waved back. I figured that if they saw me studying advanced mathematics, chemistry, or physics, then they might recall a question they had from school. They were wondering, however, what my major was, which sparked a couple of conversations, but nothing more. I was never asked to help.

I usually studied inside Wendy's until the high schoolers left. The high schoolers came after the middle schoolers, but they too never asked for help. Plus, there were not as many of them.

Alas, in 2019, that Wendy's (where I had literally been going to all my life) shut down, like so many other classic places I grew up going to around Orange County. I felt that that was it for the time being. The place later opened back up as a Chipotle, but I had Wednesday classes at Vanguard University, and later, the coronavirus shutdowns of 2020 occurred.

In conclusion, I tried my best. Simply put, I just tried my best. And now, it was time for me to enter a new chapter in my life.

–8–
From Orange Coast College to Vanguard University and Everything in Between

On December 13, 2018, I took my final exam at Orange Coast College. It was for my Physics 125 class (Electricity and Magnetism). I was done! I successfully earned an Associate of Science Degree in chemistry. I had spent five years at a two-year college, including summer semesters, working hard. Due to my Autism, it took over double the time. I could not easily handle a full load like most of my classmates.

Notwithstanding, I was determined and persevering. My grandfather could not have been any happier. "You're the first in the family to get a college degree," he proudly told me.

On May 24, 2019, I graduated in the 71st commencement ceremony at the Pacific Amphitheater.

What did I do in the meantime? Did I immediately start Vanguard University of Southern California like I had previously decided? No. Recall that it was mid-November 2017, when I submitted my final manuscript to my literary agent. After months of waiting, on March 2, 2018, I received a contract from a publishing house that agreed to publish my book. There was one problem. Nobody had ever told me how much it cost to publish a book!

I spent the next several months in a panic depression—day and night. For two months, I tried everything known to man to earn money. I got an eBay account and tried selling items on there. I tried selling handmade greeting cards that I used to make in years past (more details are in chapter 27 of my first book). I tried selling some coins that I had acquired over the years, old books, stamps, my old textbooks, and it was just not working. Pawn shops were not returning my emails. I applied and reapplied for grants that were not chosen (or flat-out ignored).

Earlier, one of my physics classmates offered to pay me to tutor him in calculus. I said I would be happy to help at no charge. Now, I was going out of my comfort zone to ask if he still needed my help, but unfortunately, he did not.

I once again felt pitifully low. I vividly remember spending months looking out my window in gloomy despair, seeing the world pass by, being tied in knots on the inside, believing my blinds to be like metal bars. I hardly had any motivation to do anything. I just waited and waited for the day when I would become an author, but first I had to somehow come up with a large sum of money.

I *believed* in this book. I *believed* it *would* cause me to start making an impact on *every* individual on earth. I *believed* I *could* help eradicate discrimination and promote not just awareness but acceptance.

In May of 2018, I remembered hearing about an opportunity at a career fair at Orange Coast College. I went online and applied to be a Carnival Ticket Seller at the Orange County Fair. This time, a job application of mine was actually accepted, and I made it to the interview round. On June 10, 2018, I was interviewed and subsequently hired on the spot. It was my first employed job! It was one of the greatest summers.

As a quick aside, as I will tie in the relevance shortly, I came back the next year to work the same job. In both summers, I juggled for passersby during my breaks and while waiting to go inside the ticket booth. A myriad of people, children and adults alike, loved it. That brought me joy.

In my ticket booths, I always loved it when children came up with their parents. If the parents paid with a card as opposed to paying with cash, then that gave me a few extra seconds to help make the child's day. I would show each child a coin trick and sometimes juggle while sitting behind the booth's window. Their eyes would light up, amazed, and their parents were usually thankful that I did that for them as they completed their transaction.

The compound where we signed in at every shift had buttons for us carnival ticket sellers to wear. These buttons either had a smiley face or a word like "Super" on them. I usually took a handful so that I could "magically" turn a coin into a button and hand it to the child. Their smiles made my day.

"You're really fun," one of the mothers said, smiling at me.

Needless to say, I loved it when I worked at Kidland (a section of the fair whose name is self-explanatory), in stark contrast to most of the other carnival ticket sellers. I kid you not, but a lot of them would give a sigh of relief when they found out that they were *not* working at Kidland for their shift. Other times, as we were waiting to be assigned, I overheard some of them express how much they did not want to work at that part of the fair.

Not me! I want to be a teacher! Plus, I loved entertaining them. Therein lies the relevance of this entire side story.

It also brought me back to Ruby's Diner. I grew up going to one that used to be on East 17th Street, down the road from Wendy's. For several years, until it closed down, I played chess with an older friend for a few hours. In between games, we both went around the diner to do magic tricks for all the children. We met on Saturday mornings when there were a ton of families who came.

Soon, at the O.C. Fair, I found out that those buttons were just for the employees, but then they said it was fine for me to hand them out. (After all, I thought that that was what they were for.)

After I was done with my first year of selling carnival tickets, I had just enough to pay the publisher in full, with a little bit left over. I sent the 50 percent down payment along with the signed contract. According to the contact, the delivery time of the books was five months. That being said, I believed that I was going to be an author around January 2019.

So, to answer the question as to the reason why I took a semester off, it was so that I could tour around with the book. I believed unequivocally that everyone would ask to interview me on television, radio, podcasts, and websites. I firmly believed that I would be asked to speak and juggle at schools, churches, and everywhere else. That is what I have always witnessed with new authors.

I could not wait to bring joy and optimism to billions of people around the world. I could not wait for universal acceptance among people with disabilities. (Although I admit that it can never be 100 percent acceptance.)

Well, let me tell you. The fall of 2018 was imbued with ominous apprehension. I was undergoing soliloquies one after the other. Again, there are more details in my YouTube video or chapter 17 of my first book, but in short, a soliloquy, as *I* call it, is when you are alone, and your mind brings up every harsh memory of your life. It forces you to stop what you are doing and talk things out for a length of time, as if you are talking it out with a friend. A closure level is there, but a small one, relatively speaking. That is the bulk of what I remember of the dark cloud of fall 2018.

I was getting ever so close to becoming an author, and hopefully, I would not have soliloquies as much. I do not know what it was, but maybe my imminent authorship made me stressed out because it was getting impossible to be patient, especially as I continued to face discrimination and hardships here and there due to my Autism.

Soon, they will understand me, I kept saying to myself. *But right now, I don't have any authority to speak. If I'm an author or a big influencer on social media, then I would have credibility and deserve a word in edgewise with those who hate me on first sight.*

Notwithstanding this, I held on to my hope of January, until I started to worry in December that I misunderstood the contract. I eventually got ahold of the publisher thereafter. He told me that his team was projecting mid-February at the latest for my book to be ready.

In the interim, on January 15, 2019, I officially applied to Vanguard University of Southern California, submitting everything, including my "Christian Experience Statement" since Vanguard is a faith-based university. I later submitted my official high school and junior college transcripts, followed by a meeting with my new admissions counselor.

On February 12, I received a voicemail proclaiming that I have been accepted into Vanguard University with a renewable academic scholarship every year, starting in the fall semester! They said that I would be a "wonderful fit for [their] community." A couple of days later, I received in the mail a Vanguard folder with a welcome letter. I felt so privileged. I even mentioned in my book that I was planning on attending Vanguard as a biochemistry major.

Earlier in the month, I continued staying busy with Royal Rangers and the aforementioned HALO Benefit for Autism. On February 2, I taught the Compass merit to about ten boys from a couple of outposts in the section. I cannot articulate how excited I was for this, preparing for a couple of months for it. I waited since the middle of 2015 to teach Compass. It was a giant success! The opportunity to teach an entire merit on my own to nearly a dozen boys for a few hours was quite an experience. I felt like I did a decent job. The boys were on task, listening and engaging with the activities.

Afterward, I rushed over to Corona del Mar High School to perform at the eighth annual HALO Benefit for the eighth year in a row—speaking, juggling, and playing the piano. It always brings me joy. Every year, patrons gave me compliments on how well I did; and said how much of an encouragement I was. In 2018, after the show, a few students recognized me and said that they loved what I did.

"Thank you so much," I said with a wide smile. "Don't ever give up on your passions," I added, turned around, and left.

"Such an inspiration!" I heard them calling out.

I continued teaching entire merits on Saturdays for the next few months at Royal Rangers, as I have done so for years past and years since, such as Tool Craft and various Leadership merits. This was on top of teaching on Wednesday nights. Again, Royal Rangers has been a tremendous help to me in building the practice, responsibility, and wisdom of teaching. The boys were respectful and loved what I brought in to teach them.

Back to the day when I got the folder from Vanguard, I believed that my book would be ready at any moment. Unfortunately, unforeseen things continued to occur. The late winter of 2018 and nearly all of spring 2019 was a continuation of my never-ceasing, inauspicious nightmare despite praise reports. I felt that I was getting closer and closer, but still out of reach. My book was being delayed, month after month, and it was depressing me again.

Finally, on the morning of May 24 (yes, the day I graduated Orange Coast College), I received the first proof of my book for my review, along with the editor's notes. The publisher let me know that the process took twice as long as usual. After three days of reading over my manuscript, I emailed back a Word document with some corrections and updates, since a lot of time had passed since November 2017. For instance, I completely reversed my plans and decided to enter the teaching field first instead of the medical field. Furthermore, I ended up getting my first employed job. Ultimately, on May 30, I officially approved the final manuscript. On June 13, 2019, I received the package containing my free author copies. It was the most surreal day of my life!

Alas, since my life tries so hard to tear me down, there was a delay in getting it on Amazon and everywhere else, but at last, on July 9, it got on. I am bypassing the details of all the stress in between here.

On July 10, I officially launched my book on social media, starting with a huge Facebook announcement, followed by my YouTube video. I shared it across Instagram and Twitter as well. I was in the middle of VBS week, being a leader for a fourth-grade patrol. This time, it was at Lighthouse Community.

Some of the other volunteers that early morning got wind of my authorship and congratulated me. I also created a Facebook page for my book too on this day.

However, if only I had known, I would have started Vanguard in the spring and saved time. At least I had a month and a half to make a difference in the world before starting a full-time semester at Vanguard. I intended to continue touring around with my book, of course, but I knew I would have less free time to do so.

To my unmitigated dismay, most people ignored my book. Not everybody, though. Michelle Tuzee of ABC7 Los Angeles shared it on her Facebook page.

I could not understand what reality I suddenly was in. I was communicating with a plethora of people via email, social media, and in person. These included news anchors, reporters, newspapers, various Christian television networks, and Autism organizations. Even Autism organizations either never got back with me or said, "Congratulations, but we cannot endorse books."

As I kept contacting and recontacting various media personnel, some congratulated me, but many ignored it. Some were simply busy. Some told me they could not do anything because it was the wrong department.

Others like Adrienne Alpert of ABC7 said that she pushed it to the assignment desk, which was the last I heard of it. George Pennacchio of ABC7 congratulated me and referred me to Denise Dador, as she reports stories on health, but she too had other things to cover.

Juan Fernandez of CBS2/KCAL9 was also happy to hear the news, but he had to refer me to Phil Berman. I emailed Mr. Berman, and he congratulated me, saying that my "book looks fascinating," but he said that they were "just booking celebrities and stars" at the moment.

As much as I am appreciative that they at least responded to me, I could not believe what was unfolding before my very eyes.

On Twitter and elsewhere on social media (including the following years), I took advantage of every trending topic and hashtag regarding Autism and disabilities that I could find. Still, it did not matter how many hashtags I found and utilized. Most of my YouTube videos, regardless of the topic, were hardly getting views, despite sharing and resharing them with all its relevant hashtags.

I forced myself to have optimism. I kept believing that at any second or any day, somebody *has* to get back to me saying that they will do a story about it.

I contacted Michelle Tuzee, who shouted me out on her Facebook page. She said that if I truly think my book will be a good, worthy news story (*and it is, I believe with all of my heart*), then write a letter to KABC's Planning Desk explaining why and enclose a free copy of the book. I later did so but never heard back.

At the fair, representatives from two different newspapers were there. One day on my break, I went up to the person in the Orange County Register tent. Previously, in December 2015, I was in a huge article about my Autism in their Life section. Before I could tell him about my book, I noticed that he kept looking down at his cell phone and kept sounding annoyed upon responding to me. Figuring that he hated his job, I just left.

I went over to the *Los Angeles Times*. This time, I ran into a representative who was beyond impressed. He gave me the number to his supervisor. After calling him up on the phone, I found out that he was in the sales department and not the editorial department.

For months thereafter, I kept emailing the *OC Register*, *LA Times*, and *NY Times*, not to mention several news networks across the world, with no success. In the interim, I kept posting on my new Facebook page about the book. There, I have been gaining a lot of worldwide followers. How? Well, just like I spent nearly all of my income from the O.C. Fair in 2018 (along with what I scraped up on my own) to get the book published, I likewise spent nearly all my income from the O.C. Fair in 2019 on Google, Facebook, Instagram, and Pinterest advertisements. Yes, I was in a couple of those YouTube ads, promoting my book.

This is because I care so much about this! Again, I *believed* I could encourage the people in this world if only I could get a word in edgewise. I believe that by proving my competence in being an international influencer that changed the world in the name of disability *acceptance* and antibullying, then for sure, every student, parent, and colleague could understand that I am competent enough to be a teacher. I should never be taken advantage of nor be denied the career on the grounds of Autism. My plan was to do both at the same time, be a teacher *and* be an influencer to billions of people worldwide.

Other renowned teachers do both too, such as Ron Clark and Brad Cohen. Movies were made about both of them, as well as other impactful teachers. I therefore know that there should not be a stumbling block whenever I endeavor to apply for a teaching position in the future.

This was not the first time I advertised on YouTube either. In April of 2018, I posted my first video in a series of Autism Awareness and Acceptance videos. Again, I knew I was far from being an author at this point, so I chose to get an early start in telling the world that I have Autism, and this is what it is like. I felt that the world needed to hear it, but seeing how little views I got on average, I got discouraged.

I therefore continued with my plan, got a Google AdSense account, and promoted it at my expense, not receiving money in return since I was not selling anything. Regardless of the three immediate dislikes I got just for being an Autistic wanting to help others, my ad proved successful. In fact, I was contacted by a United Methodist pastor in Placentia, California, via Facebook, to speak at their Autism workshop on April 29, where I spoke in front of many congregants who attended (not to mentioned playing two songs on their grand piano). I posted my speech on my YouTube channel.

This is why I tried advertising again in 2019, and here and there ever since. I wanted everyone in the country and the world to hear about Autism and how everybody should accept one another, which is in sheer contrast to what I face daily. Being discriminated against constantly for years and years proves to me that it is not over, and if it is not over, then I will unapologetically take a stand, even if it is at my expense!

Therefore, on Facebook, I targeted locations like New York City and countries such as the United Kingdom to ensure that my message would get beyond Orange County and the Los Angeles area. I was hoping like a storm that news producers, journalists, or anybody like that would see it. Unfortunately, that *never* happened.

However, again, I did get engagement from people around the world on Facebook and YouTube. One person from NYC called me "ambitious" when I described my goal, which is (in short) getting to speak in every place in the entire world, not giving up until it happens. I loved it so much that I began describing myself as ambitious ever since, because I embody its definition.

On Facebook, I started receiving positive comments, such as the following:

"Please continue to share your story. Knowing your story helps me understand my son and gives me hope."

"Keep speaking your truth."

"We need more investment of not just money over here in the UK in our schools. Congratulations and good luck!"

"You are [an] amazing soul[.] Never change[.] Always be you[.] You have given my son hope that you can do anything you put your mind to . . ."

"Congratulations and well done. You deserve this recognition and more . . . by breaking down barriers!"

This is precisely why I arduously fought to get to where I was at, but if I am proven to have given hope to a handful, then how can the news and Christian media not accept my story? Just imagine how much more people can be encouraged and have hope imparted once I get on various programs. I never asked for money. My *heart* was what motivated me.

Furthermore, I had roughly four thousand friends on Facebook, thanks to Royal Rangers, all around the world. There were hundreds of people on every continent (barring Antarctica) who regularly engaged with me and followed my book's page.

Locally, all hope was not lost. On August 20, the DSPS of Orange Coast College allowed me to be a part of a panel for incoming students who were joining DSPS. I got to share my wisdom of surviving junior college and share that I am an author that mentions Orange Coast College in his book.

Still, I was not giving up! During the summer of 2019, I also went to Crean Mariners Branch Library in Newport Beach and Donald Dungan Branch Library in Costa Mesa (a branch of OC Public Libraries) to ask them if they would stock my new book. They referred me to their websites, but for some reason, they said no to me. Likewise with a local Target along Harbor Blvd. That did not go well either. It was utterly *hurtful* to me, especially considering what I had been through just to get where I was, not to mention the bullying and discrimination since kindergarten that my mind cannot forget.

But ready or not, Welcome Week arrived. This was a three-day event at Vanguard University that gives a tour and orientation of the university, the expectations, and the whole nine yards. Day 1 concluded with a huge family dinner.

The first day was August 26, 2019. As I was practicing the piano in between classes, a conductor, whom I met at St. Andrew's Presbyterian, came in and said, "Hey, my wife bought your book!" I told him about it during Welcome Week a couple days prior.

On the second day, I met with an academic counselor and expressed my interest in becoming a middle school math and science teacher. She recommended that I get in contact with a person in the VISTA program—an accelerated, integrated teaching program to complete a bachelor's in a science discipline, including mathematics, and a single-subject credential simultaneously.

I could take one of two paths: the normal path or the accelerated path. After talking with the person, I decided to just take the normal path. She said that that would be the most advantageous timeline in my situation. The plan was that I would complete a bachelor's degree in biochemistry and then come back to take the credential program.

I continued my education at Vanguard University for the next four semesters. I took my general courses and major-specific courses and did labs and undergraduate research as a biogeochemist at SCCWRP in the summer of 2020, and even got some of my education classes out of the way. *All full-time too!*

Indeed, I told myself and my Autism, *Listen, I will not put up with my limitations as much anymore. I have gotten better throughout my attendance at Orange Coast College. I will drill myself to perform even better than before. I can and will do this!*

My classmates, professors, and resources at Vanguard have significantly made me feel like I belonged and were always there to help me out. Orange Coast College was kind of the same, but unlike OCC, Vanguard is smaller. Thus, the professors have more time to meet with students individually, which helped me extremely in the later credential program.

One of my chemistry professors (whom I had for three semesters) is the father of two boys at Royal Rangers. My biochemistry professor (whom I had the last two semesters) is the mother of another one. Additionally, on the second day of school, I ran into a theology professor who was the father to a boy whom I mentored in years past. Furthermore, students and other professors at Vanguard were quite familiar with Royal Rangers from elsewhere, I came to find out. This is because Vanguard is affiliated with the Assemblies of God, which is where Royal Rangers originates. I knew many people, including fellow commanders and their wives, at Newport Mesa Church who attended Vanguard back when it was called Southern California Bible College. Small world, to say the least!

On the first day of my first semester, my World Civilizations II professor assigned an autobiography paper. I asked if I could submit my book, as a joke. He thought it was amazing that I had just published a book and asked me to speak about it, followed by a question-and-answer time afterward. I got to do so later on, and tons of my classmates asked questions.

"What's your major?" one of my classmates asked.

"Biochemistry!" I said without blinking, nearly chuckling.

The classmate's countenance looked as if he were thinking sarcastically, *Of course, why not?*

We all began laughing. Everybody may have assumed I was going to say "English" or something, but not something difficult like a science.

I was beginning to feel optimistic on the local level, especially since I had many things in mind.

~9~

UNDOUBTEDLY, I *WILL* GET IN LOCAL SCHOOLS AND CHURCHES

September 2019 finally arrived. I was so excited to return to a few schools that I grew up attending. I waited all summer long to tell the principals there that I am an author and alumnus who mentions the school by name. I had already signed quite a few books for my friends and family.

I finally made time to walk down to Ensign Intermediate, the school I wished to teach at, on the twentieth of that month. The office ladies were impressed that I became an author. They were there when I was a student, and both remembered me quite well.

The principal was busy at the moment. I asked if I could at least go to my former R.S.P. teacher so I could tell her. Being a bit insistent about it, the office lady called her up. I wanted to share the news with my former teachers regardless, but perhaps this would buy me time so that I could have an opportunity to talk with the principal.

I walked over to the R.S.P. teacher's new classroom and showed her my book, pointing out a part where I mentioned Ensign in it. She was excited for me. Since I was on the campus, I went to a few other former teachers I had, including my eighth-grade algebra teacher and U.S. History and Geography teacher. The history teacher could not get over it.

"Unbelievable!" he kept repeating out loud as the students were entering the classroom.

Finally, I went to my seventh grade pre-algebra teacher. She too was happy for me and took a picture of me holding up the book. We both walked to the office. By fortuity, the principal was just walking out of the office toward us, about to make his rounds. I was able to introduce myself for a brief minute. I told him about my book and showed him a part where I mentioned Ensign by name. He then heard about the picture that my former teacher took of me.

He smiled very widely saying, "I'm going to take that picture and email it to all the teachers in this school."

Yes! I said in my mind. That made my day. At least the principal found out about my authorship, a little bit about me, and told me that all the teachers would find out of what I had accomplished.

I was very happy . . . until I never got one email from *anybody* at Ensign. I believed so much that at any day, I would be asked to be a volunteer speaker and juggler in a school-wide assembly, encouraging every student there to never give up on their passions and that they have a purpose, disability or not. Or at the very least, being emailed from one teacher to do so for their classes.

Three days later, I walked over to Newport Harbor High School. I mentioned that school, of course, a number of times in my book too. Long story short, I announced my authorship to about a dozen and a half teachers and faculty. They all remembered me and were proud, including one of the security personnel. (Well, let us say that most of them remembered me.) The security guard escorted me from classroom to classroom so that I could announce that I am an author to my former teachers. Unfortunately, the principal must not have been in at that time. Furthermore, I had to rush over to my Organic Chemistry lab at Vanguard.

The next day, I went to Newport Heights Elementary to juggle for my former third-grade teacher's first-grade class. The teacher had me share my book with the class too. After getting a foot in the door, I got the opportunity to share what I accomplished with the principal. She seemed deeply in a rush, though. I kept kicking myself that I did not emphasize my willingness to volunteer in a school-wide assembly. I thought I blew it and would have to somehow obtain another chance to speak with her.

My former teacher, however, ordered a few copies and donated one to the school library. That December, after juggling again for his class, I was asked to autograph it, which I did, addressing it to the school with a big inscription of thankfulness.

Now I was off to St. Andrew's Presbyterian. It was October 3, and I had previously made an appointment to talk with the new senior pastor back on September 5. We had met before.

The pastor put on his eyeglasses to take a look at my book. "That's excellent!" he said.

I was insanely nervous to ask if I could have a moment to speak in the congregation and all the different ministries, especially the children's and youth ministries. The last thing I wanted was for him (or anybody) to think that I was just selling a book. *I just want to speak and encourage; nobody needs to pay me!*

I figured that one of the only conducive ways to do so was becoming an author, since not everyone goes through writing a book.

I was stuttering all the way through my question about speaking to the church congregation. Ever since I began writing what eventually became a trilogy, in 2013, I assumed that I would be asked on the spot to speak at St. Andrew's. Besides, I served with my heart as an usher (and later Usher Captain) since 2010. I also, of course, mentioned the church by name in my book, which I showed the pastor.

"Do you know how many authors in the church ask me to promote their book?" he sympathetically replied to me.

I acknowledged his point and resigned to my fate, disappointed; but in my spirit, I would not give up. I simply accepted that it would be a much later time . . . somehow, through additional supplicative prayer. I did, however, express my interest in juggling and speaking for the children's and youth ministries. The pastor was glad to get me in contact with one of the people in charge. That brought back hope in the dark valley through which I was walking until I kept not getting an email from the person in charge. I periodically checked in from time to time. I finally met the person on Christmas Eve while ushering their service. She was exceedingly glad to finally meet me and said that she was simply too busy to contact me. She said that we could meet for coffee after the new year in January. Unfortunately, that never happened.

Later in October, my former academic counselor at Orange Coast College helped me get in contact with the *Coast Report* (the college newspaper). He was also helping me to get my book in the library and campus bookstore. I eventually got placed with a student journalist. She interviewed me over the phone for roughly forty-five minutes, followed by a couple of additional questions later on. She then messaged me that she finished the article.

I waited a long time. Finally, I went over to Orange Coast College to the journalism building and asked the person if I could see all the previous issues.

"I'm in one of these," I said.

"Oh, you are? Which story?" she asked.

"I'm the former student and author of this book about Autism." I held up my book.

"Oh," she sympathetically said. "The student dropped. We'll get you reassigned." She turned and walked away.

"Okay, well thank you." I faked a smile but appreciated her time.

I walked out of there utterly devastated. (However, in the spring of 2023, an article about my story got published in the *Coast Report*, entitled, "Juggling with 'different ability,' not 'disability.'")

A burst of hope later occurred in February 2020. That same academic counselor I had at OCC forwarded an email to me. The library purchased my book and stocked it on their shelves.

In the middle of November 2019, I returned to Newport Harbor High School. There were still some teachers and other faculty whom I did not get to talk to back in September. The principal was still not in, so afterward, I made an appointment.

Three days later, I returned and signed my R.S.P. teacher's copy that she bought. She knew that I was about to talk with the principal.

"One piece of advice, Matt," she told me. "Take your hat off when you're talking with him."

I took her advice. I waited there in front of the principal's office for quite a while. It was soon past the appointment time. The principal passed me and said hi. After waiting some more, a faculty member notified him that I had been waiting. Apparently, the principal did not get the message that he had an appointment and apologized to me. We both sat down across from each other in his office. We had quite a cordial conversation, in the middle of which I shared that I am an author and showed him my book.

Finally, the unthinkable happened.

"Do you want to speak?" He solemnly looked at me with eyes wide open. It was just like the JBQ teacher asking if I wanted to teach that morning.

Yes! Yes! Yes! I shouted in my mind.

All of a sudden, I began seeing those gray clouds over my existence depart from me. Again, I would do anything and even give my physical life to encourage the entire world, even if that means starting small and working my way up. Perhaps this would usher me into other places because there are over two thousand students whom I would speak to at Newport Harbor, not to mention the quantity of teachers who would be present.

"Yes, I would love to be a *volunteer* speaker and juggler here," I said with a huge smile.

The principal seemed excited and said that he would contact me later.

Meanwhile, a Royal Rangers commander in Panama gave an almost seven-minute story about me and my book on his Spanish radio program on November 20. I was very appreciative.

The previous Sunday, I got to speak in a Fine Arts workshop at Newport Mesa Church. The Fine Arts Festival is part of the Assemblies of God Youth Ministries. How did that happen? I was speaking with the new senior commander at my outpost, lamenting how my book had been just crumbling down to sand. And in fact, my life too.

In retrospect, I was feeling the painful grinding of a boulder weathering down to sand. The pain was all inside and out of my body. I wanted to speak, tutor, teach, mentor, encourage, motivate, juggle, and play piano. *ALL that stuff!* I knew that I was doing that, but it was merely a fraction of one percent of my time. I had *all* those lonesome hours and days that I *could* have done so, outside of my obligations.

And it was just not happening, even with my new title as "Royalty-Published Author."

The senior commander got back with me and said that he spoke with a person at the church. The person said that I could speak at the Fine Arts Festival and encourage all the youth there about what it takes to publish a book. I was ecstatic and thankful for the opportunity. I started attending their workshops on Sundays between my church and Royal Rangers, which started later in the afternoon.

The following is a humorous story that I never told them. On November 17, I arrived, and everybody at the workshop was anxiously happy to see me.

They were like, "Oh good. You're here. I'll tell the others to come in, and then you can speak to them. You didn't show up, so everyone went out to rehearse."

"Okay, sure." I smiled. "I'm sorry for running a little late."

"Oh, that's totally fine. Glad you could make it."

Here is the problem: I was never told that I was going to speak right then and there! Moments later, I delivered my entire speech on what it takes to become an author, the trials of Autism Spectrum Disorder, how I referred to the church by name and certain people in my book (including the parents of some of those listening), and my plea to never give up on anything, despite a disability.

I spoke all of it impeccably to an engaged, listening audience, mostly the youth of the church, and none of them knew that it was spontaneous. It was a fun memory that I will never forget.

I continue attending their workshops and helping out. I was almost plugged into a skit, but because I was not a youth, I could not be a part of it. Months later, I found out that all they wanted me to do was to speak at one of the workshops, which took place on November 17. All that time, before and after that day, I thought that I was going to give the speech at the entire Fine Arts Festival in April. It was a monumental misunderstanding and miscommunication with the senior commander. That is how *he* understood it and relayed the message to me.

Sure, it was a javelin pierced through my heart, but two things: at least I got to inspire people at that workshop and at least I got to help out others for all those weeks. In fact, one of them was a writer too, so I got to give her praises and critiques of her work. Another one was a guitarist. I got to give her my advice about stage fright, by saying how I combatted it at my fourth-grade talent show in 2005. I continued to help out up until the declaration of the pandemic. The festival, which was to be held in April, was ultimately cancelled.

November 17 was my second speaking engagement. My first (official) one was on November 9 at the sectional Pinewood Derby in Santa Ana, when I was asked to give a devotion and share my book.

Also in November, I began volunteering for Wednesday-night youth at Lighthouse Community Church. (Royal Rangers just switched to Sundays, freeing up my time on Wednesdays, thereby giving me another opportunity to help out students.) One of the volunteers was a commander I worked with; a few of the boys there were Royal Rangers.

Unlike the fifth-to-eighth-grade ministry at Newport Mesa Church, I was *completely* plugged in and involved, leading games, standing up to talk (even if it would be a few moments), and (*finally*) gave a few sermons over the next few years. I even got to play the keyboard too. The communications were phenomenal, and I proposed ideas that were taken into consideration. Some students I met were happy to see me upon arrival, contrasted with my time with the abovementioned fifth to eighth graders who were not given a proper introduction to who I even was. Some actually smiled and waved at me. Others could not wait to arrive themselves to see me.

Toward the end of 2019, though, one of the pastors encouraged me to intern for the youth instead of just volunteering. That way I can make "a little pocket change" to help me out as I go to school. Even though I felt funny at the thought of accepting paychecks to work with children and teenagers, I decided to take them up on their offer. I did not have a job anyway; I was merely a full-time student. I later signed a contract and began interning in January 2020. This also included working every other Sunday for the youth. I would alternate with Lighthouse Community and Oasis Assembly.

At least I *will* stand my ground and refuse a paycheck to be a Royal Rangers commander at my outpost, if ever they offer. As I went on the record saying since 2017, I would literally rip one up in their faces. One of the boys at Royal Rangers who followed me on YouTube really admired that I said that. My heart is, and always has been, one of *service* for younger people!)

Toward the end of the year, with like 2 percent ups and 98 percent downs, I was falling into discouragement again. I emailed the Administrative Director of Operations of Newport-Mesa Unified's Special Education Department, as recommended by my high school R.S.P. teacher. The director and I also knew each other quite well. This is because I would juggle or play piano at the district's annual Special Education Tea all four years that I was in high school.

One month passed. She at last got back with me, apologizing, and explaining that she was out for a month. It was toward the beginning of 2020.

She shared my request to volunteer as a speaker and juggler around the district. Toward the end of that month, I got asked to be a vendor at the Newport-Mesa's Autism Resource Fair at Costa Mesa High School on April 16.

One month later, I got asked to be one of the speakers at a documentary viewing held at Corona del Mar High School, hosted by the Special Education Department. The documentary was about people living with special needs. It was to be held on March 26. *Finally!*

Back in January 2020, I was approaching my second semester at Vanguard. I was taking the hugest undergraduate semester of my life. Five days a week and sixteen units. I took two advanced science classes, two labs, two general required courses, and my first education course: Anthropology—Language, Culture, Linguistics.

And I was completely out the entire third week too.

Right before my semester began, I continued to contact multiple news stations, newspapers, and Autism organizations to no avail. I continued to post on social media, tagging certain media outlets when appropriate, and flooding each post with as many relevant hashtags that I could possibly fit. Doing all this did not work one bit.

Another thing that did not work was trying to email and submit news tips to all the affiliates of various major news networks across the country. I thought that if I could not get anywhere in Los Angeles or New York, then perhaps various places across America would accept my story of inspiration and encouragement in the name of disability acceptance and antibullying.

I can also add "award-winning" in front of my book now! In mid-January, a few days after beginning my second semester, I was googling the title of my book and discovered that it got two awards from BookAuthority, a foremost worldwide book-recommending site that has been featured in Forbes, CNN, and elsewhere.

My book was ranked #43 of 74 "Best Autism Books of All Time!" and #9 of 16 "Best New Autism Books To Read in 2020."

I was astounded and flabbergasted! I subsequently made a YouTube video about it and posted the news all throughout social media, incredibly happy. Yet, in the long run, that did not seem to change anything. The media still decided not to take notice over the next couple of years. I must have sent my sincere, lengthy, heartfelt email to several dozen (or probably even hundreds) newsrooms.

This is the gist of what I sent to each of them:

My name is Matthew Kenslow from Orange County, California. Just over 6 months ago, I became a royalty-published author at age 23, fighting against my lifelong battle of autistic discrimination from firsthand trials. *Juggling the Issues: Living with Asperger's Syndrome* is being sold in multiple countries worldwide.

I never allowed Autism . . . to slow me down! I earned a degree in chemistry, have juggled for elementary schools since I was in high school, and play piano for seniors on Sunday mornings. I encourage children to never give up on their passions; if I can do it, so can you!

I am pleased to announce to you this incredible, newsworthy story of perseverance and overcoming. Not caving in to what people have verbally beaten me with, I got to where I am, a 24-year-old, fighting hard against discrimination. I have been making a difference to hundreds of children, encouraging them that THEY HAVE A PURPOSE.

Thank you for your consideration in this deep, ever-contemporary, large-scale issue.

And all that one Assignment Manager of WLUK-TV could say after that was, "This is Fox 11 in Green Bay, not Los Angeles," and that was it. Nothing more. And 99.9 percent of everybody else did not bother to respond.

I will say, however, I did get in communication with Kade Atwood of KMVT, a channel 11 news station in Idaho, who responded. They were doing several antibullying stories, he told me, and wanted me to submit a video. "We are excited to have you participate," he said.

I felt so honored because all I care about is making a difference, and if it starts up in Idaho, then *that* is where it will start. However, the emails stopped. He said that he was going to talk with the planning team but perhaps they decided not to use me. That was the closest yet!

And then, around January 25, 2020, I was notified that my publisher had ceased operations. At first, I fell into deeper despair. I found myself in a truck at a parking lot in Brea, California. It was confirmed to me about my now-former publisher.

I mean, it is sad for his publishing house, and I hoped that things would get better for him, but I personally felt like all hope was lost for me and the disabled people of the world. I also felt like hope was lost for all the discriminate neurotypicals who would realize that they need to change because disabilities do *not* equal alien life form.

I remember slouching in the passenger seat feeling like part of me was out of my body. That is how numb I felt.

After all the work I did. After all the discrimination I had faced. After all the heartache to get this book published for nearly two years, all while continuing to battle discrimination in my own neighborhood, including earlier that month at a Target in Costa Mesa. I felt that that was it. It was the end of me!

That afternoon, I was almost fainting with tiredness. I wondered if I would make the trip home all the way back to Costa Mesa. When I got home, I crashed on my bed and woke up at probably around three in the morning.

I felt terrible. It is hard to describe. I went over to Hoag Hospital before daybreak, and they told me that I most likely had the flu.

We suspect that I lowered my immunity with all the recent stress, not to mention my never-ending, Mount-Everest-sized stress that I have fought against for years.

I want to help people. I want to teach people. I want to get the people of this world to put aside competition, come together, and treat each other kindly with respect and peace. It should not be *hard to do*!

I believe (and still do) that I will monumentally make such a difference at all costs, but I refused to wait any longer.

I have been rejected countless times as I presented in previous chapters. Now I am an author of an award-winning book who got royalty-published at the age of twenty-three, yet just a tad under 100 percent of all secular media, Christian media, schools, churches, libraries, and even Autism organizations are completely dismissing me and my book.

Somehow, I had the optimism to continue the pursuit of my destined calling to teach and mentor, even if it would be virtually.

-10-

THE DAY THE WHOLE WORLD CHANGED
MARCH 11, 2020

Wednesday, March 11, 2020. I started the morning off attending my two morning classes at Vanguard University. In the middle of the day, I attended one of the chapels, preached by one of my professors. I proceeded to take my two afternoon classes, in between which I practiced on one of Vanguard's pianos in their music department. That evening, I went to my internship with Lighthouse's youth. That night, I listened to the United States president on television as he announced that a pandemic was declared by the World Health Organization.

The coronavirus was spreading rapidly across the planet. Again, it was a day when the whole world changed, much like the shock around the world 222 months prior on September 11, 2001, a horrific and tragic day back when I was six years old, which gave me fear.

This was in the midst of uncertain times. A couple of months prior, I remember seeing it trending on Twitter that a doctor in China contracted a mysterious illness. Later on, it was trending that he died from it. Major colleges and universities, including Orange Coast College, went remote.

We continued having classes at Vanguard until Friday. The day before, the students got an e-mail from the office of the president of the university, who said that spring break had been extended for one week with a possibility of going remote thereafter.

Later that night, all Royal Rangers activities were suspended for Outpost #33 by our senior commander. At that point, I already figured that was going to occur.

Needless to say, *all* my engagements that I *finally* had were postponed. These included the documentary viewing at Corona del Mar High, the Autism Resource Fair at Costa Mesa High, and even a Vanguard chapel that I was finally going to speak at regarding my book and testimony. I had rehearsed both my speeches many times, just to have them cancelled.

As days went on, grocery markets had lines that were around the corner, only allowing a few people in at a time. With the world on lockdown, we had the sense of being confined to our homes and quarantined, needing to wear masks wherever we went. On top of that, I dealt with bearing hundreds of memories of being discriminated against and misunderstood since kindergarten, having Royal Rangers canceled (the only consistent place where I had joy and could teach on a weekly basis), not having Lighthouse's youth to serve at (which was beginning to bring me weekly joy too) or their young adults group to attend, not having Oasis Assembly to play piano at for the senior citizens, not having elementary schools to juggle at and brighten students' days, and having uncertainty about my future and the future of my book (as well as various social media accounts that couldn't seem to go anywhere no matter how much I posted). I felt *forlorn*, a word whose definition means sad, abandoned, and lonely.

I felt that this would take my life if nothing else happened. I was *that* stressed, queasy, and demotivated. But by my strong faith in the existence of a miraculous God, I forced myself to continue.

―11―

LIFE IN A PANDEMIC

After spring break, we students returned to Vanguard via Zoom. This continued for the rest of the semester.

On April 1, knowing that April 2 was recognized as World Autism Awareness Day, and that this was going to be my first April 2 as an author of a book about my experiences, I sent several emails to various news stations and radio shows that I could contact . . . *again.*

I was like, *If they won't answer me at any other time of the year, then they* must *answer me for World Autism Awareness Day.* But again, for whatever reason, they all chose not to answer me, except one. I got in contact with a producer of the Ellen K Morning Show from KOST 103.5 FM - iHeart radio. She said that she would love to set up a phone call for the following morning.

I woke up very early, followed the instructions, and spoke for two minutes on the program. *Finally!* After nearly a year since becoming an author, I got two minutes on the radio to talk about my book and my experiences living with Autism. I was thankful and very enthusiastic about it. Later that day, I was in an article on KOST 103.5's website. I made an Autism Awareness and Acceptance video for the third April 2 in a row, featuring the audio clip of being on the program. That YouTube video I made was placed at the top of the article.

By the middle of April, I was done waiting. On Amazon, it said that my book was out of print and that there was limited availability. I reached back to my literary agent for the first time in three months. (I contacted him in January when I suspected things were going awry. He was the one who told me that my publisher ceased operations.) I found out that Amazon shut the company down; all their books are only sold through a third party, which is the reason why my book was apparently out of print.

Back in January, my agent advised me to get in contact with another publisher whom he recommended. I eventually got ahold of the publisher, and he understood, agreeing to publish my book. Plus, I decided to put it on Kindle too this time.

On April 22, I signed and submitted a contract with him to have my book republished by a royalty publisher. However, there had to be a new ISBN, Amazon website address, and everything. This had me laboriously amend a ton of hyperlinks and posts all across social media, as well as make new business cards for my book. I was also worried that all the reviews would not transfer onto the new Amazon page, but they did.

Everything was done nearly swimmingly. On June 13 (the one-year anniversary of receiving the package of my first book), I was officially republished. On July 24, I got the package containing five free author copies. Once again, I was optimistic. Plus, that was right after completing my undergraduate research as a biogeochemist, for which, to my surprise, I was awarded "Best Quality Research."

Back in April 2020, I began making a lot more Autism Awareness and Acceptance videos. I was planning on doing that before the pandemic anyway. I decided to be a YouTuber out in public, meaning that I talk about Autism topics while walking around my neighborhood. I began doing so in 2019 and early 2020. I enjoyed it and wanted to continue. To edit these videos and put them together was a fun pasttime. Unfortunately, with the pandemic, I had the fear of being arrested just for being outside, which is irrational, I know. Thus, I filmed a lot of videos in my room. I continued doing so throughout the year, including videos based on Royal Rangers and Vanguard University.

Vanguard's fall 2020 semester was remote. I took three science classes via Zoom and three labs. Two of the labs were in person (Biochemistry and Analytical Chemistry). However, my microbiology lab was at home. They mailed a huge package to each of us students, and I did all my experiments and reports in my bedroom. It was quite an experience!

Suddenly, something heart-stopping occurred in the middle of the semester. On the night of October 7, 2020, I went to my analytical chemistry lab. I did everything as normal, following the protocol. I went home afterward, and that was it. Over the next few days, I began getting messages off the hook: phone calls, text messages, and emails. They were from Vanguard's Campus Safety and Health Office, saying that it is *urgent* that I call them back.

"Hey, Matthew," the voicemail from the director of Campus Safety began.

"I'm trying to get ahold of you regarding questions concerning a recent expo-sure to COVID-19. Please give me a call when you get a chance."

I had been exposed to the coronavirus. Three students on campus tested positive at the same time. One of them was in my analytical chemistry lab that night. We never had in-person analytical chemistry lab for the rest of the semester. (Biochemistry lab, yes.)

I ultimately got ahold of the nurse practitioner on Saturday, the tenth. (Earlier that year, in January, before the pandemic began, I met her at Vanguard's Health Office, because I was not getting better with the worst flu of my life. She told me that I had to wait it out.) She started by confirming my identity and information, the spelling of my name, date of birth, student ID, phone number, email, and address. All protocol.

She proceeded by asking about my medical insurance. I answered.

"Have you ever been tested for COVID?" she asked.

"No."

She read off a litany of symptoms.

"No. None of them."

"Are you having any other unusual symptoms?"

"No."

She read off chronic medical conditions.

"No."

She then told me that the CDC recommends that anybody exposed to COVID-19 should get tested. She offered to email me information on how to go about doing that. She then proceeded to tell me the CDC guidelines for anyone who is exposed. I must enter self-quarantine, she said, for a little while, check my temperature daily, and watch for symptoms. She told me to let my professors know and to postpone any social gatherings.

She added that she could help me with any academic accommodations and to let her know if I needed any healthcare related things. "You seem *so* busy with school stuff that I'm sure this isn't the greatest news." She con-cluded by informing me that I needed clearance from the Health Office in order to return to campus.

"So sorry," she said again. "Talk to you soon."

"Okay, thanks."

After hanging up, fear of impending doom tried its best to consume me, but I immediately fought it off, as long as I didn't eat anything right then.

I emailed my analytical chemistry professor who taught lab that night, followed by my biochemistry professor.

"I am perturbed out of my mind," I wrote. I was almost in a panic for reasons I will explain in the next chapter. I asked them if they thought there was any danger. I only came on campus eight times that semester, just for analytical chemistry lab. That was all. And I just happened to have gotten exposed one night.

Both of them replied right away. My analytical chemistry professor reassured me. He had just tested negative, and he had more contact with the individual who was tested positive than I did.

My biochemistry professor said that she and others all got tested and that I should just do the same. She said the likelihood that I contracted it was slim because the lab was fully ventilated, we had been working in individual fume hoods, and we had on multiple layers of personal protective equipment.

Both professors gave me such reassurance that greatly helped out my mind. My Autism was again trying to tell me that I was going to die, but being a man in my twenties now, I had severely tamed it years prior. All throughout the pandemic, I could not imagine how I would've felt if I had been under the age of fourteen.

I additionally decided to call the mother of a friend who was also in that lab at the time of the exposure. The mother was actually the coordinator of the Fine Arts Festival and a part of JBQ at Newport Mesa. She was happy to talk with me. She said that her daughter went to a place on East 17th Street that did COVID tests. It was very easy; they were in and out in no time. A little while later, the daughter called me, and we talked with each other. Toward the end, we both prayed for one another, which brought both of us tremendous comfort.

I proceeded to look into that facility on East 17th Street and decided to go there. At that time I needed to inform my mother and grandfather. To the best I could, I calmly notified them that I was exposed to that little, tiny virus which was now a global pandemic, killing many people. To my thankfulness, they took the news okay and supported my decision to get tested the next morning. After that, I made an appointment.

That night, I watched countless YouTube videos about the COVID test. I researched exactly how the test gets administered and how people described what it feels like.

Here is the thing: deep down in my heart, I knew I was fine. I did not feel sick or anything. I knew that I would get a negative COVID test. The nasal swab to prove it, however, was what alarmed me. My grandfather had to get COVID tests at the Veteran Affairs hospital in Long Beach in preparation for a couple of procedures. That was when I witnessed one in real life. My grandfather could not stand it. He stomped on the floorboard of the truck as it was being administered, shutting his eyes. He kept blowing his nose and groaning all the way out of the parking lot.

From what I could tell from my research, it sounded like it was going to feel as if I had plunged into water, which I experienced throughout swimming lessons in my childhood.

I arrived at the facility the next morning. I stood in line outside, waiting to enter. Once I got in and filled out the paperwork, I was told to wait around the back. I walked around and stood in line. Finally, it was my turn. A man came out in full personal protective equipment, and I was a foot away from that notorious swab.

"All right, boss," he said. "Please lower your mask just underneath your nose."

I clutched my handkerchief as he gave me the COVID test.

Hmm. Not as bad as I thought.

"Okay, wait over there for your results," he said as he went back in, closing the door behind him.

Huh? I thought it was going to take two to three days, but that was what the man said.

As I was waiting for a bit, I received a phone message saying to come inside quickly. I did so and explained to the woman at the front desk that I got a call from the man. I thought the results were in.

The man came out and said, "I didn't know your sample was going to be taken to a lab, and I gave you the wrong one. I'm sorry, but I have to give you a different one right now."

He came up to me with a different-looking swab. I almost did not have time to get out my handkerchief to clutch it. If I remember correctly, I may have clutched my hat instead.

So, I took two COVID tests within five or ten minutes from each other. And I could do another one, but only if I must. Indeed, the sensation was like plunging into water. You may just need to blow your nose a few times, but then it is over. I waited three days. My results were negative the whole time! (I knew they would be.) I went on to successfully complete the semester.

Still, Vanguard did not fully open up in January 2021. My entire fourth and final undergraduate semester at the university was online as well, barring physiology lab. Students who had courses on campus were additionally required to take COVID tests every other week, so I was in one of those testing groups for the next year and a half. However, I got to take the saliva test, thankfully.

By the middle and end of 2021, new variants of the virus, such as Delta and Omicron, were lurking around. A lot of my friends and distant family members began catching COVID, some worse than others. And throughout 2020 and 2021, a couple of my friends nearly died from it.

Vanguard University opened up by the time I began my fall 2021 semester, my first semester in the credential program. However, we still had to wear masks. The masks lasted until the middle of spring 2022, my first semester of student teaching.

-12-

VIRTUAL ROYAL RANGERS AND THE EXTRA MILE

Back in April 2020, I received an email from a parent whose son goes to our Royal Rangers outpost. She has helped work at the sign-in table since 2016. She had written that her son, who was in his first year of Discovery Rangers, missed interacting with me every Sunday and that it would mean a lot to him (and everybody) if I would start conducting meetings via Zoom. Both she and I had not hosted Zoom meetings before but were getting familiar using it. I told her that I had been planning to look into Zoom as a means of holding Royal Rangers meetings, but alas, my sixteen-unit semester was getting me all bogged down.

Later on, in May, I got another email from her. This time she sent a video. "Commander Matthew, I miss you," the boy said.

The mother then asked if we could begin organizing Zoom meetings for the boys soon. She had written in the email that she figured out how to use Zoom, made an account, and that the boys at our outpost miss me.

I had written back, starting with, "I cannot express enough how that video made my entire month!" I said that the next day was the last day of my second semester, after which I would have all the time in the world.

After a couple of Zoom meetings with her and the senior commander, we launched remote Outpost #33 Royal Rangers on May 17 for Ranger Kids and Discovery Rangers.

I put together the PowerPoint slides for the opening pledges, announcements, and, later on, "virtual awards" that I had been keeping a record of. That way, when we met in person, I could hand out the badges and medals that they earned while we were remote; but in the meantime, we could all celebrate when they earn awards. After that, we split to Ranger Kids and Discovery. The mother who hosted the Zoom meetings created the slides for

Ranger Kids, and the former senior commander taught them. I made the slides for Discovery Rangers and taught. We had a pretty good showing with a lot of boys. Alas, a lot of other boys could not do well on Zoom and had to take a break from Rangers.

I was instantly filled with passion once again. I was tremendously enthusiastic about everything. Starting in September 2019, I was the head of that age group. I planned everything out. I got a sense of leadership, responsibility, and autonomy like never before. I was in complete charge of keeping all the records, which I had not been given the duty of before, even though I wanted it. I had an exhaustive list of fun games and challenges that I wanted them to try during recreation time. I chose the Bible lessons and the advancement merits that we would do. I ultimately gave each boy a list of merits that I was able to teach and had them choose for themselves which one they wanted to do. I tallied the votes for which merit to do. Right before the shutdown, I was teaching the Fingerprinting merit, which got the most votes. Had the pandemic never occurred, the next requirement would have been taking their own fingerprints and examining them.

At this point in 2020, I was teaching boys virtually using PowerPoint slides. I had to think of which merits I could do. I started out with the Safety merit and taught that over the next few weeks.

Something that I did not say yet in this book is the fact that I went PowerPoint *crazy* during high school. In all four years of high school, I spent perhaps a dozen or two *hours* per PowerPoint. I am not joking, as I packed them with animations, audio, and the whole nine yards. I think my longest bibliography took nine slides in and of itself, after forty or fifty slides of the presentation. All my fellow classmates and the teachers were impressed with them. If there was not an animation that I was looking for, then I *made* it animate like that by combining various animations together. Needless to say, when I was video editing for my YouTube videos, and elsewhere, I felt like a kid in a candy store.

I revived my creativity while crafting various PowerPoints over the ensuing months. After that first Sunday, but perhaps not to any surprise, I decided to make a YouTube video for the Safety merit. I actually wished to make merit videos all the way back when I began my channel in 2017. I just got very busy. At this point I had almost all the time in the world.

I walked over to Newport Beach and found a perfect location to film the introduction of my merit videos. If anybody would like to see what I meant by "PowerPoint crazy," then I invite readers to check out my four playlists for blue, green, and silver merits, as well as Achievement Awards for Ranger Kids. From 2020 to 2022, I have produced over a dozen blue merit videos (Discovery Rangers), four green merit videos (Adventure Rangers), one silver merit video (Expedition Rangers), and thirty Ranger Kids Achievement Awards. Previously, in May 2019, I produced a series of five videos—one for each of the four age groups and how they are set up, and a fifth one talking about the Gold Medal of Achievement and how it is earned.

I decided to share my Safety Merit video on the official leaders community page of National Royal Rangers on Facebook. I hoped that it would help out other boys, commanders, and parents. I got a lot of positive response to it.

With my life of disappointments when I built high hopes up for nothing, despite all the nerve-racking, painstaking effort I put into *everything*, I was not initially expecting the enormous impact that I would end up making. At this time of my life, I was numb. My optimism had almost disappeared.

As time progressed, I received nationwide gratitude for what I did. My merit videos were a tremendous help to various boys and commanders across the country, such as in Chicago, throughout California, Texas, and elsewhere. I had significantly helped boys who for whatever reason could not go to outposts. Now, they were able to stay on track since Royal Rangers is a merit-driven program. Boys ascend the ranks (their "track") to ultimately earn badges, advancement ranks, and medals.

Over the next couple of years, I received pictures and videos of camps where boys are watching my merit videos and following along. I have received cards and patches as thanks. It is very fulfilling to know how much of a difference that I am *finally* making on a larger scale than just in my local area, where at first, only a small percentage seemed to appreciate the heart I have.

In June 2022, I attended a huge Southern California District campout in Cherry Valley. There, a boy who benefitted from my YouTube videos recognized me and said that he had been watching my merit videos.

Through it all, this also gave me substantial practice in being a teacher! I was organizing and planning lessons via PowerPoint, coming up with virtual games, conducting those games, teaching both the Bible lesson and advancement lesson, keeping records of what each boy did each week, and communicating to a few parents via email. Some of those virtual games I thought of and put together on my own. I shared them on YouTube in high hopes of them being a resource to classrooms, Sunday schools, Royal Rangers outposts, and everywhere else. Once again, however, it appeared that I built my hopes up to no avail.

Anyhow, it was literally the highlight of my evening to credit each attending boy a Bible lesson in their tracker, taking notes on who earned which merit, virtually awarding them the following week, and setting up the next set of PowerPoint presentations. It kept me busy, without which I would physically have been *bored to death*, pitifully questioning if I had purpose during those inauspicious times of a pandemic, where nobody knew when it would finally end, or if it would suddenly get worse at any nanosecond. Now I had found a purpose regardless!

The first meeting was a success. Then it was time to incorporate the Adventure Rangers. After talking with the senior commander, I agreed to take the responsibility to teach Adventure Rangers too after Discovery. Starting on May 24, we held two Royal Rangers Zoom meetings back to back: the first for the two younger groups (where I taught Discovery) and the second for the Adventure Rangers. We did not have any high schoolers showing up, which is the age group called "Expedition Rangers."

Referring back to chapter 4, I was torn between teaching Discovery and Adventure. I assumed I would be in one of those, but somehow, the senior commander told me that I would be in Ranger Kids. Again, that turned out to be a blessing in disguise. The reason to bring this up again is to point out that now, I get to teach *both* every single week.

As months went by, we remained hopeful that things would open up again, but unfortunately, we were told that we still had to be remote. In-person activities were allowed on occasion but had to be restrictive.

After a long time, the senior commander and I set up a date, time, and location to do an in-person leadership day camp, but with restrictions. Only two boys could be at a table, one on each end, and everybody had to wear a mask or face shield.

We began promoting it as soon as it was confirmed. The boys were excited. There was only one glitch. After a fight to get a date, it was established to be on Saturday, October 17.

Remember what happened just ten days prior? Yes, my exposure to the notorious virus.

That is the reason for my panic that I said I would explain later. My heart is for those boys to make happy memories in the midst of uncertainty. Inside the email that I sent to both my professors that evening was this note:

> I guess the reason I'm so perturbed is because I was looking forward to teaching the valuable Leadership merit next Saturday like a kid going to the biggest amusement park, I was feeling alive again for once since March.

I was then told by a couple of people at Vanguard that if I received a negative COVID test result, then I could still teach the Leadership merit. Oh my gosh! Ninety-nine percent of the depression left me. One percent remained due to the improbability of testing positive for COVID.

After I got home from taking *two* COVID tests, as you now know the story, I awaited the Royal Rangers Zoom meeting for Discovery. As I concluded teaching Discovery that late afternoon, I once again (and lively) said, "And next Saturday, we will once again be together in person taking the Leadership 102 merit."

I said it with certainty because I just knew I did not have the virus. When I said that, though, I noticed something that could have wrenched my heart if I had thought hard about it. Remember that boy who really missed me? When I reiterated about being in-person again on the following Saturday, I saw that boy perk up with a smile, looking like he was taking a breath of relief.

What if I really did have COVID? What if I was never told that if I got a negative COVID test result, then it would be okay to continue with social gatherings (responsibly, of course)? What would I tell them if my test came back positive, and how would they take it? We fought to have it on October 17, and we had the boys get all ready and excited for it. *Well, thank God my test results came back negative!*

The whole big day was a success, from beginning to end—all the lessons, devotions, activities, and concluding service project. We even got a new boy in Rangers. I had to amend some of the games for social-distancing purposes, as well as create entirely new games for a couple of them, but in a way, that still got the leadership point across.

After Christmas and New Year's break, we were still told that we had to remain on Zoom. Oh well.

Throughout that time, I was beginning to have a further longing to start back up in person. It did not matter if it was morning, noon, night, midnight, or four o'clock in the morning, I would stay up thinking and contemplating ideas. I would go over the next Council of Achievement ceremony. I would go over the first day back, imagining an outpost with a ton of new boys and commanders too. I would go over how I would teach an introductory class to newly recruited commanders. I would list out the order of merits that I would teach once we get back—fun merits that could only be done in person, such as Compass, Rope Craft, Lashing, Weather, and First Aid Skills.

All this time, I kept hearkening back to my home video from June 5, 2002, which I uploaded on YouTube on the eighteenth anniversary in 2020. It was the Council of Achievement at my outpost, a remarkable evening that I remember. I watched that video innumerable times. If ever I needed a boost of motivation, I would watch it again. I had faith that one day, Outpost #33 *would* once again be as enormous and influential as we were, and it would be my honor to lead it. If I had complete charge, I would definitely focus on out-reach in order to grow the outpost, such as making our presence more known in the community than ever before.

In February 2021, I was asked by the host of the National Royal Rangers Podcast if he could interview me. I felt tremendously thankful, privileged, and honored. The theme was leading through Autism. It included me talking about growing up in the program, being a commander with Autism, helping out boys with special needs, the monumental impact I had throughout the country with my merit videos on YouTube, and more. It premiered in April, since that was World Autism Awareness Month.

Before it premiered, I was asked by my friend in Montana if I could join her live on YouTube on April 2 for World Autism Awareness Day. She is also an advocate for Autism, being diagnosed herself at the same time her young son was diagnosed. She found me in 2018 through my musician's Facebook page, where I post my piano playing videos. We have supported each other ever since. She even requested an autographed copy of my book, addressing it to her son in the inscription, soon after I got republished. After receiving the copy, she shared it on one of her YouTube videos.

During her live, I talked about my experiences with Autism and ultimately helping to answer questions that people around the country and world asked. She also let me know that my book was very special to her son and that he did not allow anybody to touch it without his permission. That put a smile on both of our faces, and I am sure on everyone listening too.

Moreover, by what seemed to be a miracle, I was asked by the pastor of Mesa Church (it had been renamed at this point from being called Newport Mesa Church) to be interviewed in his podcast, which also took place in April. I talked a lot about Autism, my book, my interests, Royal Rangers, and more.

I tried to raise my hopes up after that, but I surmise it was a good thing that I was unsuccessful in doing so. That was my final interview for a while, despite continual backbreaking efforts.

In Discovery Rangers, I had virtually taught Astronomy, Chess, Disability Awareness, Models & Design, Music, Presidents, Railroading, and Safety. I also completed the Fingerprinting merit that I began back when we were in person. In these merits, I would assign a little homework during the week, since some requirements could only be accomplished in person, like taking fingerprints. Sometimes, I got to send extra Bible lessons for boys who wanted to catch up on their track.

In Adventure Rangers, I taught Bible Knowledge, Healthy Body, Crime Prevention, Fire Safety, Forestry, Photography, and Chemistry. Chemistry is actually a high-school level merit, but having a degree in chemistry, I could not resist teaching it. The senior commander and boys were okay with it. It gave me practice teaching and breaking down science concepts to a few sixth graders and a middle schooler. After it was over, I joked that we would then start the Biology merit, which does not really exist.

With my lifelong sense of humor, I had fun a few times, such as telling the Discovery Rangers that we would be starting the Calculus merit, which also does not exist. I always say it with passion and a huge smile as if I was serious. I truly love mathematics, but none of them had to worry about me teaching it to them like that. On the contrary, I began giving both age groups a list of merits. The merit with the most votes went first and so on. Yet, one time in Adventure, three merits tied for first once all the votes were added, which was somewhat interesting.

On May 30, 2021, after being on Zoom for over a year, we concluded our 2020-2021 academic year. In total, we spent forty-six weeks on Zoom. By September, we finally found a provisional location, Lighthouse Community Church, and conducted in-person Royal Rangers for the 2021-2022 year, after which we were in Mesa Church's brand-new building.

One final thing brought me comfort. That one mother who first contacted me in 2020 always says that her son and all the other boys would *not* have completed their Discovery Rangers track if it were not for me doing what I did for an entire year when the entire world was shut down.

"What *you* did was incredible!" she said, always complimenting me. "My son would not be where he is today if it weren't for you."

Both her and the senior commander told me that Outpost #33, the outpost I grew up attending and the one that used to be the hugest in the district, would have *ceased to exist* if I had not stepped up the way I did.

However, I give that mother a ton of appreciation back because *she* was the one who messaged me a couple times to get the virtual meetings going. *She* was the one who set up the Zoom account that we used at first. *She* sent emails and texts to the parents and supervised the meetings, together with the senior commander. I, and all the boys, owe an equal amount of gratitude to her for what she did for the program too.

Throughout those forty-six weeks, boys ascended their ranks, and some of them earned their medals, which always brings me joy. They worked hard and were rightfully rewarded. It humbles me to know that I have made that impact (and still do, since I will always be a commander).

~13~

THE SUICIDE LETTERS

I felt that I needed to insert this chapter at this point. From January to March 2021, hundreds of suicide letters were being dispersed all across Costa Mesa and Newport Beach that were found in parks, schools, parking lots, residences, and sides of roads. I have seen and read several of them. I have posted about the occurrence on social media, calling for prayer, after finding one at Heller Park on January 27. I also requested that people take caution on how they treat one another.

From the ones that I read, the suicide letters said please be nice to one another, treat everybody with respect, stop bullying, say "I'm sorry" when needed before it is too late, and stop name-calling. Stop mistreating those who are homeless, disabled, of a different religion, or of a different race. Stop judging them based on sight without getting to know them.

Some of the letters appealed to parents to begin teaching their children kindness and to stop believing that everybody else out in public is a criminal. Other letters petitioned the schools (and Newport-Mesa Unified School District directly) to hold assemblies to communicate how to be nice to each other, even to those who are different.

Some even mentioned Autism, which made me shudder a bit, since I have come to terms with being in the fight toward equality. Bigotry against me (and other people with Autism) is not over yet. Otherwise, about 90 percent of everything that I have been doing in life is a waste.

The equality that this individual longed for is what I have been fighting for! I began to wonder that if all the schools would have had me speak back in 2019 and early 2020, before the pandemic, then would this be an issue? Would this person have written all of these suicide letters? Would there have been more kindness? (I personally believe so, even though I cannot prove it.)

Is this person still alive today? Is this person a student or an adult? My heart started going out to this individual and others like him or her. I started getting angry because again, this is precisely what I have fought to do since I became an author, but I was never invited by these schools or churches. Then, when I finally had three engagements scheduled, COVID hit!

I believe a lot of what this individual wrote is *true* and needs to be heard in all of society, not just Orange County. I am not necessarily advocating his or her method, but I believe it got the point across.

Soon, I began seeing schools like Newport Heights Elementary and Ensign Intermediate having kindness week, creating lawn posters about kindness, and the promotion of mental health awareness. Toward the middle of March, those letters stopped surfacing, so it seemed to have brought peace in the neighborhood, especially to this individual.

Until September. From September to October 2021, the letters began to resurface, many of which were targeting St. Andrew's Presbyterian Church. I got a chance to read a couple of those too. The individual was complimenting everybody on their efforts to spread kindness. He or she appreciated seeing the heart drawings and lawn posters. Alas, after thanking the neighborhood, he or she said that people are still bullies and appealed for schools and churches to take someone with experience of pain to speak to the students.

I once again became very angry. *Hello!* This is exactly what I have been screaming about since 2019. It is now the fall of 2021, and schools are opening back up. Why can I not be invited to speak yet? This individual would not have to write these suicide letters.

One Sunday in October, I got a Facebook message from one of the worship leaders. He told me that his wife found and brought home one of the letters that targeted St. Andrew's Presbyterian. He said that in a few weeks he was preaching about suicide awareness and mental health, and he asked if I could help him with what to say.

I felt honored, but as I should have known, the worship leader got too busy to get back with me on it. Nevertheless, I watched his sermon on Facebook, and it was absolutely beautiful. He even gave a moment of silence for everybody to pray for those who are depressed and suicidal. They put up a suicide hotline for people to call if needed. For anybody listening who was suicidal, he implored them to come to the church office and talk to a pastor, telling them to let them know how they can help.

Before his sermon and after I was contacted by him, my Autism forced me to make a YouTube video. I started the title out as "Suicide Letter Found." Autism forced me to do so because I had been up for half the night, and it would not give me peace until I filmed it. My mind was flooded with pain— pain for the individual, for the people in the world, for my longing to help the world by speaking *voluntarily*, and for all the horrible experiences that I had been facing personally.

In this video, which is just over a half an hour long, I poured out my entire heart and got extraordinarily passionate because I care so much about people. I want everyone to believe in themselves and put aside differences and competition.

The day before I made the video, I was walking by Cafe Rio alongside East 17th Street. A woman came walking around the corner and saw me. She then looked afraid but continued walking forward but not without constantly staring to ensure that I did not jump in front of her and attack her. As we were nearing each other, her lips were shut. I said hi to be neighborly, but she continued to stare and briskly walk away, not returning my greeting.

I saw the fear on her face just because I am an Autistic person she thought was going to attack her. Why else would she act like that? Her guard was up. One can easily tell. I was doing nothing more than walking as calmly and normally as humanly possible!

No wonder this individual left hundreds of suicide letters. That experience, among all the others that I will list later in this book, plagued my mind all night long.

To further show how much my mind forced me to make this video, I had categorically tried my best to focus on my assignments and tasks around me. I had been utterly distracted for roughly five to six hours. Every single time I tried to carry on with my task, I thought about that woman by Cafe Rio. I thought about another recent harsh memory. And then another. And then those suicide letters.

The majority of those five to six hours was more thinking, contemplating, and pacing back and forth in my room for *miles*! I could not concentrate on the things I was supposed to do. I had a draft to write for school, and I had to make sure that everything was in order for Royal Rangers that week.

Should I or should I not make a YouTube video about this whole entire thing? I pondered. *For crying out loud, Matthew, it's like two in the morning! Make it!*

I went on camera and gave my response to the suicide letters. Again, I back up most of the content that *needs* to be heard, yet I am not necessarily backing up the method. In my video, I expressed a sample of stories (still, quite a bit) of how I had been viewed in society by recounting a plethora of things I faced.

The content of the suicide letter is not just the issues of *one* individual. *Many* people are going through the same issues of discrimination, and people are not accepting that, causing this individual (and maybe others) to threaten suicide, thereby creating relevance for my video.

I was not ranting to *anybody* or making a mountain out of a molehill. I expressed that if *I* was experiencing discrimination, then so are many other disabled people too. Sure, I get stronger after each random act of discrimination, but I am not going to tolerate it. I am going to fight to eradicate it so that nobody else has to go through with what I constantly go through. This is unacceptable.

However, I began to firmly warn that there is a limit to what we can handle and how much bullying we can endure in one lifetime. I reiterated that message time and time again in later videos.

After my friend delivered his sermon, I made another YouTube video to give an update, applauding him and thanking St. Andrew's Presbyterian Church.

~14~

PREPARING FOR THE CREDENTIAL PROGRAM

As I noted earlier, I began taking undergrad courses that would count toward the credential program. In Spring 2020, I took an anthropology class. In Spring 2021, I took a course about integrating technology in the classroom.

In early October 2020, I began expressing to my academic counselor my interest in getting into the teaching field and subsequently completing a master's degree. She put me in contact with the program and accreditation coordinator of the credential and master's program. From there, we scheduled an appointment, and I spoke with him. By serendipity, his son also used to be in Royal Rangers at my outpost.

He told me that Vanguard has one of the fastest credential programs, and if I want to and qualify, then I can get a credential in as little as two semesters. Unfortunately, since I wanted to teach middle school, I would be going for a single-subject credential. The unfortunate part is that I cannot do both mathematics *and* science simultaneously. I wanted to teach mathematics, chemistry, astronomy, biology, and possibly physics. He helped me to solidify my choice in choosing mathematics first, instead of science.

He also made me aware that I could not get a credential *and* do the master's program concurrently. (My academic counselor later reassured me that her master's program in counseling, which was three years, was fun and went by quickly. I was just anxious to get started in a career, I guess. I love teaching and serving.)

Following the coordinator's advice, I began preparing for the California Basic Educational Skills Test (CBEST). The academic counselor said that with the CBEST, I should be able to substitute teach while completing the credential program.

I later went on the California Commission on Teacher Credentialing (CTC) Exams website and scheduled the CBEST. I chose to register for all three sections (reading, mathematics, and writing) in one test session. I had four hours allotted. I chose to take all three parts at the same time; I also chose the computer-based test at a facility. In total, there were going to be fifty reading questions, fifty math questions, and two essays. I love math, followed by writing, but always dreaded reading.

Despite some sections being easier than others, it could still take a long time for me to complete, thanks to Autism. I noticed that there were accommodations that I could apply for, but frankly, it just seemed too confusing and required a ton of communications to gain the proof I needed.

I told myself, *Matthew, you can do this. You are going to sit down in front of the computer and focus! You are not going to let* anything *distract you.*

After paying for the test and service fee, I went back to choose a date, time, and location. On the night before December 9, 2020, I studied one final time and took practice quizzes. I woke up early the next morning. I had an appointment at 11:00 a.m. at a testing center along Beach Boulevard in Huntington Beach.

When I went in, the office personnel took my temperature, processed my government-issued ID, photographed me, administered a palm scan, and asked questions to ensure that I was not inadvertently bringing in COVID. She made sure that I was not smuggling in any cheating devices by having me roll up my sleeves and turn out my pockets. Everything else went inside a locker. The personnel walked me inside the testing room, gave me a booklet to write in, logged me on, and wished me good luck.

After completing the nondisclosure agreement and tutorial, I began. I started with the reading section, compelling myself to stay completely focused. I was done within a couple of hours.

Now onto my love, mathematics. That took about an hour, more or less. It included three skill areas: computation and problem solving; numerical and graphic relationships; and estimation, measurement, and statistical principles.

The final section was on writing. They had two prompts for me that were not given to me in advance. One was on an issue and the other was personal. This is the part during which I significantly froze. Creative writing has always been my love, obviously. I have millions of things in my mind that I have accumulated for over twenty years. I went through every single grade level in my mind, starting with preschool.

Which is the perfect one to choose that I can fully and adequately write about? I was stressed.

By the time I was done with one, I believe I had twenty minutes or less to complete the other. I did not have time to proofread it. When I exited the exam room, the office personnel printed out my unofficial results, on which it said that I passed the reading and the mathematics. Phew! The writing was pending, obviously. When I returned home, I made a YouTube video about it.

Ten days later, I opened up the official results. I received it the night before, but I was very nervous and did not open it until eight hours later.

I passed writing! I therefore passed the CBEST! I passed with a 155 (passing is 123) with my highest in mathematics. Go figure. For the writing portion, they said that both essays either "met or exceeded the minimum standard."

As I said in my YouTube announcement video about passing the CBEST, I viewed it as validating the fact that with determination, Autism or not, *anybody* can do whatever they set their heart and mind to do! And if something does not work out the first time, then try it again. Do not give up. Consider taking advantage of any learning accommodations as well. Nobody is limited by the effects of a disability.

My next step was applying for the credential program. On January 26, 2021, I took an orientation via Zoom that explained everything about the credential program and the two main timelines that I could take. I was looking into the two-semester route as opposed to the three-semester route.

Throughout February, I got right down to work, so to speak, while completing my fourth semester's coursework at the same time. On the eighth, I took the Graduate Education interview, where I spoke with two coordinators. One was the person I referred to previously who helped me solidify getting a math credential. The other was the credential analyst/student teaching coordinator. They asked me general questions to get to know me, to know why I want to teach, and to describe times when I had to work with a team. I concisely explained the stories that I expounded on earlier in this book, including the time I found my passion.

The next set of questions dealt with prior experiences of working with children and adolescents, different cultures, and minorities, to which I described my role in Royal Rangers and at Lighthouse Community.

They asked about my take on the phrases, "Integration of faith and learning" and "All children can learn."

They marveled at my story about disliking science in elementary school and not taking a science class in middle school.

"And then you end up getting a degree in chemistry," one of them said. "Pretty amazing."

They asked how I sincerely and honestly react to constructive feedback, and I said that I believe such feedback is vital to receive to grow and gain wisdom. It will help shape me into being one of the best teachers.

I was then given the firm warning that I was about to enter a rigorous, graduate-level program dealing with assignments and balancing my home life, Vanguard classes, student teaching at the school site, and my job (not to mention my volunteer duties).

I acknowledged their statements and indicated that I was still up for the challenge.

One of them asked me, since I was going to be working with a lot of human beings, how would I handle stress and conflict with others. I was asked what I would do if a parent said, "I don't like the grade you gave my child."

I answered accordingly.

Next, the other one affirmed that the credential program was not going to teach me math. It is going to teach me *how to teach* math. He consequently asked me how confident I felt about my content knowledge of the subject matter.

"Well, I got an *A* in all my math classes at Orange Coast College except Calculus 2, in which I got a *B*." That was my way of saying that I was highly confident.

"Haha, that's pretty well."

This interview process spanned the first half hour. The second half hour was kind of a reiteration of what they said in the orientation, followed by time to ask questions. They talked to me about financial aid options, as well as the two routes I could take and what those semesters would look like. I was ahead since I have been completing courses in my undergrad.

Again, I decided to do the two-semester route, but in order to do so, I would have to complete the first two California Subject Examinations for Teachers (CSET) in mathematics. The CSET is a standardized test to prove content knowledge. I needed to pass the first two of the three subtests by May 1 if I wanted to do the two-semester route.

Three days later, on February 11, I was officially accepted into Vanguard's California Preliminary Credential Program. I received the acceptance email followed by another folder with a welcome letter.

My next steps were getting a Livescan/Fingerprinting at the Orange County Department of Education, a TB Risk Assessment by Vanguard's nurse practitioner, the Certificate of Clearance, and paying all the fees associated. I completed the first two in February, and I had the Certificate of Clearance issued to me later on April 8. The clearance meant that my fingerprints were cleared by the Department of Justice and the FBI. That way, the CTC can issue me a credential once I get recommended for one. My next priority was taking the two CSETs.

The first seven weeks of the semester, from January to March, were insanely busy, thanks especially to one of my core theology classes, Christian Heritage. That was a seven-week course, after which I had written on Facebook:

> I don't think I ever took a non-science course with so much work . . . It was literally 16 weeks of material crammed into 7 weeks. About 3-4 chapters a week with at least a 250-word response (or video response) to go with it, plus a 150-word reply to somebody else's response. And that was just Tuesdays and Thursdays. There were several videos [we had to watch] with 2-5 in-video questions . . . plus HUGE papers and/or videos to make that were due Sundays. Phew!
>
> And it all culminated with two [gigantic] projects (a group Church visit project with an oral presentation and [PowerPoint]), plus an independent Historical Figure project with these three things: Write a 5-page paper based on primary sources, film a 5-7 minute video saying some highlights of the paper, and watch three other presentations, followed by a short video response on all three watched . . .

And that was the past 7 weeks squeezed into two paragraphs! Needless to say, with Christian Heritage and all my other classes (including two main science courses), plus preparing for and teaching two classes of Royal Rangers every Sunday, I could not find much time to study for either CSET.

To my folly, I figured that since I usually got *A*s in mathematics, then I do not have to stress too much over the CSETs. After that seven-week course, however, I would make time to study for them.

On March 15, I registered for both CSETs. I was going to take subtest 1 on March 22 at 4:00 p.m. and subtest 2 on March 25 at 5:00 p.m. Both were held at the testing sight in Lake Forest.

Little did I know what terror I would experience right before then.

–15–

THE DAY I RAN FOR MY LIFE
MARCH 20, 2021

On Saturday, March 20, 2021, I figured that I would go on a walk. Again, I grew up hiking around the neighborhood. It is my catharsis. I get to relive memories as I clear my mind and process my thoughts.

Earlier that day, I gave a book recommendation on YouTube that was written by a fourteen-year-old boy who is mute and has Autism. He lives in the United Kingdom and had just released a book. I was not asked to do that, but I did so from my heart. I wanted to showcase his recent achievement, just as I want everybody's selfless achievements to be highlighted for the world to see. (Over the years, I shared other stories of people with Autism doing big things too.) I know firsthand how it feels to have people and places *appear* to ignore your heart in desiring to help the world, although I *know* that in some cases, they are flooded with other news tips and busy work. The family was thankful that I did that for him.

Every time I am out cathartically walking in the neighborhood, I do not know exactly which itinerary I will take, since my only destination is my origin.

This time I was walking down Westminster Avenue in Newport Beach. I heard a bicyclist come from behind me amid some laughter. I turned to him, and he slowed down, giving me a smirk. We both kept moving forward, and he matched my cadence. He was hardly looking where he was going for those few seconds as he stared at me.

All of a sudden, an older gentleman came rushing behind him on his own bicycle, and they raced down the street, laughing all the way. For the next ninety minutes, I walked all around Newport Beach with an ominous feeling. I felt hatred flying in the atmosphere like a phantom. The sunset skies had a dark, invisible sensation lurking behind it.

91

I found myself walking down the street on the other side of St. Andrew's Presbyterian. A car came from behind me and pulled into a driveway. I continued walking, but the person or people in the car did not get out right away.

Now, I am certain that this is because of my Autism, but after what just happened with that bicyclist, along with enduring one score of discrimination at this point, I tend to misconstrue a lot of things. I know when discrimination is real, but other times I am not certain. Then my Autism messes with me as it usually does. (On this note, later in 2022, I decided to append another subseries in my Autism Awareness and Acceptance playlist on YouTube called "How Autistics Interpret or Misconstrue Others Around the City." I also appended a subseries called "Autistic Walking in Public Places and Sensory Overload," where I walk around busy places, such as the beach, and articulate everything that I am feeling, the sensory overload, what I am thinking, and the whole nine yards.)

Since I just explained all that, I will now say that I interpreted it like this: the person or people did not get out of the car until I was far away to ensure their safety, as if I were a dangerous monster.

Moments later, I was walking by Newport Harbor High School, where there must have been a sports practice or sports game. A woman was walking out with her husband, I presume, but she looked at me in an odd and kind of disapproving way.

As I was looking up at the portentous skies and feeling the threatening atmosphere of doom, in retrospect, I was crying out in my heart, *Why? Why is this happening? What is the problem with me? What is the problem with being Autistic? How am I not doing anything to stop this if I have a book out and various social media accounts, all of which cannot get anywhere for the life of me?*

I kept on my journey, lamenting at the thought of an inauspicious future for me, no matter how much I fought with every microgram of my being and human existence. I was about to give up, but I decided to walk some more so that my mind could hopefully be cleared enough by the time I got back home. If not, I knew that my head would be torn to pieces in soliloquies all night long.

Keep in mind that I was studying for my CSET at the time too. Furthermore, I had realized from the practice portion that it was not what I was expecting. Many advanced concepts were in there that I was never taught in all those years of taking mathematics, especially abstract things called rings and fields.

Attempting to find some peace to conclude the hike, my darn little three-pound brain had the bright idea to go down a certain street. It was toward the end of sunset at this point. I noticed a sign with a heart and the hashtag, #BeKind.

Lately, I have been seeing a lot of these amiable messages, probably due to those suicide letters that I referenced in chapter 13. Many drawings of hearts tied with encouragements were popping up suddenly around Costa Mesa and Newport Beach. Some were signs, others chalk drawings, or still others were simply drawings of a big heart on a piece of paper that were taped up somewhere. I began taking pictures of them because they were very encouraging to me.

This is what the neighborhood needs. This is what the *whole wide world* needs!

As I was putting my camera down, I noticed a person turn his head in my direction. Then we locked our eyes.

Shoot! . . . Shoot!

I quickly walked forward and diagonally across the street. As I walked past the two guys, I heard laughter. I looked over and these were the same two bicyclists who I had seen roughly ninety minutes prior. I turned my head and continued to walk and heard more laughter. I turned around for a few seconds while still walking in the same direction. The two guys were both continuing to stare at me.

The older gentleman's arms were folded, and he had a huge, strange smile on his face. The younger had a disapproving smile, which is hard to explain, before looking down at the ground and looking back up, whilst maintaining that smile. It was his demeanor that told me that he was assuming I was a buffoon.

I did not know what to make of this. I continued forward, feeling hurt and terrible. I never met them, and here they are judging a book by its cover. A few steps later, I turned around one last time. Suddenly, I got consumed by this indescribable sensation of being in danger so I booked it out of there! I am not saying that I saw them come after me, but instinct told me to get out of there and *fast*!

After walking for almost two hours, I quickly resorted to jogging, which quickly degraded to brisk walking. I began feeling impending doom, bathed with liquid fear circulating around my arms and legs. That is what I literally, physically felt. If they were chasing me, then I only had one chance, which already had a low probability of success. I could not escape them if they were intending to harm me, especially if they decided to chase me on their bikes.

I started looking around and realized that Westminster is a longer road than I thought. If I ran into the alley and went for a wall that was protruding from the house, then I might not make it in time to hide behind it. I briskly walked past the alley, which was the last turn until the end of the street. There was no turning back now.

I began planning on the possibility of desperately pounding on doors if I had to, but that also required a wise decision since I would only have one shot at it. One, they might not be home. Two, they might not hear me. Three, and what I unfortunately believe would be probable, they might mistake me for a crazy man. Four, they might possibly choose to help.

If I went to the wrong door, then I would be done for. I could not assume that everybody in the neighborhood would act as human beings anymore. Alas, I say that because of my experience with discrimination in my neighborhood for nearly a decade at this point.

I finally reached 15th Street and decided to turn and go around the long way. Westminster takes you all the way past Heller Park a few blocks away, and the path is clear so that I would always remain visible, should those bicyclists be coming after me.

By the time I neared home, still walking briskly, I began hearing this loud, ear-piercing motorbike. At this point, I was on the other side of Heller Park, and the sound was coming from Westminster near where I stood. That is how loud it was.

I picked up the pace.

Does it all end here?! I lamented. *Right as soon I get home?*

The motorbike became louder and louder, speeding through Heller Park. I sprinted across the street and hid behind a small brick wall of an apartment complex, crouching low. I poked my head out of the side. The cyclist popped out, stopped at the stop sign, looked both ways, and sped off down Westminster toward Ogle Street and beyond. I took a deep breath, nearly collapsing. *I'm safe now.*

I stormed inside my front door and went upstairs. I washed my face and went inside my room, collapsing on my bed. Sitting there, I told myself, *I have to expose this! I must make a YouTube video about this.*

"Hello, everybody. This is Matthew Kenslow and I just got back from a hike that was about an hour and a half, give or take . . ."

That was the beginning of what became a video that made the rounds across social media and the world.

Now, just to quickly say, I make these videos as a catharsis, as I explained earlier in this book in chapter 6. By no means would I *ever* identify anybody. When I say that I expose things like this, it does not mean I expose the identity of the individual or other personal information. I would hope, however, that the individual would realize that I am talking about them, so the next time they see me, I could simply get an apology.

It was stressful, but amid queasiness and forced patience, I got the video edited and uploaded.

Within the next couple of days, I have received worldwide support on YouTube, Twitter, Facebook, and Instagram. I have received messages from people in Montana, Palm Beach County, Paterson, Sacramento, the United Kingdom, Switzerland, Nigeria, Spain, and elsewhere. Four days after the experience, I put together a thank-you video featuring all the messages I received through those four social media platforms.

Such support helped to comfort me a lot, even though it was not 100 percent. Without those kind messages and the extent of the support I have, I do not know how on earth I would have taken it.

The day after the incident, I was teaching the boys in Discovery Rangers on Zoom. Appropriately, there was a spot where my experience could help prove a point in the lesson regarding treating others fairly. When I told them that I had to run for my life the evening before, I saw one of the boys look up and have a worried face. I proceeded to make my point, tying in what I fight for in the world—a world of universal acceptance of people with Autism and other disabilities. Plus, we should be nice to those who are mean to us in the meantime, which I have stated time and time again.

Riddled with shakiness and fear, I did not go out on a walk again for precisely two weeks, except for one time that I will describe in the next chapter.

~16~

THE CSETS

On March 22, 2021, I was going to take the first standardized subtest for mathematics. Number and quantity was addressed first, then Algebra.

I experienced a couple of major hiccups because ever since my experience of being chased on March 20, I could not concentrate. I remember trying my best to practice. Every single little time I was struggling to answer a problem, I thought about those two bicyclists.

Finally, I was done with it. Next problem. *Bang!* There they were again, haunting my mind. This continued for quite a while and made me queasy. I tried going to sleep for the next couple of days. Nauseated. Amid what my stomach was feeling, I continued to dwell on how I was treated, thereby losing more sleep.

In retrospect, this seems peculiar since I have been laughed at all my life. Perhaps it was because I am an author and small YouTuber, and *still* I cannot be exempt from discrimination. (And of course, this is not a "me" issue; I want to eradicate discrimination against *all* disabilities. I am not trying to make a world who accepts me and nobody else. Such is not the case, so that is why I interjected that.) Perhaps it was also because I *have* experienced hardships all those years, and it is just not going away.

I tried my best to study, but I felt as if I were sprinting in water or fighting to run during a nightmare. I was much slower than I usually am. I kept drilling my way through the practice problems, notwithstanding how difficult a lot of them were.

Here is the other hiccup. March 22 was the seven-year anniversary of an event that I described in chapter 17 of my first book. Just like I made all those videos in August 2020 on the anniversary dates of being discriminated against, I previously decided to do likewise on March 22, 2021, and again on April 27, 2021, which is a different story. Both of which are now on YouTube. I held in all these memories for several years. I *had* to release them.

I already released what happened on March 22, 2014, in my previous book, but I was hoping for further closure if I returned to the scene, read what happened out of my book, and then expouned on it a bit *on* the anniversary date. What had occurred was I felt like a mother was truly viewing me as a kidnapper, which intimidated the daylights out of me as I walked past her.

So that is what I did. I recorded a YouTube video about it on the same day as the CSET. I could not do it afterward, for it would be dark by then. I felt a bit more confident about this subtest at this point anyway. I would have a bit more time once I got home to do last-minute studying.

As I was walking back home, a woman turned to me. I was not YouTubing at the time but rather looked like an everyday pedestrian. I smiled to be neighborly, but she gave me the strangest look because of that. She lowered her eyebrows, pinched her face as if telling me, "Who the heck are you?" and rushed inside her house.

Here I was trying to unload a hurtful experience, and my feelings were further being bruised. However, subsequent comments to these videos helped to uplift my countenance, tiding me over in the meantime as I strove to help establish relative world peace.

Once I arrived at the testing facility in Lake Forest, I went in, and it was nearly the same protocol as when I took the CBEST: picture, ID, palm scan, and ensuring that I am not bringing in any cheating devices on me.

Hours later, I walked out, somewhat confident. I was on the *border* of confidence. Again, I was trying to ascertain where those questions even came from.

For the next few days, I intently studied for the second subtest, which also included two domains: Geometry was the first, and Probability and Statistics was the second. The whole time, I was reflecting on the fact that it was precisely ten years that academic year since taking tenth-grade geometry at Newport Harbor High.

I filled out pages of practice problems that came from the sample test, as well as dozens of YouTube videos. Once again, I felt confident, but when I returned to Lake Forest on the 25th, I found that a myriad of the questions were not *anything* like I have seen before. Not even on their own study guide.

On both CSETs, I ran out of time to complete them, even though I had three hours. Both contained thirty-five multiple choice questions and three constructive response questions. Still, as a person with Autism, three hours is short anyway. Notwithstanding, for the same reasons as when I took the CBEST, I did not seek accommodations.

For the second subtest, I had no choice but to guess on several multiple-choice questions since I only had a minute left. Again, it was completely unlike what school has ever taught me.

"Now, I'm in the powerfully stressful waiting game, as it was an experience," I emailed the Credential Analyst/Student Teaching coordinator that night.

Meanwhile, I talked with that coordinator in the middle of April, just to talk about my fall classes and the schedule. She also said that she was working on my placement (the school where I would student teach). She and I were both hoping that it would be at Newport-Mesa Unified *at least*. My ultimate hope was to student-teach at Ensign Intermediate, if possible, but chances on having exactly what you hope for are always slim.

She was very optimistic that I passed both CSETs and tried to cheer me up. We assumed that I did, and she told me what my classes, days, and times were going to be during the two-semester route. Still, I could not be registered until I had both CSETs passed with documentation. That was going to come on April 30, the day before the deadline.

April 30 came. Math Subtest 1: "Did Not Pass" by *two* points! Math Subtest 2: "Did Not Pass." I was upset.

I am not surprised with my results of subtest 2, even though I studied for that one the hardest, but not passing subtest 1 by *two points?!* Just two points? I had to share the news with both aforementioned coordinators. I emailed my results.

Here is the PDF of the results of the CSETs that I tried my best on. With great lamentation and perplexity, I have no idea what the future holds now (Royal Rangers-wise, school-wise, career-wise, but those will take a lot to elucidate what I [mean]).

The Credential Analyst/Student Teaching coordinator replied, saying that we would talk the next Monday over the phone to discuss my options. "It is not the end of the journey," she said, consoling me. "It is just another pathway . . . A standardized test does not determine who you are." I came to terms with the decision, as if I had a choice.

What was additionally upsetting was the fact that I was trying to propose the perfect night to hold Royal Rangers. The senior commander and I were looking into a different day besides Sunday to hold our weekly meetings. Sundays were just not working out in the long run; we believed that more boys could show up if it were held on a weeknight. He told me that once I knew my schedule, then let him know about it. That is what I took notes on during my meeting with the coordinator in mid-April. After that meeting, I proposed that we meet on Tuesdays in the fall and permanently switch to Thursdays in the spring.

When I talked with that coordinator over the phone on May 3, she said that I had no choice but to take the three-semester route. That tore me up. I really wanted to get the credential by spring 2022, start the master's program that fall, complete it in spring 2023, and potentially begin my career by Fall 2023 (hopefully at Ensign Intermediate).

I was told the new schedule, including the dates and times, as a student in the *three*-semester route. I emailed the senior commander that everything was switched.

"Let us now do Thursdays in the fall and Tuesdays thereafter," I proposed.

However, it was ultimately decided that we would start meeting on Tuesdays indefinitely, but in an upcoming chapter, I will say how I was able to get around that conflict in schedule.

On June 13, I was officially enrolled in my fall 2021 classes.

—17—

THE SUICIDE THAT NEARLY TURNED MY LIFE UPSIDE DOWN

NOTE: Currently, I cannot divulge who this person was, or what relationship he had with me and my family. This is out of respect for friends and family. Let us just call him "a close friend."

On Sunday, May 2, 2021, I had just concluded teaching Discovery Rangers on Zoom. Of all days, I had concluded a bit earlier than normal because I taught everything I needed to.

Right afterward, I heard the truck coming into the alley. It was my mother, and I assumed that she just got off work. After parking, I heard her trying to tell my grandfather something, who had met her out there. I sprung up and listened from my window.

I heard my close friend's name. I thought I picked up on the words, "accident," "gunshot," and "gone." I began to worry that my friend had a terrible accident or something. I heard my grandfather repeat my friend's name as a question to confirm that he heard correctly. One second later, he wailed out loud. At that point, I knew.

I sprinted down the stairs, out the door, around the side, and into the alley. We all gave each other a group hug.

"[He's] gone," my mother lamented when she looked at me.

I was in a state of shock where I did not know what to do. I could not even cry. I could not believe this.

I heard somebody rush to the kitchen window in the apartment unit next to ours. As we were all processing the tragedy, I heard footsteps coming around. Our neighbor asked if everything was all right. All I had strength to do was look at her in the eyes and shake my head, unable to speak.

My grandfather told her what happened, but painfully. I saw him having the same exact physical pains that he had when he told me of his brother's passing, back on February 12, 2017.

"I'm so sorry. So sorry," our neighbor quietly said. She looked down and very slowly returned to her unit.

My grandfather and mother were holding each other during our entire trip to the front door.

"I didn't know he was depressed," my mother said. "They think it was the antidepressant medication he was taking that caused it. They just upped his dosage and that may have affected him in this negative way." He was only thirty-seven.

Later, I found out that he went to a party with his girlfriend and left early. The girlfriend soon got a call from their neighbor saying that they heard a gunshot.

After we all processed, I went back upstairs and sat down at my desk. I got the Zoom meeting ready for Adventure Rangers and just reclined there until it started.

I was thinking. I was contemplating. I hate suicide. My heart goes out to the victims and their families. However, I never knew anybody who committed suicide before, especially by someone who was that close to me. It puts suicide on a deeper perspective and deeper sorrow.

I conducted the entire meeting with all my strength and concluded a bit early. Unfortunately, the senior commander could not make it. I was the only commander there. After I finished, I called up the senior commander, followed by the mother who helped kickstart the Zoom meetings, followed by the former senior commander who taught Ranger Kids.

I let all of them know that my close friend had shot himself.

At first, I thought the suicide happened earlier that day, but later, I found out that he took his life on May 1. I had just gotten over the four-year anniversary of my aunt's death. Now this.

Later, the senior commander called me. He felt terrible for me. He was even amazed that I still conducted Adventure Rangers instead of cancelling it. He said that he took the liberty to let one of the pastors know and advised me to call her when I was ready. I did so.

"Hello, Matthew," the pastor said as she answered the phone, sounding saddened for me.

"Hi, Pastor."

We talked for the next half hour, which significantly comforted me. That night, I could not go to sleep. *This night is never going to end*, I concluded sometime past midnight. I went to bed with a headache, and I woke up with a headache.

That morning, I received a voicemail from another commander who heard the news. He almost sounded like he was going to cry at any second. He offered his condolences and his phone number in case I needed to talk to him. I communicated with him later on. The senior commander also called me and continued to do so for days thereafter, just to check up on me.

If any reader kept up with the timeline, I had just failed both CSETs on April 30, my close friend shot himself on May 1, I found out about it on May 2, and now I have to be in a phone call with the coordinator at Vanguard on May 3, who was going to tell me that I have no choice but to elongate my future study plans.

To make matters worse, my finals began on May 3. I had to take my EdTech final, not knowing what 2 + 2 was and hardly eating anything. However, I really felt confident. May 4 was what I stressed over. I had three finals between 8 a.m. and 8 p.m., all science too: Physiology, Chemistry Capstone, and Advanced Biochemistry. *Good night!*

Yes, I had the right to have an extension, but I did not want to deal with finals lingering over me while mourning over the tragic demise of my close friend. Furthermore, I was graduating Vanguard that Friday with a bachelor's in biochemistry. I wanted to be done with my finals so that it wouldn't hang over my head while being awarded my degree for which I worked two years.

"I'm going to tackle the finals on Monday and Tuesday no matter what," I wrote in an email to a couple of people who worked at Vanguard. I had shared the news with them about my friend, asking them for prayer. Again, Vanguard is a Christian university, so the university reverend was one of the people I emailed. "I have such a hole inside me right now!" I honestly told them.

Just to say, I passed all my classes! However, with such bereavement, it was tough to concentrate, retain any learning, sleep well, or eat anything. Throughout the many months following my friend's suicide, my stomach started to churn at any instant without warning. I put away food right after getting it out to eat. Whenever I walked in the neighborhood, in rare instances I would run into people who looked just like him, throwing me into a world of sadness and pain. Worst of all, the most random things reminded me of him. Perhaps it was a noise I heard outside my window, or a phrase that tied back to him somehow, or even a spontaneous movement that I made while walking. The tiniest of things brought back a memory of him, and I cannot explain how. Morning. Noon. Night. Midnight.

On May 5, I served at Lighthouse's youth group. Before it started, I asked the youth pastor if I could speak to him outside. That was when I let him know about my friend's suicide, requesting prayer from him. He felt really sorry for me and offered his condolences. He thanked me for sharing it with him.

On May 6, I attended the STEM Senior Dinner at Vanguard, endeavoring to enjoy myself, which I did. On May 7, I graduated Vanguard at Mariners Church in Irvine with a Bachelor of Science in biochemistry.

On May 11, I got an early wakeup call, so to speak. My grandfather was rushed to Hoag Hospital via ambulance. I only got a couple of hours of sleep at this point. While over there with my mother, inundated with mild queasiness, my medical passions categorically and indefinitely left me.

My grandfather stayed there all day and all night. I called up my senior commander and later, the aforementioned pastor. The commander told me to keep him posted, which I did. The next day, I was told the news that the doctor found a mass growing inside of my grandfather. The nurse said that the first thing my grandfather was concerned about was us, his family members.

I was completely lost in a state of shock. I called the senior commander to update him. An hour or two later, I walked over to Lighthouse Community to serve at the youth group. As I walked over there, scared to death that I would be discriminated again at such an inopportune time of my life, which had happened more and more often, I was bemoaning my entire life spinning rapidly downhill. *This can't be happening!*

I eventually arrived in one piece at Lighthouse, arriving there a bit early. I ran into one of the volunteers, who was walking over from the other direction. He used to volunteer with me in Royal Rangers.

"Walking today, huh?" he said.

"Yeah. I love walking," I replied.

"Good to see you. So how're you doing? You okay?"

"Well, I had a lot better days. You know, family wise. I actually had a lot better *months*."

We sat at the outdoor tables, and I proceeded to tell him about my grandfather since he was good friends with him. While we were talking, he definitely helped liven up my spirits.

During our conversation, the senior pastor of Lighthouse at the time came walking by with his wife. They decided to join in and talk with us.

"I've been praying for your family," said the pastor, a fellow author, hugging me.

"Hi, how are you? So good to see you," the wife said, before congratulating me on my recent graduation.

"I can't believe you already graduated," the pastor said, astonished. "Are we that old?"

"He's that good," the friend whom I was talking to interjected.

"How long were you there?" inquired the pastor.

"Two years at Vanguard, but like five years at OCC."

"Okay. I'm going, 'Wait a minute, that was like the fastest four years ever!' But that's still awesome."

"Well he crammed a bunch of credits together," the other friend said.

"Yeah, I had sixteen units a year ago," I informed.

"Wow. That's amazing," said the pastor's wife.

"I'm glad it's at Vanguard," I said thankfully. "Now two more years for a credential and a master's . . . Well, two and a half," I somberly corrected myself, remembering that my plans had to change against my will, yet most people were not aware of that at the time.

"You're still going to be there for a credential and master's?" the pastor wanted to confirm.

"Yeah."

The pastor told me that he went to Vanguard to get a teaching credential, but then plans changed and he decided to become a pastor instead, going for a master's in theology and theological studies. Through these minutes, we talked and shared some laughs.

"How are you doing?" It was time for the pastor to segue into a more serious tone.

"Um . . . Not a good day," I began, stuttering so much. "A lot of things going on with my grandpa and others. How much did you hear of it so far?"

"I only heard from your senior commander that it was [your friend] who took his life?"

"Yeah."

"Ugh, my heart hurts for that."

"And the service is this Saturday."

"Okay. Where's that going to be at?"

"Menifee. So we're probably going to go. My grandpa, if he's home, will probably stay home for safety."

"Is your grandpa in the hospital right now?"

"Yeah, they just discovered the mass and all that, but prayerfully, it's benign or just an infection. It's one day at a time."

They gave their condolences and sympathy.

"It's a *lot* all at once," the pastor told me. "That's a lot of things coming at you."

"Yeah, it's like this month, May, twenty seven—" I stopped myself before accidentally saying 2017, whose horribleness was still lingering over me, "uh, twenty *twenty-one*. It's just ups and downs. I mean, at the beginning of the month, we just got over the four-year anniversary of my aunt . . ."

"Right," the pastor's wife said, remembering.

". . . And then at the same exact time, my [special friend] did what he did. He was a joy to be around. And then, you know, I had graduation, but then grandpa had an emergency, and then tomorrow's a reunion that I've been praying to have for years, with another Christian circle I grew up going to, and then, the service on Saturday. The next Saturday after is Rangers, so *that's* a highlight."

For background, I wanted to do another leadership merit day like the previous October. We try to do at least two of these a year. The senior commander, wanting me to take charge and implement more responsibility, told me that I needed to set it up myself. I had spoken with this same senior pastor earlier, and he allowed me to use Lighthouse's facilities to hold the leadership merit. On May 22, I taught Leadership 103 all day to nearly a half dozen boys.

When I brought up Rangers, the pastor and I began to briefly discuss the service project that we were planning for the boys. Right before the pastor left, he said, "Matthew, if you ever need to process any of this, use my cell phone number. You can call. We can hang out. Whatever."

"Okay, thanks."

His wife felt so bad that I was suffering a tragic loss *and* the news of my grandfather simultaneously. She gave me a hug. "Keep us updated. Let us know, okay?"

"We will."

For the next couple of moments, I provided additional details to her and my other friend of what we were going through with my grandfather and how scary it was, not knowing what was going to happen next.

After the second hug, my friend said, "Okay, brother. We'll get you through. We'll be with you the whole way. You're not alone, that's for sure."

"Absolutely, that's true," the pastor's wife agreed.

At that moment, one of the high schoolers arrived. As my friend and I walked upstairs to the youth room, I asked him if he heard about the suicide yet, or if that was the first time he heard about it.

"No, I just heard now," he said, sympathetically.

A couple of moments after talking some more, he said, "Well, I mean, I would say I'm amazed you're here right now with everything you're dealing with, but God is building you up through all your adversities to present your testimony. He's been training you for this day, sharpening your skills for these moments. Just to be here, to be able to share with people, is amazing. Most people would give up and go, 'It's too much,' but I really appreciate you being here. It's teaching *me* a lot."

Those were quite reassuring words to hear, and I am so thankful to have made an impact like that. Nevertheless, the pain did not subside. Multiple pastors spoke with me and consoled me from the very beginning, but my loss caused a hole in my heart that has been nearly too great to bear. I still find myself talking to people I trust from time to time, in order to release hurt feelings over this loss and the manner in which my friend died.

This suicide nearly stopped my entire life, but I refused to allow it to. Even though people on social media begged me to kill myself for having Autism, not knowing that I am suffering from such a loss, I refuse to allow *that* to stop me either. Still, reading sporadic comments from people who desire me to be dead for having a disability that I never asked for, it makes my friend feel farther and farther away from my heart, increasing my sadness.

On May 15, a friend drove us all the way over to Menifee for the Celebration of Life ceremony. My grandfather, incredibly weak but extraordinarily strong, was going to be there at all costs. The medical staff at Hoag Hospital allowed him to leave early so that he could attend. He and I were two of the speakers sharing our memories of our friend.

While there, I ran into several friends, some of whom I only see on occasion, and we met new friends. We all exchanged hugs. One said that she bought me a graduation gift and that it was on its way. A few congratulated me on getting a book published. One of them, I believe, hates my guts, which put a depressing mood in what was already a depressing, stressful day. This caused me to once again question if I would ever amount to anything, despite what I had already accomplished.

Several months had passed, and it was nearing the very end of summer, in mid-September. I walked up the stairs and was heading toward the youth room at Lighthouse Community to serve. Suddenly, I heard the senior pastor call out to me from behind a window, "Hey, Matthew, there's no youth group tonight! You're welcome to join us, though!"

"Okay, absolutely! I'd love to!"

For the first time, I got to attend a cordial, amicable life group, which I was happy to be in. Everybody went around to unload what was going on in their lives. When it was my turn, I asked if I was allowed to say *anything* that was bothering me.

"*Anything* at all," the pastor replied.

Right then and there, I poured out my misery in the grieving process of a suicide. The reason I asked at first was because the topic was going to be heavy. I did not want to sadden anyone. They expressed sympathy, empathy, and words of encouragement. It felt great to unload the pain once again.

Sitting by me was the wife of the Royal Rangers commander whom I was talking to on May 12 outside of Lighthouse. Toward the end of the year, when I decided to regularly attend that church, I was sitting by that wife and commander. At the end of the service, the wife had a strong urge to pray for me.

"Matthew, I know that you are still sad about your [close friend]. As you were sitting by me today, I could just feel it coming off of you. I want to pray for you right now if that's okay."

I told her that she could. As she began to pray, along with her husband, she began to cry and fought to say the words. I did not have a dry eye either, and let me tell you why. Honestly, I *was* anxious during the service, but not in a way where anybody could tell. Inside, I *was* thinking about my close friend and in some way, shape, or form, that wife just felt it. My friend even appeared in a dream I had had the night before, which was not the only time, and I got to see him again.

I subsequently began feeling a bit guilty because I was not sure if my sadness would ever go away, yet she took the time and had the care to pray for it to go away, along with everybody else who had done so.

~18~
REGRESSING TO A DEPRESSING STATE
MID-2021

Toward the end of the dismal month, May 2021, I ran across a Facebook post from one year prior where I had shared an original quote/prayer that I came up with:

God, help me to help the helpless when I feel helpless to help them!

Once again, I felt tremendously useless. I felt that there was a world out there that needed encouragement, and I was there "shouting in a vacuum or through thick glass." That is literally how I described it on Facebook, but not a lot of people listened. That is because a lot of my Facebook posts, just like elsewhere on social media, were not being seen by others. Some of my Facebook friends validated my claim.

I had never stopped my endeavor to get myself out there in the media, churches, or the schools. Places were finally opening up, but hardly anybody reached back.

"While some are dreaming, others are doing, and I am that doer, but I'm getting nowhere," I put on Facebook after twenty-three months of being an author. I started believing that some of the media, churches, and schools were assuming that I was a charlatan trying to sell a book. The majority of my assumptions were false, of course.

(As an aside, there were still people who supported my book and told many others about it. For one, my Anthropology professor at Vanguard brought it up a few times back when we were meeting in person; she also had me autograph her copy before class one day. In subsequent semesters, my book became optional reading for her course. I got a few videos sent to me of students' presentations about my book, which was heartwarming to me. Later, in 2022, one of the commanders I had as a boy messaged me on Messenger.

He is a psychology and human services professor at Cypress College. He wanted to let me know that one of his students referenced me and my book in her paper. He also said that he put my book in the college library, just like at OCC. I felt extremely privileged. He had been a supporter since the beginning in 2019, meeting me in Fountain Valley to get two signed copies, one addressed to him and another being generic.)

"I do not need to be paid to . . . [help] people . . . find their belonging and purpose in this life," I also posted on Facebook. "All I ever wanted in my whole life was just to make a difference, [leave a] legacy, and [make an] impact [on] billions."

Nothing was left that I could do, as I seemed to be virtually invisible to every person, including people who needed help, as well as people who could help me help others in extraordinarily monumental ways, like getting me on the news, radio, et cetera. For years, I used the internet and social media to try communicating with more people. I contacted websites and newspapers pertaining to my expertise (Autism). I left behind hundreds of business cards and paid for advertisements. I tried these things many times over.

I solemnly believe to the point of *death* that I was commissioned to write this book, *Juggling the Issues: Living with Asperger's Syndrome*! I believe my message of acceptance, equality, equity, inclusion, encouragement, and motivation is *supposed* to be out there in the whole world. That is why I would never charge for any of my speaking engagements. The message that I was given to spread *has* to be spoken to everybody on earth.

If I am witnessing and experiencing discrimination, hatred, people who are hurting, and *even suicide*, then that means I am not crazy when I say this. There *is* a need, and I take it upon myself to fulfill it! How else are people in this world going to accept one another, believe in themselves, and put aside bullying and competition *once and for all*? But with 99 percent of everybody either saying no or ignoring me, I began questioning why I was placed on this planet.

I *know* people are already doing this, but how in the whole wide world is bullying not eradicated by now? We are one score in the twenty-first century. Therefore, I am not going to be passive, beat around the bush, cave into intimidation, or whatnot. I *will* give my life to stand for this!

I knew that somehow I would get asked to do assemblies at schools, speak at churches and on radio, and appear on television news and talk shows, but how?

I got so close in May of 2021. At the very beginning and middle of the month, I had communications with Zane North Elementary School over in New Jersey. The principal saw me on Twitter and thought that I could speak for their Special Education department. He tried so hard to make it happen, but for some reason, it did not, and the emails stopped coming. I was going to go there via Zoom.

That would have been perfect! In a world like today, I can go anywhere and be an encouragement while living here in Southern California. Why could it not happen yet?

During this year I had a close friend who shot himself and over twenty years of feeling hurt every now and again. If I was going to believe that I had *any* purpose on this planet, then I decided to once again publicly express my desire to help billions of people around the world.

I will *not* be silent!

I made a YouTube video that I titled, "IT'S TIME I BE HONEST! Most Transparent Video to Date |WATCH TO END To Fully Understand AUTISM."

In it, I shared that May 2020 quote, as well as my May 2021 quote, which is this:

I care -1 percent about myself, 101 percent about everybody else.

I subsequently decided to pour out my whole heart in this video and share it elsewhere on social media, regardless of whether or not it was noticed.

I humbly ask every reader to carve out twelve and three-quarter minutes of their time and watch that video. You will hear my heart from my own mouth at the same exact time I was facing these challenges. If you read some of the comments, then you will read how much I moved a few YouTube friends of mine. You will also read the encouragement that they gave me in the time when I needed it most. (More on this later.)

Sometimes, I am privately messaged on Instagram saying how much my videos mean to people, including this video. One individual said that he was not comfortable in commenting publicly, but this video touched and inspired him.

Nevertheless, a few days later, I posted on Facebook an over 1000 word post, in which I described myself as if I were "sweating blood" with a broken heart and a shattered circadian rhythm. I felt like any answer was "parsecs away" and compared myself to Habakkuk in the Bible. I felt as though I were "screaming in a vacuum" and that nobody was hearing the cries of help. I revealed that this was going on for over twenty-two months nonstop, making me feel anguished every single day and night.

I believed that I was not doing *enough* for others, as if I had hardly done a single thing! I believed that I would significantly help to totally eradicate bullying and discrimination. I believed *everybody* would accept us disabled for who we are and that *everybody,* disabled or not, would put aside their competition, come together, and believe in themselves.

Yet, I did not feel like anybody from the secular sphere or the religious sphere was ever wanting to give me a chance or take me seriously. (I am not talking about everyone.) Again, whatever I posted all across social media did not seem to be getting anywhere at all, no matter how much I tried, no matter how many reshares I posted, and no matter how many hashtags I used. In fact, this lengthy post (which probably took me an hour, just like dozens of other lengthy posts I ever wrote in my life) was not shown to anybody except a couple of my friends.

Now I am willing to assume that the majority of readers would contend that this is the lowest part of any human being's existence that anybody could possibly *ever* be at, and that it is *impossible* for it to have gotten worse hereafter and survive. The fact that a person who just has Autism and a heart to help and teach billions of people in treating each other with respect and acceptance has been bullied and discriminated for twenty plus years, misunderstood and countlessly told no when he just wants to volunteer his time, fought hard for years to get a book royalty-published and to *keep* it published, and lost a friend to suicide, there is just no possible way for him to exist if yet one more bad thing happens.

Well, guess again. The summer and early fall of 2021 was quite an adventure, to say the absolute least. Right now, I do not know what the heck that part of my life was. It was full of so many ups, so many downs, so many forceful attempts at optimism, and so many struggles.

In my daily walks that lasted till October, I walked farther in several directions than I ever had before, miles and miles away. I walked every single day for over one hundred days straight. I did not care about my health; I would typically walk for three to five hours at a time. I rarely ate or drank anything during the hikes and oftentimes never sat down for a break. I would walk around aimlessly to the point of pain and exhaustion, hoping for something. Anything.

The full details of June to October 2021 go beyond the scope of this book, but if I were to allegorize it, it would probably become a novel. Suffice it to say, I was in search of something. I did not know exactly *what* it was, *when* it would happen, or *where* it would come from. I may have been in search of a better life, I guess. Maybe I would finally run into people I could help teach, if they somehow happened to ask me, a random person, a question. Maybe a church or school employee might somehow ask me to spread kindness and cheer by voluntarily speaking someday in the future.

Still, I do not know what the heck I was thinking, for walking around two cities every single day for hours on end seemed hopeless. Yet, I was searching for something, somewhere, someway, somehow. In the attempt, however, I gained a myriad of hurtful feelings. (I gained an abundance of good memories too, but I will never forget the bad.)

To hammer out the bullet points, just because I am an Autistic who just wants a peaceful walk out in public, I was yelled at by a man in his car, almost hit by an SUV in a crosswalk, ran away from by a family or two, followed by a gray pickup truck, stared at by the most devilish-looking eyes that still haunt me to this day, cussed at from a passenger in a moving car, oddly stared at by various people, laughed at and teased, and even made a man take a step back and snicker just for saying hi to him. (I only said hi to him because he would not stop staring at me as I walked past him, apparently thinking I was an alien or something).

I did *not* look, walk, or act in a strange or suspicious way. When all those people did what they did to me, I was just walking down the street. I was not acting silly or crazy or whatnot.

And I was trying to help them! I was trying to get every person on earth to believe in themselves and each other. I did *not* want these bullies to get hurt themselves due to "What goes around, comes around." My message that I have been screaming to no avail applies to them too. Neurotypicals have a purpose, but it is not to bully. (I am not saying *all* neurotypicals behave in this discriminatory manner.)

I later made a lengthy post on Facebook, in which I put, "Imagine that you saved the world, and nobody cares! That's how it feels to me!"

That was the gist of the summer and early autumn of 2021, all while grieving and mourning the suicide of my close friend, not to mention seeing a couple of people who looked like him every now and again.

HOW? How on this planet did I live? How did I possibly survive all of that? How did I not die of a heart attack already? How did I not just become a hermit and hide under my bed for the rest of my life? How did I continue to believe in myself?

Well, it is just that! I forced myself to continue believing in myself. I figured that I would be a hypocrite if I dropped all of my schooling and did nothing except the little things I do. (Note: I am not calling what I do in Royal Rangers or Lighthouse Community "little." What I mean is that *I can do so much more!* That is what I have been screaming about from the top of my lungs, even though it was through a vacuum where no sound can go through. If I had all those hours to walk and all those hours to sit around at home, then that is proof that I had more than enough time to serve.)

I started reflecting on all my accomplishments thus far and the hard work it took to get to where I am. It is the promise that eventually, I *will* be an influencer to nearly ten billion people. I *will* become an influential teacher. I *will* become a volunteer juggler and speaker at *every* single school, public and private, in NMUSD and every other district in OCDE.

It is because I know that one day, I will be able to go outside my apartment for once and *never* be discriminated again because I have helped establish the awareness *and* acceptance of us with "disabilities." It is because I know that one day, I won't have to worry about hearing news stories of a person with special needs being bullied or of a child who committed suicide due to bullying, which I kept on hearing, unfortunately. *But wait,* I held on to these same hopes and promises for years, but it still never happened. My future seemed inauspicious!

Well, *here* is the immediate reason I chose not to give up on myself and what had tided me over in the meantime. True, I endured everything that I summarized earlier in this chapter, plus more experiences that I did not expound on in this book. Nevertheless, I knew that I had a loving family and countless friends rooting for me. I knew that my volunteerism had thus far made a tremendous impact for Royal Rangers around the world, the youth at Lighthouse Community, those who attended the annual HALO Benefits, and all those students I juggled for at Newport Heights and Rea. I knew that I had made an impact ushering at St. Andrew's Presbyterian for all those years, as well as being the tech guy at a couple of churches. I knew that I had made an impact on many worldwide friends on Facebook, Instagram, Twitter, and YouTube.

Speaking about YouTube, I will now explain what I meant earlier when I said that my friend's "encouragements [were given] in the time when I needed it most." The "time" meant all the times I was berated by all these discriminators (in my neighborhood and periodic "trolls" on social media). After those malicious, horrible experiences that I suffered throughout the middle of 2021, I would eventually talk it out on YouTube. If I did not, then my mind would not let me hear the end of it.

For instance, on June 19, a man at Westcliff Plaza's parking lot gave me a mean death-stare just for being who I am. As is usually the case, it was on first sight; we had never seen each other before. About ten minutes later, we ran into each other outside Ralphs, and he was tremendously mad, storming off in the other direction upon seeing me. *What the heck did I do?*

That night, he appeared in my nightmare, pointing at me, saying, "I just called the cops!" before morphing into the appearance of that man at Heller Park from August 18-19, 2017. The next day, I made the YouTube video entitled, "I Have to Talk This Out." This Video is for ABLEISTS and to Encourage People with DISABILITIES. Therefore, since I have Autism, in order to have the minimum closure to live my life, I *need* to talk things out, but as I said in a previous chapter, it must be done responsibly.

In March 2020, I decided to wear bodycam because of who I am. Thus, most of the experiences that I described were caught on bodycam, and they are now circulating throughout social media. If the person was too close, I would blur them out, of course. I am not against them; rather, I am against their bigotry for people who are different. If I were the only person to save them from death, then I would do it. I would even take a bullet for the worst "troll," which is actually something I said in one of my YouTube videos answering a troll.

In fact, to get this off my chest finally, a person from church had me blocked on Instagram for commenting on a few posts, complimenting them. I did not realize how much she strongly disliked me when I did nothing but be an Autistic, I guess. We both volunteered with the teenagers at a church. Whenever we ran into each other, I always smiled and said hi, as I do with *everybody.*

She sometimes said hi back, but after a while, I figured out that she felt obligated to. If I missed the opportunity to greet her by even one second, she quickly turned her head away from me or walked briskly away.

For nearly a year, before I realized what was happening, I followed her on Instagram like several other leaders from the church. On her posts, a lot of mutual friends from the church and youth ministry commented. I would comment as well, usually followed by a Scripture verse for inspiration. That was it. This is what I did for *several* friends whom I followed, so I was not targeting this profile.

Suddenly, one night in early 2021, I was blocked and kindly told by another person to stop commenting on her posts. That was confirmation to me. *Why?* Why did she simply not tell me herself, instead of allowing me to comment many times all those months, making me think I was simply misunderstanding the social cues and that she was indeed a nice person?

In the past, I had tried giving the benefit of the doubt before assuming the worst. She may have just been a shy person, even though she was really involved with the church. What I have a problem with is suspecting a church leader (to some degree) of hating Autistic people. I do *not* have a problem if they admit being shy.

Regardless, what was my problem? I am just an Autistic trying to bring cheer, equality, equity, and encouragement to the world! I am here volunteering my time for children and teenagers, not being paid, because I see potential in *all* of them. I tried convincing myself that it was merely a misunderstanding on my part. I did not want to believe that I, a person discriminated against since kindergarten, yet an author, was *still* being discriminated against in this manner, especially by a person who is involved at a church.

However, I ran into her again on September 4, 2022, while volunteering my time for the church. They were having a barbeque. As I was helping, she was coming down with her plate. My heart started to pound, and my stomach was queasy. I felt as if I were going to get weak and possibly collapse due to my lightheadedness. I had not seen her in over a year and a half. I was reminded of the hurt I felt when suddenly, I was rebuked, even though I was not explicitly told beforehand.

This was the moment when I would find out for sure.

Sure enough, before she got to the end where I was, by the eating utensils, she quickly turned her back and walked briskly out of there. She would not even look over in my direction. Her new husband, on the other hand, was happy to see me again and thought it was amazing that I appeared in *Newsweek* Magazine a month prior.

Now back to my earlier point. If I had never made the friends on YouTube from all across the country and world, then I do not believe I would be writing this today. I had no idea if I would be as far in my education as I am today. I had no idea if I would have become a student teacher. I had no idea if I could have physically and mentally pushed on. My friends on YouTube (who are typically firebuffers, planespotters, railfanners, and more), would come to me in the moments when I the most needed encouragement. They would often-times defend me if I had a troll in the comments section.

I started to build this camaraderie in 2019 and even more by the end of 2020. By March and April 2021, I had significantly built the friendships I have today on YouTube. They were the main ones who helped me during the low, dark valleys of my life. They supported me and shouted out my channel, and I supported them and shouted out their channels. We would watch and comment on each other's videos. I somewhat owe a part of my life to them. They motivated me, sometimes unbeknownst to them, to carry on with my life and calling.

Furthermore, throughout 2021, my channel began to grow. Because of my Autism videos, I also gained a lot of support from parents and fellow Autistics, among others.

One final thing before I conclude this chapter. Remember when I said that I made some good memories on my walks throughout 2021? Here are two of a few incredibly timed moments that I had the privilege to experience.

In the first story, on August 21, I was walking around Newport Mesa Plaza on East 17th Street one night. Suddenly, I heard, "Wait! Do you do magic? I think I remember you from like second grade."

I turned around to see a handful of teenagers looking over at me. I said the name of the teacher whom I juggled for. Indeed, I had juggled for some of them several years in the past.

A couple of them said, "That's awesome," and "Nice to see you again." "You, too."

"Do you have any magic on you?" one asked.

I searched my pockets. "Uh, unfortunately, no," which is surprising since I always carried many things on me that nobody else would.

"Aw, dang it!" the teenagers said, groaning.

"I left it at home, sorry."

"It's okay. Thank you. It was nice to see you," all of them said.

"You too. See ya." I turned around and walked away.

Suddenly, I got a strong feeling inside that they might be interested to know that I wrote a book, in which I talked about juggling for their class. Going out of my comfort zone, I pulled out my book from my jacket, which is what I *did* carry, and turned around.

"I'm really sorry to bother you, but since the time you were in second grade, I got a book published," I boldly said, combatting my lifelong shyness with each word, "talking about Newport Heights Elementary . . ."

"Oh, wow!" one exclaimed.

". . . and how it got started."

"What's your book called?" a couple inquired.

"*Juggling the Issues: Living with Asperger's Syndrome.*"

"*Whoa!*" they all exclaimed. "That's awesome."

"I thought I'd share my story and hopefully encourage the world, so . . ." I knew I was about to stutter soon. "I talk about juggling at Newport Heights."

"That's *awesome*," they repeated with huge smiles.

"We'll definitely have to check that out," one said.

"Thank you. Have a good night," I said and turned around and walked away.

For a little while, that one experience completely reversed the majority of all my hardships, pain, lonesomeness, and stress that I was enduring, which is just what I needed at such a time as that. Hearing all my friends' encouragements on social media wasn't enough to suffice, although that did help to tide me over. Experiencing something like this *in person* takes the serenity to the whole next level. I once again felt noticed and valued. I obviously made a difference in how some remembered me, even six or seven years later.

(In fact, really quickly, in 2022, after I crossed the street nearby the plaza, a passenger in a car called out, "Yo, you juggled for me in sixth grade. Dude, I remember that so much. That was awesome. Do you still juggle?" From there, we had a small conversation before the light turned green. In 2015, I was visiting my R.S.P. teacher at Newport Harbor, and a student remembered me from juggling in 2011, thinking that my little juggling assembly was amazing. Knowing that I had left a lasting impact like that, and that I was recognized by them several years later, provided unfathomable peace in my heart.)

In the second story, on September 19, 2021, I was taking an evening walk around the neighborhood. Once again, I regressed to despair, praying to God in my heart, for nothing else seemed to be happening. I then saw three boys biking on the other side of the street in the opposite direction where I was walking.

Unexpectedly, I heard a "Hello!" from one of them.

"Hi," I said and smiled.

"How was your day?" another one asked.

"Excellent! Have a good evening."

"You too!" he said while biking away with his friends.

The rare feeling of acceptance and inclusion in society once again imbued me, and I finally gained that momentary peace for a while. It was the perfect day too. Earlier that day, I was introduced to a daughter by a parent who was happy to see me again. However, the daughter stared into my eyes, unspeaking, pushing back against the seat, wide-eyed in fear. It was unmistakable, and I am not making this up. All I did was smile and say hi after being introduced.

I do not think that the parent noticed, but that shattered me. It gets to me more when children and teenagers seem to be scared at my presence, run away, or laugh at me (which happened many times, even in my nightmares consequently, for years).

I am the one who wants to spend my life helping them, encouraging them, mentoring them, putting smile and joy in them, motivating them to succeed in life, as well as tutoring and teaching them!

Then, at the time I felt the worst, those three bicyclists who never knew me showed up.

All that matters in my life is that I am influencing others and eradicating bullying, whether that is through social media, in the classroom, at churches, or wherever. It is my joy and daily motivation to give back and pay it forward.

On social media, reading people's comments about how much I have given people hope, as well as watching shout-out videos to me, I *know* I am on the right track in making an impact. Therefore, I *know*—if given the chance—that I will be a benefactor to society. I *will* change and leave an everlasting impact on everybody in my community and on this entire globe.

―19―

TAKING SUBTEST 1

For about ten days straight in August of 2021, give or take a day, I intently restudied for the CSET Math Subtest 1. After what happened in March, I was not taking any chances. I got right down to business, watching a litany of videos and doing a myriad of practice problems.

I still could not get over the fact that I failed by two measly points. I actually appealed it at the beginning. I paid a fee to have them take a second look, and on my birthday in July, in the midst of the chaos that I was living in (as explicitly told in the last chapter), they kindly gave me a gift saying that they confirmed my original score during the verification process, and that they would not alter my score. *Ugh!*

However, upon restudying, I felt very confident, but I was not buying their study guide one bit. I knew most of this stuff beforehand for years, and from what I remembered, most of it did not appear on the test I took in March.

I continued to research deeper, especially "Abstract Algebra," which covered rings, fields, and all that abstract stuff that I had never learned about, and frankly, stuff that I won't be teaching to middle schoolers anytime soon.

Nearing the big day, I scrutinized the sample test off of CTC Exams' website, which is something I did in March too. I practiced and re-practiced several of those questions many times over. August 24, 2021 was the big day. Fighting off queasiness, I arrived at the testing facility in Lake Forest. Passing *both* CSETs would mean the entire world to me. I packed my brain so hard for several days straight. At the time, it was the only way to prove content knowledge to the State of California, unless you majored in it. I took one final glance through everything, as well as did a practice problem or two. Once again, I went through all the formalities. I sat down in front of the computer and began.

Later, I came out with thirty-two seconds to spare, *excited and confident! Phew*, I felt so reassured inside, knowing that I had to pass after all that. Now onto studying for subtest 2, which I began later that day.

~20~

MY FIRST SEMESTER
IN THE CREDENTIAL PROGRAM

Three days after my CSET, I attended the mandatory Credential Orientation via Zoom. Three days thereafter, on August 30, I entered Vanguard University's campus to attend my first class. I YouTubed it. It felt so surreal to be back, especially to attend a normal class in person, and in the fall too. (Fall semesters are my favorite.)

My first class started at four in the afternoon and would last three hours. I walked inside Heath Academic Center, down the hall, and into room 105. Upon entering, the professor gave me a peculiar look at first. After one second, we passed by each other. I proceeded to go to the front row, which is where I usually choose to sit. I looked around to see if I recognized anybody from my undergrad. One looked familiar but ended up being a different person.

However, I was consumed with an odd sense, as if I were in the wrong classroom, or that I was conspicuous in some way. I looked around at my classmates who were talking with each other or waiting for the class to begin. And then I got it! The professor's look. That student. Everybody else. *Masks!*

Oh shoot! I quickly dug a mask out of my pocket and put it on. Apparently, nobody told me that it was still mandatory to wear masks indoors, and I am thankful that I was not rebuked for coming in without one. Thank goodness I always carried a couple of unused masks just in case, but just like in any classroom, there is a box full of them anyway.

The class that I was in was a five-week course called "Language Acquisition for Secondary Students," followed by an additional five weeks taking "Metacognition and Reading Strategies," concluded by a final set of five weeks taking "Literacy/Content Areas." Same days, times, classroom, and professor. (Metacognition is studying how one thinks, which is what we discussed throughout those five weeks.)

Some of my classmates were in their Beginning Student Teaching (BST) semester, which means that they were in the two-semester route, already student teaching at their placement site. Others, like me, were in the three-semester route, anticipating our BST semester come January.

In this trinity of Monday-night classes, we learned a wealth of teaching strategies and practiced several of them with each other. That way, we got a feel for what our future students would do if we chose to implement them. We learned various Specially Designed Academic Instruction in English (SDAIE) to help our English-language (ELL) students. We often referenced the California English Language Development (ELD) Standards to guide us in carrying out instruction that would help each ELL develop proficiency in English.

At the end of each of the three classes, we had to choose about ten to fifteen strategies, write down their purpose, and tie them in with our content knowledge. For instance, how can I use a particular strategy in a mathematics lesson?

Since I was not a student teacher yet, I had an opportunity to complete a big assignment at Royal Rangers. The professor wanted us to get experience actually teaching a person or group of people. For BSTs, they were already set. For the rest of us, our professor told us to teach a friend or family member. In the assignment, we had to collect data from a pre-assessment and a post-assessment. I raised my hand and said, "I'm about to start teaching the Compass merit to the boys at my Royal Rangers outpost. Can I do that?" The answer was a yes.

For my pre-assessment, I asked the boys to answer questions on what they knew. I told them that I was not expecting them to get a lot correct. I asked them to fill out the eight major directions, what they know about angle measures for when we start talking about bearings, questions where they would need to know certain terminology and such.

Within the next two lessons, I taught all the boys the material needed to ace it. I gave them the post-assessment afterward. Now I have two sets of data. I inputted them into Excel and calculated the statistics. I found this to be a very interesting way to prove that learning has occurred. Indeed, I was not teaching them things that they already knew, and I was finding out how effective my teaching was.

For another project I needed to interview a former or current ELL. I got to interview the senior commander from Outpost #68 in Santa Ana. Afterward, I gave a reflection as well as stated what actions I would consequently take in my classroom.

On Tuesday evenings, we had the course, "Foundations in Teaching for Secondary Teachers." In this semester-long course, we were taken on a journey through the history of education, the different philosophies of education, and the psychology of cognitive development, among other things. Some of the meetings were on Zoom, and the others were on campus.

The first in-person meeting was a field trip to Westminster in September. We all met at the Family Resource Center within Sigler Park. Zigzagging all across Orange County, I finally found the place. After the learning portion from our professor and Westminster's transportation manager, we took a walk around the Mendez Freedom Trail and went to the construction zone of the Mendez Tribute Monument Park. Our professor, the director of Vanguard's Graduate Program in Education, happened to have had a hand in it, partnering with the city. He also happened to have been the Chief Academic Officer of the Orange County Department of Education.

In one of the many interesting assignments for that class, I had to interview a teacher in my content area. I emailed my former prealgebra teacher from seventh grade and set up a Zoom meeting with her. She still taught in the same room where she taught me. It was great to speak to her again. She was happy to know what I had accomplished and where I was heading.

As I said earlier, Royal Rangers began to meet on Tuesday nights, but I got around that. The professor allowed me to leave the two-hour class a half an hour early. He would later fill me in on what I missed.

My fifth class was the graduate course of integrating technology in the classroom. I had to enroll in it so that I could have enough units for financial aid. However, it had a humorous start.

I was still hiking every single day at this point. I thought I would have enough time to order a coffee to go at The Coffee Bean & Tea Leaf at Costa Mesa Courtyards, which is one of the few new places I tried in the summer of 2021. (It was one of the good things that took place during the storm of 2021, trying new things and expanding my horizons.)

Upon entering Costa Mesa Courtyards, I calculated that there was no possible way I could get a coffee and arrive back in time. I began walking briskly all the way home, which was just under a half an hour's walk. A red light jumped out in front of me, and I had to wait. Further panic ensued. A few blocks later, I rushed inside the apartment.

I'm late! I'm late! I'm late! I kept repeating in my mind as I sped walk through the living room and up the stairs.

I opened up my email account, and I did not see a Zoom link, which further caused me to panic. I emailed both the professor and Credential Analyst/Student Teaching Coordinator.

Suddenly, one of my classmates I had met in my undergrad (because he also majored in biochemistry) texted me. He could not find the Zoom link either. *Phew*, I am not the only one. I was still catching my breath. He said that his friend was also having a problem.

Later, I found out that the course was only a five-week course that began on November 9, even though on Degree Tracker, it said otherwise. This class ended up being easy for me, since I already learned a lot in my Spring 2021 semester. It-was mainly asynchronous, where the Zoom meetings were typically there to ask questions. The assignments were given on Canvas.

On September 13, I received the surprising email of a lifetime. It congratulated me, saying that I was a finalist for the Teachers Test Prep 'Pass the Torch' Teacher Scholarship of 2021. It informed me that there were many applications that year, but mine was one of ten that were chosen.

Previously, on June 10, I had submitted a video talking about my former (and late) United States History and Geography teacher from eleventh grade at Newport Harbor High. I described how he had been one of the few influential people who further inspired me to get into teaching. My video was put on their website, among the videos of the other finalists. I was one of ten finalists in the entire country. I shared this news with my Foundations in Teaching professor. He was proud of me and shared it with the entire class.

As part of the reward for being a finalist, I was given free access to Teachers Test Prep's Core Plus Online Prep Programs, which are meant to help students pass the teacher certification exams, such as the CSETs. It contained several videos and practice tests. I got access to math subtests 2 and 3, as well as science since I wanted to teach that as well. That was also two CSETs to prepare for. One caveat they gave me was that I could not share it publicly on social media for two weeks.

And then on September 17, I received the email bearing the results of the CSET. I was nervous. I opened it. I *passed* this time!

I was overjoyed. I emailed the PDF to the aforementioned coordinator for my records. I let her know that I had been studying for the second subtest in math for nearly a month at that point. The two main domains were geometry and statistics, but at the time, I was still restudying geometry.

Throughout the rest of the semester, I continued learning various strategies, models, and theories in teaching and education. (I endeavored to implement a couple of the strategies while teaching the Compass merit at Royal Rangers.)

We learned about special education and neurodiversity. My research was in Gifted and Talented Education (GATE). We developed a classroom management plan, our own philosophy of education, our mission statement, and more.

My mission statement is as follows:

My mission is to encourage, mentor, and equip children and youth at churches, schools, and in the community with the goal of instilling a sense of purpose and optimism.

We got a taste of planning lessons, while abiding by the six TPEs (California Teaching Performance Expectations), CCSS (the Common Core State Standards), the California Curriculum Frameworks, and the ELD Standards.

On top of all my classwork, we had periodic journals and essays to write. We usually referenced books, videos, podcasts, and websites. One week, for my Metacognition and Reading Strategies course, I thought I would have some fun since it was appropriate. I found a spot where I could reference my book and then just left it there to see what would happen.

Later, my professor inquired about it.

"I had to do a double take when I read that and had to look it up," she said. "I want to read it over Christmas break, but is it okay if I borrow a copy for a week just to look through it?"

"Sure. I just have my traveler's copy on me, but I can bring one in next week."

Per her request, I brought in the copy for her to borrow.

On November 1, I had an advising meeting with the aforementioned coordinator to plan and discuss my Spring 2022 semester. As soon as I walked in, she pointed at her copy of my book and asked me to sign it.

Later that evening, my professor spontaneously asked me if I would be willing to take five minutes to speak on my journey of becoming an author.

"Sure." I was enthusiastic and grateful for the opportunity.

After we returned from a small break from classes, the professor said, "A few weeks ago in one of the learning journals, somebody referenced this book, *Juggling the Issues*. And I thought it was very interesting and made me want to investigate the book a little bit more. So, that's what I'm doing with the five-minute book pitch. I am going to go ahead and hand this over to the author." At this point, in my periphery, I saw some of my classmates perk up. The professor continued. "So that he can explain to us a little bit of the background of where this book originated and what its journey has been. There you go, Matthew."

Classmates began clapping, and I got to share my story. In the middle of it, I got to recite the biography of a couple of presidents by their number from memory. It was a very rewarding experience. I could not resist, but I filmed it to keep it as a special memory.

For the Foundations in Teaching class, we all created a "Professional Portfolio" website, in which we put most of our papers and philosophies. For the rest of the credential program, we continued to pack our websites with more assignments, lesson plans, our feedback from our Mentor Teacher (described later) and University Supervisors, and more.

The first semester, I felt, was phenomenal. I enjoyed it because of the interactions with my classmates, the practice, the knowledge I learned, and the fact that I had professors with a strong commitment to us teaching candidates.

~21~

A Little Dematerializing of My Storm Clouds

In September 2021, I was still feeling sad and lonesome that I could not simply juggle and/or speak at schools. I was upset that the current status of the coronavirus in the world still called for restrictions.

By this time, students were back in school. I decided to text my former third-grade teacher at Newport Heights Elementary to ask about the current protocols of visiting jugglers. He texted back, saying that volunteers and visitors were still not allowed yet.

Over an hour later, he texted me to say that the PTA was hosting a Fall Festival Trunk or Treat. One of the PTA mothers was asking if I could juggle at it.

My eyes lit up at that point and I texted back, "I'd be honored to."

I got in contact with the person and on October 26, I had the privilege of juggling at Newport Heights' Fall Festival. It was a marvelous experience. Afterward, I had to rush over to Royal Rangers. However, that was not the end to what I dubbed "my miracle week."

Earlier that day, the senior pastor at Lighthouse Community called me. He said that it was put on his heart to ask me to juggle for all the children during *their* Fall Fest Pumpkin Decorating event. You better believe I said yes!

It took place the next evening, Wednesday, October 27. I would have been there anyway since I intern for the youth, but it was quite a highlight for me to see the wonder and amazement on all the faces of the children when I juggled. But even *that* was not all. In fact, that was just the beginning.

The Sunday before, I decided to attend St. Andrew's Presbyterian again. It was my first time there in about ten months. It was wonderful to run into several friends again. I even got to meet a Facebook friend in person; we had been following each other for years at that point. The senior pastor (the same one I spoke with in his office two years prior in 2019) was walking down the main aisle. It was during worship, and I was standing at the end of one of the pews. He stopped to say, "I haven't seen you in a long time. Great to see you again, Matthew!"

I attended both services, after which I ran into ushers I volunteered with. One was happy to see me but then the look on her countenance dropped. She brought up my Facebook posts.

I had been expressing how drained I felt not being able to juggle, speak, or play piano as often as I had time for. Again, after Vanguard classes, Royal Rangers, and Lighthouse's youth group, I still had *hours* of time. I could have spoken somewhere at my expense. I could have been interviewed by some television, radio, or podcast company. I was still feeling invisible. Here is what I had written in one of my posts:

For months and years, my heart had just been hurting for other people. As Jesus sweated His blood in the garden of Gethsemane, likewise, I'm almost sweating blood to make a difference in everybody's life, whether that be in schools, churches, or even on television and radio if God leads. It was quite a depressing summer, not to mention the past two years. This very thing had been one of the greatest causes of my insomnia and daily/nightly distractions. I was hardly helping anybody when I prayed to. (I know I'm helping some, but not as much as I believe I can.)

She subsequently reassured me and implored me to continue looking to the Lord, no matter how mucky things were. Another usher came up to me soon after, her eyes tearing up. She begged me not to be hard on myself, for she had read a lot of my Facebook posts too.

"You've always been an asset to me. You've always been a joy. You're brilliant. You have so many gifts. Don't be too hard on yourself. You are so much loved." She sincerely looked me in the eyes. "Come to Trunk or Treat— the Fall Fest."

I nodded. "Oh, yeah. I was thinking about it." A huge banner was outside the church promoting it.

"Or volunteer, so you don't have to pay. They need volunteers for the games and stuff like that. You know, the different stands."

I thought I would throw it out there, so I said, "Yeah, I wonder if they could use a juggler."

Her mouth dropped. "Oh my gosh! Of course . . . That's *right*!"

"That's what I'm going to be doing Tuesday at Newport Heights."

"Yes, they need a juggler. Listen you're going to call . . ." She thought of the name and told me. At least I was putting my foot in the door, but I was not yet assured, since it was not set in stone.

The senior pastor was standing beside us talking to a couple of congregants. I started hoping that he would get me acquainted with somebody in person so that I would not have to call anybody. After talking with my friend, I walked over to the pastor. I had also been eager to show him the picture I took of the Jupiter-Saturn Conjunction of December 2020. That Christmas Eve, the pastor was talking about it in his sermon.

I began talking to him but had a little interruption.

"Do you know Matthew?" the usher friend I was just talking to came up and asked the pastor.

"Of course, I know Matthew." The pastor smiled. "Every year, he comes to Christmas Eve and ushers."

"He used to usher all the time. He was a great help. He was an asset to our church."

"Absolutely."

After we had a nice conversation about Astronomy and how my education plans are coming along, my friend told the pastor, "He's going to juggle at the Fall Fest."

"Oh!" the pastor exclaimed, looking at me, impressed.

Well, it's not set yet, I said in my mind, a bit nervous. "Uh, yeah, actually, I was just wanting to . . ." I stuttered. "I heard about the Fall Fest, and I said, 'Maybe they need a juggler.'"

"That'll be great! Can you dress up as something and juggle?"

"Well, uh, I don't usually dress up these years."

"You don't have to do much. Just a vest or something, like an English countryside juggler. What do you juggle?"

"Jugglebugs and clubs."

"You juggle clubs?"

"Yeah."

"Kids will love that."

"I'm doing that on Tuesday at Newport Heights."

"Good for you!"

Just then, the pastor got caught in another conversation, as people were leaving and cleaning up. The pastor was weeks away from retirement, so people were saying their goodbyes.

"I got to run," the pastor said. "It was good to see you. So glad you're here."

"Thank you. Is there anybody I should contact if I am going to be volunteering here?"

"Let me see. I'm going to find somebody."

Standing nearby was another minister I happened to know. Her daughters and I attended the high school youth group together there. The senior pastor called her over and told her that I expressed interest in volunteering as a juggler for the Fall Fest.

"Wouldn't that be a cool thing?" the pastor asked.

"That would be so fun," the minister said.

"And I'll buy some candy to have in a bucket in front of you, so kids can watch you juggle and grab some candy."

Right then and there, the aforementioned worship leader came up and hugged me. "I'm so glad you came."

"Yeah, and I really enjoyed the sermon last week online," I said. Again, in his sermon, he addressed suicide awareness in response to those suicide letters.

"Thank you. I really appreciate that," he said.

After talking to the minister for a few seconds, she bought me coffee at their church's café, Corner Café, and texted the new Director of Children's Ministries. The director came over and after *all* of that, I was an official volunteer!

On Friday, October 29, for two hours, I entertained hundreds of passersby with my juggling tricks and math shortcuts. For instance, I can multiply two numbers between 100 and 109 mentally in seconds, that and squaring numbers easily between 5,040 and 5,060. It was the largest event I juggled for that week. I juggled up to four "jugglebugs" (beanbag-like juggling cubes), three clubs, a basketball, and two soccer balls. Not all at the same time, though.

While there (as well as at Lighthouse), I got to deliver my "Juggling Analogy." Juggling represents passion and not giving up on what you want to do in life. If whatever you are juggling with in life drops (and I drop one on purpose), then bend down, pick it up, and keep going. At that point, I either do trickier tricks with three or I start juggling four, saying that you will eventually do more and more amazing things.

Afterward, I took to social media, starting with YouTube, to express how this was the best and happiest week of my entire life. I had written:

> *Right when I was about to lose all hope indefinitely, God graciously gave me this miraculous week.*

Nevertheless, I was earnestly hoping that this week was not a fluke. I have been depressingly disappointed many times before when my life started to appear to get somewhere, just like this week, but right afterward, there was a long-term, deafening silence. I was hoping so much that that would not follow, but since I am recounting this over a year later, I can say that that is exactly what happened.

In the beginning, I was holding on to that tenacious hope that this week was a springboard to skyrocket my volunteerism. I kept holding on to it with my life, like fighting to sustain a campfire once that first tiny flame begins to glow.

At least I was able to do what I did for those three occasions, and I am quite grateful for that. I texted back my former teacher to tell him the news of that week. I said, "It honestly instilled a lot of joy in me that's hard to explain, and I'm quite appreciative for everyone who was a part of it."

Toward the middle of November, I turned back to Facebook, explaining the relapse and requesting prayer, since I have not been asked to volunteer since late October. (And likewise in December, just to say.)

In December, I was on a Zoom call with my professor who was the CAO of the Orange County Department of Education. I told him everything. I wondered if he would have connections all throughout the county. My goal is to juggle and speak voluntarily for *every single* student and staff at *every single* school in the entirety of OCDE at least! Maybe I will get to branch out sometime in Los Angeles Unified and in other counties.

I did get a bit of hope in November. A friend messaged me about a new BBC documentary, "Inside the Autistic Mind," which is now called, "Inside Our Autistic Minds." Enthusiastically, I made a submission and talked about it on social media. A few friends from YouTube around the world told me that they had also written to them on my behalf. (Alas, by the end of January 2022, they apologized to me and rejected my story.)

What sustained me was the promise that I was called to be a teacher and that I would work hard in school to obtain that career, as well as be an influencer to everyone around the world. I was going to begin student teaching in January. I was going to continue being a commander in the Royal Rangers and a youth minister at Lighthouse. I was destined to juggle and speak in every school in the county. I chose to never lose hope on these promises!

This was always about *other people*. How do I seem to be a failure most of the time if all I want to do is to encourage others, especially children and teenagers? *I am not after money.*

I am after following my heart in donating my time to be an encouragement to others, disability or no disability. I do not need to take up juggling or piano playing to survive. I did not do all those years of endless practice for myself. I did not even earn two hard science degrees or an Eagle-Scout equivalent for myself. I am not studying hard in passing those CSETs or my credential classes for myself. It is –1 percent me, 101 percent others! What is the point of all my talents and knowledge if I am going to keep them to myself and not share them with other people, either for their entertainment or benefit?

As fate would have it, around this time in my life, the pianist at Lighthouse Community had to move away with her husband. I had already expressed interest in playing there from time to time. On December 5, 2021, I played the keys during their Sunday morning service for the first time and have been doing so ever since, including special events such as Christmas Eve and Good Friday. In February, getting my foot in the door again (or on the sustain pedal, if you will), I started to play hymn/praise medleys as a prelude for the five-minute countdown whenever I am there.

For St. Andrew's Presbyterian's Fall Fest and Winter Wonderland in 2022, I had the opportunity to juggle there for all the families once again.

–22–
Taking Subtest 2
and the Panic That Ensued

From the day I retook CSET Math Subtest 1 in August, until the beginning of October, I studied hard to retake the second subtest. Once again, I watched at least dozens of YouTube videos, practicing and going over what I learned on paper. And then a diversity of circumstances happened that made me pause studying for a couple of months.

I picked the studying back up in December. I watched and studied every single video from Teacher's Test Prep. I scrutinized their practice tests as well as the sample questions provided by CTC Exam's website. The date of the exam was December 22. This time, it was at a testing sight in Anaheim along East Katella Ave. I signed up for it the day prior.

I was a mess inside, not because I felt underconfident, but because of the time. I wanted to retake this exam in September or October, but many factors prevented that. I was to begin student teaching on January 3.

I wished to have been explicitly told that if I did not pass both CSETs yet, then it would be okay, as long as I get them passed sometime soon. I thought that I passed the deadline because I would not have my results back until early February, over six weeks later.

However, despite my *high* confidence levels, studying for *months*, and doing some last-minute studying right before entering, I walked out feeling, *What the heck was that?* I felt so down and depressed again because that CSET was unlike *anything* I studied for. I felt like my life was completely over!

Now I can't student teach, I thought. *Or at least for a long while. Still, I would have to retake it for the third time, pay the expense, and somehow pass it. If I couldn't pass it this time, despite studying* every *single resource* out *there, including an incalculable amount of YouTube videos, then how the heck can I pass it next time? Oh gosh! If I cannot pass, then I can never fulfill my dream of being a middle school math teacher.*

I started to panic. After several days, I came forward on Facebook and posted the entire story. This is the bulk of what I said:

This has been running me (and tons of other family and friends) ragged, day and night. For months, I studied for this CSET, referring to a couple hundred YouTube videos . . . I took the CTC practice exam that they offer freely on their website again. I watched all of Teacher's Test Prep videos twice with notetaking for this particular CSET, plus consulted additional resources, such as YouTube, for tougher concepts in statistics. I also took two CSET practice exams on the Teacher's Test Prep's website, plus analyzed over half their tutoring videos regarding the practice exams, not to mention day-and-night studying. The night before the CSET, after staying up most of the night and saying my prayers regarding this standardized exam, I went to bed thinking about formulas and all, and woke up soon thereafter thinking about formulas, and writing down all I remembered on a blank sheet of paper plus additional practice problems and proofs. Carpooling over to the Pearson place in Anaheim, I further studied and tested myself with the CTC practice exam.

I felt pretty confident. Not 100 percent, but like over 90 percent confident. Geometry and Stats formulas, methods, etc. At that moment in time, I'd probably be able to do every single problem on all three practice exams I had and get every single one right! I sat down at the computer taking the CSET, and almost none of it had been shown to me before! Like 90-95 percent of my exam was nothing I had prepared for. Sure, the concepts were there, but nothing prepared me for what I witnessed. The Teacher's Test Prep videos and practice exam bore nearly no resemblance to the actual test. What's funny is that the CTC practice exam said that the practice exam was supposed to be harder than the real exam. It was vice versa! I did the best I could, and I was confident on a lot of my answers, but gee whiz! I was forced to leave one of the constructive responses blank. A lot of the things I kept in mind (concepts, formulas, and such), I tried to employ and apply, but nothing [could] possibly prepare me.

I know math! I know Geometry and what I was able to study from

Statistics! But that CSET is something else! I mean, I always loved mathematics with straight *A*s mostly, and this is utterly depressing me!

This is very important for my near future. Obviously, God won't change my test answers, and I'm not asking Him to. My prayer is that all my answers [are] correct (there's a difference), including my "educated guesses," and that by leaving one of the constructive responses blank, I'd still pass, because I did most of the other two constructive responses. I'm hoping I got all 35 multiple choices correct by some miracle. As I was taking the CSET, I kept praying and supplicating all throughout.

And let's not bring up how I ran out of time again. Every single CSET I took (4 total), as well as the CBEST, I ran out of time. There's just no way anybody can possibly do them in the short, short time allotted. When I was doing all three practice exams, I estimate it took me at least six to eight hours each.

Okay, well, with all this said, I still have hope that I passed, but not confidence (there's a difference). If they fail me over this nonsense, then pray that I'll get a waiver because this is utterly ridiculous, after all the time, prep, and study I put into it. [I also had] confidence that what they had prepared me for was actually going to be on the exam, which it wasn't hardly. This is why I'm panicked. Without this, I cannot student teach, and without student teaching, I can't be a teacher. And student teaching begins soon for me . . . Again, if they asked the questions they prepared me with, I would've passed the test.

With a few more details, I also sent what I wrote above to the Credential Analyst/Student Teaching Coordinator, prefaced with the request to read all of it whenever she has the convenience to.

It was just unfathomable. I told her in the email that I love mathematics with all of my heart. From seventh grade to Orange Coast College, I took Prealgebra, Algebra AB, Algebra 1, Geometry, Algebra 2, Intermediate Algebra, College Algebra, Trigonometry, Precalculus, Calculus 1, and Calculus 2. How the heck could I not pass the CSET after all those years of taking mathematics? In fact, as I told her, I took Trigonometry for fun, not knowing that I would need it. And those were strictly mathematics courses, not counting all the math and statistics that I learned and implemented in all my physics and chemistry courses too.

I hope nobody blames me, but at the start, I asked my grandfather to call up all his pastor friends. I later went to Lighthouse Community and St. Andrew's Presbyterian to tell some friends, especially the pastors, of what was going on. I needed major intercessory prayer over this.

"Hmm, sounds like a setup," one of the fellow worship musicians at Lighthouse said, shaking his head, when I told him about the CSET debacle, to which others agreed when I later quoted him. A couple of pastors there prayed for me right on the spot.

"It'll be okay," the interim pastor at St. Andrew's consoled me after a brief encouragement. "Don't worry."

By the time I made my Facebook post at least ten pastors from across the county were praying for me. After my post, friends all around the world in multiple continents joined in. Again, I was not praying for God to cheat and change my answers. I do not know exactly what I was asking God to do, as a matter of fact. In retrospect, I guess I was praying that my choices and guesses were correct. I was highly confident on two of the constructive responses, so I was hoping that that would boost my score.

Nonetheless, that evening on December 22, right before attending the Christmas Eve band rehearsals, I decided to call Pearson. With immense passion for becoming a teacher, I was wondering if a service was available to grade my CSET early for a fee. I could not wait over a month! I guess it really shows how much this was bothering me if I am willing to make a phone call. (Recall how much I dislike phone calls, as a person with Autism.)

Finally, a gentleman answered. He sounded like he either hated his job or that he was just sleeping when the phone rang. As I stuttered through my request, he interrupted me and shouted, "No!"

I paused for a few seconds, wondering if I just heard correctly.

"I'm sorry, what'd you say?"

"We will not expedite the grading process."

"Oh, okay. Thank you so much and have a good evening," I said, hanging up the phone, feeling hopeless.

Notwithstanding despair, December 22, 2021, was actually one of the most victorious evenings of my life. It all started after rehearsing for the Christmas Eve service at Lighthouse. I was telling a person there that I was two subscribers away from 1,000 on YouTube.

Previously, a few boys in Lighthouse's youth and children's ministries were anxiously eager for me to hit 1,000. I, personally, was getting very antsy, as my Facebook friends could tell you. I am not one for telling people to subscribe, but when I got closer and closer, let us just say that I gave the invitation more than once.

After the person became my 999th subscriber, she remembered that she had another account of another family member. My heart started beating. We went outside since the Wi-Fi was terrible inside. I took out my camera to film her press "Subscribe" and refresh. There it was—"1,000 Subscribers" under my name. I cannot tell you how accomplished I felt over this milestone, especially since I posted at least one video on the platform almost every single day for nearly four and a half years.

I went over to St. Andrew's Presbyterian to usher their "Travelers Christmas Eve Service." I could not help but share the news with my friends over there. They were all very proud of me. That made my night, despite all the anxieties of the CSET. The next day, I made a big 1,000 Subscriber Special video, thanking everybody, as well as taking viewers on the journey of milestones since 2017.

~23~

My First Day as a Student Teacher
January 3, 2022

January 3, 2022 was, and still is, one of the most surreal days of my life. It was my first day as a student teacher. Since elementary school, I have had student teachers (including one for math during high school), but now, I was actually one myself. Furthermore, I felt very accomplished in taking the next step in my journey of becoming a teacher.

Where was I placed at? I count it as a miracle. In mid-November 2021, I received an email from the Credential Analyst/Student Teaching Coordinator with the subject line, "Student Teaching Placement." I opened it. I could not believe it.

I had been placed with a math teacher at none other than Ensign Intermediate School—the school I attended for two years! The school where I hoped to teach as a career. The school I first thought of when I decided to teach middle school math and science back in 2016. The school where some of my teachers still taught.

Oh my gosh! I felt so privileged and honored, except one thing—the dark cloud of the CSET retake was hovering over me.

I was told in the email that NMUSD opens back up on January 3. I was also told to contact my Master Teacher. The Master Teacher is the professional who was going to train me in teaching for two semesters. I would be in her classroom to teach, co-teach, and grade—the whole nine yards.

After a couple of emails, we determined that I should come in on Monday and Tuesday and take it from there. She said that she was excited to have me. Monday, January 3, 2022, arrived. I was to report to her classroom at 9:30 a.m.

I walked inside the front office. Two of the office ladies still remembered me from when I was a student there. They were amazed to see me and how much I had accomplished to get to where I was. They asked how my family was doing.

After signing in and getting a visitor's sticker, I walked over to the room and knocked. The teacher opened the door.

"Hi, come on in!" she said, smiling. "You can sit at the table over there, and then I will talk to you in a moment." She pointed before resuming her instructions to the class. I walked over to set my stuff down.

The students were working on a project and setting goals for the new year. I soon found out that it was Advancement Via Individual Determination (AVID). Her math classes were third and fourth period, whereas the first two periods were AVID. I looked around the entire classroom in awe—the students, the walls, everything.

After the bell rang, the Master Teacher gave me the workbook that her math students were using. "We're on Unit 5, Lesson 14. You can keep that. Kind of follow along, you know? You can take notes there. And I would look mostly for classroom management. That is like the *biggest* in middle school. That's what's the most important, seriously. And then you probably know the math."

I opened the workbook and wrote down on top "MR. KENSLOW (Student Teacher)," and underneath I put the name and room number of the Master Teacher, the school, and the semester (spring 2022). They were learning interest rates and percent change.

After the five-minute Nutrition was a third period. The teacher opened the door, greeted the math students for the first time in 2022, and told them all to come in.

Students poured inside the classroom and took their seats. One who sat at the desk next to my table looked at me, probably wondering who I was. I waved and said hi. He waved back. Not a lot of students seemed to notice me there, but soon, the teacher gave me a quick introduction.

"Over here, we have Mr. Kenslow. He is going to be observing me this quarter. And you guys. So, from Vanguard, right?"

"Right," I said, shuddering inside, because I have to get used to being called "Mr. Kenslow" now.

"So yeah, we're just welcoming him. Just to let you know that's what's going on."

In fourth period, it was a different story.

"Do we have a guest today?" one of the students inquired, wondering who I was sitting at the table on the side.

"Yes. This is my next thing. This is Mr. Kenslow," the Master Teacher said.

All the students swung their heads over to me.

"He is a student at Vanguard, getting teaching credentials. He's going to be observing."

"Hi, Mr. Kenslow!" a student said from the back.

"Hi," I said back, thankful to have gotten a greeting from a middle school student.

"He wants to teach math, so he's going to be in here observing, helping with whatever. Two days a week, I think; we're not sure."

In both periods, I followed along with the lesson and took down observation notes inside the workbook. For instance, I noticed the teacher handing out tickets whenever anybody answered a question. After third period, I asked about that and found out what that incentive was. At the end of the period, two tickets would be drawn for a small prize, like candy, pencils, or stickers.

I noticed that the teacher was using an iPad that had pictures of their workbook pages. This gave the teacher liberty to move around the classroom and through the aisles while she taught. As she taught the lesson, students would answer, and she would fill out that portion of the workbook on the iPad. I estimate that two-fifths of the class time was devoted to homework.

Overall, the first day was remarkable but numbingly surreal. I felt excited yet nervous. Both classes of students seemed nice and respectful at first sight, which gave me a little reassurance. I still had to introduce myself and gain their respect.

How successful will that turn out to be? I thought to myself, trying to give myself optimism. Nobody here yet knows me, or so I thought. Later on, I found out that one of them was a Royal Ranger I had mentored several years prior; we just did not recognize each other at first. And talking about a small world, my Master Teacher's husband is a P.E. teacher over there. I met him on September 4, 2007, which was my first day as a middle schooler. He filled in for my P.E. teacher for the first few weeks. Soon after, he told me that they had bought my book.

Speaking about the Royal Rangers, I began using her idea with the tickets and prizes. She thought it was neat that I began using her strategy elsewhere.

On that first day of student teaching, I left around noon. Before I did, all of a sudden, a few students started to run up to me. "Hey! Hey! You know [this teacher], right?"

"Yeah," I said, smiling.

"Yeah, you went to Rea! And you performed. I was at Rea when you performed."

"Oh, the juggling."

"Yeah!"

I began feeling respected and as if I belonged, honored to have made an impact on students who remembered me years later . . . again.

Honestly, for years, I have heard about the mannerisms of middle schoolers. A couple of years prior, I was inside Alberton's in Brea, self-studying physics by their Starbucks. At one point, all my papers dropped.

"Oh no," an older lady said, looking over from the couch, seated by her husband. She was curious what I was studying, and I told her.

"What do you want to do?"

"Become a middle school math and science teacher."

"God bless you!" She closed her eyes and leaned back against the couch. We had a cordial conversation thereafter.

One of my former teachers, years before, told me, "Um, they're good kids at heart, but why not become a high school teacher? That might be better for you."

These were only a couple of comments that I received. Still, even though they were not trying to be mean with their recommendations, I was determined. I *would* teach middle school.

Again, on that first day, the students seemed to be kind, respectful, and on task. Furthermore, those other students recognized me from juggling for them a few years previous.

As I left, I spontaneously decided to make a video journal about the first day. I had already chronicled my journey through Vanguard since 2019, so I figured that I would do likewise throughout my student teaching. Tons of my friends, including fellow planespotters and firebuffers across the country and world were congratulating me and wishing me luck. These included friends from across the United States and the United Kingdom, Australia, and India.

Nevertheless, I was not entirely excited inside. I was worried the entire time that I was going to get kicked out of student teaching at any second. Again,

I did not realize that it was initially okay not to have both CSETs passed. I truly dwelled over it all day, thinking it was over a 50 percent possibility.

However, a couple of lights were shining in the tunnel. The afternoon before, I got an email back from the aforementioned coordinator. She understood that my CSET experience was frustrating. She wanted me to come by her office to discuss a new option that might work. She said that I could possibly use my Orange Coast College coursework to prove subject matter. I actually did not open it until the next day after I got back from Ensign, standing to reason why I was worried. I guess I was nervous to open her email and worried about what it might say.

I nearly had a heart attack of relief. I replied, "This just really brightened me up and gave me some potential hope." I asked what time I could come over; she said that she was in her office all day so I rushed over there.

She first let me know that she read every word of my email. She told me that many people have complained over such standardized tests. She assured me that standardized tests do not show *everything* about a person, which was quite a consolation. In reality, a person could be knowledgeable in a specific subject, but standardized tests only select a small portion of the whole scope of a human being. Furthermore, such tests do not show a person's character or other abilities that individual has.

In my email, I said that I overheard some of my classmates saying that their CSETs were waived because they majored in mathematics. I was wondering, due to the immense amount of mathematics that I learned at OCC and Vanguard, if my CSET could miraculously be waived somehow.

She proceeded to tell me how my coursework at OCC might cover the requirements in proving content knowledge. She informed me of a brand-new California Assembly Bill, AB 130, that the governor signed into law that past July. In the most basic terms, as it pertains to me, it says that Vanguard could verify my competence in the subject matter by seeing if I took and passed qualifying, pertinent coursework.

"Right now, let us just wait for the results of your CSET," the coordinator told me. "If you do not pass, then we'll send the details of what you learned in your coursework to the department chair for mathematics and see what he says."

The department chair happened to be my chemistry professor for three semesters.

"Regardless," she continued, "go to the course catalog of OCC and send me the descriptions of all your math classes. We will compare them to the details that you are required to know, according to the CSET domains, and see if you could be waived. You might be waived for subtest 3 and if you are, then you can go for a full math credential instead of a foundational math credential. That way, you can teach *all* math, all the way through high school if you want to."

This brought peace to my soul. I wasn't even upset over all the hundreds of dollars I spent on the CSETs, not to mention the dozens of hours studying and the immense amounts of stress.

-24-

CONTINUING MY BEGINNING STUDENT TEACHING SEMESTER

Overjoyed, I continued to student teach and arrived back at Ensign the next day. It was sporadic at first. I only went there seven times in the month of January. I was being productive, however, mostly taking observation notes and helping out. I would usually stay between two and six hours throughout this semester; my Master Teacher and I would keep a log of everything for Vanguard.

We soon tuned into a Vanguard orientation meeting on Zoom with all the Master Teachers and student teachers. That was when my Master Teacher got a greater sense of my responsibilities and what was expected of me. I consequently gained experience in a lot more areas.

My former teachers still worked there, and they were all proud of me. However, I inquired about one of them. He was an aide to me and other R.S.P. students for about a year and a half. We followed each other for nearly a decade on Facebook, and I always wanted to see him again. We had not seen each other since June 2009 when I graduated Ensign.

"Oh, Matthew," my R.S.P. teacher responded, sounding very sad, "he just died during the break. It was sudden."

She proceeded to give me some details and I was in shock. I later shared my condolences in a Facebook post that I had missed.

In the middle of the month, I began my coursework at Vanguard, taking Instructional Design, which taught us innumerable teaching methods and strategies. We learned about different types of instruction, such as direct (teacher-centered) instruction and indirect (student-centered instructions), the latter of which included cooperative learning and inquiry-based learning.

We were introduced to Social-Emotional Learning (SEL) and Universal Design for Learning (UDL). UDL and all of its checkpoints help make it possible for all students to learn through multiple means of engagement, representation, and action and expression.

Four times that semester, we teaching candidates additionally attended seminars that thoroughly went through all the rubrics and expectations for the California Teaching Performance Assessment (CalTPA) Cycle 1. As a resource, we all had a digital copy of the handbook. Cycle 1 focused on planning instruction based on student assets; in order to do so, we had to learn about our students.

On January 31, I formally introduced myself to fourth period students (followed by third period on February 9). I had just handed out a one-page questionnaire that I had written so I could get to know the students and their assets.

It was a little hard to keep a straight face. "Uh, in case you guys didn't know, I do have a sense of humor, so this last question is Calculus 2, which I took four years ago, so you don't have to worry about that one." (I asked if a series was converging or diverging. Some of their answers were hilarious.)

After collecting most of the questionnaires, I gave my introduction.

"Here's just a little bit of who I am. I am actually a former Seabee. I'm class of 2009 here. It was the fastest two years of my life, around the time you were born, 2007-2009. And then I went on to Newport Harbor High School, class of 2013. And then I went on to OCC, where I got an Associate of Science in Chemistry. And then went across the street to Vanguard where I got a Bachelor of Science in Biochemistry last May. And now I'm in their credential program. And a couple of fun fast facts about what I love to do is I love juggling. I've been juggling for thousands of people in the past fifteen years or so. I also like playing piano, and I'm an Instagrammer, and small, professional YouTuber as well; that is who I am." At the time, both social media platforms began growing rapidly. On YouTube, I had just become monetized and had surpassed two thousand subscribers. That is why I usually included the adjectives *professional* but *small*.

Toward the beginning of my student teaching, during lunch, I remember walking around the campus, going somewhere. By the gymnasium, I overheard many whispers, saying, "It's the juggler" and "He's the juggler." I presumed I was recognized from Rea Elementary and probably Newport Heights. As time went on, many more students said they remembered me juggling for them at either of those schools.

Furthermore, throughout the semester, I ran into *several* former Royal Rangers from Outpost #33 whom I had not seen since before COVID.

In the math periods, I followed along with the lessons in my copy of the McGraw Hill workbook for Algebra 1. At home, I would get ahead of the game and pre-study upcoming lessons. Interest rates had not always been my strong suit actually. Regardless, as we later got into exponential function and quadratics, I still reviewed the lessons, summaries, and homework. That way, I got a feel of *exactly* how the State of California wants the standards taught and how they formulate the activities and questions.

"These are the honors kids," my Master Teacher told me one day toward the beginning. "So they all love math."

That was when my observations began to make sense. That was probably why they answered questions in a way that surprised me, as well as being quiet and mostly on task.

One morning, I asked the Master Teacher if it was all right to take questions whenever I saw hands raised during their homework time.

"If you feel comfortable, go ahead," she said.

It still took me a little while to get up and go to a student. In my heart I wanted to, and I tried to lean over and help at times, but I still faced timidity. I could *know* how to do the problem, but upon being asked, especially spontaneously, my brain needs a moment to get my bearings straight. That is a part of Autism, and I was not sure how many people would understand.

Then I began to worry. *What if I got it wrong? Or what if I'm taking a long time to answer? What if I have to raise my hand and ask the Master Teacher? Oh my gosh! How will I redeem myself? How would students trust me again in being a competent math teacher and tutor?*

Eventually, I was able to gain the confidence needed.

On day four for me, I was asked to grade the study guides, which I did. It was once again a surreal feeling that I was actually going to grade a student's work for the first time. I did so at Royal Rangers for years but not at a public school yet.

On day five, I got to rotate as an AVID tutor for the first time. Being an AVID tutor would be just as beneficial since most of the questions were about math. On rare times, some had a science question.

The teacher's seventh period was seventh-grade Basic Skills. She advised me to stick around for seventh period if I wanted to. That way I could help the seventh graders who needed a lot of math help. Additionally, it would give me more experience.

I remember helping out a student in the Basic Skills class for the first time. It was systems of linear equations. One student had a word problem. To be honest, I began to panic inside because I had not seen it before. My mind got in the way. If I had to call the Master Teacher over for help, then how would that make me look to her, *all* the students, and my immediate future?

Rereading the question, however, I got it! It was a basic slam dunk from there, and I did my best in articulating the method of solving. In subsequent weeks and months, I would float around during AVID tutorials, answering tons of questions, helping students in understanding.

Yet, there is one story that I lost sleep over, which I shared on YouTube. I must have been deeply thinking about something, looking out the window. All of a sudden, I began hearing voices, "Help! Help! Help! We need help!" The audible voices crept up to me, getting louder and louder and louder.

Suddenly, I snapped back into reality, looked in the foreground, and saw an entire tutorial group turned back in their seats, looking at me with raised hands. *Oh my gosh!* I thought as I quickly walked over to them and helped them out.

During seventh period for a few days, I helped out a particular student in math with fractions, operations with signed numbers, and more. I felt confident throughout those days of working with him, but one word problem stumped me. I had to look at him, resign to my fate, and say something to the effect, "Well, you can never be too old to ask for help." I turned to the teacher and raised my hand up high. That was not the last time, but it was only on occasion. I counted these times as learning experiences.

To my Master Teacher and other experienced math teachers at Ensign, I inquired about different methods of solving problems, learning how *they* teach it. I also remember one of the first times I helped out during a math exam. I felt pressured because I wasn't supposed to help them in a way that leads them straight to the answer. When a hand was raised, I took a deep breath and pushed myself forward.

"How do I cube numbers on this calculator?" the student asked.

"Uh." I was not sure if I was allowed to give her that information. "Let me ask to see if I'm able to answer that."

"Okay," she said and nodded.

I rushed over to the teacher, and she said it was okay. I went back to show the student how to do so.

Another student raised his hand. I took a deep breath and went over to him. He talked through the solution as part of his question. I was frazzled because I was not sure how much information I was able to share.

I stuttered throughout my response as I gave him a little information that I knew was acceptable.

"Oh, it's okay. I got it now. Thank you." He smiled widely behind his mask, I could tell.

Phew.

~25~
My First Lesson
February 1, 2022

For my Instructional Design course, we were required to do four formal lessons. For each of them, we had to fill out a daunting "Grad Ed Lesson Plan." By the time each of these were completed, they were over ten pages long. It was the same professor who taught me the Foundations class, the director of the Graduate Program in Education and former CAO of OCDE.

Here is a taste of what needed to be included (hold on tight):

- The California Teaching Performance Expectations (TPE) Target Skills that we chose to improve on

- The state standards and/or the curriculum frameworks for the lesson, learning goals, the rationale behind the lesson, and how it smoothly fits into the unit

- ELD standards and ELD learning goals

- Essential questions, academic vocabulary, the demographic profile of the class as a whole, the details of our three chosen "Focus Students" (including their backgrounds, assets, interests, aspirations, and considerations to accommodate for in their learning)

- SEL strategies, SDAIE strategies for our English-Language Learners, UDL strategies and any modifications needed so that *all* students can learn

- Differentiation strategies to meet special needs

- Higher-order thinking strategies so that students can ascend the pyramid of Bloom's Taxonomy

- How the students will be engaged, what educational technology we will employ, and any visual or performing arts we will incorporate

- A description of our formative assessment, a description of our summative assessment, a description of the student's self-assessment, a rubric that we created, and which instructional method we chose

- A summary of what the students learned before this lesson, a summary of the lesson objectives, a list of all the resources and materials utilized, a detailed procedure of the lesson (including the open, body, and close), how I would communicate the next steps of learning to the students (a foreshadow of what is coming next), the rubric data, an explanation of what was successful and what was unsuccessful, an insertion of graded student samples of the three focus students, and a complete reflective writeup (answering a *series* of multi-part questions), including self-reflection.

Good night! Nevertheless, what they were preparing us for were those templates for the CalTPA since the Grad Ed Lesson Plan is almost mirrored after them. Furthermore, Vanguard and the State of California is significantly molding us to become state-of-the-art teachers, so that *all* students can (and will) succeed. Most of the seven parts of the Grad Ed Lesson Plan were tied to various TPE subpoints.

Again, Vanguard holds a strong commitment to us teaching candidates. Being a small university, professors and staff have time to meet with us and help us out on-on-one, keeping every one of us updated on what we need to do and what we still need to turn in. Other places, I heard, give you resources to where you need to figure everything out. Of course, I am certain those other places would help each candidate but not as readily and promptly as Vanguard, due to class sizes. Furthermore, those four mandatory seminars thoroughly took us through every bit of the rubrics that we had to follow for our CalTPA submission.

I talked to my Master Teacher about what my first lesson could be. We settled on Unit 6, Lesson 5, which was part one of building quadratic functions, and we planned to use them to describe real-world scenarios. I was to teach that on February 1, beginning at 10:55. The teacher was going to teach third period, and I was going to teach fourth.

I got straight to preparing. I read through the entire lesson, filling out what I could, including notes on what I should say at certain parts. I later went to the teacher's edition to ensure that I was including everything that is recommended. Of course, not every teacher can hit every single point that is suggested. When I was done, I went through all the pages, notes, and ideas with the teacher, who gave me feedback.

The day before my lesson, during lunch, I practiced using the iPad. February 1, 2022, arrived. I had rehearsed the lesson several times by then, just in case. That is what I told myself I would do from the beginning. I had previously told a couple of people about my upcoming first lesson, including my former R.S.P. teacher and prealgebra teacher.

"I will try and stop by for a second," said the R.S.P. teacher. (She ended up being busy and had to hear of how it went later.)

During Nutrition, I went to the Master Teacher's husband, the P.E. teacher. It had previously been arranged for me to borrow a basketball and a volleyball, which are of two different masses. I had brought a soccer ball from home for a surprise at the end.

In third period, I sat at the table on the side, opened up the workbook, and followed along. I made a couple of quick final notes for my consideration as I watched the lesson being taught first by the teacher.

The bell rang.

Now was the time.

I took the iPad and went to the front podium, on which I placed my opened workbook with all my notes.

The teacher gave me a little pep talk. I felt ready and exhilarated, with a smidgen of eustress.

Before the bell rang and while the students were being seated, the teacher said, "We're going to have Mr. Kenslow do a lesson with us today."

A couple of students gave a little cheer.

"So I need your full attention, just like normal. Raise your hand. Participate. Thank you so much. So we're doing lesson 5, tomorrow is lesson 6, and then a quiz on Thursday."

When the bell rang for the class to begin, I used my nerves to push me forward.

"Well, good morning, everybody," I began.

"Good morning," a student replied.

I started by imparting to the students that I am still getting used to talking through a mask and that I will try to enunciate clearly, although I subsequently told them to raise their hand if they needed me to repeat anything.

I really had no idea what to expect teaching a class of middle schoolers through an impediment. I spoke better, relative to when I was diagnosed with a speech delay at the age of three, thanks to speech therapy all throughout school. I would have loved it if I had given them a *complete* introduction to who I am, as a person with Autism, my limitations, and the successes I had thus far, despite a "disability."

The teacher sat at that side table where I was at, filling out the Lesson Observation Protocol (LOP). Throughout my lesson, she evaluated me, scoring and commenting on various TPE subpoints.

I started with the warm-up and first activity, which was designed to help students build and use a quadratic equation. I asked questions and allowed them to ask questions. When one student raised his hand and derived the equation, $y = 16x^2$, I asked him to share how he figured it out, to which he explained all of his steps in thorough detail.

Moments later, I showed them a neat trick in determining what type of function you have, given an X-Y table. Is it linear, exponential, or quadratic? While I was doing so, a few of the students participated, jotting the trick down.

"And that's how you know that you have a special type of function called, what's this unit about?"

"Quadratics," many students said.

Linear functions have a common difference. Exponential functions have a common ratio. Quadratic functions have a constant second difference.

At this point, I remember being a bit nervous because this was a bit extra. I had not gone through every single detail of my lesson with the teacher. I never knew if I was going to be told to move on or hear, "That's too much" in front of everybody. However, I went through it efficiently, and the students understood it well.

I led them through two activities, which took up the bulk of the lesson. They dealt with a rock falling from a skyscraper and free-falling objects. Students were challenged to find out the distance that the object had fallen after a certain number of seconds, followed by the general expressions. Several students participated. Sometimes, a couple of different answers were offered, and we addressed them to determine the correct one for the situation. I continued encouraging new voices.

Halfway into it, I proposed the hypothetical of the object being something other than a rock. Suppose it is a boulder or a car. Would it accelerate faster?

If the object drops faster, then that would mean we must have an equation for every single object on the face of the planet.

It was time to do the classic science demonstration. I took the basketball and soccer ball (I ended up choosing that over the volleyball), explained that they are of two different masses, and asked them which one will hit the ground first.

A lot of students pointed toward the heavier object.

"Probably the basketball. Also, it looks bigger, so it has an increase in volume," one said.

I took a quick poll.

"Let's test it! So three, two, one."

Both landed at the same time with a loud thump.

"Whoa," some of them said.

"Do an eraser," one student called out.

I was not expecting that, but I thought it would be good for students who were curious to know. I took the eraser and one of the sports balls and dropped them. Sure enough, they landed at the same time.

A student then handed me a pencil to test it.

"What about a staple?" another student blurted out, to which some laughed along with him.

"No," I said, chuckling. "Last one." I smiled, entertained that students were expressing their curiosity and wanted me to test it. I took the pencil and one of the sports balls and dropped them.

"Whoa." Students continued to be impressed as objects seemed to drop at the same exact time.

"This is something you'll learn more about in physics later on," I said. "So, that's just a little demo. Yeah?" I called on a raised hand.

"Can you juggle those for us?" a student asked as I was about to put them away underneath the podium.

"Let me say that, uh, 'We're moving on here,'" I quickly answered, "and if you guys are well behaved, then I have a surprise afterward. Just a little surprise, just a little . . . okay, moving on!"

Some students laughed.

"Okay, five point three. Galileo, oh, one of my favorite scientists." I rushed on to the next activity, yet I was truthful in what I said, due to my interest in astronomy.

I had a student read, followed by my advice on how to approach word problems. Soon after, the screen froze, which I knew was going to happen. It had been happening during fourth period at the same time in multiple classes. The teacher rushed forward to fix it.

As she was doing so, I thought I would show that I can keep a class from losing focus by asking, "Does anybody have any questions so far?"

Dead silence.

"No? Okay."

I then told them to take a look at the tables in their workbooks and see how they are alike and different. I did not necessarily need the iPad to introduce that, since the tables were in their textbook. I sent them off to make observations for a few seconds before the connection was restored.

I continued with the lesson. Before I sent them off to do the homework, I took out the soccer ball that I brought from home, and as an incentive, I said that I was going to juggle them. That is why I stammered earlier when that student asked me to juggle because I was planning on surprising everybody.

However, something strange happened. It is easy for me to juggle, say, three soccer balls. I can juggle a beanbag, a club, and a basketball at the same time even. I have been doing so for several years at this point, yet it was harder to juggle a basketball, volleyball, and soccer ball for some reason. I had no clue how it happened, but one kept on going outward instead of upward, to where a student caught it. Oh well, I got to make it up later on. At least I got to juggle a little for them and they applauded.

Once I completed the lesson, I went back to the side table where the teacher was sitting.

"Great job!" she whispered with a big smile.

"Thank you," I replied, taking a seat and watching for any hands raised.

Being my very first lesson ever, I was intently concentrating on everything I was saying and teaching. I am a person who typically gets nervous at the thought of being asked a question in front of everybody, not knowing the answer (or at least *how* to answer it *concisely*). However, I believe I did a great job, and I knew the content well enough to answer immediately.

I was also confident in answering questions that a couple of students asked during the homework portion too. There was a thirty-second hiccup toward the end with a student's calculation. I walked over to him, and he showed me what he did on the calculator.

"Oh, my bad," the student eventually said. "I clicked the wrong button."

"Okay. You almost gave me a heart attack there," I said, walking back up to the front. "I'm like, 'Math doesn't do that.'"

Toward the end of the period, before the bell rang, one of the students noticed something on the table. I almost always carried my traveler's copy of my book. I got to show my former eighth grade Language Arts teacher, among others.

"You have a book?" the student asked, probably noticing my name as the author.

"Yeah."

"Oh, nice. When did you write that?"

"2019."

"That's so cool. Wow."

"Wait, you wrote a book?" another student overheard and asked.

"What's it about?" the first student asked.

"About my Autism. I mentioned Ensign fourteen times in it. Let's see if I can find one really quick," I flipped through the pages. I had red memo cards bookmarking places where I mentioned Ensign specifically. "Ensign Intermediate School," I said, pointing.

"That's very cool."

Then the tickets were being pulled, followed by the bell ringing.

"Thank you," a student told me.

"You're welcome. Have a good day."

A few seconds later, the teacher came over, opened up the LOP that she filled out, and gave me her constructive criticism. She had a ton of praise for my first lesson, which made me feel wonderful, but a few things that I may have not noticed. Some of the students started to go on and finished the next page. She told me that I should monitor that next time and told me I can use the seating chart to "cold call" students if I want new voices. This would help them participate since they sometimes won't do so in situations where I say, "Raise your hand." She noticed that students started calling out here and there in lieu of raising their hands, which I did not address.

She liked how I went very deep in my explanations, had high expectations, and was clear about them. She complimented how I used a visual science demonstration, tried my best to engage all students in participating, and had students read at times. She said I was very knowledgeable in what I was teaching, had planned and designed the lesson in-depth, had time management, spoke with academic language, encouraged the students to speak with such vernacular, and handed out the tickets.

"Do you feel like it went well?" she then asked me.

"Yeah. Of course, in my mind, I always critique myself."

"Totally."

"I always look back. Maybe not 100 percent."

"Well, I think next time, you should do the lesson twice. Do it in third period *and* in fourth because I saw that you did a very good job. Then you have the opportunity to do it twice. I always remembered that I did it so much better the second time."

"Yeah, I kind of observed that too in weeks past."

"Oh, for me? All the time. I'm always better in fourth period because I have done it twice. So, that's also an option next time. Now that you've done one, we can try to do two, *if* you want."

"Yeah, that'll be good."

"Cool. Awesome. Good job!"

As I was leaving to return the sports balls, she complimented me again, saying, "Great job, buddy. That was great."

After a while, I found the P.E. teacher. Turns out, he was in the gymnasium presiding over Sustained Silent Reading (SSR), which is a half an hour for students to read, study, or do homework.

"I returned them," I whispered.

"Good. Thank you," he said. "Everything go well?"

"Yeah," I said, nodding.

"Great job, buddy."

"Thanks."

Afterward, I returned to the classroom.

"So, when are you teaching your first lesson?" the art teacher asked me. He usually ate his lunch in that room with a couple of other teachers. In fact, he used to teach math there.

"It was today."

"Oh!" He was enthusiastic. "How'd it go?"

"Excellent." I smiled.

A couple of weeks afterward, I volunteered to re-teach a part of my lesson to all of my classmates at Vanguard. For each of the four required lessons, spaced out within the semester, the teaching candidates got in groups of four or five to rehearse our lessons. Our class was four hours long, and on rehearsal days, we typically spent about an hour of it practicing our lessons and getting feedback. The professor would make the rounds, since each group got our own room in Heath Academic Center.

I was one of the students who already had the first lesson completed. That was typically the case each time. On this evening, February 17, the professor called me up to teach part of my lesson, pretending like I was in my classroom teaching my students. I brought the tickets and prize box that I purchased for Royal Rangers, as well as my soccer ball and basketball. I made a PowerPoint slideshow, as we all did, which gave the background (lesson title, standards, learning goals, and such), the rubric, and the lesson, culminating with a time for questions and answers.

The lesson portion of the slideshow was divided into the "Anticipatory Set" (the warm-up activity), the main content of the lesson, how I modeled the math for them, the guided practice for the students, and their independent practice. As soon as I got to the Anticipatory Set slide, I jumped into my character as a middle school teacher. I kept it concise since I was allotted about ten minutes total. It turned out great, and my fellow classmates participated, and I handed out a few tickets as a result.

During the science demonstration, something unforgettable and humorous happened. I asked them, "Based on the given information I just told you, which one is going to land first?"

"They're both going to land at the same time," one of my classmates said a few seconds later.

"Yeah, because we're all in a university. You all know it!"

Everybody began roaring in laughter.

"But a couple of my students," I explained once I regained composure myself, "thought the heavier one was going to land first, so I went like this: 'One. Two. Three.'"

I dropped the items, saying, "And they landed at the same time. And one of them gave me a pencil, so I took a pencil and a ball, and they landed at the same time."

After class, the professor and I were the last two left.

"That was a really great lesson, Matthew," he told me. "I *really* believe that Royal Rangers has significantly helped you in your ability to teach. I really enjoyed it. Bravo!"

I categorically concurred that all my years as a commander in Royal

Rangers had given me the practice and the patience for teaching, instructional strategies, and in various reward systems. I repeated all of this to my senior commander, who had always been interested in hearing of my accomplishments and teaching updates. He works at Newport Elementary, a school whose backyard is literally the sands of the beach. The senior commander agreed with my professor without question.

And now, my courses and experience in student teaching is, in turn, improving me in being an effective commander, so they complement each other greatly.

-26-

THE FATE OF SUBTEST 2 AND BEYOND

On February 4, my phone began to vibrate while I was in class at Ensign. It was the Credential Analyst/Student Teaching coordinator, and I could not answer it.

Yikes.

During Nutrition, I emailed her the explanation that I was in the middle of student teaching.

She immediately emailed me back, saying to call her when I was finished, that she would be in her office until two.

Oh dear. This is serious! I began to assume the worst.

I could not wait until after school, so I called her during lunch.

"Matthew," she said, "I know that you have been really worried about your CSET. I just wanted to let you know, *you passed*!"

"Oh my gosh!" I almost collapsed. "Oh my gosh."

"We get the results a day early, and I didn't want you to wait until tomorrow. You passed. Congratulations!"

"Thank you so much."

After hanging up the phone, I pulled out my camera. Right there in the parking lot of Ensign, I recorded the update. I walked back into the classroom with a huge smile. A few teachers were there eating lunch. When I told them my news, they all were very happy to hear it and congratulated me.

Three days thereafter, the coordinator emailed me saying that the department chair in mathematics, who was my former chemistry professor, was going to sign the document that would officially waive me for subtest 3. The professor had written, "That seems reasonable to me; I have also observed his applied calculus skills, and they are more than adequate."

I was jubilant. The next morning, the coordinator obtained the signed document and told me that I was now eligible for a full math credential.

$-27-$
MEETING WITH THE SUPERVISOR

One week after my first lesson, I had my initial meeting with my university supervisor, who was in Kenya. I logged onto Zoom, followed by my Master Teacher a few moments later. He was in Kenya because he spends about three to six months at a time over there, helping with eight schools and setting up their own school. For the teacher and me, it was about 7:30 in the morning, but for him, it was 6:30 in the evening.

"Hey, Matt," the supervisor said as we waited for the teacher to log on.

We began talking about my first lesson and how things were going. Normally, the supervisor would come in four to six times throughout the semester, observe me teaching, and give me feedback afterward. Due to the restrictions and him being on the other side of the world, I only had to meet him on Zoom twice.

The meeting was essentially an introduction to the teacher and me, how we were getting along, and about my first lesson. The second one was to analyze a lesson, which I will write about later.

"I heard you wrote a book," he said. "I'm in the middle of writing a book too, so maybe you can give me some tips on that later on."

The teacher soon joined in, and after introductions, she gave her input on my first lesson. She explained how I watched her teach third period and that I taught fourth. She said that I came in super prepared with a ton of notes and the science demonstration. She was impressed that I was able to do the ticket reward system, even though it was my very first lesson, as well as involving as many students as possible.

"Good! That's awesome. I love that," the supervisor said.

"Yeah. He did all the right steps. I was impressed," the teacher continued. "He's even going to teach again tomorrow just because he wants to."

"Hey, you know what? I'm all for throwing into the deep end and getting as much teaching experience as possible," the supervisor responded.

The teacher began talking about her AVID classes and how I was helping out in tutorials. The supervisor happened to be part of a large AVID program up in Riverside.

"It's not like being a clock watcher; it's being a time manager," the supervisor said, imparting some wisdom and giving me a pep talk for my future lessons. He assured me that it was rare for even experienced teachers to have a "perfect lesson." He proceeded to tell me about the importance of "crisp, clean transitions," checking for understanding, focus on not just teaching but teaching *and* learning, scan the whole class as much as possible, monitor the students, and more impactful pedagogical wisdom. (Again, pedagogy is the art and science of teaching.) He told me that next time, he would watch a video of a lesson and coach me from there.

The teacher then gave me additional advice that she forgot to say earlier. After I was done with my first lesson, I went and sat down. I *had been* alert for raised hands, and I went to them accordingly, but the teacher told me to still walk around and monitor.

We soon concluded the meeting. The supervisor said that he was more than happy to answer any of our questions and to give me coaching any time I feel like I need it. After this great meeting, I went over to Ensign for the day.

~28~

BUILDING CONFIDENCE AND TRUST

I continued teaching lessons, even if they were not toward the four required ones. I was eager to gain as much experience as possible. Not only that, but teaching is what gives me a sense of purpose and daily motivation, *clearly*, as I laid out earlier in this book. For nearly a decade, I labored to teach and tutor at my expense, but the bulk of what I got was Royal Rangers, JBQ, and Lighthouse's youth. Everywhere else . . . well, you know the story now. (I am thankful for what I had, do not get me wrong, but I could have done a *million times* more within that entire decade if given the chance.)

It had been my joy to be at Ensign. My Master Teacher and I decided that I would teach one lesson a week. I also started going there for five days of the week instead of just two. The same day I had that meeting with the university supervisor, I had completed fifty hours of the 100 minimum. I later exceeded the minimum by over double.

A peculiar thing happened after both my second and third lesson, however. The second lesson took place on February 9. Both periods I taught Unit 6, Lesson 10 regarding the standard and factored forms of quadratic functions and comparing such functions to their graphs. Toward the end, I included the Zero-Product Property as an effortless way to find the X and Y intercepts.

The teacher interjected this remark: "Make sure you're all writing this down, because it's going to be important for the future."

(Later, one of the students commented on one of my teaching update videos on YouTube, thanking me for teaching the Zero-Product Property, which I thought was nice.)

"Great job!" I said, about to conclude my lesson in fourth period. "Thank you, everybody. Just go and do the summary, two to three annotations, the rest of the practice, and I am available for questions and clarifications if needed."

Then a peculiar thing happened.

Suddenly, every student began applauding me.

"Boy, thanks," I said, not knowing what to make of it. "I'll go on tour. No, I'm kidding."

Some of us laughed. I then apologized about not handing out tickets. It was a Wednesday, which was early-dismissal day. Classes were forty minutes as opposed to fifty. It took a lot of concentration to get through the lesson twice, especially considering that the lesson was five pages in the workbook. Thus, I was nervous to hand out tickets, wondering if I would get through everything if I did. The teacher encouraged me not to teach on Wednesdays as I first practice teaching.

I tried cold calling, but the teacher recommended that I should stop using that method for the time being. I was wanting everybody to participate, but I began forgetting who I called on. I also wanted to be fair and alternate between boys and girls. For these reasons, I took valuable seconds in choosing the correct person; I had the seating chart on a clipboard in front of me the whole time.

The teacher gave me the seating chart to memorize the names, but I thought, *I'm good with dates, but I'm horrible at memorizing names, despite their school pictures being on the seating chart.* Nevertheless, through determination and spending a lot of time with the students, I soon got all the names in fourth period memorized, followed by third period students sometime thereafter. After teaching third period, I had a brilliant idea. I would highlight the names of those I had cold called.

However, the teacher insisted, "Just don't do it."

I suppose that I was a bit hesitant to cold call regardless. What if the student did not know the answer? What if he or she really did not want to get called on? That is why I was always comfortable calling on raised hands instead. The teacher helped me with my hesitancy later on in my student teaching.

Notwithstanding my stuttering during cold calls, the teacher said that I had "great use of time." She also loved a method that I guess I invented.

"Hold up one finger if you believe it's this, and hold up two fingers if you believe it's that," was the gist of my strategy. I continued using it throughout my student teaching. It is probably not original but is something that I thought of myself.

In this lesson, I made brief use of the whiteboard, writing the general expression of factored form and likewise with standard form, numbering them one and two, respectively. It was quick, but I asked them which one was standard form. "One finger if you say it's the top expression, and two if you say it's the bottom expression."

Another thing that was recommended to me after the lesson was moving around the class more. At first, it was not the easiest thing to do, since all my notes were in the workbook on the podium. When I got farther from the podium, it felt as though I were swimming out farther in a pool or ocean. The teacher said that I was better at it during fourth period. This was another thing I improved on throughout student teaching.

I also employed a strategy that I learned in one of my fall 2021 classes called "Think Aloud," where I walked through a problem step-by-step, explaining everything that I was saying in my mind. The students just watched and listened.

Overall, the teacher said that my lesson "flowed well!"

My third lesson took place on February 17, after which the peculiar thing reoccurred during fourth period. After teaching Unit 6, Lesson 14, all about using quadratic equations to model real-life situations (like a frog jumping or a pumpkin being catapulted) and their graphs, all the students clapped for me. I also got a hand in more educational technology. Desmos is a graphing software that students can access on their Chromebooks. When appropriate, in certain lessons, the teacher would have students take out their Chromebooks and open up the application. This lesson was the first time leading the students to Desmos, to which the teacher said, "Good job."

She liked that I was explaining *all* the math, but I do not have to write every single thing down on the iPad. She also appreciated that I was calling on students using their names but warned me about some of them who called things out without raising their hand.

She encouraged me to walk around some more, yet I still felt tethered by the podium. Again, I may know everything, but my Autistic brain usually draws a blank, especially when I am in front of others. I have been noticing that at Royal Rangers for years. I could rehearse my lessons a few times flawlessly, but once I got in front of others, I would fear that I forgot something. Then I got tied up in a sea of stuttering, making myself appear incompetent when I am not.

She gave me great tips on how to respond when students are incorrect. I sometimes did not know what to say other than, "No," followed by an explanation. The teacher encouraged me to lead the students through the solution together, as well as to ask other students for their input while arriving at the answer.

At this time of the semester, about a month and a half into student teaching, I began feeling like I fit in. I described it to the aforementioned coordinator like this: "Student teaching at Ensign is just *wonderful*! And that's the simplest (yet understated) way I can describe it without writing a novel."

Students appreciated me teaching and helping them. One time before I taught a lesson for third period, I was standing by the door, greeting the students while holding the iPad. I usually do that regardless, thereby maintaining a positive and safe learning environment. It is my joy greeting students coming in, and I surmise that the usher ministry at the nearby St. Andrew's Presbyterian helped me out with that.

"Are you teaching today?" one student asked, eyes lighting up.

"Yes, I am." I nodded with a smile.

"Let's *go!*" the student said with excitement.

That made an impact on me. I always hoped to get that type of reaction, but I refused to cave into wishful thinking. I figured that it would take a long time to build that trust and confidence for students to have in me.

Previously, I had begun to feel a little discouraged inside. At Vanguard, one of my classmates was sharing aloud to the class, describing his experience as a student teacher in history so far. He had a similar experience with the high schoolers who became excited upon seeing him, saying, "Let's *go!*" During one of our breaks, I was talking to him outside, and he gave me some encouragement, not knowing that I was questioning whether I would truly gain such a response from students. And there it was, right before third period one day.

Furthermore, by the middle of February, whether it was in school or out of school, several students would say, "Hi, Mr. Kenslow!"

One day, I was walking down East 17th Street to U.S. Bank.

"Hey, YouTuber who goes to my school!" one student called out from the vehicle, to which I waved back.

Further down East 17th Street, a student on his bike yelled out, "Hi, Mr. Kenslow!"

"Hi." I waved.

Just then, I saw two adults by Mountain Mike's Pizza looking around, startled. Then they saw me and realized what was going on.

As I approached, I said, "I'm a student teacher, and he is one of my students."

"That's what we figured," they said, smiling. We carried on with a small conversation after that.

This happened nearly a year ago, as of writing this, and I can say that within the past year, *hundreds* of students have said hi to me out in the neighborhood. During one hike, I ran into a few different groups of students. Several have called out to me from the car, bicycle, restaurant, store, you name it! Situations like these significantly brighten my day or even my week. I would say that about 97 to 98 percent of all students at Ensign are nothing but kind and respectful toward me.

To reiterate what I said in a previous chapter, when I was telling people over the years that I want to be a middle school teacher, 99 percent of them warned me against it and even attempted to deter me from teaching that age group, but I never listened. I am thankful because my passion is to teach at a middle school. I believe in all of the students and see great potential. Sure, I have witnessed middle-school behavior all of my life, but I still have no idea what some of those dissuaders were talking about. I ran into many who are nice and courteous.

Part of the reason why it changes my mood to hear many students say hi to me is because when it happens I finally begin to feel worth and value. It is as though I am contributing to their lives and not being an invisible person, like before—a person who was never noticed, standing in the background. That has always shadowed my life, as I described in the beginning of the book. Furthermore, I have been utterly discriminated against in this neighborhood in the past, which I also expounded on.

I have spent my entire life endeavoring to make a difference in other people's lives, and now, I feel as if I am doing so in greater ways by a factor of a thousand. I am thankful for the opportunity to serve in this manner.

During free time, students would ask me what it was like when I was a student there. I told them, among a couple of other things, "For one, there were no Chromebooks. We also got to use the lockers."

In April, students found out that I knew all the presidents—their presidential number, birthdates, death dates, term dates, and other fun facts—from memory. They began testing me by picking a number between one and forty-six. It brought a sensation of timelessness, because when I was a student there, that is exactly what all my friends would do.

One day in May, when I went to several classrooms to deliver call slips to the teachers, many students in nearly every classroom were surprised to see me, saying, "It's Mr. Kenslow," and "Hi, Mr. Kenslow."

A lot more students began finding out that I was a YouTuber as well.

"Hey, aren't you on YouTube?" one student called out to me after school, recognizing me.

"Uh, yes I am."

Another day, right after school got out, I was standing outside the office. A student came up to me asking if I was the YouTuber he heard about.

"Yes," I replied.

After a brief conversation, he concluded with, "I think you're very cool."

From that point on, every time I walked by, he would say, "Hey!" and wave. One time, he said sympathetically, "Sorry about your grandma," which I appreciated. Valentine's Day 2022 was the ten-year anniversary from my grandmother's unexpected passing at the age of sixty-three. I made a YouTube video about it, explaining for the first time publicly what that day was like and concluding with a short tribute to her.

Sometime later, I was walking toward the library or office for something.

"Hey! Hey, can we get a picture with you?" I thought I heard in my direction but figured I was mishearing. A few minutes later, I was walking back to the classroom, and I heard it again. I looked over, and a bunch of students were sitting at a bench.

"Can we get a picture with you?" they repeated.

I was much obliged, but I said as I was walking toward them, "You think five thousand subscribers is that notable?"

"Yes, I enjoy your videos! Can I please get a selfie?"

Just then, a few students got selfies with me. (For background, they chose to study outside so they would not have to wear masks; their substitute teacher was out there with them. Also, the last day we were required to wear masks came a little later on March 11.)

"I appreciate your support," which is what I always say. I do not believe I am famous (nor will I ever be). What I put out on social media is to encourage and motivate others. I am not showing others what my talents and accomplishments are to gloat. I am not believing that I am the only person with the abilities and nobody else. In fact, I hold true to what I said in one of my early teaching updates in mid-February regarding my chronicling of this journey:

"I also like using this journey to show that you can do whatever you set your heart and mind to do, despite a disability. Just don't ever give up on your passions—persevere and keep going. Have a nice day!"

In March, I was student teaching when suddenly, an AS350 Écureuil helicopter came circling around and hovered, very loudly. Lots of students, teachers, and staff were distracted by it and on-edge. I was helping a student with the graphs of parabolas when they were either stretched or compressed. I heard a distant man's voice yelling, "Hey!" coming from outside.

We are going on lockdown at any second, I thought, dreading it. I distracted myself by helping the student, yet I was prepared to hear the all-call announcement. It did not happen. For some reason, I had to go to the office. While there, I inquired about the helicopter.

"We don't know yet why it's there," one of them told me. "Our on-campus safety officer said she hadn't heard anything about it."

She asked me to give a description. I said it was an AS350 Eurocopter, but I did not notice any design that would suggest it came from a police or sheriff's department.

Once I came out of the office, the same students who were on the bench a week prior were sitting there and called out to me, saying hi. They said I should make a YouTube video. Since I had a few seconds, I walked over to the side to take pictures and a video of the helicopter. I like documenting things, so if this becomes a major news story, I can at least show my grandchildren that I was there, and here is my footage of the helicopter.

Those students continued to laugh and make comments about the helicopter. When they saw me filming a YouTube video, one said something like, "Matthew Kenslow's first."

I was like, "In action!" as I started to zoom out.

As it turned out, it was a news helicopter. *Phew!* When I got home, I found out that a police chase with a stolen yacht had happened. By coincidence, we had just had a fire drill prior to the helicopter coming.

Later in the semester, when I crossed ten thousand subscribers on YouTube and 100,000 followers on Instagram, I said on YouTube that these milestones are *proving* that anybody can do anything, even with a "disability."

Essentially, my message is that nothing is limiting us. People from all around were encouraged when I said that.

Before I continue, I am *not* saying that *all* "famous" people or "social media stars" are arrogant whatsoever. Just in case, that is why I do not want to put words like *famous* or *celebrity* next to my name.

Speaking of which, in March, one of the third-period math students asked me how many followers I have on Instagram. This was right after I crossed the 100,000 followers milestone on Instagram.

"Oh my gosh," he said, stunned when I showed him at the end of class. He leaned over and whispered, "He's got 102K."

"Was I just being taught by a celebrity?" the former Royal Ranger in that class exclaimed.

"Uh, well," I stuttered, "I would never call myself a celebrity."

"Oh, how humble," another student said.

Later in the spring, several students told me, "You should get TikTok, and it'll help you reach more people." After much persuasion, that is what I did, which is why I got the account.

As the year continued, I taught more lessons and helped out. I tutored in AVID, SSR, and Basic Skills to the best of my ability, mainly in mathematics and science. While doing so, it was strictly professional, and I was not getting carried away with my life as a social media influencer. Students asked me to help them with their assignments, and they learned in the process.

Periodically, outside of their learning, students continued to request pictures with me, complimenting me on my YouTube channel. On rare instances, students requested my autograph. I counted it more as being accepted than being treated as a celebrity. That is why I appreciated their support. Again, I have had over twenty years of teasing, name-calling, discrimination, and loneliness due to my Autism. I honestly had no clue on what to expect with middle schoolers after hearing about them so much, not to mention witnessing first-hand how some of them treat others. I always believed in them regardless.

I *know* the content. I love teaching. I desire to make mathematics and science super easy and explainable. Would they even give me a word in edgewise? I feared that they would not believe me, much less believe *in* me, if that makes sense.

Now, the tempests are beginning to dissipate for me, thereby helping me focus more on my teaching, tutelage, jobs, volunteerism, education, upcoming career, and so on.

At this time, I need to make an important note: I am allowed to make all my teaching updates as long as I never put students, names, or personal information in them. If anything is accidentally in the background, such as names or students themselves, then I either crop or digitally edit them out. Several students have asked me to be in a YouTube video of mine. I apologetically say that I am not allowed to.

Because I abide by the rules, I have never once been asked to take anything down. On the contrary, several teachers, staff, and even school board members and district personnel have said they loved my YouTube videos that kept them posted on my journey.

-29-
OBSERVING OTHER CLASSES

"You can feel free to go observe other classes, even if they're not math classes, just to see different ways and methods that teachers teach," said my Master Teacher. "I'm sure they would be okay with it, but just ask them first."

I had already run into my former teachers, including my seventh grade prealgebra teacher. In late January, we planned where I could observe her class. I walked inside the room and sat in the back corner. It was unequivocally surreal to sit there in the same exact classroom I was in, hearing a math lesson being taught by the teacher who had taught me.

The teacher, excited, introduced me to everyone as her former student. Sometimes, while I observed her, she would ask me if I remembered certain things from her class that she still uses. At another time, she had me share my knowledge of the U.S. presidents with everyone. I continued taking observational notes of her strategies and periodically inquired about them afterward.

One day, I was walking out of her classroom door, and upon seeing me, a couple of students started dancing. "We got a sub!" they sang, but I had to tell them I was not.

I expressed to the teacher how much I was willing to help. That is what got me started in helping her SSR students with math.

Nearly every day of the first half of my first semester, I would go to her classroom during my lunch break.

"All right, who wants to work with Mr. Kenslow?" she would ask.

Usually, but not always, students did not raise their hands, but the teacher picked around three to five that she knew needed help. The incentive for them being singled out was being able to take their masks off, for we would sit outside the classroom. We all got whiteboards, erasers, and markers and did problems from their packets.

Pretty soon, if I missed a day, those students would ask me where I had been. I began getting several compliments from a couple of them such as,

"You are actually making me understand this," "Okay, *now* I get it," and "Can you please be our teacher in eighth grade?"

On February 3, I had an extraordinary experience. I got to witness the same lesson being taught by three different math teachers. Getting different perspectives on how to teach and seeing different strategies being used are beneficial. All day, I made notes on how they taught, their strategies, and their incentives.

In fourth period, I got to observe a seventh-grade math teacher for the first time. His classroom used to hold my Foreign Language class during the spring semester of seventh grade. The teacher was happy to have me come in. I sat in the back. Some students chattered amongst each other, wondering who I was. Once class began, I continued with my notes.

While he was teaching, I kept noticing one student turning back to look at me, sometimes for several seconds. After class, he walked by and put a sheet of paper on the desk where I sat. On it was an incredible detailed sketch of me. It was technically my first gift from a student, and I still have it today. I talked about it in my video the next day when I announced that I passed the CSET subtest 2. One of my YouTube friends, a fellow planespotter from Texas, heard that and asked if he could draw a picture of me and mail it over. He did so and once I received it, I featured it in a reaction video, where I reacted to one of his trip reports.

When I talked about it on Facebook, a mother of two brothers who used to be in Royal Rangers commented, "Frame this to keep in your own class-room one day. Your first of many teacher gifts." She had also been a teacher herself.

After observing the seventh-grade math teacher in fourth period, he told me about four other math teachers I should observe, two of which taught Specialized Academic Instruction (SAI) math. I ultimately introduced myself and observed each of them.

For seventh period, I observed the same lesson for the third time that day with another math teacher. In my page full of notes, I captured a ton of strategies and made comparisons of the unique approaches that the three different teachers used. Afterward, the teacher suggested an additional teacher to observe. He called an eighth-grade math teacher, asking if I could observe. She agreed.

As the math teacher and I were walking over to the classroom, he and I had a conversation about my future plans and who I want to be. He said it was great that I wanted to get credentials in mathematics and science. "That'll put you high up in the totem pole when you look for jobs," he said. "We need a lot of teachers right now who can teach those things."

While observing the eighth-grade math lesson on time-distance graphs, independent variables, and dependent variables, I jotted down a few notes, including how the room was set up. This I did in other classes as well. I was curious how different teachers arranged the desks and decorated the walls. I admired the different posters of motivation from class to class. I noticed where they wrote down the weekly schedule and the homework assignment of the day. I took note of where some teachers put daily handouts, makeup work, the late bin, and the no-name pile. Additionally, I found that some teachers preferred low lighting, and others had their classrooms scented with a fragrance.

I once again felt a push to help students during moments of independent practice. However, I had no idea if I were allowed to since I was just an observer. Diving out of my comfort zone, nevertheless, while observing the eighth-grade math class, I whispered to a student who needed help and explained how to do it. Other students began teasing him for getting help from me. I looked up at the teacher, who did not seem to notice. They softly laughed it off, and it was immediately over, so they were probably joking amongst themselves about something else. I got a little nervous at first. The last thing I wanted was to be kicked out for trying to help, especially in front of eighth graders.

Observing the same math lesson taught by three different teachers that day was quite an interesting experience. Later in March, I observed the same lesson by the same teacher in multiple periods, which showed me how she modified and adjusted as needed. There, I was taught a neat version of Simon Says to help the students remember lines, segments, and the different types of angles. I also viewed it as an assessment to find out what they retained.

I continued to observe a couple of those teachers every now and then, especially the second teacher I observed that day in fourth period. One day when I went to observe his class, a student said that he found my YouTube channel and thought it was neat that I wrote a book. The teacher was all right with me helping his students during independent practice. It took a while for a few students to get used to me being there, however.

One time, I was standing at the side of the room, waiting for a hand to be raised, when I overheard chattering. I looked over and overheard the teacher reply to his student, "Oh, he's just a student teacher. He's in here to help with math."

Another time, a student was complaining that the math was difficult. I asked if I could help her.

"No, thank you," she snapped at me.

A few moments later, I turned around and saw the teacher answering her question on that same math problem. *Oh well.* I knew most of the math and if students were struggling, then I desired to help them, but if they wouldn't accept my help upon offering, then I once again felt underused and helpless.

Nevertheless, toward the middle and end of my semester, during most Wednesdays, I spent several periods in that same room. Wednesdays were usually practice days where students work in a packet.

"You have *two* math teachers in this room willing to help you out," he would call out before sending them off to do work. Soon, students who walked into the classroom were surprised and excited to see me. I got to help several of them out through these opportunities.

Back in early February, I entered a science classroom during lunch to introduce myself to a teacher. I told him that I recognized his name from years past, giving him the years that I attended the school. He said that I could come by anytime.

"Thank you," I said. "By the way, that periodic table is now outdated." I could not resist sharing this information, since I memorized all the elements. We both got a laugh out of that.

I was thankful that I had gotten the open door to a science class, for I had been wanting to observe various science teachers too. For the next few months, I sat in several seventh- and eighth-grade science classes.

"Thanks for taking the initiative," one seventh-grade science teacher told me. Both he and his student teacher were caught up helping others, so I started going to students who were raising their hand. It took more nerve to do so, since science became easy later in my life. However, some questions were about the Chromebook or navigating the website, which I was not savvy in. Other questions were things that were highly specific. Never seeing the computer program before, I was not sure exactly how it wanted us to answer.

By the time I was done with the semester, I had a stack of papers filled out with all my notes—instructional strategies, management, incentives, and a whole lot more. I wanted to eventually integrate everything that I saw work best.

A couple of times during this semester, I observed student teachers from my cohort at Vanguard—one science and the other U.S. history. One of them later observed me, whereas the other one helped in AVID tutorials once or twice. We saw each other in class every Thursday, but it was neat for all three of us to see each other in action. Our professor thought that that was amazing as well. We had quite a camaraderie.

—30—

"Hey, Matt. Can You Teach My Class?"

On the morning of March 3, I introduced myself to another math teacher who taught Enhanced Math, but to seventh graders. I told her that I recognized her name and that she was there when I was a student. She allowed me to observe her class during first period, followed by an eighth-grade math class further down the hall. I had an entire page filled with observational notes by the end of second period.

At Nutrition, I ran into my former prealgebra teacher.

"Hey, Matt?" she said nervously, "Do you think you can teach my class in seventh period. I need to pick up my kids from science camp."

"Sure," I said, feeling honored. "We just need to let my Master Teacher know."

After the teacher called her, she said that it would be totally fine.

I decided that I should observe her third period class, so that I would know exactly what would be taught and the style in which she teaches this particular lesson.

Suddenly, in the middle of third period, the teacher gasped, looking down at her cell phone. Her sons needed to be picked up early. She began to panic and called the office, followed by her substitute teacher. The substitute was going to be in the classroom as I taught the lesson since I do not have a substitute teacher permit; I cannot be alone with students if I am just a student teacher.

When the substitute later walked in, the teacher thanked her greatly and left. Now, I was kind of in charge. I was tasked to handle the rest of third period, and instead of teaching just seventh period, like we planned, I got to teach fourth period too. It was multi-step equations. By this time, a lot of the students knew me.

At fourth period, I greeted them in the same way the teacher does. "Good morning, mathematicians."

"Good morning," they responded.

For the next length of time, I taught them the material step by step, writing each one on the board. They were quiet, listening, respectful, writing everything down, and following along.

I sent them off to do problems one at a time on their whiteboards. After each one, I asked them to hold it up over their heads, just like the teacher. I chose one of the whiteboards to put under the document camera and went through the students' steps. Those students who allowed me to display their math work got a million-dollar bill to spend on prizes later.

Afterward, they spent the rest of the class doing homework in that packet. I walked around to help as needed. After fourth period was SSR, wherein I also walked around and helped.

Seventh period went just as flawless as fourth period went. In both periods, I gave an additional incentive. I told them that if they were very good, I could convert three small pieces of rope into one long piece of rope. Both times, they were perplexed on how I did it, and it baffled the daylights out of them.

Teaching an entire lesson twice to a full class of seventh graders was quite an experience. During one part, I realized I was going a little fast. I immediately stopped talking and looked up at the substitute standing in the back. She was just about to say something too, so we both laughed silently about it. A development that was enhanced during student teaching was further patience. As I love math, believing it to be fun, I am excited to get to the answer. That day, I completed my one-hundredth hour in student teaching.

When the teacher returned, she asked her students how I did. When I went in to see her, she shared their critiques with me. Her students told her the good attributes that they saw, such as me being a very nice person. They all enjoyed my magic trick. However, I could improve in some areas such as not being as soft-spoken. I felt fortunate and grateful for the feedback from actual students.

In this semester, while interning for the Lighthouse's youth group, people from Ensign were there, a few of whom used to be Royal Rangers I had taught. Sometimes, in small groups, they complained about certain things at Ensign. One night, afterward, while I was supervising their kickball game, I asked one of them, "As a middle-school student, what do *you* recommend I do when I become a teacher? How can I be effective in a way where you would actually like my class?" He gave me his honest answer, which was to have students be more engaged in the lesson and working together.

I desired to take twenty-first-century style instruction to the classroom. Consequently, as a teacher candidate taking classes at Vanguard and student teaching at a middle school, I was learning, observing, and employing a plethora of new strategies that were designed and created to make school fun and a safe space to learn. We were not hitting them with standards through boring rote memorization that they would forget two days after the exam.

I determined that I would do my best in employing various UDL, SEL, and SDAIE strategies and mix them in my own unique personality and teaching style. To this day, I intend to take the best of what I have witnessed *all* my life, along with my strategies that I came up with and developed since high school, and utilize all of them whenever I get my own classroom.

-31-
Becoming a Substitute Teacher

Toward the end of January, my Master Teacher encouraged me to become a substitute teacher. That way, if she couldn't make it on a day, then I could sub for her. I remembered people at Vanguard encouraging us to become a substitute too. Some of the teaching candidates in my cohort were already subs. So I emailed the Credential Analyst/Student Teaching coordinator to remind me of the steps.

One day in February, during seventh period, while sitting in the back row of the Basic Skills class, waiting to help a student, a woman walked in the door.

She looked at me and asked the teacher, "Is this your student teacher?"

"Yes, he is."

"Hi," the woman says to me. "I'm from the district office of NMUSD. I heard you wanted to be a substitute teacher, so I'm giving you this packet to fill out. Here is the business card to the HR Technician. Reach out to her if you have any questions."

"Thank you so much," I said, smiling as I received the super-thick packet.

The packet contained a litany of forms to fill out and the procedure for becoming a substitute teacher. When I found the time, I began filling out everything I could.

The next steps included communications with my accountant, paying a couple of fees, and having a doctor's appointment for a physical and risk assessment. I had to send over my official transcripts and CBEST results, since basic skills proficiency and a bachelor's degree were required.

I called the Orange County Department of Education to make an appointment for the OCDE Clearinghouse Fingerprints and livescan. The appointment date had to be made roughly a month in advance. Furthermore, I had hours of online Keenan training videos to watch and get tested on.

Pretty soon, a couple of staff members at Ensign became anxious, wondering when I would get the substitute permit. Around this time, California and other states were facing teacher shortages to some degree.

"Hey, Matt? When do you think you'll get your substitute permit?" my former prealgebra teacher asked me. "Do you think it'll be soon?"

Upon answering, she told me that she was about to take a six-week leave and wondered if I could be her long-term sub. "You're at the top of my list," she told me.

I was enthusiastic. We began talking more as the days and weeks went by. I was ahead in my class at Vanguard and only had a couple of more lessons to teach, including the one for the CalTPA. I knew it was doable to complete the lessons before I would start subbing. The teacher gave me the workbook and showed me the lessons that I would need to teach.

Then one morning, I got to Ensign early, and my Master Teacher had some news for me. "I don't believe your program is going to allow you to be a long-term sub," she said, looking into my eyes, sincerely apologetic. "I've emailed your coordinator and talked about it with the teacher."

That started to bring me down, so I later emailed the coordinator when I had the chance. Twenty minutes later, she emailed me back, telling me to come see her before that evening's class to discuss the situation.

Once I arrived at Vanguard, I ascended the staircase of Scott Academic Center, walked through the hallway, and entered her office.

"Matthew, we are not going to allow you to be a long-term sub. We don't allow *any* BST to do so. We just don't want to set you up for failure or cause you to have a burnout. We want you to take your time as you approach the field of teaching and not throw you out into the deep end. You still have a lot to learn."

I was crushed, but I knew it was wise.

The date of the orientation for us prospective substitute teachers was the next day on March 18. That morning, I went over to the district office of Newport-Mesa Unified, and it lasted for three hours. I had to bring my Social Security card, government-issued ID, voided check, and all the paperwork. At the end, after being greatly encouraged, I signed up for SchoolsFirst Federal Credit Union, which everybody (including Vanguard, my senior commander at Royal Rangers, and my Master Teacher) said was really great.

Afterward, I rushed over to Ensign to at least serve for part of the day. Unfortunately, I was too late to help students in my former prealgebra teacher's SSR class. A couple of her students ran into me, saying, "Hey, why weren't you over there today?"

I told them that I was taking an orientation to become a substitute teacher at the district office.

Later on, I was helping a student in math again out at the lunch tables during seventh period. My former Language Arts teacher saw us and found out that I was tutoring him in math.

"You have the patience of an angel, Matthew. Patience of an angel," he said, walking away.

I have worked with students who did not have much motivation to learn math or any subject, but I still believed in them and helped out the best I could. I took the time all period to get through whatever we could without rushing it, working with students one-on-one most of the time. I re-explained how to do it using an alternate way of thinking about it. I then had students work on the next problem, trying their best to walk me through the solution themselves, through which I guided them when they got stuck.

Within the next week, it was official! I became an employee of Newport-Mesa Unified School District as a certificated substitute teacher. Soon thereafter, I was issued the Emergency Thirty-Day Substitute Teaching Permit. I got my own employee email and an account on Frontline Absence Management System to start accepting substitute positions.

$-32-$

MY FIRST DAY AS A SUBSTITUTE TEACHER
MARCH 25, 2022

Once I announced to my Master Teacher that I received the permit, she congratulated me. On March 23, I was assigned my first substitute position. I was to cover my Master Teacher's third, fourth, and seventh periods, plus SSR.

On the morning of March 25, 2022, I went over to Ensign and YouTubed about what I was about to do for the first time.

I walked inside the office, and the people inside were very proud of me. This time, I did not need to sign in or get a visitor's sticker like before. I walked into one of the rooms to sign the sign-in sheet for payroll and get the substitute folder, in which was the key, substitute teacher lanyard, and important general information.

"Good morning, class," I said as I started both third and fourth period. "You noticed that the teacher is not here today, and, in the past, a substitute teacher had to be here in order for me to be in here teaching you guys. Well," I took the lanyard from the podium, "today is the very first day in my life as a substitute teacher."

In both classes, all the students clapped and cheered as I put on the lanyard. I proceeded to teach them Unit 7, Lesson 9, which dealt with the use of factored form to solve quadratic equations.

I told them, "If you earn it, I brought something special at the end to show."

My incentive for them was a juggling act, this time, using my jugglebugs and clubs.

After school, I concluded the video for my teaching update.

"First day as a substitute teacher," I excitedly told my neighbor who lived in the apartment unit next door.

"What?" she stretched out the word with a big smile. I told her a little bit about how it went.

Before, during, and after this, several of my YouTube friends around the world complimented me, rooted me on, and said that they wished I was their teacher.

$-33-$
THE CALTPA CYCLE 1

"Hi, Matthew!" my Master Teacher said when she answered the phone.

I called her one day to request teaching Unit 7, Lesson 11 for my TPA video. It was all about perfect squares of quadratic equations and two methods in solving for the variable.

"Sure, go ahead. Let's see, that will be taught on Friday, April 1."

"Perfect." I was so relieved to get this settled.

In preparation, I continued writing in the five CalTPA templates, which are Word documents with questions to fill out. Since I knew *what* I would be teaching, I could start adding specifics. Each template consisted of multiple pages that I had to fill out. It was like the Grad Ed Lesson Plans, but not exactly. Again, those lesson plans were meant to help us as we filled out these templates, and they did.

Once again, hold on tight.

The templates asked us about the class, the students, their assets, prior knowledge, learning needs, demographics, specific information on my three focus students, the standards and learning goals of the lesson, rationale behind the lesson, an exhaustive narrative of the lesson, how I will adapt and accommodate based on the learning needs, every resource I used (including the worksheet that I made and the workbook), all the strategies that I employed (including UDL, SEL, and SDAIE), how I will assess and check for understanding, how I will engage them in high-order thinking skills, how I will know if the learning goals are met, how I will communicate what the next steps are, and a comprehensive reflection afterward. By the time each of the five templates were finished, they ranged from three to six pages.

Furthermore, I had to film my lesson, take three clips up to five minutes, and upload them. Not only that, but I had to annotate each clip with timestamps to thoroughly explain how and why I did certain things, such as how I established the expectations and how I connected the lesson with things previously learned. I had previously given all the students permission slips for their parents to sign, allowing me to submit the video clips to the CTC. I was required to have at least a few students in the video.

In the workbook, I packed those pages with notes. I had more or less written a script all throughout the lesson. For days, especially the night before the filming, I rehearsed that script repeatedly. Compared to earlier in the semester, I felt comfortable at this stage of the game, but for the CalTPA video, I was not going to take any chances.

Then it came time for filming. The Graduate Education Department at Vanguard provided an extraordinary robotic mount called the Swivl. This was offered to check out as an option. In class one night, we saw it demonstrated. The Swivl is set up on a tripod, hooked up to an iPad, and once everything is ready, you press a button on the marker (which is situated in a lanyard), and it records you. Not only that, but the marker has a microphone to capture sound and a sensor so that the robotic mount can swivel, thereby following you around the classroom.

The first time I used one was in February so that I could film a lesson for my university supervisor in Kenya. They gave me a live demonstration to show me how to work it. I had to sign a form to check it out, assuming full responsibility. Everything is not cheap, just to say! Additionally, I was allowed to borrow an iPad, since I did not have one myself.

On March 1, I used it for the first time, and the product was amazing. The video and audio were clear. Nine days later, before school began, my supervisor and I met on Zoom to analyze the video. He paused at times and told me some techniques and strategies that I could use for the next time. I filled out about a half page of good notes from him. He said that overall, I looked comfortable in the classroom and was doing a fine job. Once again, I credit Royal Rangers for that.

April 1 arrived. I rehearsed a bit more as I got ready for school. I got to Ensign about a half an hour before third period. I had the opportunity to teach my lesson first to third period (kind of like a dress rehearsal) before teaching fourth. As everybody agrees, the second lesson is typically better than the first.

It was minutes before third period began. I had still not gotten the Wi-Fi working. My brain was scrambling.

I used this before. What was happening? The teacher took the iPad as calm as any human being could possibly be, punched in her password, and handed it back to me, saying, "So this is why it's a good idea to come *before* school starts, so that you don't get panicked right before teaching a lesson. You get to relax that way."

I nodded in agreement, unbelieving that that just happened. I was not really panicked, or at least visibly; it was just what was in my mind. Furthermore, I thought the teacher and I agreed that I should come in at 9:30. I just said "okay" and came at that time. Whatever the case, it was over.

Third period went smooth, but there were moments I tripped up on my words, probably undetectable by everybody else. Since I knew everything that I wanted to teach, I knew what I missed in my sentences that I spoke.

Now it came time for fourth period.

"Thump! Thump!" spoke my heart.

I pressed the button on the marker to record my lesson.

Students began pouring in like rain.

"Good morning," I said to them as they walked in. "Can you please take out your worksheet to pass forward once you're seated?"

That was something that nearly messed up the entire period.

In third period, the teacher wanted them collected at the beginning and likewise with fourth period. I began to panic inside since there was hardly any room according to the schedule. Again, I needed three video clips. The assessor will strictly stop watching after five minutes if it goes beyond that. For the first video clip, I needed to show how I created the positive learning environment (such as greeting the students as they walked in) *and* my thorough introduction of the lesson, saying how it connects to what they had previously learned.

"Oh, they would want to see that," the teacher had told me, "that you are able to have students pass forward their homework before starting a lesson."

I *could* do that, but I still expressed that I might go beyond the five minutes.

"It'll be quick," the teacher said, not taking no for an answer, encouraging me.

Okay, I thought as I resigned to my fate. I simply had a *ton* on my mind, all the targets I needed to hit throughout my lesson, even though every single lesson that I would teach in my career would never require every single thing the TPA wanted to see, or at least in super-short, five-minute intervals. (To an Autistic brain like mine, *time* is usually not in my favor, regardless of being thoroughly observed by others.)

I got the papers passed forward, but my brain told me to begin. All the students were quieted down. The teacher noticed that I was starting and quickly grabbed all the homework from the desks in the front row.

When I recited my script, it was flawless. It felt like muscle memory was taking over my mouth. This continued throughout the entire lesson. One time, however, I set the iPad down on top of my workbook on the podium. I began reciting the next part of the lesson, which was explaining the partner activity.

All of a sudden, *wham!* I did not account for the absence of friction that was needed. The iPad slid down the workbook and onto the floor. I picked it up and apologized. Looking at the teacher, she shook her head but remained silent and continued facing her computer. Thank goodness that iPads are durable. I backed up a sentence or two and continued my instructions. When I was done, all the students spontaneously clapped once again.

I am being *utterly truthful* when I say this. At the end, after I said the very last part of my script and the students began clapping, I almost physically collapsed! My legs started to give out, but I quickly rested my arm on the podium to catch myself.

It was subtle, so nobody else caught that. When I told the teacher afterward, her countenance immediately changed to a concerned one.

That is how much I care about being a teacher and how much stress this TPA caused me. In fact, the following Thursday, I had to email my professor saying that I could not make it to class. I was feeling physically ill throughout the day, probably due to stress.

At one point in my semester, I entered class, and my professor asked me how I was doing. I told him about a few compliments I had received for student teaching, followed by blurting out half-jokingly, "And I'm a nervous wreck!" We both started laughing, and he reassured me that it was normal. Becoming a teacher is extremely challenging, and they warned us about that, but Vanguard was there every step of the way.

My lifelong goal is to teach and serve others. I do not know what my purpose would be (career-wise) if it weren't being a teacher. And acknowledging that I must hit *every single tiny point* of the TPA, I feared that it was out of reach, even if I thoroughly did fill up those TPA templates in massive detail. I felt torn that this was the only way to become a teacher.

As I always started saying, "Teaching is the easy part; the CalTPA is something else!"

Nevertheless, I persevered!

To conclude describing this day, in case nobody caught it, it was April Fools' Day. Now, being a lifelong comedian, I obtained permission from the teacher to say the following:

"One more thing, before I send you off: I want to remind you about the homework. You have the McGraw Hill homework, the Khan Academy, and the teacher wants you to do the next two lessons on your own this weekend about Completing the Square."

Students began to jerk their heads up at me, almost getting up out of their seats. Each lesson consisted of the warm-up, a few activities, the summary to annotate, and about ten homework problems. Thus, I was assigning a *lot*!

"And this is the first time as a math teacher that I get to say, '*April Fools*' on April 1! I couldn't resist."

Student were very much appreciative when I said that. I heard sighs of relief, mixed in with some cheers and claps. (Previously, I had my first Pi Day as a math teacher (March 14), albeit a student teacher.)

When I got home, I ensured that the video successfully worked and was saved. For the next week, I got busy filling out those templates and video annotations. On April 7, at 11:35 p.m., I officially submitted Cycle 1 of the CalTPA. I immediately emailed one of my professors to share the news, thanking her for her help and guidance. She was the one who hosted the four seminars on Zoom.

After that, I emailed my Instructional Design professor, thanking him for the prayers and letting him know that I am starting to feel much better. "It has become a major stress" I wrote, "physically and mentally since everything they require has to be articulate and precise. It's like when a person graduates high school or boot camp; it's quite the feeling of success. However, I can tell you, with giant relief, that I just now submitted the CalTPA on Pearson, and the mission is categorically, irrefutably, unequivocally accomplished!"

The professor seemed immensely proud in his reply to me. "Congratulations, Matthew! This is a huge accomplishment, and I'm confident that you did outstanding work! Bravo! Now take some time just to rest."

-34-

FIRST TIME SUBSTITUTING OUTSIDE MY MASTER TEACHER'S CLASSROOM

On Sunday, April 3, I got a phone call offering me a substitute-teaching job. The call was automated, in that it prompted the recipient into accepting or rejecting the assignment. It first said that it was a one-day assignment at Ensign Intermediate School. Then it said the name of the teacher, which I recognized. It was an eighth-grade science teacher I had observed a few times before.

I pressed the number to accept.

"Good-bye," the robot-voice said.

I did it. I had just accepted my first substitute job position outside of my Master Teacher's class.

On Frontline, the teacher uploaded his sub notes and link to the slides. I prepared my incentive for each period. It was a magic trick that I had not done since COVID started, before which I would do it in classrooms where I juggled. I asked everyone to think of a three-digit number, but they couldn't tell anybody. I chose three of them to write their number down in my notepad. A fourth volunteer came up and added the three numbers together. The sum was inside an envelope that I sealed the night before. (Later that year, I changed it to multiplication for a greater wow factor since the product would have eight or nine digits.)

The next morning, I arrived at Ensign, signed the sheet, grabbed the folder, and entered the classroom. I got everything set up, the slides displayed on the pull-down screen, and the music playing for when students would enter and leave. The latter was something that I was both taught and had observed before, in order to hopefully get students feeling good and ready to learn.

In each period, as students entered the classroom, some of them recognized me from my Master Teacher's class; others, I have met within the past three months. They were surprised and stoked that I was going to be their sub.

Once class began, I was to show them a couple of YouTube videos about what they were learning and then send them off to continue a project they were working on. At this time, they were learning about DNA, as well as CRISPR, which is something I learned in Microbiology.

The bell rang. As always, it seemed to ring longer than it actually did.

Here was the time when I needed intense focus and concentration. I believe that everybody in the Enhanced Math classes understood who I am and that I have some limitations with my speech. I oftentimes jumble up my words if I do not stop myself and slow down. Over several years, I have greatly reduced the effects of my impediment. Being outspoken on YouTube, especially as an advocate for Autism, not to mention a Royal Rangers commander, I have significantly built confidence and improved my enunciation. I did not mask the fact that I have Autism; students found out one way or another. Students at Ensign were totally accepting toward me . . . about 97 percent of them.

Starting the class once the bell rang was the first hurdle. Students usually came in with conversations, some louder than others. I usually said, "Good morning, everybody!" over them, which typically quieted them down. Some periods were easier to commence, whereas others took a few moments. In one of the periods, one of the Enhanced Math students got frustrated on how I was being treated and loudly said, "*Shhhh!*"

Even though I can easily command a room full of boys at Royal Rangers, elevating my voice appropriately, I still did not feel comfortable doing so in a public middle-school classroom. The boys at Royal Rangers get it. They understand the procedures. They know that I am building the *leader* inside them. Yelling out loud to middle schoolers with various kinds of backgrounds was a different story. I simply did not want anybody to get offended. I am just trying to help them succeed in both education and life. I do not want them to mistake any yelling as hatred or anything else negative. For these reasons, from January 2022 to the present day, I have usually been the soft-spoken teacher.

In fact, I was subbing for an elementary school later on, and the students thanked me, wishing that I could come back because their teacher yells at them all the time. It is simply a difference in philosophy. I believe yelling

190

might have its place in dire situations, but still, I do not want to inadvertently deter anybody from coming to school, frightening them away from their education and future.

(Just in case somebody is wondering, I am not implying that I would give drill and marching commands to middle schoolers like at Royal Rangers. It was simply the notion of yelling out loud that makes me take caution. As I once said, I am coming to schools *not* as Commander Matthew, but as Mr. Kenslow.)

My Master Teacher was insistent on this, trying to get me to use my voice in a disciplinary way. One day in her class, I was teaching a lesson, and I had to politely ask a student to stop talking.

"Can you please stop talking for now? It's just a little distracting."

He was quickly apologetic and said, "Okay, sorry."

"I'm sorry," I said under my breath, closing my eyes to regroup, and continued teaching.

Later, the teacher told me how proud she was of me. Telling a student to be quiet was never the hardest part in classroom management. The harder part came later on, when I was substituting for that teacher again. A few students in the back would not stop chattering.

"Please sit over there," I firmly told one of them.

"But we were just—"

"Right now, please."

"But—"

"Right now!" I said louder, continuing to point to his new seat. My mouth was closed.

"Okay, I will." He walked over to take his seat.

"I'm sorry," I whispered under my breath and continued.

Later that day, in eighth period, I went over to observe that eighth-grade science teacher I was subbing for on April 4. That student I had told to move was in there.

When it was appropriate to do so, I said his first name, and he turned toward me. "I'm sorry about what happened in third period, but you were just being distracting toward me and the other students."

"Oh, it's okay. I was misbehaving and deserved it." He was understanding. "I'm sorry."

To this day, we have no hard feelings between us.

Back to April 4, all the periods went great, some greater than others. Once I got them going, it was a piece of cake. The magic trick impressed everyone; I almost messed up in SSR, but it is done and over with! Most students are respectful. Afterward, one student who previously began following me on YouTube and Instagram kept saying that he enjoyed having me as his substitute teacher.

(One year later, in mid-April 2023, I was in the crosswalk at 19th and Newport Boulevard. Another student who was in one of the periods biked past me, saying, "That was such a fun day. Thanks for being an awesome sub, man!")

During the teacher's prep period, I went over to my Master Teacher's classroom to help her Enhanced Math students if needed. Later, she communicated with me that she got worried when I left, for she did not know that I was substituting that day. I assumed that she saw my badge or that one of the students told her by now.

Since I was finished with the CalTPA, most of the required lessons, and my clinical hours by far, we agreed that I would come in every Tuesday and Thursday for the rest of the semester. If I was not substituting, then I could always come to volunteer, which gave me reassurance, since this is my daily motivation.

The fear of not being there to help students for a while can cause me an idiosyncratic, depressing phenomenon, which I found out the scary way. I tell that story in the next chapter.

~35~
THE BEWILDERING HEART WRENCHER
APRIL 8, 2022

Compared to other things that I am hesitant to reveal, they don't even compare to what happened on April 8. I will honestly and sincerely preface this chapter by saying that I am nervous to divulge this, but nevertheless, I believe in my heart that it has its place here.

The week went amazing. I subbed on Monday (as I told in the previous chapter), took a trip to Newport Harbor High School on Tuesday for the incoming-freshman orientation and campus tour, substituted for my Master Teacher on Thursday, and passed my 200th hour of student teaching.

Friday, April 8, on the other hand, was a different story, after school. I walked to the office slowly, signed myself out, and said, "Well, that's it for one week."

The following week was spring break. There were no schools to go to; no students to encourage, tutor, teach, and motivate; no wheels to see turning or lightbulbs to go off.

At *least* I had Royal Rangers and Lighthouse's youth ministry where I could serve. Recall that for years, that was pretty much *all* I had. Now, I have the opportunity to be at a school every day of the week, which, as readers know by now, was what I had fought for—for nearly a decade at this point. I desired to be a tutor, to work at Discovery Cube Orange County, to be an assistant teacher at St. Andrew's Presbyterian, to be a volunteer speaker at every school in assemblies, et cetera.

At the same time, I was pounded with discrimination, hammered with pain, riddled with loneliness, ignored by most news media (when all I was trying to do was to make a difference for billions of people), and torn to pieces trying to consume all the information needed to get two degrees and pass the CSETs.

I still pushed on with my life despite living with all those challenges. I was getting closer and closer to my goals. I was at a place where many people respected me for who I am and do not tease me for my Autism like a couple of places did. (In fact, a couple of students have talked to me about Autism, hearing that I am speaking out for its universal acceptance.) I was assuming a lot of responsibilities instead of being viewed as incompetent with most of them. Students were asking me to help them in their studies. Students' eyes were lighting up when they saw me on campus.

I was at a place where people said hi to me every single day—*all* day—and sometimes have a small conversation. I was at a part of my life where I could walk anywhere in my neighborhood and hear, "Hi, Mr. Kenslow," or, "Have a good day, Mr. Kenslow," quite often, in lieu of a yell, laugh, or cuss word that others have hurt me with.

When I was walking home that day, several students who just got out of school rode by on their bicycles, waving or saying hi to me.

"Hi. Have a great spring break," I would say back.

Walking around a sandwich place along East 17th Street, somebody rushed out the door, calling out, "Have a good spring break, Mr. Kenslow!" before I walked out of sight.

I turned around to thank him. It was one of the Enhanced Math students. When I got home, I was sitting in front of my laptop, putting together my teaching update video for YouTube.

Suddenly, something strange and bewildering happened. What I am about to divulge requires 100 percent acknowledgment of the life I lived, as described in this book. My plea is for the reader to have read everything up to this point, fully understanding the horror that I lived with just to get to where I was at—discrimination, being bullied and teased, being nervous to go up to my friends, name-called, ignored, cussed at, laughed at, yelled at, ran away from, stared at, rejected, being underused, thought of as a joke, suffered a suicide of a close person, constantly feeling lonely and left out, begged not to have children a few times, and more. Everything I have written in this book does not come close to *everything* that I have endured within the past twenty years.

On top of all that, I still fought to pass all of my classes at OCC and Vanguard. I fought to get a book published and social media accounts growing. I fought to volunteer in schools, churches, and Autism organizations all across Orange County to nearly *no* avail. I fought to encourage people with Autism and their families online with little success.

Right there alone in my room, while editing my video, someone or something unexpectedly turned on the faucet in my heart. For one darn hour, it would not stop. I managed to get a wrench to tighten it, but it leaked for one additional hour. In case nobody understood that, let us just say that I was emotional for two full hours. It felt scary.

What the heck is going on? Why the heck am I feeling this sad?

It was because being a student teacher (and now a substitute) was a great, much-needed fulfillment in my life, as well as gaining the respect from those I wanted to teach and encourage. It made me feel alive and valued as a human being a million times more than ever. It helped me acknowledge that this *is* my passion, and this *is* where I belong. I was on the right track. (Earlier, my Instructional Design professor told me with a huge smile, "You found your passion," when I explained to him after class that this is my daily motivation and what gets me out of bed in the mornings.)

I had no clue what I was going to do during spring break! I was so close to calling my professor, requesting to see him in person. I ultimately emailed him, saying that I prefer to speak to him face-to-face, *not* on Zoom or over the phone. Alas, he was out of the city but could meet me the following week. I was additionally tempted to call my Master Teacher but decided against it.

How on earth was this going to sound? I wondered. *Is it even normal for a person to feel this way, considering the context?*

I began fearing that I was getting "emotionally involved" somehow, but quickly determined that I was not. I was not getting myself involved with a student's problem, so that was not it. In fact, it did not have anything to do with students, per se.

Then what was it?

I deduced that it was the fact of being accepted by everybody on a grand scale for the first time in my life. It was the fact that everybody at Ensign brought me joy. It was the fact that I *finally* got to do what I love, which is teaching, by teaching part of what I love, which is algebra.

About one quarter into this incomprehensible phenomenon, I took to Facebook, not knowing what else to do but to ask for thoughts and prayers.

Everyone, I am . . . so emotionally distraught right now for a half hour or more, and I didn't want to post here . . . but I'm like, forget it! . . . I've dreaded this day for about a week now. But today was the final day before spring break. There is no school next week. No students/teachers to serve. Nobody to encourage, mentor, and motivate at Ensign (or any NMUSD school). No teacher to substitute for. The hurt I feel now is as if I am moving far away and have to say good-bye to hundreds of my friends and family. About 98 percent of the students over at Ensign have been nothing but truly nice to me and made me feel purpose, value, worth, alive, and belonging in life. Outside of school, many students recognize me everywhere and say, 'Hi, Mr. Kenslow' to me. Teaching, now, is one of the only things that . . . [is] giving me daily motivation to live out the day. And now, in lieu of two days, I have to wait nine days before I return . . . If I'm getting this upset for one week off, I can't imagine after my semester is done in early May . . . If I do get allowed to come back on days I'm not substituting, then what I really dread is two months of summer break. I pray for many substituting days of summer school, but I don't have any guarantee. All I have next week is Royal Rangers, Youth on Wednesday, playing keyboard at the Good Friday Service, and playing keyboard the next two Sundays . . . but no school to serve my time (even volunteer time) at. I can't believe this. I disliked the week off in February for President's week, but jeez, I didn't get this upset. And no, to be clear, I'm not against giving students breaks; they deserve it. As a student, I counted down the days. As a teacher, it's Mondays I love, and Fridays I hate.

Soon, my mother read the post, which upset her. She tried reassuring me. She also reminded me of something I must have forgotten. After high school graduation, we were all happy and celebrating, but soon after, the depression hit because a lot of my friends were moving across the country to attend universities.

After the two hours of lonesome, tearful misery, I decided to take a walk. Right beforehand, I was talking with my grandfather about what was going on when I said, "I just need some fresh air right now." I quickly rushed out the door because I was starting to choke up again. I immediately brushed it off. I put on my sunglasses, despite it being evening time, for obvious reasons.

I was walking by the Circle K on Santa Ana Avenue and began to text my mother. She knew I was going for a walk, but I did not want her to continue worrying about me. Just then, I saw two bicyclists riding across the street.

"Hey! It's Mr. Kenslow!" one of them said.

"Hi, Mr. Kenslow!" They both waved.

"Hello." I smiled and waved back. "Have a good spring break."

Being reassured by that, I immediately added that experience to the text, hopefully reassuring my mother that I was feeling better.

I honestly had no clue where I was going. Usually, my itinerary is haphazard anyway, but I was moving myself toward Lighthouse Community. By some miracle, is a pastor there?

In that direction was the pastor's house. Was somebody perhaps outside? Alas, no. I continued walking around. *Maybe I'll run into my Master Teacher*, I thought wishfully. I knew it was a long shot. I kept rehearsing in my mind what I would say if I ran into *anybody* who could help.

On Sunday morning, I went to Lighthouse Community for band rehearsal since I was playing keys. As I was trying my best to set everything up, the keyboard, plugs, cords, the whole nine yards, I broke down. I just broke down. The drummer gave me a hug. Just then the senior pastor entered and hugged me next. The pastor and I went in a back room.

Shakily, I said something to the effect, "I can't believe this is happening. This is going to be a long week. If I'm upset like this now, then what on earth is going to happen during summer break?"

The pastor proceeded to deliver quite an impactful consolation, encouraging me that I have been used by God to reach students far outside this school district. I have reached students to the ends of the world through social media. The pastor himself has followed my journey of what I do on social media, with my book, in the community, and in the classroom.

"I love that about you," he said, "but your identity is not that: *just* being a teacher. It's *definitely* something that gets you out of bed in the morning, and I love that you found something that does that for you, but that's *not* just who you are. And if *that's* what you're living for, then you need to rethink your values . . . All right?"

"Yeah," I said softly.

"Because you are just as valuable if you aren't teaching math than if you are. I get that given how short a period of time you've had to enjoy the fruit of this longing, you'd be like, 'Yeah, I don't want to wait another whole week!' Kids are lucky to have you."

"Yeah, so, well, thank you," I stuttered, appreciative of all his advice and prayers. Indeed, as he conveyed, I am valuable in their youth group, worship ministry, Royal Rangers, and whenever I get to usher at the Presbyterian church. However, those have been once a week, and I began questioning how I'd survive.

"You need to go for a walk at the Back Bay," he suggested to me as we walked out of the room and back into the sanctuary. "That's been my source of replenishment. I just walk and appreciate God's beauty. For me, photography is something that I like to do." Referring to his career as a pastor, he said, "I love this. I absolutely love that I get to open God's Word and teach it, but this isn't all I am. In fact, I'm finding that the greater impacts are the one-on-one investments. It's moments like this where you go, 'Oh, there's an opportunity here to meet a need.' I'm going to do it because I find joy in it. And then I find joy in going for a walk and seeing the beauty of God's creation. And I take my phone with me." He began sounding more joyous. "And I take pictures. *You* love to document planes, and you get to share that with people. *I* love to document beautiful flowers, beautiful vistas, and the birds I get to see. *That* brings me joy, and I like getting to share that with other people."

After we concluded our talk, I went back to the keyboard and began to rehearse.

After rehearsal, the electric guitarist sympathetically said, "You had a tough morning?"

"Yeah, actually for about thirty-six hours."

"Really?" He sounded surprised.

I called over another pastor, who is also part of the worship team. That way, I would not have to repeat it again. I gave both of them the rundown, describing my emotional oppression for the past thirty-six hours.

The pastor made a frightful look. "Well, stop that!" he snapped, as if it were an easy thing to do.

"I know!" I nodded, wishing it was that easy.

"I like when people tell you that, right? 'Just don't do that,'" he said sarcastically.

"It's because next week is spring break, and I have literally no school to serve at. No students to teach. No teachers and staff to support. And it-it's just . . ." I began to stutter but took a firm grasp with my words, "I don't get it! It's just one freaking week." I knew I just broke character.

"Okay," the pastor said understandingly.

"And I cannot imagine what it's going to be in summer when . . ."

"Well, I got news for you then. That means you just told me that you have time this week to help me do what we have to do to get ready for next Sunday."

"Yeah," I said, understanding that keeping extra busy is unequivocally the best option.

"Okay? Let's go in here and pray with Matthew." The pastor called a few other musicians in the back room. As we were walking in, the pastor told me, "I have a bunch of stuff that's got to get done. I did not know how I was going to get it all done. Now I do. I'll be calling you, probably tomorrow."

He proceeded to tell me the setup of the stage for the Good Friday service while the other musicians came in and surrounded me. He then began to pray, and they all laid hands on me.

My eyes began to water.

"It's going to be okay, brother," the pastor said after finishing the prayer. "It's going to be all right. I understand."

"Thank you." I was grateful. "Yeah, those students really make me feel alive." My voice was shaking. "It gives me purpose and hope."

"Also, continuous responsibility means that you need breaks," the drummer encouraged me.

"I agree," I said, smiling. "As I said on YouTube, I'm not against spring break. They deserve the break."

Less than a minute later, it was time to play the five-minute prelude.

After church, I spoke with a third pastor who also stood by me since 2018, when I first got involved in the young adults ministry. Both of us help the junior high small group. He gave me his advice for when God tells him to take a week off of ministry, which involves both prayer and community service.

Walking home, I went through the 17th Street Promenade, as I always do since it was in the itinerary. I kept thinking, *This time next week, I will be seven days closer to helping students and teachers.*

When I was in eighth grade, I did the same thing. However, in *that* context, it would be a week closer to break and being able to visit my family friends in Lake Elsinore for a few days. Those friends were a couple of years younger than me, but they brought me similar peace and joy in ways that I rarely found over here, nearly sixty miles away. They were accepting toward me, despite my disability, making me feel welcomed.

I am not saying that my friends at school or church were bad, but I never really hung out with any of them. They rarely asked me, and I was too nervous to ask them myself. (This is a topic that goes beyond the scope of this book, but I have produced several YouTube videos about this, especially later on in 2022.)

On Tuesday, I went to Vanguard University to talk to my professor. I was both nervous and embarrassed.

"Hey, Matthew! Come on in," he said with a huge smile. "How's it going?"

"Good," I replied.

"Good. Have a seat. How is life today?"

"Life is going good," I said as we both sat down at the table.

"Tell me a bit of what was going on."

I told him everything down to the last detail for over a minute and a half.

I concluded by saying, "I'm not sure if you can relate or what advice you have. It doesn't make the time go by faster, but that's what's been going on."

"Wow, that's amazing. Um, in a sense, on one level, it sounds as if God has really put these students on your heart, and He put this passion in you to serve them. And you've like, been on this track full speed ahead, right?"

"Yeah."

"And then all of a sudden, *boom!* It stops for a week."

"Yeah, and I was good during president's break. I mean, I was sad during president's break, but not like this. If I'm like this for one week, what happens after the semester ends? What about summer?"

"I don't know if I ever mentioned to you in class, but at the end of every school year, I said good-bye to my students for the last day of school. And they go running off, and they're excited about summer. And I would sit at my desk, and I would be completely depressed at the end of every school year. This is like what you're describing. It felt like, 'Ah! You're going and I'll never have you in my class again.' But it's because God has put them in my heart and called me to this. There's that love and compassion that God put inside of you when you're a teacher. It has a sad side."

"Bittersweet."

"It's bittersweet. In a way, it's like having your own kids. They go off to college and you're excited for them, but at the same time, you miss them like crazy because they're your kids. And in a way, does that resonate? Like, God's kind of giving you a little taste of that?"

"Yeah, probably. I guess that's what it feels like."

"But still, that's so much a part of who I am and am called to, that if I'm not doing it, I *feel* it, you know? And I think that's maybe part of what you're feeling."

"I think so. I've expressed this to my friends on Facebook and pastors, and everyone's just telling almost the same thing: 'Take a break,' 'Take a rest,' and 'When you're a full-time middle school teacher, you'll be *waiting* for the breaks.'"

"Yeah, that's true," my professor said and chuckled. "Now, this week is spring break. So, what you were feeling last weekend was in anticipation of this week?"

"Yeah. In fact, to tell you the truth, I was dreading last Friday for at least a week and a half," I boldly stated.

"Is that right? You kind of knew you would feel that way?"

"I just knew it inside."

"Have you experienced this with Royal Rangers, when it comes to the end of an academic year?"

"I was thinking about that. I think yes, to an extent, but I never broke down for that. When I had to say good-bye for the summer, and if they don't have summer Royal Rangers, then it's like, there's nothing to do. Royal Rangers was at the *top* because it was the highlight of my week. Now with student teaching, that's up to five days a week."

"So there's been a little bit of that too, but not to the same level of intensity."

"Right. There was a time a couple of years back. We took Christmas break in December 2019, and the church didn't allow us to come back until February 2, and that's never happened in all my years I've been in Royal Rangers. It had never been that long, and the senior commander and I were on edge about that, but we came back."

"I bet you really missed it when you were gone."

"Yes, *really* missed it because that's what I *really* live for. I mean, music ministry is really good and other things, but serving the future generation in either leadership or education is like, my heart."

"Well, one thing that's been so impressive to me is how well your Royal Rangers experience prepared you for teaching. You've been able to draw on all kinds of things that you did at Royal Rangers—the way you relate to kids, the way you organized lessons, the way you have cooperative learning, all kinds of things that you've been developing for years in Royal Rangers has become transferrable skills."

"Yeah, I have to credit Royal Rangers, big time. And I was telling that to my senior commander. He totally agrees."

A couple moments later, he asked if I felt good about how the TPA came out.

"Yeah, I feel confident."

"Well, you've done really, really well on the lesson planning. I think you were prepared for the TPA because the quality of your work on your lessons was outstanding."

"I'd say the Grad-Ed lesson plans helped, and class of course. I just have one more to do: the inquiry-based one."

"You're very close, Matt." He smiled. "And then you have your Advanced Student Teaching next semester."

After a few more minutes of talking, he prayed for me. He was glad that I was transparent enough to share with him. He agreed that it was better for it to be in person and not on Zoom, phone call, or email.

During our conversation, I told him that I remembered my sixth-grade graduation, back in 2007. The teacher warned us ahead of time that she always cries during graduations. When I was a few classmates away from receiving my certificate, that is when I noticed her beginning to choke up, which got to my heart. When I got up a few more steps and it was my turn, she said, "And how can I ever forget Matthew?" As I was walking off the stage moments later, I saw one tear fall from my eye and onto a stairstep. I hoped nobody saw me, but one of my classmates asked me about it. After speaking with my professor, the next step was talking to my Master Teacher.

After all week, Monday, April 18, finally came. For the first day back after spring break, I got to sub for a U.S. History and Geography teacher at Ensign. A couple of the students remembered me from juggling at Newport Heights throughout their second-grade year, six years prior. Throughout the week, students asked me how my spring break was.

"Well, despite the lonesomeness of not being at a school, I put together like forty or fifty YouTube videos that needed editing, so I'm good for several months."

At the end of the day, I spoke with my Master Techer.

"All right, what's happening?" she knew that what I had to say to her was pressing.

"Well, uh, do you want the urgent one or the less urgent one?"

"Go for it."

I got the milder one out of the way, which was getting her input on what was needed during inquiry-based lessons. We established the one I was going to do for my fourth required lesson, which took place three days later.

"Well anyway, there's *that*. Now what's the second thing?" she asked.

"Uh? Yeah, the second thing is something that is really, really dire." I kept looking back at the open door. I had been worried about students overhearing this, which is why I told the teacher that I preferred to speak when nobody was in the room. "And I had to talk to my professor about this in his office."

"Okay. Do you want me to close the door?" she asked, concerned.

"Well, I don't think that'll be necessary. Anyway, I was this close to calling you on Friday." I held up my right hand with my thumb and index finger pressed together. "Not last Friday, but the Friday before."

"Okay."

"I have no idea how to preface this, but on Friday, after school, when spring break was ahead of me, uh . . ." I looked back at the door, just in case. "I don't know how this is going to sound, but someone or something turned on the faucet in my heart for an hour. Someone or something tried to close it, but then it leaked for another hour, because I knew I was going to miss everybody. One week and no students to help, no teachers to help, nobody to motivate or encourage, and everybody's been kind and respectful since January 3. So that's what happened Friday. Um, on Sunday, I was at Lighthouse Church's rehearsal, and I broke down in front of the band. And the pastor and I went out to the side room and talked. And he encouraged me to just rethink my values because I am just as valuable there as I am here and everywhere else. And I was talking to my professor about that on Tuesday. He totally related to what I shared since he was a teacher. He's like, 'I love graduation. I'm so happy for the students and the families, but I'm like, "Don't go yet. You're my students."' And he used the word *compassion* as an explanation for what I'm feeling. It's just like my Art History teacher at Harbor, when I told him I wanted to be a teacher. He said that the feelings that I felt were passion. So I just wanted to let you know. What am I going to do in May, and what am I going to do in the summer? I inquired at Vanguard and NMUSD about summer school to see if it's possible to sub during the summer, but I'm still waiting to hear back from them. Either way, that will probably tide me over for one of the two months."

"Yeah, for sure, and if there are summer opportunities, then I bet they'll say yes."

"I mean, on the contrary, when I was a student, I would count down the days to the vacations and the ultimate vacation of all, summer. But now as a teacher . . ."

The teacher began laughing, knowing what I was about to say.

". . . everything's flipped for me."

"It's so different," she said. "I totally remember those feelings in the beginning, and it is sad, but it's so different how time changes that. You're going to miss them, but that feeling probably won't always be there. As you get older, you'll have some classes that you'll probably start counting the seconds until they're gone."

She continued to give me advice and said tons of alternate opportunities were available in the summer, such as STEM and Enrichment programs.

"That's something you can look forward to also," she said.

"Yeah, and segueing into the third thing, after the first week in May, I'm technically not a Basic Student Teacher anymore. I'm also not an Advanced Student Teacher until August. Nowadays, if I don't get a subbing job, I just come here for the day, and if it's after the first week in May, and no one calls, am I able to come here and volunteer?"

Her answer nearly changed me at that point in my life.

"I mean, you can come here every Tuesday and Thursday for the rest of the year!"

"Okay, well what about Monday, Wednesday, and Friday?"

"Oh, *any* day. Totally. I think you should because you want to stay here as much as possible and gain experience. To be here with other teachers is really valuable."

"That's a giant relief."

"I have no end date in my head. You're going to be here until December."

We proceeded to take a lot of time to plan out my inquiry-based lesson, based on the infamous Quadratic Formula, its derivation, and where it came from.

I soon expressed a little worry about being asked questions by students that I do not know the answer to. For that reason, I always like prereading the lessons and worksheets. Recalling my past, I always tried to retain knowledge in such a way that I can answer anybody's question, even if they came from random people in the neighborhood. However, many times in Royal Rangers over the years, I realized how much I can forget.

The teacher said that that is why AVID is great for me, since I get thrown a lot of questions on the spot as an AVID tutor. Indeed, being a tutor for three months at this point (as well as helping her basic skills class and students from other math teachers) has significantly built my confidence on a grander scale. This teacher has strongly influenced me since I was able to watch how she handles on-the-spot questions.

She proceeded to give me tips. "That is a challenging part of teaching, but I've been here so long, so I know a lot on how to answer. But sometimes I get stumped too. I'm like, 'How do I even solve that? I have no idea.' Um, but then I'm like, 'Okay, I *know* the topic. I remember that we do this.' So, the more you're here, the more you'll get used to doing that."

The next morning, I gave a big praise report update on Facebook, pouring out my gratefulness of the news that it was guaranteed that I would either substitute or volunteer at a school, from then until the graduation in June. Plus, there was a probability of serving in the summer.

My inquiry-based lesson went phenomenally. I took construction paper, glue, and magnets, and on the whiteboard, I showed them a visual representation of completing the square right before their eyes. At the end of both math periods, I got to explain the Quadratic Formula, which is what I was excited about.

Prior to this day, the teacher gave them a song. I said that I had a mnemonical story that I learned as a freshman at Harbor, but there was not any time to tell it.

"I want to hear Mr. Kenslow's story," a couple of students said.

Once there was time, I got to tell the story twice, which was equally as fun. The first time, I told the story; the second time, I told it while writing out the formula.

—36—

THE ULTIMATE PROOF

The first week of May 2022 had a lot of ups but some downs. I *dreaded*, I mean, nightmarishly *dreaded*, May 1! It was the five-year anniversary of my aunt succumbing to cancer and the one-year anniversary of my special friend's suicide.

"But for months, I've seen that this day was going to fall on a Sunday," I told a group of pastors and fellow musicians in the back room before service that morning, "and I'm like, there's no better place I would rather be than here at church, surrounded by my church family."

I thanked them for all of their past prayers, but I was still depressed every single day and every single night. That Sunday, they all laid hands on me and began to pray. I will say that I did not have a dry eye. I had the picture of my friend and me on my phone during the prayer. Afterward, we went back in the sanctuary, and, after my five-minute prelude, we did the opening worship set.

That evening, I took one of my normal cathartic hikes. I walked all across Costa Mesa and later, Newport Beach. It was risky for me, because I was so worried about being discriminated against on this day of all days. Nevertheless, I ran into three students who said hi to me at three different times—one sitting outside a restaurant at Westcliff Plaza, one on his bike along Newport Boulevard, and one in a car driving up East 17th Street. The person at the restaurant asked if he could get a picture with me.

I said, "Sure, if you want. A lot of people have been asking for one lately."

"Yeah, because you're like famous or something."

"I would never call myself famous."

"Well, uh, can I get a picture really quick?"

"Sure."

Just like those bicyclists who asked me how my day was going (of *all* days), back in September 2021, those three students, unbeknownst to them, really helped me as I was mourning two losses, as well as walking in neighborhoods that had been so wretched toward me.

That was only the beginning!

That week was Teacher Appreciation Week. To my surprise, I got cards from seven students, appreciating me for being their teacher, albeit a student and substitute teacher.

One student included a whole bunch of math symbols and formulas. Another said that I am helping him with a better understanding in math. One appreciated the fact that I was a sub who could *teach* the math instead of making them figure it out on their own, like other subs did, he wrote. Another said that I make math class entertaining. One appreciated the fact that I had always been kind to him, helped him, and said hi whenever we saw each other.

Some of them added that they like my tricks and juggling, and they congratulated me on ten thousand subscribers on YouTube.

One day toward the end of the month, after third period, one of the Enhanced Math students came over to me and handed me a folded piece of paper. "It's just a little letter of gratitude," he said, smiling before he left.

I read it. It was quite articulate. It brought me peace and joy (along with the other letter, of course). Still, this one was extra special to me. Later on, in December, he ran in to me while I was out walking around the neighborhood.

"Oh, hey, Mr. Kenslow," he said, stopping his bike. We had a little conversation, in the middle of which I asked him permission to use excerpts from his letter for this book, as long as I won't mention any names (obviously). He said I could.

This is what he wrote:

Dear Mr. Kenslow,

I am proud to say I am your student. You are an inspiration and all around good person in this world. Although my middle school life is coming to an end in the next few weeks, I would like to share that you are an amazing teacher. I have taken an example from you, not only in school, but in life as well. You have shown me how there are many solutions to the tough sides of life than we see. It is rare to see someone be as calm and collected as you. I hope to have half as much patience as you when I am older. Teaching and helping others is definitely your specialty, and I believe you will be even more successful . . . Know that everything you do is greatly appreciated by everyone and that your academic help has more of an impact than you may perceive. On a math test, you always explain things as much as possible, and the knowledge you share with the class is great. I also want to thank you for your patience with teen humor and patience with the repeating questions you ask. Any effort you put in goes a long way, and your joy in teaching is amazing. I am proud to say Mr. Kenslow was my teacher. I hope you remember your first year teaching at Ensign. No one can thank you enough.

Let me tell you: that letter (plus *all* the letters) was a *treasure*. I put them all in a safe place, along with the drawings of me that I received earlier in the year. I felt so fortunate that I made such a difference in these lives.

That is *all* I am living for. Them. Not me.

My first student-teaching semester was unforgettable. Nearly all the students were exceptionally nice. Some of them had a sense of humor. For instance, when I taught a review on radicals, one told me, "The lesson's going to *be* radical." Likewise, I would implement humor when appropriate. After all, I got the most-sense-of-humor certificate on the last day of fifth grade.

"If you hear me, clap once."

Clap!

"If you hear me, clap pi."

Huh? And yet, some students endeavored to do that.

Sometimes, instead of "pi," I said, "ten to the tenth power," or something like that, which just led to applause.

Sure, there were times I made calculation errors. Students were always patient with me, knowing that I was in the learning process.

Rare times, I made clumsy mistakes while walking around the classroom, such as accidentally knocking over a Hydro Flask, creating a pool of water on the student's desk. The student lifted up his Chromebook as fast as lightning before it could potentially be destroyed by the water.

Something I found mindboggling was the fact that half my life ago at this point, I was a student at Ensign. Not only that, but that was when all the students were born, around 2007-2009. Most of the eighth graders were born when I was in seventh grade, and most of the seventh graders were born when I was in eighth grade. In fact, when they told me their birthdays, not only did I retain most of them, but sometimes, I was able to tell them where I was on the day they were born (or around that date). For a couple of them, I had their birth date in my book. For a couple of others, I had a home video of that date on YouTube.

Furthermore, substituting has been phenomenal too. However, it never fails, but pretty much everywhere I sub at, students ask me, "How tall are you?" (Students ask this even a year later, and it will probably last for the rest of my career.)

Toward the end of my semester, we teaching candidates were asked to journal in class, week by week. We usually journaled about SEL, such as self-management and social awareness. We began to share what our lives have become through student teaching. I was one who found my daily motivation and a balanced circadian rhythm. In one of my journals, I wrote the following:

> *One thing I . . . confirmed is my capability of building confidence, especially in a classroom. I learned many strategies . . . as well as ways to teach, even if I get stuck. It built my confidence in being able to teach math and tutor in mathematics and science. I learned I can be a respected, professional teacher and oftentimes, gain the attention of students. My Master Teacher sincerely packed tons of critiques, strategies, and opportunities to teach in me.*

–37–
CALTPA CYCLE 1 RESULTS
AND BRANCHING OUT!

On May 3, 2022, I had an exit interview with my Instructional Design professor in his office, after which I YouTubed a summary of how life has been going through this journey. I also gave my encouragement about not giving up, the sky's the limit. I was officially done with my semester, and I ended up serving for fifty-two days (239.5 clinical hours) as a BST.

I would be getting the results of my CalTPA Cycle 1 any day now. And that day came two days later. The morning after it came, on May 6, I went public with the news that I *passed* Cycle 1 of the intensely stressful CalTPA!

That was not all that occurred that day. I was branching out. The afternoon before, I accepted my first substitute position at another school. Not only that, but it was for an elementary school, 5th grade, at Rea Elementary, thereby having multiple subjects in lieu of a single subject. I had attended there for summer school in 2004, right before fourth grade, and I juggled there from 2017 to 2019, as I have noted earlier in this book.

I arrived early in the morning and filmed the beginning of my teaching update video, explaining my accomplishment with the TPA and the fact that I was branching out. I went over to the office, and surprise, nobody was home.

I waited outside for quite a while until an office personnel arrived. (We knew each other from when I came in and juggled in the past. We also worked at the OC Fair at the same time too.) Apparently, not all schools started around 8:00. Rea started at 8:35. On Frontline, the time said 8:05, and I assumed that that was when school began. Thus, I came around 7:30-ish. What I soon figured out was that the displayed time was for substitutes to *arrive*, which was a half an hour before the bell rang.

There were a lot of similarities of procedures. I signed the payroll sheet and got a substitute folder with a key. Right afterward, the principal walked out.

"Hey, Matthew! Great to see you," he said, smiling.

We met back when I was in high school. Every year, NMUSD held a Special Education Tea, where I juggled and played piano. He said he always enjoyed my juggling and story. He was one of the people who helped me juggle at a few events at Rea, such as their Spring Festival in April 2019. The other person who helped me get involved was my former fourth-grade teacher, who moved to Rea after she taught me. She had just retired in June 2019.

I went to the classroom, which happened to be the same room number as my Master Teacher over at Ensign. Once I got everything set up, I walked around the classroom in awe. I guess I somewhat felt what Brad Cohen must have felt as portrayed in the movie *Front of the Class* when he entered his classroom for the first time.

I saw the class pictures from years past that the teacher had displayed. I recognized two of them who were currently seventh graders at Ensign.

As it drew closer to the start of school, I walked outside. Being a Friday, a Flag Deck was there, which was the first one for me in ages. There, I ran in to a teacher who used to teach sixth grade at Newport Heights Elementary. He did the physical education rotation when I was a sixth grader, and he is a fellow juggler. He remembered me well. It was great running into him again and catching up. After Flag Deck, I walked the students to the classroom. I introduced myself and started with a brief icebreaker activity that I would use at Royal Rangers.

Substituting at an elementary school is quite interesting. There is usually a mountain of papers, packets, magazines, and/or books on the desk, stacked in the order of the day's schedule. Akin to when I was an elementary-school student, the general order is language arts, recess, math, and lunch, after which there can be science, social studies, and/or physical education, depending on the day and the school.

For my first day as a substitute at an elementary school, I divided the schedule up into parts, based on main assignments, at the end of which I would do a magic trick. Every trick that I showed them on this day had really baffled them—converting three pieces of rope into one, changing a playing card right before their eyes twice, and opening an envelope that had the sum of three numbers that they chose. During downtime at one point, a student had me solve his Rubik's Cube.

Throughout the day, a couple of students recognized me from YouTube and Instagram, saying hi to me. I was talking with a teacher at the time, and that melted her heart to see that. Others recognized me from juggling in years past.

The students were very kind and respectful. At the end of the day, to reward their good behavior, I juggled for all of them. Overall, I really enjoyed my first day as a sub for an elementary school. I described it as an "outstanding, phenomenal, exquisite day."

Quite an interesting thing happened, however, at recess. I was by the basketball courts, and a teacher came up to me, recognizing me from juggling for her class and the class of my former fourth-grade teacher. Both classes were inside one classroom. My former teacher happened to communicate with her twenty minutes prior, wondering how I was doing these days.

The only regret that I have was missing the principal. He had a meeting by the time school was out. I wanted to ask him if I could do an all-school assembly, volunteering to juggle, speak, encourage, and motivate.

At the end of my teaching update video, I told anybody listening, "Never give up, persevere, keep going, and you shall succeed. Have a nice day!"

–38–

Adventures (and Lessons) in Substitute Teaching

Since I was done with my semester of studying, I could now relax for a month, substituting at various schools. Again, if I did not have a position (which had been the case a few times), I would volunteer at Ensign. On days when I was back at Ensign, some students came up to me, happy to see me again.

The boys I had been mentoring at my Royal Rangers outpost knew that I was a substitute teacher now. Many of them were telling me to please come sub for them. Unfortunately, a couple of them were in a different school district.

Once at Ensign, a person in the office told me that another substitute said that she knew me. I later went to see her in the classroom, and it was a classmate from third grade.

The Monday after subbing at Rea, I subbed at Costa Mesa Middle School and High School (two schools in one). It was the first time I got to be inside. I had previously spoke, juggled, and played piano over there for the 2020 and 2022 HALO Benefits.

I subbed for a science class. Great, one of my specialties, although nobody asked me for help, even though I offered. Just being there to sub, it was kind of a relaxed day for the students, when they could review some material or do silent reading.

Mondays at Costa Mesa held all periods on the same day, instead of block schedule. That sort of made the time go by quicker. There were two prep periods that were a little boring.

My incentive was juggling if they reminded me. By the end of the day, students would enter, saying, "Aren't you the sub who juggles?"

The first lesson that I learned that day was about the technology. I could not get the darn computer to work; they were also out of Chromebooks. The front office told me to call IT. I did so and explained to the gentleman on the other side everything about the computer before me. He sounded surprised when I said, "Oh, it's a desktop; not a laptop." I soon found out why. Baffled, he said that he would send someone over.

After a couple of hours, another gentleman from the district came in to examine the problem at hand.

"Oh, without a Chromebook, this monitor won't do anything," he explained.

"Thanks," I gave the smile of shame, humiliated.

At least there were no hard feelings. We both chuckled and he left.

Now I know, I said to myself.

I ended up not needing a computer the whole time, but at least I learned something.

In the middle of the day, I ran into one of the student teachers whom I had classes with during the Fall-2021 semester. He had just finished up his AST semester, for which I congratulated him.

Then came the final period.

As students began to enter, one asked me, "Are you the sub?"

"Yes, I am."

"Oh," he looked sorry and in a low voice, warned me, "Good luck handling this class."

Oh boy, I thought. *Uh, thanks . . . I guess.*

Sure enough, I could not sit down one bit. I kept walking around in circles, monitoring the students, asking many to stop talking out loud, and offering to help others. By fortuity, they were learning about the circulatory system. That is my absolute specialty when it comes to human anatomy. I was thinking about it earlier, but thought, *What are the chances?* Alas, they told me that they were understanding it, which is good, of course, but I have been eager to help explain cardiology for nearly ten years, as I have done *extensive* research in it.

Up to this date, that was one of the toughest classes I ever subbed for. And at the end of the whole day too. Nevertheless, I had no hard feelings. I just wish I could have done some SEL with them, encouragements that they can take out of the classroom and apply to everyday life, motivating them to choose to succeed.

After school, I stuck around for quite a long time. Earlier that morning, I ran into the principal and got to meet him. I asked if I could speak with him in his office after school. He said I could, but by the time school ended, he was in a meeting. After a half an hour or so, the office personnel told me to just email him, which I did, to no avail. I asked him if I could speak voluntarily and juggle for every single student for both the middle school *and* high school.

Later, on Wednesday, it was one of the most special substituting adventures to date. I subbed at Ensign Intermediate School again *for my former eighth-grade U.S. History and Geography teacher . . . in the same classroom!* Talk about full circle.

All the students in every period were impressed by that, including the teacher the next time I saw him. He still has something that I wrote in 2008 stapled to the wall.

I found out something funny, though. Somebody said that she thought I was the mailman when I first began student teaching. In fact, that was not the last time I heard that, just to say.

The next day, I just volunteered at Ensign, due to no sub jobs available. After school, I went back on Frontline and accepted another special opening for the following day. The next morning, I walked a few blocks to Newport Heights Elementary, carrying all my magic and juggling incentives. It was the place I went to for four years and the place where I came back to juggle since I was a sophomore in high school. I was subbing a fourth-grade class. It was nostalgic to be back there, seeing what remained and what changed.

I am not superstitious, but it was my first Friday the thirteenth as a teacher, albeit a substitute teacher. The only thing stressful was a dream the night before, where everything went wrong. Dreams always bring me down whenever I am excited about something.

Alas, my former third-grade teacher was also off that day, but I texted him about it. I did run into teachers who remembered me but did not have me as their student.

Another one of the most remarkable happenstances to have occurred was that I was subbing in my old third-grade classroom.

During Flag Deck, one of the students recognized me from YouTube. The teacher's class was one of the best and most well-behaved set of students that I have ever taught. The day before, I went over there to talk to the teacher, and she gave me a copy of the sub plans. She told me the rundown of the schedule, as well as all her incentives and rewards that she gives. All the students enjoyed the tricks and juggling. I also taught them a coin trick and a math shortcut trick. By the end, the students wanted me to come back.

I also got to run into the principal again for the first time since 2019. I reemphasized my heart to juggle and speak at an all-school assembly someday, at my expense. "I'd give anything to be an encouragement and motivator," I said. She truly thought it was great that I had such willingness.

The following week, I was subbing at Ensign. From Monday to Thursday, I taught statistics to the Enhanced Math periods—histograms, box and whiskers plots, dot plots, mean absolute deviation, and all that fun stuff. For a couple of those days, I was teaching about volume to AVID from their study guide.

I definitely saved my skin on one of those days! I forgot to hand out a simple worksheet about histograms, despite the teacher reminding me. During lunchtime, I took those worksheets, a clipboard, the seating chart, and a pencil. I went out and found almost every single one of those students and handed them the worksheet. The one or two I did not find were in the teacher's SSR.

I took a sigh of relief. *Phew, everybody got one.* No one had hard feelings; I just saw smiles and heard chuckles from the students.

Word got out that I was subbing for a seventh-grade social science class for Friday and the following Monday. Students were stoked to hear the news. I had accepted the two-day assignment nearly a month before. I introduced myself to the teacher and observed her class a couple of times. She shared with me her instruction strategies and talked to me a lot about SEL and how she helps a couple of her students. She had been as resourceful to me as other teachers I observed, taking the time to talk to me.

On Friday, my incentive was the magic trick that I did for the eighth-grade science students in April. On Monday, it was juggling. When I arrived on Monday morning, I was telling everybody, "Thank God it's Monday!"

Yeah, I was like the only person celebrating. Oh well.

At lunch, I ran into the on-campus safety officer, telling her that I was happy it was Monday.

"Yay, just a couple more weeks before summer!" she said.

"I'm not happy about that." I proceeded to tell her that it is my joy and motivation to serve, even if it must be voluntarily. She thought that that was very admirable about my character.

The Friday before, one of the custodians ran into me and said, "Hey, it's almost Friday!"

I was like, "No, uh, I don't like Fridays; I like Mondays."

"Oh. Well, then it's almost Monday!" He smiled just as wide.

Within these two days, I got to substitute teach a couple of people from Lighthouse's youth group, one of whom used to be in Royal Rangers. They were amazed to see me as their sub at last. Many students greeted me as I greeted them. One even jumped up and down, shouting my full name, "Matthew Kenslow! Matthew Kenslow!"

However, with the majority of the experience being positive, I did have to call for a student to be escorted out. It was the first time I had to do that, which was a hard decision. I patiently talked to him throughout the entire period, trying to employ SEL and giving him a pep talk. I figured that for the benefit of the class, who were getting distracted, I should call the office after a million and one chances that I gave him.

I dialed the specific extension.

"Oh yeah," the person said after I said the student's name. "I'm coming right over." She knew exactly who I was talking about.

I figured that if given the chance, I would be able to encourage him later once I did not have an entire class to manage. He was not necessarily mean as in being hurtful, but rather, was seeking attention.

Other than that, a couple of periods started to get on the hectic side, such as not quieting down during work time. I simply walked around and used proximity control.

In my notes that I gave to the teacher, I told her which periods were good and which ones were were on the noisy side. I gave her details about the most disruptive one, where some (not all) of the students kept yelling out, throwing things around, and printing random things out of the printer.

Later on, after the teacher returned, she gave me two stacks of apology notes that she had every student in that period write—one for each day. It was quite heartfelt. Again, not every student was bad, but they still apologized for the way I was treated by the class as a whole, saying that I did not deserve to be treated like that. The couple of students who were on the disrespectful side sincerely apologized to me.

Just like the letters from Teacher Appreciation Week, these letters significantly brightened my life, as they were more affirmation to me that I am positively influencing their lives. One said that he found me as an enjoyable teacher. Others said that I was one of their favorite subs, that my juggling and magic trick were fun to watch, and that my memorization skills were insane. Some hoped that I was doing well and that I would not be in such a situation like that again. One apologized that I kept having to walk around to ask students to do their work. Others, according to their words, admired my empathy, leniency, and patience. One apologized for the class taking advantage of my kindness. A few of them drew me a picture, one of which was an incredible drawing of me juggling.

Soon thereafter, I was walking by the former Yogurtland along East 17th Street and ran into a few students. One sincerely apologized for how the class behaved, being a bit upset about the students who were disrespectful. Another time, a student yelled out across the street, apologizing to me.

Nevertheless, there was an amazing occurrence on those same two days. The teacher's prep period was eighth period. On both mornings, I got a call asking if I were willing to sub eighth period for another teacher.

Absolutely!

On Friday, I stepped right in and subbed for my former R.S.P. teacher, and on Monday, I subbed for the U.S. History and Geography teacher whom I subbed for right after spring break. On Monday, the students were thrilled to see me substitute teach.

Wherever and whenever help is needed, sign me up!

As I continued to substitute, I once had to manage amid Wi-Fi issues. There was another class period that was a feelings bruiser, which I do not want to go into detail about. However, the majority of the time, subbing created great, rewarding memories. When students saw me at Ensign, they asked me if I would be subbing for them.

"No," I sometimes had to say.

"Well, I wish you were. You're my favorite sub!"

Another special memory was made on Wednesday, May 25. I had the privilege to sub for a science class at Newport Harbor High School. During the break and lunch, I went around to say hi to as many teachers and staff as I could. Tons of my former teachers still worked there and remembered me. I told them that we were now working at the same school together. Some of them were asking me about how my book was doing.

My former R.S.P. teacher, whom I had for four years, was shocked to see me, stood on a chair, and gave me a hug. She could not help but introduce me to an office personnel as her former student, author, and presidential encyclopedia. At one point, I got to meet the principal again.

"What's the name of your book again?" he asked, remembering that I wrote one.

I told him, followed by my acknowledgment of how COVID changed a lot of things. However, since schools had been opening back up, I was still interested to voluntarily speak and juggle during an assembly. He said that he would be in touch about that.

The only downside of subbing there was being bored to death during class. I quickly remembered how *long* high school classes with block schedules are, roughly an hour and a half. All I got to do was introduce who I was, take roll, and explain what they needed to do.

That was all I could do. For three periods. I had one of my magic tricks ready but told them to remind me before the period ended. Only the middle class reminded me on time.

Later that week, more special blessings continued to unfold. At Ensign during lunchtime, one of the students came up to me, saying that the librarian wanted me to donate a copy of my book for the library. I felt immensely privileged. After speaking with the librarian (whom I remembered from when I was a student), I personalized an autographed copy and donated it the following week when I subbed for my former history teacher again.

On that day when I subbed history again, as I was greeting the students coming in, that same student from earlier came up to me and pulled out a copy of my book. Later that day, another student pulled out her copy and had me sign it. Back when I was subbing for the social science class, a couple of the students said that their parents were buying a copy. Another student referenced a part in it. This all meant a lot to me.

I had made a YouTube video back in the middle of May talking about this very thing. Students at Ensign and around the neighborhood had referenced my book or said that they had bought my book. A few asked for my autograph and several got a picture with me. In my video, I gave an important message. All I ever want, besides being a teacher, is to be a benefactor to society. All I care about is to help many people in realizing that they have purpose, "disability" or not.

However, I am not feeling as if I am famous; I am not trying to attain those feelings either. When people, such as the students, talk about my book or social media accounts, get a picture with me, or get an autograph, it is simply affirming to me that I am being noticed and heard, that I am being an influence in their lives. I do not view it as celebrity status.

It helps me because, if you have read this entire book, you know what terror I have been living with. Therefore, it makes me feel alive, that I have purpose, that I have belonging in life, that I am not invisible, and that I am being accepted as a human being. Also, I am making other people's day, and I am helping them out.

As I have gone on the record ever since March without apology, I will never stop fighting for equity, antidiscrimination, and relative world peace until the day I get to heaven, whether that day is soon or whether that day is a hundred years from now.

As I conclude this chapter, I have a couple more subbing experiences that meant a lot to me. What I am about to tell makes up the bulk of my YouTube video that I titled "*MOST SPECIAL TEACHING UPDATE OF THIS SCHOOL YEAR*" As of the publishing of this book, this video has gotten almost 30,000 views and over 7,000 likes. It takes the viewer from May 31 until summer break, thereby concluding my first academic year, during which I was a student teacher and substitute teacher.

On May 31, I substituted for fifth grade at Kaiser Elementary School. It was special because I went there for summer school twice, in 2001 and 2002.

As soon as I walked inside the classroom, I saw a picture of a familiar face on the cabinet door, where the teacher had everybody's picture up. It was one of the boys at Lighthouse's youth group, whom I see every week, along with his older brother, whom I have already subbed for. Both of them used to be in Royal Rangers for years.

"Oh, let's go!" The boy's eyes lit up when I opened the door to greet the class.

After I commenced the class, another student recognized me from something that happened one night in the summer of 2021. Three boys were out skateboarding, and the youngest one broke his arm. I rushed over to help, but unfortunately, I did not have any splinting materials (not even improvised). Thankfully, the person watching them that night was there and called the boy's mother, who took him to the hospital. I felt horrible because I was completely helpless. I just stayed for moral support. Somehow, this student remembered me. He reintroduced me to that boy during recess, and I said that I was glad he was better. At lunchtime, I walked around to the places I still remembered from twenty years prior, reminiscing.

During recess and lunch, I searched for the principal. At one point, I saw a lady walk up to me with a smile. "I heard you were looking for me," she said. "I am the principal."

I was happy to introduce myself. I then told her that I am an author of a book and am willing to volunteer my time in an all-school assembly to speak and juggle. She was very pleased to hear of my accomplishments and heart for service. Her eyes especially widened when I told her that my book is being read and reviewed in the UK, Australia, and India, demonstrating that my book is internationally making a difference. She asked for my information and told me she would keep me in mind.

The students in the class were impressed with my magic tricks and juggling skills. By lunchtime, students were asking me if I was going to sub for them the next day. Others asked if I could teach sixth grade to them in the next academic year. At the end of the day, nearly all of them were begging me to come back.

On Wednesday, I was back over at Newport Heights Elementary. This time, my former third-grade teacher was there, and for the first time, we worked at the same school together. He was standing outside his door with his class at the time and introduced me to his students.

The teacher I was subbing for was there when I was a student; we remembered each other quite well. The students were great. Some immediately recognized me from juggling for them when they were in first grade. I got reacquainted with the P.E. teacher as I dropped the students off at P.E. that morning. After telling him that I was a student fifteen years prior, he remembered me.

The day only got rambunctious during an interesting trading game, which the teacher told me was going to happen in his sub notes. It was social studies related.

After lunch, I got to teach science: the rock cycle. It was not as easy as teaching the water cycle, but it still went well. I observed a seventh-grade science teacher at Ensign earlier that year teaching the rock cycle using Laffy Taffies, but alas, I could not find Laffy Taffies or Play-Doh in the classroom.

By the time school let out, one student said that the whole day was a ten-out-of-ten for her. Once again, students all liked my incentives throughout the day. Before class began, a teacher told me about a student I could send over if he got out of hand. While I was there, he and others were commenting on how he was behaving well all day, eager to see all the tricks I brought.

My schedule is day-by-day. Sometimes, I know where I will sub at the day before. Other times, I know the morning of. Such was the case the next day; but not only that, it was another special opportunity.

As soon as I woke up, I saw a position available to teach third grade at none other than College Park Elementary.

How is that special? College Park was my very first school *ever*! I attended there for preschool, starting on September 9, 1999. I still have dozens upon dozens of vivid memories from being a student there, not to mention home videos and pictures, many of which I already have up on YouTube.

As I was setting up everything inside the classroom, I noticed students looking in from outside the window, waving at me and smiling.

Being a Friday, there was Flag Deck. I had already introduced myself to staff and teachers that I was a former student there twenty-two academic years ago. As I approached Flag Deck, looking around and wondering where my class was, a student from the class came up to me.

"Are you looking for [this teacher's] class?"

"Yes, I am," I said, smiling.

"It's over here. Come this way." He navigated me to the spot.

A person soon came up to me saying that she could not come in during the first half hour. According to the sub notes, she was going to come in and continue to teach Mandarin to the students, but something came up. She basically told me to stall for the time being until the next task on the agenda, and then she would come in later that day. (The class I subbed for was dual immersion, where students learn both English and Mandarin.)

As I continued to stand there, suddenly, I heard, "Matthew! Oh, my gosh! You're here! It's so good to see you again."

It was the principal. I knew him since Newport Heights Elementary, back when he was one of the teachers. Since graduating Newport Heights, we ran into each other multiple times, but this was the first time seeing each other in years. Not only that, but I was standing there with a Substitute Teacher badge.

"Boy, I'm starting to feel very old this morning," the principal said once he got up in front of everybody. "I just ran into a former student from over ten years ago, when I was a teacher at Newport Heights. We're very happy to have *Mr. Kenslow* over there substituting today. Thank you for being here."

Once I got everybody in the classroom, I took attendance, played a brief icebreaker, and conducted their morning procedures per the sub notes. After all that, we still had several minutes before the person said she would come. Students had found out that I was a YouTuber and were quite eager to watch a video. Since there was a change in the schedule, I searched up a home video I had of being at that school. I chose the one called "College Park Elementary's Christmas Choir + a Party with a Piñata" from December 17, 1999.

All the students marveled from beginning to end. They noticed things that were still the same and things that were new. They even recognized a person from the staff in the background who still works there.

Later, the third grade had a Spring Sing performance in the multipurpose room. It was surreal to be back in there, especially after showing a video that partly takes place in there. It looked the same, down to the blue theater curtains.

Afterward, the principal said, "Hey, Matthew, I was bragging about you to the other third-grade teachers. We're wondering if you brought your juggling stuff with you."

"Yes, I did."

"Are you willing to juggle for the entire third grade? It'll be during the last thirty minutes of school."

"Absolutely," I said, managing to contain my enthusiasm. "It would be my pleasure."

At lunchtime, I walked into the part of the school where I had attended preschool. I stood there outside, absorbing the ambiance, and reflecting on countless memories. I turned around and saw one of the students walking toward me.

"Having memories, Mr. Kenslow?" he called out with a huge smile.

"Yes, I am. You better believe it," I said, nodding.

Toward the end of school, all the third-grade classes sat out on the field. All the students and the teachers were impressed by my juggling. I was significantly proud of myself for pulling off a big card trick while standing up in front of everybody. Getting that perfected without a document camera took more concentration than juggling. It was an unbelievable day, and I am thankful for the opportunity to substitute there. I went back to the area where I had preschool to YouTube about it.

"Bye, Mr. Kenslow!" one of the students screamed out while walking with her mother from beyond the fence.

"Bye. Have a good day."

"You too!"

A minute later, one of the third-grade teachers said to me, "Thank you so much. That was very fun. The kids really enjoyed it so much. They were like, 'How did he do that? That was amazing.' You did great. Thanks for doing that. It was a nice way to finish our Friday."

I then found out that she teaches in my former preschool room. The custodian happened to come by, and we three began to reminisce on how the outdoor area used to look, including its similarities. The teacher was working there for twenty-five years up to that point. I showed her and the custodian the class photo from 1999-2000. They recognized a couple of people, but not the teacher I had. I also showed the teacher a picture of the outdoor area from circa 2000, pointing out that the picture was taken right at that spot.

When I turned in my sub badge, I knocked on the principal's door. I was eager to say how well the day went, as well as the juggling. I was hoping to talk to him about having an assembly where I could volunteer to juggle and encourage.

"Hi, Matthew," he whispered. "How'd it go?"

"I survived," I said, smiling.

"Good. Fantastic." He smiled. "Hey, it's great to see you. I'm in an IEP right now, but I hope to see you back, okay? We can catch up a little bit more."

"Okay, thank you."

"Take care."

As soon as I walked out the door, a couple of older students from Costa Mesa Middle School started yelling out, "Oh, what's up!" and "Hey!"

One said, "I knew I saw you. I still follow your YouTube channel."

Right after I hit one thousand subscribers, I was telling one of my barbers about it. They overheard. As I was paying for the haircut, they inquired about it. A week or two later, they saw me inside the truck at a red light. I first heard, "Hey, isn't it that guy? It's that guy," I looked over and they were waving at me. I waved and said hi back.

Once again, we ran into each other. "Thanks for your support," I said.

"I *knew* I saw him." One of them still could not get over it.

"Bye," they called out as I was leaving a couple moments later.

"Have a good day. Have a good *weekend*," I called back.

Afterward, I was getting one of my usuals at my local Juice It Up! place. While entering, students in a golf cart at the nearby Target pointed me out, saying, "Matthew Kenslow! He's a YouTuber." Others began shouting hi to me.

"Hello," I called out.

About a minute later, a couple of other Ensign students walked in, one of whom was in Enhanced Math that I student taught. He was wondering why I was not at Ensign teaching him anymore. "Wait," he said. "Where were you? You weren't even in my math class."

I told him that I was at College Park and explained that my semester was over. Thus, I was just subbing around. I congratulated him and his friend on their upcoming graduation, which was just five days later on June 8.

~39~

FINALLY!

Thanks to one of my former elementary school principals (who is now the Executive Director of Elementary Education), I got in contact with the principal at California Elementary, where I attended summer school in 2003. I had been asked to juggle and speak for two classes of fourth graders in the multipurpose room. On June 9, I arrived at the school, got acquainted with the principal, and took a walk to the MPR. Soon, my former principal arrived. It was the first time seeing each other in over a decade, but he looked exactly the same.

Once the thirty-nine students came in and took their seats, the principal talked to them, starting out by saying that the school year was extended two more weeks. After hearing the groans of the students, he revealed that he was just joking. He asked the students to show the Executive Director and me their best behavior.

The Executive Director gave a five-minute introduction about me, how much I have inspired him in the past, and what they are going to take out of the assembly. He said that I was a person who took what he has, never gave up, and kept going.

It was my pleasure to juggle for the students, talking about who I am as a person with Autism. I got to tell them about Autism/Disability Awareness *and* Acceptance, along with antibullying. I delivered my juggling analogy about not giving up on what you want to do in life. If things fall in life, then pick them back up and keep going.

I told them that the Executive Director was the person who encouraged me to juggle four items for my sixth-grade talent show back when he was my principal. I was not yet good at four, but he motivated me to keep practicing.

While juggling clubs, I got to share my presidential knowledge and math shortcuts. After my science-demo analogy about not bottling things up inside, I proceeded to juggle my basketball and two soccer balls.

Finally!

I gave my "Be Number One" encouragement about not setting standards based on other people, but rather, basing them on themselves. Everybody is unique with distinct skill sets and various levels of mastery per skill. If I were driven by jealousy, then I would not have gotten as far as I did, that's for sure.

In between my encouragements, I performed my rope trick and card trick. They provided a document camera for me to have my tricks displayed up on the stage. At the beginning, I had an envelope displayed under the camera, saying that I will open it at the end if everybody is listening. At the end, three students wrote a three-digit number in my notepad. Another student added the three numbers shown and the sum was in the envelope.

The entire experience was just incredible. All the students could not get over everything that I said and did. I was told afterward that they all became very motivated after hearing me.

The Executive Director told me to keep him updated on my future schooling and student teaching. I could not wait to plan the next few times and hopefully perform in front of bigger and bigger audiences.

The next day was the last day of school for elementary schools. Middle and high schools officially concluded that Thursday. I had already planned to juggle for three first-grade classes at Newport Heights Elementary. They all went inside my former third-grade teacher's first-grade classroom. A couple of people from Vanguard student taught there, so it was amazing to see each other.

The teacher introduced me, explaining that I was his former student, an author, and a Gold Medal of Achievement recipient. Juggling, doing the math shortcuts, motivating them with my analogies, and all the magic tricks underneath the document camera had created an unforgettable experience for all those first graders. The teacher concluded by playing the trailer to my YouTube channel.

Afterward, I was outside talking with the teacher by the lunch tables. One of the second graders came up to me, remembering when I subbed for the fourth graders. There was something called "buddies" where the fourth graders spent time with a second grader. I would go around and periodically pull a coin out of their ear, before making it disappear. While talking with the second grader, he and his friends found out that I could juggle, so I gave a little encore performance.

Later, the teacher and I were walking together and saw two other teachers.

They both taught there when I was a student. They were all proud of me. I got to step inside the two fourth-grade classes I subbed for that year to say, "Have a great summer" to the students.

"Whoa, they treat you like a rock star here," my former third-grade teacher said, astonished.

Subsequently, I walked down to Ensign Intermediate to give my final words for my special teaching update. I ran into teachers and staff while I was there; I said that I hope they would have a great summer. They appreciated that.

On the way home, I began feeling very special and proud inside that I could call myself a teacher, albeit a student and substitute teacher. Nevertheless, I began feeling more pride in my accomplishment and happiness that I could tell the community and world that I gladly invest my life for future generations.

~40~

My Efforts During Summer

One day at the end of May, a student biked up to me during an evening neighborhood walk. He asked me if I was excited for summer.

"Uh, not as a teacher."

"Not as a teacher? Why?" He looked confused.

"Because I don't have any place to serve at in the summer."

"You can't serve in the summer?"

"No, they said that they won't keep the sub list during the summer."

"Oh, that's not cool." He sounded sympathetic.

That had been some difficult news to hear. However, I sent back a letter to the district office saying that I was willing to stay employed during the 2022-2023 academic year. They later sent me the Offer of Employment form in August. After signing it, I remained a substitute teacher. In the interim, I filled out an electronic form expressing interest in serving during the summer. However, all summer long, they never reached out to me.

"I'm trying to remain optimistic," I told that student on his bike. "I'm turning twenty-seven in the summer, so that's a good thing."

"So I'll see you around Ensign next year?" he asked.

"Yeah."

"Oh, okay. Good. I'm going to have to get in the *advance* math classes now," he said, smiling, hoping to have me as his teacher. "All right, have a great one."

"Thanks. You too."

Well, on top of the news about NMUSD and the uncertainty of summer, Royal Rangers continued for only half of the summer instead of all of it. I still served at Lighthouse's youth group, but it was quite lonesome. Most people had plans for the summer, including Wednesday nights. Toward the end, before school restarted, a new boy came to youth group. I knew him from Royal Rangers, and I mentored him for a couple of years. I also saw him around Ensign when he was a seventh grader. I found out that he was in Enhanced Math and asked who his eighth-grade teacher was going to be. It was my Master Teacher.

"I'm going to be teaching you," I said, smiling.

His eyes lit up, and he whispered, "Let's go!"

Even though I was faced with an uncertain summer, I was not going to just sit around! There is no reason why I could not be helping my community and the world in the meantime.

As the school year was winding down, I thought about Mariners Christian School. Some of the attendees at Lighthouse's youth group attended there; one of the pastor's daughters substituted there. I ultimately found out from her that they do not have summer school.

One Sunday morning, while playing with the band, the guest drummer (who happened to be that same pastor's brother-in-law) was saying how excited he was to teach geometry in the summer.

"Hey, would you need a sub?" I blurted out.

"Yeah." He smiled. "If I need one, sure."

"Okay. Where do you teach at?"

"Pasadena."

Ugh! In case you do not know the geography of Southern California, Pasadena was an hour or two away, depending on traffic, past Los Angeles.

One day, I walked past a sign that advertised a VBS at Bayside Church OC. *That's it!* I suddenly felt empowered with a boost of optimism. At that time, I was enthusiastically on a mission to be a volunteer juggler and speaker at as many VBSs as humanly possible. I was requesting to do so for part of one day (not all the days).

I contacted Bayside Church OC with a formal email explaining all about who I am and what I have accomplished for others. I additionally contacted St. Andrew's Presbyterian Church.

One of the young adults at Lighthouse was working at Mariners Church at the time for the children's ministries. The lead youth pastor helped me get in contact with her, but it was seeming to be that Mariners was already filled up. Nevertheless, I decided to still email Mariners Church directly. After all, I was just asking to be there for one part of one day. I have proven in the past that I made a lifechanging difference motivating thousands of children and teenagers throughout my life.

I went online and found several churches across the county who were having VBS. I contacted Mission Bible Church, Calvary Chapel Costa Mesa, Rockharbor, Liberty Baptist, and Newport Center UMC. I then took to social media and asked my church friends in the county to help me out and to pray with me about it.

On June 10, after I was juggling for those three classes of first graders, one of the things I was talking to my former teacher about was this mission. I asked if his church was holding a VBS. He said that he would let them know about me.

One day, St. Andrew's Presbyterian got back with me saying yes! All I had to do was get fingerprinted, and they would run a background check on me. Once I was cleared, I was officially a volunteer. On June 23, I juggled for four rotations of children and a little spontaneous encore once everybody gathered back together. I was ever so grateful for them. They told me that over three hundred children were there.

I continued to periodically check in with the other churches. Their responses varied. One said that I was not a good fit for them. A few others said that everything was already planned. A couple of them gave me hope for the following year. (I did contact a lot of churches a few months early in April 2023. Still, for some of them, like Bayside OC, they were already booked that early. A couple of others declined. St. Andrew's and Liberty Baptist, however, were two who accepted me.)

As the rest of the summer of 2022 was being shattered before my eyes, one by one, I still endeavored relentlessly to appear in the news media, talk shows, radio, and all that stuff. I have never stopped since 2019.

Earlier that year, I was talking with my doctor during my annual checkup. He began asking about how things were going in my life. I laid out all of my stress about feeling perpetually underused and devalued. I poured out my feelings about how much rejection I got by Autism organizations, news, newspapers, and other media, not to mention all the places in Orange County and surrounding counties I wanted to go to in person, just to be an encouragement at my expense.

That's all. I was not looking for money.

Around this time of my life, I publicly described my physical feelings and stress on Facebook. I described it like thin (yet resiliently untearable) dental floss being wrapped around my heart thousands of times over. Then, hands are pulling on it from both ends, pulsating back and forth, attempting to slowly slice my heart to shreds. That's precisely the pain my heart has felt, 24/7/365 the past few years, trying to get out there to make a difference to billions of people, yet the majority of the world, including my own county, is not allowing me to volunteer to speak and juggle.

The reason why I wrote the book in the first place was to make an international difference through it but also to speak and juggle everywhere else. I started to assume that most people had written me off as a quack or charlatan, in spite of stressing the word *volunteer* to them.

All I am trying to do, besides teaching at a middle school, is fight to end and eradicate bullying, discrimination, teasing, suicide, and such. I looked up the stats, and at the time, one in six teens in America planned to commit suicide. I am not trying to be a celebrity or earn money. There is a *dire need* out there, and I believe (even today) that I was born to fulfill that need! I am here to call on humanity to finally put aside differences and competition, come together, and accept one another, despite their disabilities.

When this happens, the world would be at "relative peace," as I call it. Even though I acknowledge the impossibility for humanity to achieve 100 percent world peace, I am simply striving to help this world reach the highest percentage humanly possible.

My doctor understood what I was describing to him and said that he would get me in contact with somebody at the clinic who might help with that.

Soon, I got a phone call from a clinical social worker at UCI Health. After explaining to her what my lifelong goal is, she put me in contact with a clinical psychologist at The Center for Autism & Neurodevelopmental Disorders. After a couple of months of emails and Zoom meetings with her, I was given the opportunity to be a presenter at a virtual Spring Mental Health Symposium on March 19. It was like an interview, where she asked the questions and I answered. She told me that there were twenty-nine people (all of whom were doctors) who listened in. She added that many of them reached out to her afterward, applauding my presentation.

Notwithstanding, in early June, I wrote a long and thorough email to my publisher, explaining to him everything about my never-ending nightmare with the media. I did everything known to man for nearly three years.

Word of mouth, business cards, social media, emails, in-person announcements of my authorship, you name it, didn't seem to make a difference. Every single little thing I could do, I tried. To this day, I do not believe I missed *anything*. I would bet a million dollars if I had it.

My publisher referred me to a publicist. I did so immediately. Within the next month, I got everything written and filled out. I requested prayer over it from my pastors, friends, and family. I described this upcoming journey as driving on the edge of the world's sharpest and precarious knife. One wrong move, one slip, and I felt as if I would fail. I was extremely close to getting out there to help change this world, and this was definitely the one chance that I was going to take!

My one-month Public Relations campaign officially launched on July 5, and I started getting several leads a week. My first opportunity was a radio interview that took place on my 27th birthday, July 22, 2022: CHVN 95.1 FM radio up in Manitoba, Canada. It was my first radio interview since KOST 103.5 FM on April 2, 2020.

One week later, I was live on Doctor Radio – Sirius XM early in the morning; that evening, I was on another live radio program. The latter was quite something. This one was via phone instead of Zoom. As I have expressed earlier in the book, I strongly dislike phone calls. The interview was very cordial; the host and I enjoyed every bit of it.

However, there was one hiccup roughly twenty minutes in. "Oh, it looks like we lost Matthew. We'll try to get him back, but until then . . ." I was just answering a question when the host suddenly said that. A few seconds later, they called back, and I was reconnected. The program was flawless after that. One of the two major things I stress about with phone calls was being disconnected. The second thing was hearing. I get worried about not being able to hear well. I also worry about my surroundings becoming too loud at such an inopportune time. Outside my apartment window, people sometimes come over, talk, laugh out loud, and/or play loud music. Other times, garbage trucks, motorcycles, or lawn mowers come by and seem to amplify their noise as if it is a popular sold-out concert.

I started to be featured in magazines and blogs around the world, including the United Kingdom creativity magazine, *The Table Read*, as well as *Newsweek* Magazine. My publicist was incredibly blown away to find out that I made it in *Newsweek*, as did my former teachers I shared it with. Whether it be live interviews or in articles, I would oftentimes mention my student teaching at Ensign Intermediate School, NMUSD, Orange Coast College, and Vanguard University.

Over several months, I began seeing my follower count grow rapidly on various social media accounts, as well as a great increase in book sales. Several of the leads wanted me to mail a physical copy of my book, which I did. For others, I kept following up many times over. There were a couple of the programs that I was really eager to get on, but the communications stopped. One day, I was contacted by Gayle Anderson of KTLA 5 News, who forwarded my information to the producers and editors. She told me to contact them to determine when my story could be broadcasted. After many attempts, however, I never heard back. The same thing happened with others. I surmise that things get busy in life, which I must understand.

From July to October, I continued being featured in an enormous amount of articles, including *Authority* Magazine, *e27*, David Meltzer's Instagram live, and many others. A couple of times, I was interviewed early in the morning, right before going to Ensign to student teach. Such were the cases with my WSAZ Channel 3 news interview in West Virginia via Zoom, as well as the Northeast Ohio Parent podcast.

If I could just expound on one thing that was very special, it would be this: In July, I got in communication with Zarina Khairzada, a multimedia journalist for Spectrum News 1 SoCal. After phone calls, texts, and emails, on August 3, she came over to the apartment and filmed a news story about my journey through Autism. Afterward, we met at the Back Bay for a special part of the news story.

Earlier, the journalist was asking me if there was somebody with Autism that I significantly helped, whether it be from student teaching or at Royal Rangers. After thinking for a little while, I contacted the mother of a boy I used to mentor at my outpost. She later said that the whole family was okay with it. She got in contact with the journalist.

At the Back Bay, I got to see that boy (now a teenager), his sister, and their mother for the first time in a few years. While being filmed for the news story, he and I walked around the Back Bay, catching up on everything. We were both interviewed individually.

The news story, called "Man using his diagnosis to help others with autism feel included," came out on television and their website on August 5.

I am exceedingly grateful for the PR campaign, and I count it as the start of more extensive opportunities for the future, which I am *never* giving up on.

Later that year and in early 2023, another PR firm that I invested in wrote three articles about me, my book, and Autism. Each article went all across the country and world. One of them even became a trending story. I was featured in *Bloomberg, Insider, MarketWatch, Digital Journal*, and several dozen other websites and online periodicals.

Then, by early February 2023 (thanks to both PR firms, everybody who supported me, the innumerable interviews and articles over the course of several months, and a reel that went viral), I reached the prestigious milestone of one million followers on Instagram. It was an incredible and monumental moment to see *1M* next to my name. Nobody can believe what joy I had.

Yet one million is currently 1/8000 of the world's population. I soon signed another contract with my original PR firm. Over the following months, I have been interviewed on *Afternoon Live* (KATU ABC 2 in Portland), twice for *Scripps News, ni4kids* magazine in Northern Ireland, *News10* in Detroit with Nick Monacelli, the *Parenting OC's* magazine, 91.9 KVCR/PBS (NPR Radio), live radio in the Virgin Islands, live radio in Spain (*TRE Talk Radio Europe*), *Good Morning Augusta* (WJBF) with Shawn Cabbagestalk, *Exceptional Parent* magazine who gave me a cover story, and too many more to include.

I was substituting at Killybrooke Elementary one morning in March 2023, when suddenly, Denise Dador of *ABC7 Los Angeles* texted me. Seeing my article from the PR campaign, she reached out and wanted me to comment on the recent news. The CDC increased the prevalence of Autism in eight-year-olds to one in thirty-six. Gigantic story short, I was on the news that afternoon. Many people I knew watched it, surprising them, including teachers and school personnel throughout the district, students, and a pastor.

This was only the beginning.

~41~

THE NIGHT I WAS ALMOST
BEATEN TO DEATH
AUGUST 12, 2022

August 12, 2022, started like any other morning but seemed more special. I walked down to Ensign on this sunny day with spectacular clouds, running into students on the way who said hi to me. I went there to volunteer for the eighth-grade registration. Students were there to take their school photo, pick up their P.E. clothes, and the whole nine yards.

Once I got there, I was directed to where I could go help. On the way, a student said hi to me and asked if she could get a picture with me. "I enjoy your YouTube videos," she said. I thanked her for her support.

Well, all I got to do was stand by the cafeteria door for quite a while, periodically directing students to go in. It was not too exciting, but it was great to say hi to several students who remembered me.

I got the invitation to come because I was communicating with my Master Teacher. I was eager to contact her regarding the fall semester. I was going to do so on August 1, but the day before, while at Lighthouse, I got a surprise. I was playing the keys during the opening set when I looked up and saw her waving at me. Afterward, I told her of the coincidence that I was just about to call her the next day. She later texted me information about what is going on the week before school starts. She recommended a couple of those days that would be advantageous for me to attend.

After I left Ensign, I took the long way around back home, since again, I love walking. In the neighborhood hike, I ran into many students, each of which said hi to me. Throughout the entire summer, an innumerable amount of students have said hi to me, whether they be across the street, at the beach, in a store, at a park, on their bicycles, or in a car. A couple of them asked if I would be returning to Ensign. They were quite excited when I told them I would. Others asked to get a picture with me. One even wished me "happy birthday" the day after I turned twenty-seven.

Just in case the reader had not drawn the connection yet, this was in stark contrast to the summer before. Nevertheless, the discrimination was not yet over. That evening, I went out for a normal cathartic hike. As I walked by Rite Aid on East 17th Street, I noticed people standing outside and a police officer who was probably writing his report. Earlier, I heard sirens and saw a fire engine in that direction. It looked as if a car had run into one of the windows.

As I was standing there, a man asked me who I was. I presume to this day that he was one of the higher-ups for Rite Aid and was there to assess the damage. However, I am not positive. Regardless, he was concerned because of my YouTube hat, asking if I am from YouTube. Well, I do not work for YouTube, but I kindly informed that I was nothing more than a professional YouTuber.

He and the people around him began to cacophonously laugh at loud because of that. One of them gave me a look telling me that she thought I was an idiot (to use a euphemism).

I was asking him, "What the heck happened?" but he simply lied to me saying, "I don't know."

I continued my walk, feeling terrible about myself once again. I am trying to change this entire world to be nice to one another. I was just in *Newsweek*, *Spectrum News*, and a litany of other places, but I cannot seem to eradicate discrimination and promote self-confidence in the bullies here in my hometown.

Readers might wonder if I misinterpreted them. I am not writing the full story here, but in short, I know beyond a doubt. Again, if I had it, I would bet a million dollars. I found myself walking in Lion's Park. Suddenly, a bicyclist pulled up behind me.

"I'm from Rea," he said. He recognized me from subbing his fifth-grade class.

After leaving, I felt rejuvenated once again, nearly brushing off the harshness that I had dealt with in recent times, which I will briefly list out later in this chapter.

I looped around Costa Mesa Courtyards before nearly getting hit by a car crossing Newport Boulevard. I started hearing honks from behind me. I looked up, and the car in front of me was turning onto the boulevard, not seeing me. It made an abrupt stop with headlights beaming in my face. I continued walking. This was certainly not the first time this happened to me, but I had no hard feelings.

Ultimately, I went inside the Extra Mile at the Chevron Station by East 17th and Orange. There, I made a cup of cinnamon coffee for like the hundredth time. It was one of the many new things I tried in the summer of 2021 amid the chaos in my life.

While making the coffee, the door opened, and a young man asked to use the air pump outside for his bicycle. After I paid for the coffee and a couple of snacks, I walked outside. It was just past 8:40 p.m., and I had been walking for a couple of hours at this point. It was dark outside, but the lights of the gas station brightened everything. I saw the young man kneeling down while filling up his bicycle tires with air.

Standing next to him was another young man, probably the same age, with his skateboard. In my periphery, I knew that he was staring me down, probably wondering what thin, strange-looking clown or monster was about to walk past him.

Here we go again. I knew in my heart what was about to transpire. I kept looking forward, never even glancing at him. Of course, if he really needed help, I would try and help, but until I knew, I was not going to look at him. (I am not callous, however, but I never want people to think that I am ignoring them.)

"NPC," he tells me as soon as I walked past him.

I stopped and turned to him. "What?" I asked.

He just stared at me behind his disposable mask.

"I'm sorry, what did you say?" I was sincerely having a bad, uneasy feeling, but I was set on not cowering this time.

"Nothing!" he sternly raises his voice.

"Nothing? Okay—"

"NPC," he cuts me off from what I was saying as I was turning around.

"MPC?" I repeated what I thought I heard.

"Yeah," he said.

"Okay, well, what does that stand for?" I honestly did not know.

"I don't know," he shrugs.

"I don't know either," I immediately said.

"All right."

"All right. Well, have a good night." I turned and walked away.

"Later!" he said, unenthusiastically.

"Thanks. See ya."

A few steps later, I hear him saying something like, "[Blank] off, man! [Blank] off!"

I immediately swung around and yelled back, "What are you saying? Hey, what are you saying?"

Listen, I have been putting up with being treated like a wild animal for over twenty years. I was *not* going to just walk away like previous times. I guess my media appearances and book was not enough yet. *This* was *exactly* why I was begging to get in the media, schools, and churches nonstop for years. *This* was why I labored and stressed about getting a book published and *keeping* it published, insofar as lowering my immunity, and giving myself the worst flu in my life in 2020. I did *all* of that to prevent this from happening again! Not just to me, but to anyone.

Plus, part of my message is telling discriminators to start believing in themselves. My philosophy is that bullies feel hurt themselves. If I could have just gotten in every media outlet, church, school, you name it, at my expense, then I believe that this night would not have happened. I could have helped such discriminators begin to believe in themselves, that they *have* a purpose. However, their purpose is not to bully. (Again, I acknowledge that it is impossible for us humans to achieve 100 percent world peace.)

As I continued to stand up for myself and all Autistic people, both the skateboarder and bicyclist were mildly making fun of me. The bicyclist had the same disapproving smirk as that person on March 20, 2021, when I nearly ran for my life. It was a smirk that told me that I am a quack and a lost cause.

Bear in mind, we were all shadows and silhouettes at this point. I continued to maintain distance. I began to put one foot in the street, just in case I had to run, but suddenly, a car comes rushing around the corner toward me. I quickly get back on the sidewalk. *Suddenly*, at that exact moment, I looked up at the most horrific sight that I had ever witnessed in my life.

That gentleman who had essentially called me a Non-Playing Character, which is one of the greatest insults for an Autistic person, was *charging* at me at full speed! His skateboard was up over his shoulder, tightly held with both fists.

In that instant, my stomach dropped. I was holding the bag of snacks and hot coffee in my hand. I had walked for two hours at this point. There was no way I could possibly outrun him if I tried. Time slowed down as I thought about three possibilities.

One, I could try to sprint in the dark parking lot to my left. Probable outcome: I would collapse out of exhaustion really quickly and be killed.

Two, I could dash into the street behind me and try to make it across Orange Avenue. Probable outcome: I would be hit by a car and be killed.

Three, I could try to sprint to the right. Probably outcome: I would be cornered at the corner, thereby being killed.

When I say *killed*, that could mean different things. I could have been physically killed and died. Or, as a pastor later told me when I recounted this horrid experience to him, the man could have beaten me to where I could never teach again, if you know what I mean. Thus, I could have been mentally killed. For a less severe scenario, I could have been brutally beaten to a bloody pulp. Sure, I would not have been killed, but at the same time, I would not want that to have happened either.

As I was realizing that I had seconds to choose, suddenly, out of literally nowhere, a loud voice thundered in the air. By an irrefutable miracle, a police officer just happened to look over. He got on his loudspeaker and yelled out, "*Hey!* What the [blank] you doing? Move it!"

The soon-to-be-assailant quickly stopped dead in his tracks and turned around.

Not only was I physically shaking as I have been typing this entire chapter, but I was almost getting emotional out of sincere gratitude for that policeman. I could have been maliciously beaten to death for having Autism! I still, to this day, have no idea where that police officer was at or which city he was from. Furthermore, how on earth did he happen to be looking our way? Not only was it dark, but we were not loud enough for anybody to hear from that distance. He was probably sitting at a red light, which means that he happened to be there at the most extraordinary instant in time, but I repeat, how the heck did he know to look our way?

A lot of my family, friends, and I count this as an unquestionable miracle. I firmly believe with all of my heart that I should be dead! *I am positive!* However, it was not my time yet. This immediately proved to me that I *will* make an everlasting difference to all my future students, to all the churches I serve at, and to the entire world someday in news media and on social media. There is no other reason why I was kept alive that night. This told me that I *will* pass all my schooling to get a credential, earn a master's degree, land a teaching career, and appear everywhere, thereby motivating and encouraging eight billion people and the next generation(s).

I had no time to lose! After that officer went on his loudspeaker, I was getting the heck out of there! I quickly zigzagged across slow-moving traffic to get to the other side, only to be greeted by smirks.

Apparently, many people were still outside of Rite Aid. I walked past two people in the middle of the parking lot. One was giving me a smirk. Looking inside Rite Aid, I saw a gentleman smirking at me too, the one who laughed at me and lied to me earlier in the evening.

"I was just getting coffee," was all I could say. "That was . . . weird."

Afterward, in retrospect, I started to realize that they did not get the whole story. I was assuming that the people standing outside saw me almost being attacked. What if they only turned in my direction just because of the cop and his loudspeaker? To that gentleman standing inside, I realized that he could not have possibly witnessed the altercation. Therefore, his countenance told me that he thinks I am nothing more than a mentally insane Autistic who acts like a child and has a disposition of an egotistical teenager. To this very day, I still lose sleep over this. I still feel intense hurt in my heart. Likewise with everyone else who was staring at me that night. They probably did not realize that I was almost killed.

(Really quick, I am not saying that all teenagers are egotistical or that all children act childishly. Those are the darn stereotypes that some adults hold. I have witnessed that all my life—in movies, television, and in person. It always made my blood boil. *That* is a valid reason why some of them become rebellious in the first place, because certain adults degrade and underestimate them. *That* is part of why they become demotivated in life, resorting to act in certain ways to gain attention. *That* is why I started encouraging and *believing* in children and teenagers at a very young age even when I was that age.)

Why else would I devote my life to them? Why else would I convey to certain adults to start believing in them too like I do? Some have masters and doctorates, but they still cannot understand that the younger deserve a chance in life. Such chances are compromised when the younger feel devalued by the older. (This may have been the case for that man who almost killed me.)

As I sped walk further down, I suddenly remember that *all* of it was just captured on my bodycam. Before I could rejoice some more, I had to get home safely. It was the most intimidating walk home since March 20, 2021. I braced for the possibility that those two young men were going the other way around and would meet me somewhere. As they were on a bicycle and skateboard, I would be of no match to them. But I made it back home, safe and sound!

I quickly got up to my room and started making the video about it. I was going to expose this. This must be stopped! (Again, if those two were close enough to being identified, I would have blurred them out, like in times past, but both of them were too far away, relatively speaking. I am not against people. I am just against their discrimination.)

Suddenly, for the first time by my apartment, I started hearing the most blood-curdling screams. They were off and on for a while. Just bloody murder. I began wondering if those two were lurking around and ran into a person who they thought was me. What if it was a coincidence? Needless to say, I was too queasy to take a sip of my coffee for a while.

The bodycam footage was not perfect, alas, but it caught the gist of what happened. The audio and visual were always out of sync. Furthermore, between five-minute video files, there was a split second that was not recorded. Synchronizing everything and adding my annotations and commentary, I made the video and got it ready for posting.

One thing was stopping it. I first had to let my close family members know. I did not want them to hear about it from anybody other than me directly. I did not want my mother to see it in her notifications unexpectedly.

The next day, I tried to get my mother to stop work and come to the apartment really quick under a pretense. I just did not want her to worry all the way over if she knew something was wrong. I had to wait. While waiting, I heard commotion outside. This was not abnormal where I live. I peeked out the blinds.

But suddenly, I was nearly thrown into PTSD. Right there, outside my window was that skateboarder who almost attacked me. Next to him was a bicyclist that looked exactly like the one from the night before. They happened to have met there. Immediately, they were off.

My stomach turned. Now I know that they roam in my part of the neighborhood. Gosh, what if I were taking a neighborhood hike at that time?

Soon, my mother came. Once she came in, my grandfather and I were already sitting in the living room. I had told my grandfather that I had something to say. He figured that it was distressing. However, I prefaced it by saying that everything was okay now. He calmed my mother down better than I could have, for she figured that I must have had some bad news.

It was now time to divulge everything. I did so as gently as humanly possible. I pretended that it was not bothering me as much, for their sake. However, there was nothing I could do. After I explained what happened, my mother cupped her mouth and got very emotional. I sighed. I do not like it when my family is upset or sad, although I appreciate their love and care for me.

Per their request, I showed them the bodycam footage from the night before. Both of them told me to just walk away next time. I felt that that defeats part of my purpose on earth as I believe I am called to change the mindset of every single discriminator on the planet (to the best of my ability), as well as empower the younger into believing in themselves, thereby preventing such bullying before it even happens. That is part of my mission as I continue with Royal Rangers and Lighthouse's youth group, not to mention my future career as a middle-school teacher. Not only *am* I (and *will* I) teach the content, but also employ SEL strategies, thereby equipping the younger with truths that they can take out of the classroom and apply to their lives.

I soon posted my experience all over social media. Just like my experience in March of 2021, I immediately gained worldwide support, but at a massive level.

On YouTube, I gained an outpouring of sympathy and empathy. To date, the video has over 6,500 views, 2,500 likes, and nearly 100 comments. Not all of them were nice, however. One user sided with the discriminator. Nevertheless, several of my friends stood up for me in their replies to him.

On Instagram, I put the following for the description of my post:

> *Last night in Costa Mesa, I was almost brutally beaten to a bloody pulp, but a true miracle saved my life! No, this guy was not on drugs or alcohol. This is Autistic Discrimination that I faced for 21 years, but this is by far the most horrific experience that I've ever experienced. Like I publicly said without apology, including in YouTube videos, I will NEVER stop fighting to ERADICATE discrimination until the day I get to heaven—whether that day is soon, or 100 years from now. Myself, per-*

sonally, I got stared at, laughed at, mocked at, cussed at, called names, followed by a vehicle, gone near ran for my life last year due to discriminators in Newport Beach, ran away from, given the strangest of looks, had a handball chucked at my face, and now this. NOBODY should have to put up with being such a doormat to neurotypicals, and if it's happening to me, it's happening to 1,000s if not 1,000,000s of other neurodivergents/disabled around the world. I will put an end to this!

In the interim, I am thankful for the backlog I have with media personnel (and counting, for I get several leads and interview requests frequently). I was just in Newsweek, *several radio/podcasts, a United Kingdom magazine, and a couple of blogs. This world will FINALLY get the message that we Autistics are not aliens from some exoplanet, deserving of such discrimination.*

To date, that post has received over 75,000 likes. On Facebook, I continued to receive the message to just walk away next time. Indeed, I have to contemplate that. I believe I am here to change the world, but if I am not going to speak in person at many places, or on the news and radio, or for newspapers and magazines, or wherever, then how on earth will I reach them if I do not risk my life?

I still remained hopeful that I *will* get on every news channel, radio program, talk show, podcast, and newspaper in the country and in the world. I mean, honestly, what is possibly stopping me? Why can I not appear on an affiliate news station somewhere in Green Bay, for example? What is preventing it? My message of acceptance, equality, and ultimately equity is *universal*, not just for Los Angeles. If I am seeing a lot of hatred, discrimination, suicides, and homicides on the news, then certainly I am not out of volunteer work.

I believe once that happens, then these scary occurrences might die down nearly 90 percent or higher. One hundred percent is world peace, yet I can hear a lot of people now saying that that is impossible. I agree with that, but still, what is stopping humanity from at least coming together and just getting *close* to world peace? What on earth is inhibiting that?

Moving on, I suffered with PTSD for a while. I contacted a couple of pastors at Newport Mesa Church. Later that evening, I called one of the pastors at Lighthouse Community who happened to be a police chaplain. He already knew full well of all the horrible monstrosities that I had endured throughout life. He was the one who said that they could have roughed me up to where I would never be able to teach again. He earnestly urged me to therefore walk away next time. Just for my proactiveness, he told me to buy pepper spray and to begin carrying it. I was hesitant at first for reasons that are superfluous to describe, but the next morning, before church, I got some for the first time.

The only place where I have seen pepper spray was Rite Aid. Yes, *that* Rite Aid. Not wanting to go near that place for a while, I went over to Circle K instead, which was on the other side and across the street. Unfortunately, they did not have any. I had no choice but to go to Rite Aid.

The window was all boarded up. I felt the PTSD while walking inside for a couple of reasons. I did not know if I would run into one of the people who thought I was insane back on the twelfth. I also did not know if I would run into the attacker. Again, this Rite Aid was across the street from the scene at which I was almost beaten; it was the closest that I was there since Friday.

After purchasing the pepper spray, I went over to Lighthouse for early-morning band rehearsal. In case anybody was wondering, I definitely was *not* walking from my apartment to Circle K and all the way to Rite Aid. My grandfather drove me. After church, I texted my grandfather, and he picked me up.

My PTSD was getting to me. I did not go out for a walk again until August 15. While walking around for the first time since nearly being attacked, I made a heartfelt, lengthy YouTube video explaining everything about PTSD life and working through it.

Day, night, and midnight, whenever I would be in the kitchen, I kept staring out the window. I had no idea if the attacker would happen to roll by. While preparing food or drink, or washing the dishes, I kept looking outside the window, ready to crouch down if necessary. Sometimes, the tiniest of sounds made me shudder in fear, causing me to crouch down anyway. I kept imaging the skateboarder *everywhere*. When I thought about playing the keyboard on Sunday, I imagined looking up and seeing him skateboard across the foyer, staring at me with those eyes behind his COVID mask and underneath his vivid baseball cap.

I had to rely on family and friends for transportation. Whenever I was in the family truck, I was always looking around. I always kept the windows rolled up, despite the hot weather. I locked the door just in case the man would run up to it at a red light. There were times when I quickly leaned down underneath the glove compartment.

There were a few friends and acquaintances across Costa Mesa who said that they would have my back if they ever came across me getting attacked.

Now, knowing that pepper spray is considered a weapon at public schools, my joy in walking to and from Ensign *ended*! Once again, I had family (and sometimes friends) drive me there and back. I just cannot trust this neighborhood anymore without pepper spray.

For months, I was panicked. I knew that the *one time* I went out without pepper spray, I was going to be killed. I knew that if that attacker happened to look inside my apartment window and see me, then I would be done for.

As I have alluded to toward the beginning of this chapter, this was not the first incident of discrimination in the summer of 2022 either.

One day, I was walking by Target on July 25. I looked up and saw a white car coming down Santa Ana Ave. The front passenger looked at me in the eyes. I looked down. All of a sudden, I heard this insane, deep monster yell that was as loud as fireworks on the next street. I looked up. I kid you not, but he had the most angriest, fiercest, disgusted look at me.

I am just a person walking in a parking lot, and I have never seen him before in my life. You see? This happens to me all the time upon first sight. I am trying to stop it through my book, social media, and news media. I immediately filmed my commentary for a YouTube video since I got it on bodycam. This was among a few other things that occurred from July to September 2022, some of which I posted my bodycam evidence. I have received an unintelligible comment from a man. I was literally called "disgusting" by a woman when I was just walking past her as normal as I could possibly walk.

Still, nothing in my life compared to what happened on August 12. Just previous to the experience, on July 26, I served at Royal Rangers. It was the last night of the summer session. As we were cleaning up, I was carrying items with one of the younger boys in Discovery Rangers to the upstairs storage area.

"Oh no!" I said.

"What?" called out the boy, halfway up the stairs.

"The door's closed and it's locked, and I don't have the key with me, so we can just leave these right here."

A few seconds later, the boy said, "Wait. Why do people laugh at you again?" He looked very concerned, having known what I go through.

"Uh," I took a deep breath, "because of how I look. Because of how I walk, I guess. Um, people just think I'm a weirdo. People have um, done a lot of bad things." I then switched from stuttering to boldly proclaiming, "But I'm trying to educate the world, so that they could recognize us that we're not aliens from some exoplanet, that we're real human beings with a heart, and that behind the disability, we have a heart and a mind."

As we descended the staircase, the boy thought for a second and told me, "You don't look that weird. You look like any other normal person."

"I really appreciate that, but a lot of people just give me the weirdest looks. This happens every day I go out of the apartment."

As we walked back to the room, the boy continued to give me his advice, concluding with, "Just ignore them."

"I try to ignore their insults, but at the same time, I try to support them. Yes, it pains me. It makes me feel hurt that they treated me like that, but at the same time, I believe that they have potential, that their calling in life is not to be a bully. They have purpose too, but it's not to bully others, so my heart is for them at the same time. And I pray for them too. Yeah, sometimes it's hard, but you know, I just got to pray for them. That's what we all should do."

I enjoy mentoring children and teenagers by talking to them and giving my encouragements. However, it was very moving to talk with that boy, hear *his* advice, and knowing that he, being that young in the middle of elementary school, accepts me as a human being and took the time to lift me up.

I definitely know many other children and teenagers (not just in Royal Rangers) who equally support me as an Autistic, such as several students I substituted for. That is unquestionable. However, it has been rare for me to hear such support, sympathy, and advice live and in person, specifically coming from them.

Later, in my AST semester at Ensign, one of the students inquired about that experience I had of nearly being beaten. He suffered bullying too and told me to just ignore them and walk away.

To conclude, I was giving a devotion at the sectional Pinewood Derby later that November. In the middle of my talk, I was saying that we were created for a purpose and even through adversity, we can overcome obstacles. Some, like me, have Autism Spectrum Disorder. Others have Tourette's

Syndrome. I continued on from there and quoted a bunch of Scripture verses to make my point, but during lunchtime, I was sitting with the other boys at my outpost, and one asked me a question.

"What did you say you have again?" one of the youngest Discovery Rangers asked me.

I said that I have Autism and gave him a summary as to what it is.

"You don't seem shy at all," he responded, "and you speak just fine. I can understand what you say."

I thanked him, telling him that a lot of things took practice in my life to get to where I am today, including my enunciations and social interactions.

~42~
THE GREAT RETURN!
AUGUST 22, 2022

A week before school began, I took a day of teacher training that all the teachers had to go through every year. It was held inside Ensign's library.

That night, I observed a board meeting at the district building for the first time in years; it lasted nearly two and a half hours. I was there because one of the board members told me that it would be a pleasure to meet me and for me to introduce myself to everyone on the board. She was replying to an email that I sent to NMUSD about my *Newsweek* article and my story on *Spectrum News*. Many of the board members, some of whom remembered me from the past, were proud of my accomplishments. They shared it around with others who might benefit.

When I got there, I ran into a couple of people who work at Ensign, including my former prealgebra teacher, who was speaking that night. A few board members and other district personnel came up to me, amazed to see me again. One knew me from all those Special Education Teas I performed at during high school. Additionally, it was wonderful to see a board meeting on this side of education, being a student teacher and substitute teacher. I also ran into the former principal of Ensign, the one I talked to in 2019, announcing that I am an author.

The next day, I returned to Ensign for the teacher prep day and New Student Orientation. During the prep time, I talked with my Master Teacher in her room about the upcoming year. I was placed on top of the syllabus as the student teacher, along with my school's email. In the first week, we were going to refresh on volume; the students did an extensive summer packet on it. Their exam was later in the first week.

"Their grade in this class goes on their high school transcripts. This is the hardest class at Ensign," the teacher explained to me.

After that, we were going to start on Unit 2. The teacher advised me to start looking at it. She told me that she likes having a planner and planning at *least* two weeks in advance, which means having the worksheets printed out and everything. She also told me that the school was discussing having me teach (or at least co-teach) in one or two eighth-grade math classes.

Sign me up! I was enthusiastic.

However, they were just talks. One ended up getting her own student teacher (who happened to come from Vanguard too), whereas the other one decided not to have help. Later, there were also talks about me teaching something to her AVID classes, giving me additional experience with students who were not all honors students, but I only got to teach math to them. I loved teaching math, but we were talking about teaching something other than that subject.

After saying good-bye until the twenty-second, I went to the gymnasium to volunteer with the orientation. (It was quite surreal. Fifteen years prior, in August of 2007, I was there for my orientation.) I was a part of the Spirit Tunnel. After the introductions in the gym, the students were off on a scavenger hunt. They were to find all of their classrooms and get stamped. I floated around the campus to help point students in the right direction. A few times, I got to share that one of their teachers was my teacher back in the day. A couple of them recognized me from juggling at VBS at St. Andrew's Presbyterian earlier that summer.

"Hey, I know you!" one incoming seventh grader said, pointing at me.

"Oh, Newport Heights Elementary?" I was assuming that I juggled for him in the past.

"No, from YouTube."

"Oh, thanks," I said, smiling.

A few others found out that I was a YouTuber too.

"I appreciate your support," I said, as I always did.

Finally, August 22 arrived. I got a ride to school, walked up to the front, made a short video journal for YouTube, and entered the office to signed in.

"I thought you weren't going to come," my Master Teacher said, sounding a bit rushed and looking busy, glancing at her computer. The bell had just rung, and dozens of students poured into the halls, rushing to their next class.

Incredibly bewildered as if I were in the Twilight Zone, I said, "We agreed that I should come at second period, didn't we?"

"No, we said eight-thirty."

I was totally flustered, barely remembering that.

"But it's okay," she reassured me.

Students began to enter the classroom. Several of them remembered me from the previous year. Likewise with all the periods. This year, first period was her prep period. The next two were Enhanced Math, followed by two more for AVID.

She later recommended, based on her observations of me, that when I get a job, to choose first period as my prep period. That way, when I arrive, I can relax and have more time to get everything turned on and ready. I previously determined that if I want to teach everything I want to, then I would not be able to have a prep period. Regardless, I love teaching and planned to opt out of having a prep period if possible.

For both math classes, I got a part in the introductory slideshow. I briefly went up to introduce myself.

I wanted to see how other teachers started their first day of school. During eighth period, which was the teacher's second prep period, I chose a seventh-grade math teacher to observe. While observing him, I was in a classroom filled with seventh graders. I could only imagine how they were feeling toward the end of their first day of middle school. I definitely remember my first day of middle school so clearly, September 4, 2007. (To be honest, I was on the nervous side starting middle school. Having Autism, it took time for me to get used to the transition, but I soon got dialed in. I started feeling amazed that I sat in the same classroom all day all throughout elementary school.)

My Master Teacher and I discussed which period I should choose for the CalTPA.

"Third period!" she said in a heartbeat, which was her second and final math class of the day.

In that period, I handed out permission slips again for the parents to sign, just as I did for the previous semester. Underneath her signature, one of the parents wrote, "Good luck!"

I later met a lot of the parents at my first Back to School Night, which took place on September 15. I introduced myself as the student teacher and former Seabee, class of 2009. One of the math students was there that evening and applauded after I was introduced.

A few of the parents were happy to meet me, being asked by their son or daughter to look out for me and say hi.

"My son told me to look for a very tall guy and to know that he is my student teacher," one of the parents said to me in the classroom. "He's never asked me to say hi to anybody before, but he asked me to make sure I say hi to you."

The reception that I get as a student teacher has been very reassuring to me.

While I was standing in the classroom, waiting for parents to arrive, there were student volunteers outside the door, walking by. However, every time they looked in my direction, they paused and looked surprised with their mouths open. I was curious as to what it was about, but later on that evening, they walked by me. One of them said, "I love your YouTube videos" and seemed happy to see me in person. Lately, students have told me that my content is inspirational, which is the point. That means the world to me.

At this part of my life, I began telling others, "What Vanguard and the State of California requires to be a teacher is a lot of work and stress, but once I am in the classroom in front of students and teaching, it is joy!"

My first lesson of the semester came on August 26, which was on platonic solids, algebraic constraints, and coming up with algebraic equations in order to model relationships. We also had an assembly that day with a motivational speaker.

One peculiar thing happened later that day, however, during the seventh-grade lunch.

"Hey, are you an eighth grader here?"

"What's that?" I turned around and asked.

"Are you in eighth grade?" the seventh grader repeated, not joking.

"Uh . . . no," I hesitantly said and smiled. "I'm a student teacher."

"Oh."

I continued walking. Once inside the classroom, I told the teacher that I was just mistaken for an eighth grader.

"You've got to be kidding," the teacher slowly said, shocked.

Well, that story kind of made my day. After school, I was mistaken for a mailman for the second time in my student-teaching life too.

The following week, I began the courses of my final semester in the credential program. They were Curriculum Unit Planning for a single subject, which introduced us to Understanding by Design (UbD), Clinical Practice Seminar, which provided guest speakers and substantial help in our lesson planning, and four additional seminars to help us with the CalTPA Cycle 2, just like Cycle 1. We also had another orientation meeting via Zoom for the student teachers and *Mentor* Teachers. (A recent change switched the title of "Master Teacher" to "Mentor Teacher," which is what I will use for the remainder of this book.)

Unfortunately, however, two of my classes were on Wednesdays, which meant that I could not serve the youth at Lighthouse. One week before classes began, we made the announcement that I could not return until December. Students booed.

Toward the beginning of the semester, I ran into one of the history teachers out in the hallway. His student teacher was my cohort at Vanguard. I was asking him how things were going in his class and with the student teacher.

"Great!" He smiled widely. "He's completely taking over a couple of my periods."

That excited me. Before long, I would receive such an experience as a full-time student teacher. I figured it would take a few weeks before my Mentor Teacher completely handed over her class to me, with her supervision and mentorship, of course. Not only was I going to teach many more lessons, but I was sure I was going to do more grading, creating assignments, entering scores on Schoology, making phone calls as necessary, and answering emails with my district's email account.

─43─

THE ROLLER COASTER OF BEING AN ADVANCED STUDENT TEACHER

In hindsight, I guess I viewed my AST semester like playing a chess game. I overthought on *when* to move my chess pieces and *how* to move them. It took a lot of *strategy* as I finalized my move.

For the next few weeks, I thoroughly went through each upcoming lesson in advance, making my detailed notes, and sometimes writing in what I would say. I also began coming up with worksheets to hand out after the lessons. My Mentor Teacher said that nearly every lesson should have a worksheet. However, she told me that she has her own in case I couldn't find any.

"So, I saw you emailed me a worksheet," the teacher said one morning after I arrived.

"Yeah . . . after like two hours of creating it."

Slowly she turned around with wide-open eyes. "Seriously?"

"Uh, yeah."

Here is where I can interject something about Autism. I am *overly* meticulous on creating the *perfect* set of questions that pertain *exactly* to the lesson. The teacher told me to just Google a worksheet. She said all I have to do is put the lesson title and "PDF" in the search bar and dozens should pop up.

"We don't need to reinvent the wheel," she told me.

Nonetheless, I could never find the *perfect* worksheet that way. Sometimes, within a worksheet that I found, unrelated questions were included, or topics were missing. Therefore, I began finding more worksheets and PDFs of textbooks. I also opened my own math textbooks that I collected over the decade to help me with examples. I endeavored to pull various questions and insert them in one concise worksheet. Some questions I tweaked, and others I came up with in order for it to match the student's lessons and the corresponding standards. Not only that, but I was doing the problems myself to ensure that it was feasible, adequate, and aligning with the standards.

After I told the teacher that one of the worksheets took me hours to craft, she told me to forget it. We would just use her worksheets. I tried to explain what I said in the last paragraph, wanting a second chance, but that did not come until later. Since there was no use arguing for it, I was planning to resign to my fate and not be as meticulous.

Most of the worksheets that I made already were great, adapted from various worksheets I found, but one of them I will probably lose sleep over. (Not really, but it was quite an extraordinary memory)

Enter one of my hugest blunders.

"I'm in hot water this morning," I told the teacher as she walked inside the classroom.

We were in Unit 2, the first half of which was all about linear equations in one and two variables, as well as application problems, graphs, and systems of linear equations. The day before, after I was done teaching the lesson, I handed out one of the worksheets that took me a long time to put together. It contained four questions. The main goal was to have students manipulate equations by solving for a variable. That was it. After all, the lesson was all about rewriting algebraic equations and being able to explain each step. The teacher approved of the worksheet but did not thoroughly scrutinize it.

Later that day, I was helping one of the students, explaining how to solve problem one. The teacher overheard and interrupted me, giving me a Post-it note on which she wrote down how she would solve it, which was a different method than how I learned it. With my brain being in the middle of helping a student understand with very limited time, I did not have time to analyze her method. Inside, my brain suddenly shut off. Here I was, tutoring a student on how I would solve it, which makes logical sense to me, but the teacher stopped me and told me to consider her method instead, which she claimed was easier.

I just could not do it. I only knew my method. And as time was running out and the pressure was on, I was starting to forget how to do math.

To this day, my brain completely blacked out on what happened after, but I do know this: there were no hard feelings at that instant in time. I am all for teaching students multiple methods and allowing them to choose which one is easier for them, but I could not look at a completely new method with only minutes and seconds left to help a student. Anyway, this is not even close to explaining the full picture of my blunder. The teacher was already upset with me. During her eighth-grade SSR period, I was out supervising the seventh-grade lunch, which is what I started doing in the latter half of my BST semester.

I am a person who tries to do everything. I mean every single thing. I want to help out wherever and whenever I can, even if it is as a volunteer. I endeavored to do both. During the first part of her SSR period, I would circle around at the lunch tables, basketball courts, and field. Then, I would return to her classroom to see if I could help her SSR students, many of which were in the math classes I was teaching. Sometimes, hardly any questions were asked, and I was either sitting at the front table or standing in the back, waiting. Other times, I kept being called, one after another. Every day was different.

On this day, however, I must have lost track of time. I walked in. SSR was over halfway done. The teacher looked up at me with an overwhelmed, wide-eyed countenance as if telling me, "Finally! You're here!"

I found out that some Enhanced Math students I taught were confused about that worksheet I handed out. At the same time, she was grading quizzes that the students took the week prior.

The bell soon rang, and it was over. I felt terrible, since I could have helped with the worksheet that I put together, adapting the problems from a couple of sources. I simply stayed outside longer than I thought. For those of us who have Autism, it is sometimes easy to lose track of time.

The teacher continued to be upset, rightfully so, explaining what she had just been through. She added, "All these students were coming up to me for help, and at the same time, here I am grading these quizzes when *you* should be doing it because *you* taught them the material."

In my defense, the night before the quiz, I was excited to once again be grading quizzes, which is probably unlike most teachers. However, as I was about to start grading period two's quizzes, the teacher asked me if I was sure I could do it, and if I felt ready to grade them all.

"Is that too much?" the teacher asked.

Am I in the Matrix? I thought to myself. Having the key to the quiz and everything, I felt ready to grade!

"Because if it's too much, then I'll grade second period, and you can grade third," she said.

I did not know what to say. I was ready and willing to start grading right then and there. Just then, the teacher told me that she would grade period two's quizzes. Once students in period three completed their quizzes, the teacher asked me the same thing.

"I can do it," I said.

"Well, since I graded period two's quizzes, I should probably grade period three's," she said, believing that both sets of quizzes should be graded by the same person.

"Uh . . . um . . . okay?" I agreed, confused, knowing that the person who taught the material (me) should grade such assessments in order to see how well it was taught. Plus, I could clear up the common confusion that a lot of students seemed to have on a particular problem.

Now SSR just concluded, and the teacher, who had just insisted on grading both quizzes, is now telling me that *I* should be the one doing it. Again, I was feeling my passion for teaching getting stronger the night before the quiz, excited to be grading again. I was also getting experience inputting scores in Schoology, which I continued doing throughout the semester.

Oh well. What can I do about it now? How can I recover? How can I redeem myself after this?

To this day, I put total blame on myself. I lost track of time during SSR. I do not know what to make of those quizzes, but right now, it is over and done with.

Let me now get to the climax of my worksheet blunder. The next morning, before school began, the teacher said that she was inundated with emails regarding that worksheet, especially the first question. I expressed my confusion as to why none of them emailed me about it. I could have helped. They had my email from the syllabus, and I check my emails nearly every day. This was when she finalized the decision that I should not make worksheets anymore.

The teacher had to go to the office for a while. I was getting set up to teach later that day. Before first period began, the other Enhanced Math teacher called out to me from across the way and walked over, looking concerned.

"Matthew, this morning, *several* of your students I had last year came to me. They were asking for help on the first problem of your worksheet. This is a high school standard. This is not a standard that they need to know right now. Did you *teach* them this before you gave it to them?"

During the entire time she was talking to me, I was stuttering, trying to formulate my response. All I was trying to do was to check their understanding on manipulating equations and solving for the variable. That is all. However, I understood that a couple of the problems that I chose were based on advanced formulas, such as "$D = r*t$" and the gravity equation.

She left and I went back inside the classroom. I was all set up and alone. I had plenty of time to contemplate.

I am about to be kicked out of student teaching, I thought, dreading what I thought would happen. I was reformulating what I would say to both classes at the beginning of each math period. My Mentor Teacher walked in, and I told her that I was in hot water, describing what the other math teacher said to me.

The bell rang. As always, I stood outside by the door to greet the students, but this time, I did not know what to expect. Everybody walked in and took a seat. I was expecting some rebuke, but thankfully, I did not get any. However, students were commenting about the darn worksheet. I told them that I would explain once everybody was there and seated.

"Okay, class," I said nervously, "I'm a Royal Ranger. And part of what we learn in Royal Rangers is leadership. And part of being a good leader is owning up to your mistakes and apologizing if and when necessary. So, you know that worksheet I handed out yesterday?"

Students nodded.

"Burn it!"

Some laughed.

I told them not to literally burn it, but they could throw it away if they wanted to. It was not counting toward their grade. Some, especially students in third period, cheered and ripped up the worksheet to shreds. At least one smirked at me while slowly tearing the paper, exaggerating the process. I was utterly apologetic before, during, and after class.

Toward the very end of my student teaching, during lunch one day, I was talking with a few of the students by the basketball courts. Somewhere in our conversation about how student teaching has been for me, I brought up that worksheet debacle.

"Listen," one of them said, "don't worry about it." Both of them continued on, emphasizing that it was an honest mistake and now a funny memory. Overall, they said I did great as a student teacher.

There were other times when I had to own up to little mistakes, whether it was to my Mentor Teacher or to the class in the middle of a lecture. At one point, one of the students kindly said, "Oh, don't worry, Mr. Kenslow. We all know that you're learning how to teach us." (As an aside, that same student, being an avid reader, said that she always wanted to buy my book, and if she does, she asked me to sign it. I thanked her and said that if she reads it, then she will read "Ensign" mentioned inside.)

I took in joy, considering that all of my mistakes are merely opportunities to learn. I was once again reminded of my former (and late) eleventh-grade U.S. History and Geography teacher. He once allowed me to teach his second-grade son all about Theodore Roosevelt, but it had to be written and not in person. His son received 100 percent on the test. I told him that I *learned* in the process and that Theodore Roosevelt is now one of my favorite presidents.

He told me that I learned one of the most valuable lessons in all of teaching—that I *learned* in the process. Ever since then, I have held on to having a growth mindset.

Taking hands during student's mid-unit or post-unit assessments continued to pose a challenge. I could not help them *get* to the answer, and all I knew how to say was, "You're on the right track." Oftentimes, I got looks that told me that they were still struggling. I gave additional guidance, but I usually resigned to my fate and said, "I'm sorry, but that's all I can help you with."

They usually nodded and/or said okay.

As I slowly backed up, I felt as though I were taking the walk of shame. I wondered if any of them felt that I was incompetent, as if I could teach the material that was provided to me but could not actually do the math in real life. I am sure that was an irrational conclusion, but still, in my mind, I really want to help them understand. I felt as if I failed them.

To various teachers, including my Mentor Teacher, I asked and asked again on what to do in times like that. I took in their advice, such as these:

"Rephrase the question."

"It might help you if you ask yourself, 'What am I trying to test them on?'"

"Tell them to think back on what they took notes of."

By the end of my student teaching experience, I told the teacher that I was feeling more confident in going up to raised hands during assessments.

To segue into a less stressful part of my AST semester, on September 6, I began being observed by my Lead University Supervisor. This semester, I had a new one, and she got to watch me in person. She needed to do a minimum of two informal observations and four formal observations. The two informal ones were simply to observe a lesson and talk and reflect on it afterward. The formal ones required that huge, multipage Grad-Ed lesson plan. Prior to the observation, the supervisor needed me to fill out and send her what I could of the lesson plan. I was kind of a natural at the Grad-Ed lesson plan by now, having filled out four of them in my BST semester. Additionally, both the supervisor and Mentor Teacher had to fill out the LOPs. After each lesson, the supervisor and I would privately discuss how I did.

The first observation was an informal one. Serendipitously, it was the same day I passed out that now-notorious worksheet, unbeknownst to any of us on what would ensue. Afterward, she and I talked up in the lounge. She always started by asking me on how I think it went. I usually said that it was better than second period to an extent. By the end of the semester, she laughed, "You always say that."

Indeed, the second time you teach something is usually better than the first. That was my case 99 percent of the time, but not 100 percent.

For every observation that she did, there honestly was not too much she could say. She asked questions to clarify some of the things I did or said. She offered advice on what I could try next time. She said that I was hitting a lot of the California Teaching Performance Expectations (TPEs).

She also told me that she observed other students working, asking a couple of them about the material. She said that I was helping them understand it.

By fortuity, she used to be a math teacher. She could hardly get over how much technology has changed. Back in the day, she used to write on the board, feeling terrible that her back was toward the students. With the iPad, I have the liberty to face the students, walk around the classroom, effortlessly change colors to color-code things, and more.

There was one day when she informally observed me teaching second period and then formally observed me teaching the same lesson for third period. That way, she could see and comment on how I effectively transition from one period to the next, modifying my instruction if needed.

On the first day that she observed me, after talking about the lesson together, she gave me a copy of her book and took out a copy of mine that she bought. We both took a minute to sign each other's books, so it was quite a neat little book signing.

While continuing the semester, in late September, Royal Rangers started back up for the academic year. This time, it was at Mesa Church's new building in Irvine. It was the commencement of my tenth year as a commander and my twenty-third year in Rangers. I continued to keep myself busy, especially when I went to El Dorado Park in Long Beach on September 24 to teach the entire Compass merit to several boys at a multi-outpost camp. I was also still a part of Lighthouse's music ministry, taking up Thursday evenings and Sunday mornings.

Time continued to move forward, and I was still trying to find my place. I continued teaching math lessons, preparing for them well in advance, and helping out in AVID, such as various projects, tutorials, and grading TRF forms, which I have graded hundreds of throughout this semester. TRFs are Tutorial Request Forms. Before and during tutorials, they fill out this form, explaining a problem that they are confused with, steps in solving the problem (which is what they do as a group), and a reflection afterward. I expressed interest in knowing how to assign their McGraw Hill and Khan Academy homework, as well as finding their results, since I would probably need to know that for when I become a math teacher.

She showed me step by step how to do it, and I took notes.

"However," she firmly said, "I am going to do all of that myself, just to make sure it's done right. This is a big, important class that counts toward their high school transcripts, and I don't have the time to check if you did everything correctly or not."

Oh well. At least I wrote down the protocol. I'm sure it's easy, and after a couple of times doing it, it will be second nature to me, like always.

"You should start coming to the meetings," she told me at one point. "Once you're a teacher, you will need to attend them."

"Yes, I've been wanting to do so," I responded, desiring the whole time to use my experience to simulate what it would be like to be a real, full-time teacher. I was quite eager to observe such meetings. That is why I came in August a week before school began. "When are they?"

She told me the different types of meetings, depending on which

Wednesday it fell on. For instance, the first Wednesday was a staff meeting in the library. The second was just a department meeting. She told me that I would not need to attend the third or fourth Wednesday meetings.

My first meeting was the first Wednesday in October, which was exciting for me to witness. That night, I got to surprise Lighthouse's youth group since I did not have to attend Vanguard.

As this chapter's title conveys, this semester was still a roller coaster. I made mistakes. I had misunderstandings and miscommunications. I had to make apologies (gladly) to my Mentor Teacher. I also had mountains of work and many learning opportunities.

I am thankful that through it all, I was given the opportunity to succeed and have the strong support of my Mentor Teacher. Truth be told, toward the beginning of the semester, there were moments when the teacher could not figure out what I was saying or doing. It is common for a person with Autism like me to misunderstand or be misinformed.

At the start, I would observe other classes during eighth period. After days of doing so, the teacher said that I should not be rushing out of her classroom as soon as seventh period ends to go observe other teachers. Eighth period (as well as first period) is a time to plan, get organized, and ask any questions.

Well, I must have not realized what I was doing, and I usually ask the teacher if there is anything I need to do. She usually says no, and that is when I "rush out." I do not like walking into classrooms that have already started, even though the teachers are usually okay with me observing them.

During this semester, I realized that some of the things I nonverbally do are wrongfully perceived. For instance, when I have my backpack on, the teacher assumes that I am trying to run out and escape, in lieu of doing work, which I am passionate to do if needed. Again, I usually ask first if there is anything I need to do before exiting the classroom.

As a person with Autism, I am quite shy and nervous to ask questions. This is especially true when I notice that people are working. This is compounded when we are in a dead-silent room. This happened dozens (if not hundreds) of times throughout my entire student teaching experience. I simply had important questions to ask. Sometimes I emailed them, but some ended up being unread (much less replied to) because they were too long-winded, which is another trait of Autism. I simply had to discuss my questions in person.

To be brutally honest, the teacher sometimes got uncomfortable with me just standing there, waiting to ask something. In my mind, I was ensuring that I could ask the darn question without stuttering to death. Other times, she was talking with one of the administrators. When it became conversational and not business, I walked over and stood a few yards away, looking out into the empty classroom. I had a question, but I was not about to interrupt my elders, due to how I was raised. Unfortunately, the teacher later got upset with me on how uncomfortable I made her feel, despite being yards away, waiting.

Another time, when I was standing still, thinking about how to phrase my darn question for the hundredth time, she simply broke the deafening silence, slowly saying, "I *know* you have a question for me, so go ahead and ask it."

I hate interrupting anybody, but this is my explanation of what was going on: at the beginning, when I would arrive at Ensign before school started, I would straighten out all the desks, sit down at the front table, take out the workbook, and read through an upcoming lesson where I left off previously. I was getting several lessons prepared as much ahead of time as possible.

Eventually, the teacher said that it was not what I should be doing after I arrive. That is what should be done *at home* and not there. What I *should* be using the time for, especially as a teacher, is to prepare and get things done for the class, such as making copies, which I already started getting familiar with.

The overall message was that I should not use that time to plan. That was an eye-opener. After that admonishment, among all the others, I felt that I was getting bolder. Soon, she began to compliment me. "See? Now you're asking me, 'What can I do for you?'"

That *was* my focus the entire time, but, having Autism, it was hard for me to have the boldness to ask that. Most of what I did, however, was make thousands of pages of copies throughout the semester up in the copy room of worksheets, quizzes, exams, and such. Every now and then, I had to deal with printer malfunctions, which goes with the job, I guess.

Another task that was suggested was taking the job of writing the upcoming weekly schedule on the whiteboard. Every Friday, I made a point to do so, but most of the time, the teacher beat me to it since she wanted it done by SSR or seventh period. Sometimes, I saw her coming over to do it herself. I usually kicked myself because it slipped my mind.

"I was going to do that," I said, feeling bad about myself.

"I love how you always say that," she said and kept looking at the board, writing everything I had planned to write myself.

I kept offering that I could do it, but she told me, "It's fine. I'll do it."

I felt terrible. I was trying to do everything I could. I *want* to take over like my classmate who is student teaching history, but I cannot even assign homework online for fear that I would do it wrong.

I desired to make phone calls or answer emails if necessary. I was *trying* to do things before being asked to do them. These sorts of things are what I tossed and turned over, night after night. I am not joking.

There were simply miscommunications where I simply misinterpreted things, thanks to Autism. Furthermore, Autism has given me great timidity, and I have been working for a lifetime to get over it completely.

At one point toward the beginning of the semester, after school, the teacher expressed severe concern about my performance or the lack thereof. Despite working hard to show myself approved, as well as using her teaching tips that she gave me after each lesson, she began laying out a ton of requirements that I was supposed to do as an Advanced Student Teacher, many of which I have been wanting to do. Others, I have either not yet been given the opportunity, or I have, but she did not notice that I was actually doing them.

Let us just say that as she continued to talk for what seemed like an eternity, based on her word choice and tone, I firmly feared that at any second, she was just about to say that she gave up on me.

My heart continued to beat. She said her last sentence. She did not say anything about giving up on me. *Phew!* I nearly collapsed.

It was just the way she was talking to me. I was also perturbed because a lot of what she said, I was already doing, but she happened to not be looking when I did it, whether in class or out of class.

She made a point that I should start building teacher-to-student relationships, which included more than saying hi and wishing students a good morning as they entered the classroom. Sure, that was part of my go-to greetings, but sometimes, I said, "Happy birthday" when I knew it was somebody's birthday. Other times, I had a small conversation about the hobbies that students had as they entered.

Not only that, but everywhere I went throughout the day, as well as in the neighborhood, several students still came up to me. They said hi, asked me questions, and sometimes requested help on something they were learning. A couple of times during lunch, students encouraged me to take a shot at the basketball court, reminding me of when I was a student there. (Let us just say that I was out of practice after fourteen-ish years.)

To me, personally, it sounded like the teacher did not know any of that. I knew that I would get overwhelmed if I tried to prove it. I *have* been building such teacher-to-student relationships since the middle of my *first* semester. That is how most of the eighth graders (including those in all four of her classes) knew me before August 22 arrived.

I also endeavored to lead by example (including places I substituted at too) by nonchalantly picking up trash on the ground. Sure, I have done so my entire life, since litter simply juxtaposes the cleanliness of a location, thereby causing me to shudder. I was hoping that this would solve the litter problem, but it did not entirely work.

I have also been holding the door open for people since the middle of ele-mentary school, as it gives me a feeling-alive sensation, knowing that I am making somebody's day, even if it is short-lived. Again, my hope was that students would catch on to what I was doing. I enjoyed them asking me ques-tions, and I would interject jokes and one-liners.

"What's up, Mr. Kenslow?"

"Uh, the sky?" I would respond.

(In 2020, I made an Autism Awareness and Acceptance video about that phrase, "What's up?" and how it is difficult for some of us with Autism to decipher exactly what that question means. Thus, I made up that joke. Not only did several students laugh at the joke, but some said that they would start using it.)

"Mr. Kenslow's so fun!" an AVID student exclaimed right in front of the teacher.

Thus, I was kind of in a quandary.

The teacher also said that I should start building such relationships in her SSR period too in lieu of volunteering to supervise half of seventh-grade lunch. That way, *trust* can be made between her SSR students and me, show-ing them that I care enough to help them. That was when I decided to simply stick with helping out in SSR.

However, those students (or at least most of them) seemed to trust me already. So far, they had already allowed me to help them and even called on me specifically to help them. I was able to help them for the most part, especially in math, but even though I love science too, some physics problems I had to resign to my fate, taking almost the rest of the period to work through it with them. Chemistry, anatomy, and astronomy are good subjects for me that I can help with easily, but my aptitude for physics is not my strongest.

Some of the faults of mine that the teacher noticed were a result of little mistakes I made. Here is something I cannot believe I absentmindedly did. I used to work ahead in the workbook to plan lessons while students were taking an assessment. I would be attentive to raised hands, keeping the class in my periphery, but I happened to look down at the most inopportune time.

A student raised their hand. The teacher went over to them when I should have done it. *Ugh!* I thought I could have done two things at once.

You can take it to the bank that the teacher gave me a long talk about that afterward. Indeed, I should not have had the workbook out to begin with, but rather sat facing the students, periodically walking around the room.

After all of that, *that* was when I completely had a shift in my teaching life. *That* was when I came back the next school morning and asked if there was anything I could do, to which she complimented me, happy that I understood her advice.

I knew more of what was expected of me. By the end of the fourth week, I genuinely felt as if I had greater purpose and involvement, including her AVID periods. It was quite exciting, and I did not feel as lost. My worry was not getting a full student-teaching experience.

Enter the next conundrum, however. Other times I had nothing to do, and I copied all the worksheets and exams. Since I just straightened out all the desks, the only thing I could do was plan lessons again out of the workbook, getting much further ahead. Recall, however, that the teacher told me that planning lessons was reserved for home only, or so I thought. I worried that if I took out my workbook during first period, then I might get in trouble for it.

Toward the middle of my student teaching, I did not know what to do, and this was not the first time either. I thought that sitting there would make her feel uncomfortable. The silence was awkward. I could not just rearrange all the desks for the second time in five minutes. I asked if I had her permission to plan lessons in the workbook. It did not go too well upon asking that.

Apparently, that "permission" should be assumed if I had nothing else to do. However, I thought she told me a categorical "No" (implying *never*) a couple of months prior. Thus, I never brought the workbook out unless I had a question. For that reason, the previous time that that occurred, I simply took a couple of moments to look at old yearbooks that the teacher kept. She was talking with an administrator at the time. Afterward, she mentioned it but did not seem upset. On the day I asked permission to plan lessons, she referenced that time when I looked through yearbooks, calling it very rude that I did that. I did not ask permission then, so why now?

I was just trying to placate her, because in my Autistic brain, I was *told* (or so I thought) to never plan lessons during first period, ever, but to do so at home only. I simply misunderstood, and I know that now. I *could* plan lessons during first period, but only after everything else was done.

If I could do it all over again, I would have made it a point earlier in January to sit down and articulate everything about my Autistic brain instead of codeswitching, or what others might call "masking." I was not hypocritically masking to make myself out to be a neurotypical, as I have encouraged the world to just be yourself just the way you are. I was simply putting high confidence in myself when I still had some struggles with Autism.

It is okay to accept limitations, but we cannot pretend that they do not exist. We just need to work at it and learn to get *through* them. Over time, we shall get better and better, but they may not completely go away.

Perhaps a mistake on my part was assuming that being older, I could understand and remember more things that are spoken to me. I do have quite a memory, as everybody who knows me will tell you, but I cannot remember every single thing that is spoken to me, compared to a lot of other people. The teacher became frustrated with me at times because I asked her to repeat things when my Autistic brain could not keep up with how fast information was given to me. I sometimes walked away, telling myself to remember it, but I clearly forgot it two seconds later.

Furthermore, I would have told the teacher at the beginning that I cannot easily figure things out right away when all neurotypicals can. I *must* be told things explicitly, such as expectations. I *must* be told things clearly to avoid making such mistakes as I described, such as not planning lessons during assessments or during AVID, for instance.

It was all an adventurous, thrilling roller coaster, especially in hindsight. My Mentor Teacher was truly supportive of my endeavor, or else she *would* have given up on me. Student teaching has done much for me, including making me bolder and more assertive.

In addition to that, I have increasingly been breaking away from social shyness. I almost always stood by the door, welcoming students in, which would surely make me feel welcomed if I were a student. They typically replied with a hi, smile, and/or wave back. However, by the fifth week of the semester, I had been saying hi and "have a great day" to all students and not just those of my Mentor Teacher. Plus, before first period and eighth period, I would step out of the classroom to greet students and then come back in and organize. Even while walking back to the classroom after Nutrition or lunch, with the hallways being flooded with students, I would encourage them to have a good day and that they would do great. I would also get out my mental thesaurus and pull out various adjectives other than *great* or *good*.

It is my categorical joy to bring encouragement, cheer, and optimism, regardless of the reception. However, students all appreciated it. Eventually, some started to tell me hi and "have a great day" before I did.

Thanks to my Mentor Teacher, I was informed about after-school tutoring that was starting on September 20, which was going to be held in the library for one hour every Tuesday and Thursday.

"And it's paid," she told me.

Well, I'd do it for free, I thought.

I got plugged in right away. Later, I was told by a couple of people that there was a problem with the district about payroll. It was soon established that I could not be paid.

"But I'd still like to come and volunteer," I told one of the administrators.

Soon after, I ran into the principal while helping to supervise the eighth-grade lunch. She started to inform me about the payroll issue, but I told her that I already heard of it. Upon hearing her imply that I did not have to come anymore, I quickly said, "Well, I'm still going to go and volunteer. I'll be a volunteer."

The principal marveled, put on a huge smile, and said, "You're so nice! You're so nice!"

For the remainder of my student teaching, that is what I did every Tuesday and Thursday with an emphasis on supervising and tutoring mathematics. I only missed one day due to a commitment I had. The students and faculty really appreciated my help, especially the librarian, whom I remembered from when I was a student there.

~44~

Persevering after My Most Nightmarish Lesson!

The first formal observation, which was about a couple of weeks before getting deep into the CalTPA, took place on September 23. I taught Elimination, a technique for solving systems of linear equations. I felt ready and had printouts of my self-assessment rubric, which is required for all four of the formal lessons and the TPA. I handed out self-assessment rubrics as exit tickets, on which I put each learning goal. Students would rate how they felt about each one by circling a thumbs up, thumbs middle, or thumbs down emoji. In this manner, I would get a survey on how the class felt in understanding the goals. The quizzes helped me know if they could demonstrate such goals, or if I needed to clarify anything.

The formal observations took place during the third period. Alas, during second period, it did not take long for me to conclude that I was in hot water. Solving by elimination is easy, but the way it was to be taught was a bit complicated. I needed to take my time so that the students could comprehend it. It was not just that, but I had a lot of things on my mind; I had things to say and get through for the Grad-Ed lesson plan. Every single lesson that a teacher teaches would not ordinarily include all the requirements to hit.

I needed to get through the activities. I needed to find a way for them to use Desmos for the technology component of the lesson. I needed to allow them time to self-assess afterward, which meant I had to explain what a rubric is and how to use one, which was going to be a requirement for the TPA. I had to pass out the worksheet. The entire lesson was already *packed* as it was. I only had fifty minutes allotted, *maximum*. Plus, it was the first time ever teaching it to students.

I found myself stuttering all throughout the lesson, juggling all that I needed to say and do in my mind.

269

I am thankful to have had a very nice and understanding set of students, but I was fearing that I was failing them, trying to get through everything I needed to cover. Again, not every lesson required as much as I needed for each formal lesson, as well as the TPA lessons. Thankfully, the TPA lessons were broken up in three to five lessons, plus one more (which I will get to later on). In Cycle 1, I had to include *everything* inside the same lesson, all while fearing that the fire alarm would go off in the middle of it, thereby ruining the whole TPA, including a few of the templates that I spent days filling out.

Later that day at Ensign, my mind was preoccupied. I *had* to talk about what happened, my take on it, and my encouragement to the world. I could not hold it in my mind any longer. A couple of times, I found an empty place at Ensign and began filming for my YouTube teaching update.

"Everything is a learning experience," I said. "But what I love is what I'm learning out of this about what to do next time and what *not* to do next time. Being a student, I have to acknowledge I am a student. I'm still learning. I'm learning *how* to teach plus other things that go on. And having Autism adds to the difficulty. For instance, a common trait is that we know what we want to say in our heads, but when we actually say it, it could sound like [we're] stuttering. There's a lot of things that have to go on inside my mind when I'm teaching."

I went on to explain that when I teach, I have to assess myself on how much time I have, how much I have left, and what to do to complete that particular lesson on time (or at least get through what I could with exceptional quality), and at the same time, check for how well the students understood.

After second period, I did not want to face my Mentor Teacher who witnessed the fiasco, but I did not have a choice. She told me as she was walking out the door, "So you're going to stay in here during Nutrition and *reflect* on what happened, right?"

"Absolutely! You bet," I said, nodding. And reflect I did, big time.

Well, although I had quite an ordeal teaching second period, third period went totally better, which was what my supervisor observed. I blocked out what happened during second period, choosing not to keep it in my memory, other than my optimistic, pedagogical lessons that I took away from it.

In second period I did get through all the material, and the students understood. Overall, there were no hard feelings; none of the students said anything to me about it. Perhaps I am just being overly hard on myself, which is unfortunately a specialty of mine. Still, I strove to do better.

I continued to say in my video, "I find in life that sometimes when I make the mistakes and usually the biggest of blunders, *that* is when I remember the most about how not to repeat it." I know math, but now I am learning how to teach math firsthand, along with strategies in UDL, SEL, SDAIE, and the whole alphabet soup. I was not going to take what happened and kick myself over it. Rather, I was determined to continue to get better.

"I'm going to persevere, learn from mistakes, and get better. I just believe that by the end of this semester, I will be a much more effective teacher. I'm very excited to learn, and I like the fact that I get to be honest. Hopefully, this can encourage other aspiring teachers, especially those who are 'disabled,' any disability and not just Autism . . . People can do whatever they set their heart and mind to do. In my heart, ever since I was probably in first or second grade, I wanted to be a teacher. I didn't know it was middle school until six years ago, but I am following my dreams."

—45—

AN UNEXPECTED MEETING

On October 3, after I was done student teaching for the day, I went over to Vanguard to pick up the Swivl. While there, I ran into one of my former professors, the one who was currently the director of the Graduate Program in Education.

"And I'll see you tomorrow at the meeting, right?" he mentioned as we were concluding our conversation.

"Uh, what meeting?" I was confused. That was the first time I heard about it.

When I got home, I saw the email that was sent earlier that day and opened it. It was a Candidate Performance Assessment Committee meeting, the purpose of which was to find ways to support my success in the program.

Oh, I thought. *Just one of those mandatory mid-semester check-ins that every candidate must go through.*

But then, I read further, which said that this "formal meeting" will discuss ways to improve my performance, while addressing concerns that were raised about me. My heart started sinking at that point.

It said that this mandatory meeting would be held the next day at 2:00 p.m. The next day, I told my Mentor Teacher that I had to leave early, and she understood. At Vanguard, I walked inside the conference room and put my stuff down, being greeted by everybody. I took a seat at the end of the long table. Present before me was the director, the department's Program Coordinator, the Credential Analyst/Student Teaching coordinator, and connected via Zoom on a laptop, my Lead University Supervisor and one of my current professors.

The meeting, which lasted approximately forty-five minutes, addressed a variety of concerns with my current placement for student teaching and was aimed at "strengthening the working relationship" between my Mentor Teacher and me.

"I just want to start us off by expressing what a blessing you have been to all of us and how grateful we are that you're in the program," the director said. "You've been doing *really amazing* lessons, and I got a chance to see the quality of your work."

He proceeded to emphasize how they were all a part of my team and wanted to find out how they could effectively support me while navigating this noble endeavor in becoming a teacher. They wanted to hear my thoughts on how I felt about my student teaching experience up to this point. They wanted me to describe what I felt was going well and what I felt was posing a great challenge.

"Ever since I began the program last year, the experience has been very good. Last year, I felt that my confidence was being built more. I am now understanding more on what to do—not just teaching, but being able to make all the copies and the worksheets and all that, having more autonomy with grading and such."

"I want to really quick repeat what you just said, because it's really, really good," the director interjected. "You talk about two things that are related but are not exactly the same thing. One is *teaching* and the other is *being* a teacher."

"Yeah," I said, nodding.

"The beginning of the program is about learning to teach, the lesson plans, and all that. Then there's the *being the teacher* piece, including all the other things that that entails, right? You mentioned a couple of them: copying, making the tests—"

"Fire drills," the Credential Analyst/Student Teaching Coordinator interjected.

A moment later, I continued, saying, "I feel that my Mentor Teacher really solidified all what is entailed very explicitly. She's also given me a lot of stuff to do for her AVID classes as well, including grading those papers. I think so far, so good, but I believe I could be doing a little bit more. I believe as time goes on, I'll be able to *do* that more." I was trying hard not to stutter. "I've been inputting grades. But assigning things and putting them *in* the gradebook on Schoology, um, my Mentor Teacher is wanting to do that part in case I make a mistake. But she showed me twice how to do so, as well as how she assigns the McGraw Hill and Khan Academy assignments. She hasn't yet given me, um, where I input those things in myself, but I believe I could do those things."

"You mentioned some of the things that have been challenging," the director said. "But what are the things you've really enjoyed about the experience?"

"Enjoyed about it? Um, I guess building my confidence. Uh, finding that I could just believe in myself to be able to answer the questions. One of my number one worries thus far is getting stuck on a question in math that a student asks. Last year and this year so far, my Mentor Teacher really helped me by encouraging me to go for it and to not overthink things. And I've observed how *she* approached problems by students, which has really been inspiring to me. I saw how she went into math problems that she probably never saw before."

The director said, "You mentioned that you had a conversation a few weeks ago with your Mentor Teacher where she laid out some suggestions or coaching. Can you share with us some of the things she said?"

"It was a few weeks ago. I don't think I fully understood exactly what I needed to start doing. I knew we were going to get to the point where I eventually take over the classes, and I just wasn't sure when, and I wasn't necessarily expressing it, um, on the outside."

"Hmm."

"But on the inside, I wanted to eventually get to that part, and I thought that maybe it would be in October."

I explained for a moment how I got started making copies, which was not a problem for me. The teacher simply wanted me to take the initiative, which, as I described earlier in this book, I did, which she was happy about.

The director said, "So, if I'm hearing right, you sort of were operating on the assumption that you were preparing to take over the classes by October and teach them fully on your own."

"And build up to that."

"Indeed, but you felt like she wanted you to do other things, which would include, for example, making copies. What other kind of things did she include in there?"

"Making sure I observe her as she teaches, *including* AVID, so that I can see how she teaches a non-honors class, a class that I would typically be in. She keeps saying that I won't be starting out teaching an honors class once I get the job. Preparing for future lessons is for outside of school. I need to participate and answer questions during school."

"Yes."

"And since I never took AVID before, I'm learning a lot more about AVID. I've been answering a lot of questions. Most of them I've been able to answer, and some, I had to refer to the teacher since she knows a lot more about AVID."

"Okay, so, it sounds like in a nutshell, what she's saying to you at this point is, 'I just want you to *participate* in class. I want you to *interact* with students. I want you to *assist* in the other stuff I'm doing as a teacher. I want you to be responding to student's questions and be engaged with everything that's going on in the class.'"

"Yeah, building relationships," I said, quoting my Mentor Teacher.

"And being fully present," the Credential Analyst/Student Teaching coordinator added.

"Yes, and that's not really a problem. I've been doing a lot of that anyway."

"So, how have you felt in those few weeks since you had that conversation?" the director asked.

"We both saw a significant difference. She seems to be very happy that I'm taking that charge, as well as asking her, 'Could *I* put those in the gradebook?' And most of the time, she says 'Sure.'"

"Okay, so you're taking more initiative," the director said. "Well, this is all really, really helpful, Matthew. Part of what you are unpacking for us is really the distinction between the mode of creating lessons and teaching them in particular context, and you have done that really, *really* well. But *now*, you're in an environment with *all* this other stuff going on, and you've laid out for us what all those other kinds of things are. And all of them are essential to becoming an effective teacher. It's just as important as lesson planning and instruction, right?"

"Yeah."

"And seeing how those pieces fit together. What we really want to talk about today is how *we* can be supportive of you in that process. We have tremendous confidence in your abilities, and we've seen you at work in terms of lesson preparation and lesson delivery. And where the challenge has been, based on what you're telling us and what your Mentor Teacher told us, are these other dimensions."

A moment later, the Credential Analyst/Student Teaching coordinator took over the conversation. "I love what you said about *teaching* versus *being a teacher*. That sums it up greatly because *teaching* is 'Okay, I've got my lesson plan. I got everything done.' *Being a teacher* is being *fully* present. You have your radar on 24/7. You know what's going on. You know that Johnny had a late night last night, so he's kind of grumpy over there. You know that, over here, these two just got in a fight outside, so you probably need to separate them. There are *nuances* that are very hard to pick up. I think your Mentor Teacher wants you to take such initiative. If you're unsure, take a moment and tell her, 'I don't know what you need from me. What would you like me to do?' or 'I don't know what that looks like.' Ask her what else is going on in her mind while the students are doing their SSR.

"Those are some of the parts of being a teacher. You got the teaching part down pat. Your lesson plans are flawless; they're beautiful. Ask the questions and don't feel as though any question is not worthy to be asked. I think that that would be *really*, really beneficial. And like you said, you've seen a turn-around in a few weeks, so we know that there are things to do, but it's being fully present and being able to understand the nuances. And sometimes that might be a struggle for you, so you ask. Ask her to help you, and it's going to be training yourself, just like what you've done remarkably to get to this point in your life right now. You retrained yourself. So that's what we're here to help you with."

A couple moments later, the director segued into another concern raised. "One of the things that we've heard from your Mentor Teacher is that when she was trying to get you to do some of the tasks, you were initially resistant. Did that come up in your conversation with her?"

"Yeah, it did."

"Okay. Talk a little about that."

"I have not been resistant, but that is how it was conveyed, I guess. I may have accidentally expressed that." I imparted the entire story of when the teacher graded both sets of quizzes in the beginning of the semester and then got upset at me for not grading them myself, even though I was just about to grade them. I described the feeling of being in the Matrix when the teacher decided to grade one set herself, followed by the second set.

I said, "It's not that I was resistant. That day, I was *expecting* to grade a lot of quizzes."

"So there were some communication issues. You weren't intending to convey resistance, but she was picking up resistance."

"Yeah. Again, she asks sometimes, 'Is that too much for you?' or 'Are you sure that you can handle it?' But I've been willing to do all of it."

I then expressed that we would discuss the answer keys of assessments together. In this semester, I began making my own keys and scores instead of taking a look at hers, followed by a discussion, which made her happy.

"It sounds like both of you have taken good steps in addressing what some of those early communication issues might have been. That's all good and heading in the right direction."

A couple of moments later, the conversation turned to my Lead University Supervisor, who joined via Zoom. She simply reaffirmed how competent I was as a teacher and how self-reflective I was after the lessons, based on her observations and our post-lesson conferences up in the lounge after the period. "I feel that there are those connections there that he's making with the students. He's understanding where they're coming from in the math solution, where their mistake was, and how to pedagogically correct them. So all of that is coming together. I haven't seen the issues that his Mentor Teacher is talking about."

Next, it turned to one of my current professors. "The main thing that I want to share, Matthew, as we were talking about this before you came, is how proud we are of you. Honest to goodness, *you rock*! Your conscientiousness. The sheer integrity of your work. And your desire to do well and your desire to do things right. There were *several* times where you came to me after class to make sure you did things well. I love the idea of students getting to have you as their teacher, the person who you are. The lesson plans, as we all said, are great. I just look forward to seeing how your continued efforts are going to play out so that you can be the teacher I know you want to be. And that's all I have. I look forward to your lesson plans."

"Thank you," I said and smiled, reassured.

As the discussion continued, they recommended the "co-teaching" model to find additional ways for me to be engaged in activities, communications, and further responsibilities. Essentially, it is standing side-by-side with the teacher in the classroom. It is like riding a tandem bike where sometimes I am in the front of the bike and other times I am in the back. In this manner, I can still meet the requirements for the State of California to get a credential.

Here was my take on the co-teaching model. I see its value, especially in the beginning of the journey. My Lead University Supervisor witnessed the teacher and I using this model before, commenting on it. A couple of times I felt stumped. I looked at the teacher and she jumped in. Other times, the teacher felt that I left out an important detail, causing her to jump in. I am completely supportive of that, but in this model, I felt that I would never feel the independence of taking over the class.

I felt as if I would be cut off at any point, even if I was about to explain what the teacher assumed I would leave out. I feared that I would not get the full experience like all the other student teachers get, making me feel overly scrutinized.

I still checked my district emails nearly every day, but I never received one email from a student or parent. I still never called and talked to a parent, which was probably a good thing in retrospect, unless the reason was for something other than behavioral issues.

They exhorted me to continue with my growth mindset as I transition from "how to teach" to "how to be a teacher." There is a difference and I fully understood. I knew everything that went on behind the scenes, not just the teaching aspect. I knew full well of the planning, grading, assigning, inputting of grades, meetings, and the communications with faculty and parents. I was all for that since the start.

While student teaching, I devoted dozens and dozens of hours in preparation at home or elsewhere. I wanted to teach my entire life. Thus, I passionately devoted a lot of time to ensure that I do the best job as humanly possible during my student teaching. I indeed took in, considered, and implemented *all* the advice of my Mentor Teacher, other teachers at Ensign, and professors at Vanguard.

I know what "being the teacher" truly meant. I told my Mentor Teacher that that is exactly what I have been doing in Royal Rangers for years and years. Not only did I do those things, but I enjoyed every minute of it. I not only taught Discovery Rangers (including both Discovery and Adventure on Zoom for a year), but I kept scrupulous, painstaking records of every single boy, their progress, and the badges they earned. I planned and set up every meeting per my responsibility.

For Zoom, I planned and set up both sets of PowerPoint slides and conducted the beginning of every meeting. I strongly communicated with my fellow commanders, writing out emails to send to the parents, and also emailed the parents directly when necessary. I set up meetings and merit-day camps myself to help boys catch up, such as at a local park or on Zoom.

Whether on Zoom or after reconvening in person, I continued to communicate with boys and parents, discussing with them commander-appointed leadership position opportunities, leading the boys to assume some of the roles that I do, thereby leading the other boys, as that is one of the main principles of Royal Rangers.

After the forty-five minutes of this meeting, we concluded with a big prayer. It was quite cordial and reaffirming to me. All of us, including the other faculty and my Mentor Teacher, made up what the director later called "Team Matthew." I truly felt like I was a part of a great, highly committed team who indeed wanted me to succeed in this endeavor.

They told me not to think of this as if I am doing things wrong, but rather as a way to find out how they can support me through the rigor of becoming a teacher.

Afterward, being a Tuesday, I rushed back over to Ensign so that I could volunteer tutoring in the library for an hour.

I decided to keep all of this private for the time being and didn't share it with anybody. Only my team at Vanguard and Mentor Teacher knew the details. On YouTube and elsewhere on social media, as well as the students at Ensign, I withheld these facts. This is part of what I meant at the very beginning of this book when I noted that certain things that went on behind the scenes might be surprising.

As expected, on October 6, I received the letter from the committee meeting for me to sign, summarizing everything that we discussed and our plan for moving forward.

Later, I walked inside the office at Ensign. Of all the days, the teacher told me that I could arrive later.

"They're all waiting for you in there," one of the office staff told me.

Oh boy, I thought to myself as I signed myself in.

I walked inside the classroom and was greeted by the director and Credential Analyst/Student Teaching coordinator from Vanguard, talking with my Mentor Teacher. This was the "site visit" that was to happen in accordance with the aforementioned letter. Both of them suggested to us the value of the "co-teaching" model for student teaching.

For the minute that we had together, they asked me if I had any questions.

I do not believe I thought of any, but I believe I expressed how the verbal and nonverbal communications were difficult for me. My Mentor Teacher further gave me her advice on how to improve conveying information between us.

Both the director and coordinator smiled, thanked my Mentor Teacher, and gave her a book on the co-teaching model as well as a gift. Then they left.

Out the door, the director turned around and waved at me with a big smile before walking away. Inside, it was reassuring, along with everything else, but I was still nervous about the future. I was still not entirely sure if the teacher had total understanding about me and my mind. I also had other things I wanted to say deep down inside, but I did not know how to express it concisely without sounding incompetent.

~46~
THE CALTPA CYCLE 2

By the fifth week of the academic year, I knew exactly what I was going to do for the CalTPA Cycle 2. In a nutshell, this cycle was assessment driven, preparing the teaching candidates with various types of informal and formal assessments, collecting assessment data, and from the results, making an appropriate decision about where to go from there. I had to both thoroughly plan and teach (therefore film) three to five lessons, pulling out four video clips up to five minutes maximum. For each video clip, I had to prove through annotations how I met certain criteria, such as the building and implementation of academic language, for instance. Afterward, I had to either do a re-teach lesson or an extension lesson based on assessment results. For that, I also needed to film it, include an annotated video clip, and fill out a template.

Vanguard prepared us candidates extremely well. The classes and seminars were meant to help us through Cycle 2. The Grad-Ed lesson plans closely paralleled what the TPA was going to ask.

I was going to do Unit 2, Lessons 20-24, which was about writing, solving, and graphing linear inequalities in one and two variables, culminating with finding solutions to systems of such inequalities in two variables. I felt so relieved about knowing what I was going to do.

As far as my teaching updates on YouTube, I decided to make one big video chronicling my entire journey through the CalTPA Cycle 2.

In late September, I began filling out some of the templates, which, like Cycle 1, asked an entire panoply of questions about the class, the lessons, the rationale behind each lesson, instructional strategies, how I would modify each lesson upon certain things, and more.

The big first day was October 6. I was nervous, but excited, and comforted that I did this once before in the previous semester. However, instead of filming for one day, it was going to be a total of six days for me. Part of my nervousness was the technology, which has not always been my friend.

And on this first day of filming, that is *exactly* what occurred. I walked inside the classroom and started to set up. Suddenly, I entered into one of the most technologically hectic mornings that I have ever faced. The Wi-Fi would not connect at all to the iPad that I was borrowing. The teacher and I tried to fix it. After many different ideas, the teacher decided to turn off the iPad and turn it back on. Yep, that did the trick!

However, *her* iPad was not connecting to the app that allowed screen sharing, despite working flawlessly up until this day. Without screen sharing, the lesson could not be projected up on the board. I would have to use the document camera and write in a workbook. That is doable for me, of course, but was not my preference, since I would be strongly tethered to the podium.

The teacher did the same trick of turning it off and turning it back on again, which seemed to work. Then, as I was teaching the second-period class, the Apple Pencil stopped working. The teacher quickly gave me a little stylus that was not easy to use but I made do.

Now it was third period. I clicked the record button for the video. The students had quite a sense of wonderment upon seeing the Swivl for the first time, as it operated without hands. The marker in my lanyard was causing it to follow me.

After teaching the lesson, the teacher praised me for adapting well, responding better to student questions, and having good in-the-moment modifications. I felt mostly confident.

Later that day, the teacher received an emergency call, so I substituted for the rest of the day. I graded TRFs for AVID and volunteered as a tutor/supervisor for an hour after school. Not until I got home did I realize that I forgot the highly expensive Swivl somewhere at Ensign. I rushed back to school, got access to enter the library, and found it. *Phew!*

The next day went equally as well with working technology. The beginning of the lesson was going to stress on the building of academic vocabulary, such as "inclusive boundary," "non-inclusive boundary," "solution set," and "half-plane." Not only did I need to teach the definitions and usage of such terminology, but I needed to show that students understood them.

I took a full page of hand-written bullet points to serve as a script for me. Pressured to do it all in five minutes, I felt tongue-tied during third period, but I pushed through it. I did not fit everything in five minutes, but I felt satisfied with what I got.

My third lesson came the next week, on Wednesday, October 12. I went upstairs in the lounge and waited to make copies of the self-assessment rubric for that day, as well as the card-sorting activity for the next. I was utterly queasy. October 12 was the birthdate of my special friend who committed suicide in 2021.

I was *so* very close to breaking down in the classroom during first period while I was getting the iPad ready for the Swivl. To make it worse, being early-out Wednesday, I had ten less minutes to do *everything* that would satisfy the CalTPA requirements, which included the teaching of what a rubric is and how to self-assess. Again, teachers would not ordinarily do what the CalTPA requires for *every* single lesson of their career, but we were required to present such evidence.

I was able to get everything done with confidence, while re-mourning a loss due to suicide. I started the day out feeling queasy and had *so much* inside my mind. A peculiar thing that occurred was the clock's hands clicking and winding around uncontrollably. I figured that I had to resort to my wristwatch or phone in order to see how long I had left.

After third period on Wednesdays is Nutrition. While walking around the quad, a student asked me if I could still juggle.

"Yes, but I don't have anything on me, unfortunately," I said.

"Well, could you juggle my two pens?" another student asked.

"Uh, well pens are hard."

"Wait, I have a tennis ball," he said, opening up his backpack.

I was carrying a water bottle and had on my sunglasses. Once I was given the tennis ball, I gave a little performance with it, my water bottle, and my sunglasses.

However, even though that brought me cheer, it was short-lived. After my duties were done and it was eighth period, the teacher and I were talking about the stress the CalTPA was causing, making sure that I included all these things in the lesson, as well as fitting certain points within five-minute clips. I then told her about my friend, which made this particular day extra hard. I showed her a picture of my friend and me. It was the last day I got to see him alive, just under a year and a half before he took a gun and shot himself. She was understanding and I left.

I remember walking down the hall, tears welling up in my eyes. I went upstairs to the lounge. Two people who worked in the office were just concluding their conversation. I walked toward the paper towel dispenser.

"Hi, Matthew!" one of them said to me with a big smile. "I saw you juggling for the students. That was really impressive."

I gave a little smile and nod, trying to hide my tears, but it was no use. After wiping my tears with a piece of paper towel, she and I walked over to the table where the other person was. They were both very concerned. I told them everything about my special friend and showed them the picture of him and me on my phone. We talked for a bit, and they consoled me. One asked if they could call somebody for me or if I needed a ride home. I said that I get rides. They suggested that I stay up there in the lounge for a bit, which I did.

After school ended, I went down the stairs and was on my way to the department meeting with all the math teachers. I ran into the principal who just exited her office.

"Hey, I saw you juggling and giving those high fives to the students," the principal said and smiled.

Being very tall, every time I give high fives to students, I extend my hand as high as it can go and tell them to jump for it. As they smile and jump for it, I jump in tandem with them as a joke. Then I give them a real high five.

The principal and I both entered the classroom. The desks were arranged in a circle. One by one, the math teachers entered and took a seat. This was something I wanted to prove—that I was willing and excited to attend these meetings. It was the second one that I attended since the academic year began.

But I had a problem. After an emotional and stressful day, I had a horrible headache! In the middle of the meeting, my Mentor Teacher leaned over and whispered to me, "You really don't have to stay. You can leave if you want."

I continued insisting that I could stay, but she told me that it would not be of much benefit to me.

"Okay," I said and left.

Now on to my next problem. I had to force myself to stay awake for a few hours so that I could attend my two classes later that afternoon at Vanguard, beginning at four o'clock.

I managed to survive it all, fighting my headache, mourning, and enduring continual stress. Again, being able to teach students (i.e., the future generation) means more to me than nearly anything else, as it is my passion and life's motivator.

I had just one more thing I needed to do after both classes, which was to pick up my First Aid and CPR card. The Saturday prior, I retook the six-and-a-half-hour course and training at Vanguard, taught by a former commander at my outpost. He works for Campus Safety.

One problem: I could not remember where the Campus Safety office was. I literally wandered all around the campus with a headache (and in the dark) and found myself walking around all the different dorms. I knew it was by one of the dorms, but I began to fear that I was going to be mistaken as a trespasser.

The next day was my fourth lesson for Cycle 2, which was going to emphasize the use of technology, which I used Desmos, followed by the card-sort activity.

However, I was downright nervous. I needed to provide evidence that students were transferring their knowledge, meaning that they were gaining higher-order thinking skills. How will students apply or transfer the contextual use of inequalities to other things in real life? In doing so, I had to give actionable feedback, which I planned to do during the sorting activity.

Before this day, I came up with a list of questions that I could ask as part of their actionable feedback, but this caused a reliance on the students to answer my questions. These students were very good in math and its applications, but I needed to form my questions to where it made sense. My line of questioning dealt with asking *why* they sorted the way they did, how they can *apply* this with other things in life, and how they could *present* it to the layman. Still, I felt that everything was haphazard. My mind felt like a hurricane containing all these things I needed to do and say.

I arrived very early. To my surprise, my Lead University Supervisor was sitting at the table outside the classroom. We talked for a while, and she gave me generic input on good actionable feedback questions. A few moments later, I walked up to another math teacher to ask his advice. Once my Mentor Teacher arrived, I got everything set up and the desks straightened out, which was my daily routine.

I took out a blank sheet of paper, and in order of importance, I listed out all of my questions that I could ask. Second period, as always, was like my dress rehearsal, but it was *quite something* to say the least! After I sent the class off in groups of two or three, I went up to one of the groups with my list of questions. It was the first time implementing actionable feedback like this.

Let us just say that it was not going so smoothly.

Finally, the teacher rushed up to me and told me that I had to move on. I told her that I was still asking questions.

"No," she whispered. "We've really got to move on. This is taking way too long."

I surmise I took too much time finding the perfect group to practice on.

In third period, I felt more prepared after doing it once. I realized that I just needed to find a group and stick with it. I chose one. Although it was not 100 percent perfect, it went splendidly, getting two partners to think of ways to apply what was being taught to other situations and to describe what points or key features meant on the graph.

I am my biggest critic. Whether playing piano, reciting a script I wrote, or teaching a lesson, I always kick myself about things that the general audience does not have a clue about. Typically, people do not hear me get jumbled up on my words or hitting the wrong note, but *I* do. Sometimes, I lose sleep over these experiences, tossing and turning at night, even if it occurred a decade or two ago.

Later that day, I asked students how I was doing with teaching. As typical, they said I am doing great, and they like how I teach. Still, I always felt bad for second period, since third period got the better lessons, 99 percent of the time. I feel like I stuttered a lot more throughout second period than third period, despite rehearsing the lesson at home many times over.

Notwithstanding, I always learn in the process, thereby causing me to modify as needed between periods. I also consider the advice of the teacher in between periods on what I could improve on for the next lesson.

The final lesson in my series came the following day, the 14th. After the instructional part, I gave a formal assessment, which I adapted from their workbook. It was a large application problem where they had to identify the variables, set up their own system of linear inequalities, and graph them with all the trimmings. Based on their results, I would either do a re-teach or extension.

The entire lesson was super amazing! That weekend, I graded all of the assessments based on the rubric that I had to make for it, giving them rubric-based feedback. Also, throughout the weekend and prior to this, I spent an incalculable amount of hours filling out those templates, all six of them. Three nights in a row, I was up until one or two in the morning. Recall that I have already started filling out those templates for a while up to this point. Again, there is simply a myriad of questions to answer, most of which require a lengthy response. I had to explain the things I did, *why* I did them, relate them to the learning goals and standards, et cetera. One of them was just under thirty pages long, but most of the others were typically between two to five pages.

Not only did I write narratives, but I had to provide descriptions and blank copies of my informal and formal assessments, rubrics, student self-assessments, and student samples with rubric-based feedback on them.

However, as I continued to upload them on the website, marking them "Ready to Submit," I increasingly felt more and more weight lifted off my entire being and not just my shoulders.

Vanguard continued encouraging and motivating us teaching candidates. They told us that they were not lying when they said that this was going to be a *tough* and *rigorous* program. They imparted how proud they were of us for sticking with it and with what we had accomplished thus far.

One professor kept pointing us toward the light at the end of the tunnel that was beginning to shine. Toward the end of my experience, I added that that light was getting brighter and brighter for me.

By Sunday evening, I felt as if I had time for a walk, which was quite cathartic. I additionally cleared my mind with a video journal for my YouTube video, getting to release a lot of things that were in my heart.

Finally, October 17 arrived!

After grading all of the formal assessments, I concluded that I should do a re-teach. Seeing common errors among the student's work, I felt that it would be good to go over it with them, clarifying all the little things that may have been easily missed.

Now was the hard part: telling my Mentor Teacher about it. She was exceedingly set on a schedule, saying that certain lessons must be taught when each day arrives. I had to find some way to concisely explain it while acknowledging that I would still teach the planned lesson. All I needed was a matter of minutes, not half the period.

After explaining it to her, she agreed. After the brief re-teach lesson, I moved on to the next lesson, which would have served as an extension anyway.

After school, I went to Vanguard to return everything I borrowed. I was very grateful for Vanguard and my Mentor Teacher. The teacher thoroughly ensured that everything went right for me with the technology and during the filming!

By the next morning, I was walking to Ensign and felt extraordinarily relaxed. All I had to do at that point was to complete one of the templates and video annotations. I felt more energized and alive than ever!

The teacher and I were both so happy that I was done with my series of lessons. We both kept saying that I can finally get into normal, stress-free teaching without worrying about saying all the stuff that the CalTPA required me to say. I admire, however, what the California Department of Education wants out of their teachers, making us state-of-the-art, and Vanguard did a phenomenal job preparing us for that.

On October 21, 2022, at 5:34 p.m., I officially submitted my Cycle 2. I could almost hear my heart beating.

I filmed my reaction for the YouTube video, emphatically imparting how it was a *lot* to do. Afterward, I went on a neighborhood walk, which was the first one that I had been able to enjoy for a while.

That day, I emailed my Mentor Teacher, professors, and other faculty members at Vanguard, telling them that I submitted Cycle 2 and how thankful I was for them.

"Bravo, Matthew!" the director wrote back. "Submitting CalTPA Cycle 2 is a huge milestone on your journey! Blessings and peace."

When my classmates at Vanguard found out that I submitted the CalTPA, they were all like, "You *submitted*?!" and congratulated me. Not only was I the first to submit it, but I would be able to receive my scores a month earlier than expected. In thirty-three days to be exact, according to one of my professors.

Now, it was onto preparing for Unit 4. I was going to prove to my Mentor Teacher that I *could* be (and *am*) a dedicated, industrious student teacher, willing to do *everything* it takes to *be* a teacher.

I was going to prove myself if it was the last thing I would ever do.

-47-
WHY I NEEDED TO PROVE MY SINCERITY

Near the end of teaching the lessons for the CalTPA was the Mid-Evaluation Student Teacher Evaluation Profile (STEP) Survey, required by each student teacher, their Mentor Teacher, and their Lead University Supervisor. Here, I was scored based on certain TPEs, similar to the Lesson Observation Protocols (LOPs).

I have noticed a stark contrast between my Mentor Teacher's STEP and LOP comments and scores, versus those of my Lead University Supervisor. This led to an immense quandary in my mind. I believed wholeheartedly that I was doing my absolute best in literally *everything* I did, implementing all the teachers' advice.

Furthermore, when students would come up to me outside of class, I would sometimes ask them about how I was doing or if I was making anything confusing by accident. They would always give me high praise with a thumbs up. The fact that they always smiled, waved, and/or said hi to me throughout the school day or out in the neighborhood was confirmation to me. If I was making school hard, stressful, and/or confusing, which was completely the antithesis of who I always wanted to be as a teacher, how could this be?

Throughout *this* semester, my Mentor Teacher was a tough grader. She typically scored me as average or below average in most of the TPEs. My supervisor, who saw the same exact lessons, would score me fives and a couple of fours. (Fives were the highest scores.) A lot of the scores were followed by a paragraph of notes. The notes were usually targets that I hit well; a couple were suggestions for the future.

The supervisor saw that I was asking guiding questions to help students develop strategies in solving math problems. She noticed that I was great at monitoring student learning, reiterating aloud how students arrived at their answers, and focused on building academic vocabulary. Several times throughout the semester, she quoted me in the LOPs on important statements that I made in the lesson. She also recorded how students responded to me when answering their questions, causing them to express their consequent understanding and being able to correct themselves.

On the day when she observed both second and third period, she commented on how I adjusted my teaching, insofar as alleviating some points of confusion that second period faced. When such adjustments were made, it was due to me talking with the Mentor Teacher in between both periods. I also took mental notes in second period on how to amend parts of the lesson for third period.

As the semester waned, the supervisor commented in the LOP that I created a learning environment where students came in and automatically prepare themselves to learn, having their workbooks opened to the lesson. I definitely credit the teacher for that. That is something I observed her doing in my first semester.

In one lesson, the supervisor liked how I divided the class, where one half explored one graph and the other half explored the other. This then led to a whole-class discussion about both graphs and the real-life context. In another lesson, about average rate of change, she commented on how I had a student contextually explain aloud what a number represented in the given scenario.

Also, in lieu of correcting students with the answer, I oftentimes asked a question to give them hints toward the answer. Additionally, instead of assuming that the given information was intuitive, I took extra time and instruction to ensure students understood the hidden information precisely, such as tables and corresponding graphs in context, as well as reinforcing concepts that they learned previously.

She said that my lesson plans had been "very thorough." She noticed that I write out questions in advance based on the lesson's learning goal, asking students such questions in order to monitor their understanding. She added that I teach and solve problems "with precision." Her recommendations for me were to continue taking the lead of my Mentor Teacher and to practice analyzing student's reactions more throughout the lesson.

One thing the teacher herself always told me to do was to read people. As a person with Autism, interpreting facial expressions accurately is sometimes difficult for me. However, I *have* scanned the room and I *have* noticed confused looks, to where I simply reiterated and reworded the solution and its context. I also checked for understanding by asking for a quick thumbs up, middle, or down, followed by a time to allow students to ask any questions they may have.

At first, the teacher told me that I was not doing enough when given such information. Sure, most students held their thumbs up. However, upon seeing thumbs in the middle or down, all I did was ask if anyone had questions. She told me some students may be too shy to ask. I should alternatively summarize what they just did, which is what I began doing. She also encouraged me to find a variety of other check-ins to increase participation instead of resorting to the same one, as well as to develop a plan upon the results of such checks for understanding. She challenged me to think on how I should re-teach part of the lesson in the moment for better understanding.

To quickly explain the mind of Autism, in-the-moment adaptations are sometimes hard as we tend to be slow processers. I usually have to think quite a while beforehand about how I would rephrase something. However, that is what I always try to prepare for when rehearsing. Still, even after an alternative way of describing something, students sometimes do not seem to understand. Other times, they ask outstanding questions, but I do not know the answer to them. As time went on, I felt that I got increasingly better at these.

The teacher pointed out that a lot of lessons of mine were planned well, but sometimes, I had been following the workbook and its Teacher's Edition too closely, instead of bringing in my own personality and students' assets. She told me a couple of times, "It is not the Bible. It is not something that you follow and live by. The book is just your *tool*. Plan outside the book. *I* usually skip or modify activities whenever I think it's too much or too confusing. In all my years of teaching, I taught out of a few curricula, so it keeps changing."

I believed her, of course, yet I was still practicing on covering the standards and learning goals *while* interjecting the other things.

Moreover, she was also a bit annoyed that I seemed to be following a script of what I was taught in school. She said what I had been doing was more of a laborious procedure.

"Well, when I stand at the door, I *do* greet people," I said before blurting out, "in order to maintain a safe and positive learning environment."

"You see?! Right there! You just proved my point, quoting what you memorized. When *I* stand at the door, I don't just say "hi" or "welcome." I ask questions about their weekend. If they had a game to play, I ask them how it went. That comes by *knowing* your students."

"I *do* that," I said, defending myself. "If I know it's their birthday, or near their birthday, I say 'happy birthday,' since I have them all memorized by now. They're usually happy and surprised that I remembered. Also, I had a great conversation with [this person] a while back as he was entering. He and I share the same hobby."

She was happy that I said that, but she told me to do more of it in lieu of being like a robot reciting a script. Okay, sure. My go-to greetings are "hi," "glad to see you," and such, but not always. Furthermore, as I said in a previous chapter, I say, "Have a good day" and "I know you'll do well" to all who pass by, who expressed appreciation thereafter.

In her LOPs, informal observational notes, and in our conversations, the teacher continued to point out a lot of good things I was doing, as well as several critiques and suggestions to improve upon. She said that I usually modify the lessons between periods greatly.

During her Mid-Evaluation STEP Survey, she addressed some of the concerns I described so far. She said that I need to work harder in engaging students with their interests and reading facial expressions better. I found out that I still needed to prove to her how hard I plan for these lessons, as she wrote that I was not planning much. I totally was. I also found out sometime in the semester that she told Vanguard that I always seem "flustered" whenever I entered the classroom or started to teach, which is certainly not the case.

It is Autism. That is why I look and act in certain ways. That is how I inadvertently portray myself as incompetent or confused, even though oftentimes, it is just the opposite. In short, the outside of me does not always reflect the inside of me.

I will admit absentmindedness. Once I had an entire lesson planned out, including a big activity. Everything was all set. The desks were straightened and ready for the students. The iPad was on and working. The lesson was projected onto the screen. Copies of the activity were printed out and everything. Then, within minutes before the bell rang, the teacher reminded me of one tiny thing I forgot—the colored pencils, scissors, and glue for the activity, which she had all along in the cupboards.

As far as the worksheets go, in general, she said in the survey that I did not make any so far. However, I did, but she told me to stop after that notorious one from the beginning of the year. If an Autistic brain is told to stop, it usually complies, and she told me that we would use her worksheets from then on. This is in spite of the fact that I was set on doing a better job afterward, but she insisted that we would use hers. Then she said in an annoyed tone, "I've been giving you everything on a silver platter."

She continued to express frustration about me not grading those two periods of quizzes at the beginning. However, she told me that she would grade them in the face of my expressed willingness.

She also explained that I had not been designing my own assessments. This is true, because what she *told* me at the very beginning is that she has all the assessments. Furthermore, I understood that the assessments came from McGraw-Hill and were aligned with the workbook, meaning that all I had to do was make copies.

She did conclude by saying that I am tremendously kind and work hard, using her suggestions and tools, eager to hold conversations with students, telling them about my experiences at Ensign from when I was a student back in the day, and that I am heavily involved around the community and with my mission to spread Autism Awareness.

As for her recommendations, it was an extremely long paragraph. It really took me off guard because I either knew (or was already doing) at least half of it. I realized that I was sinking in the ocean with the Mariana Trench below me. I simply had a difficult time *proving* that I understood much more than she thought.

I deduced that there was nothing I could say or do. (After all, there was a time or two when she gave me suggestions and immediately said something to the effect, "But I know you're not going to follow my advice.") To be honest, that was a bit hurtful. I immediately countered it by saying, "I absolutely *do* take in your advice." However, I was just speaking words. They were true words, but I cannot prove my sincerity just by speaking it.

"I just want to say that I truly am thankful for you and sincerely take your advice," I said one day.

"Thanks," was the gist of what she said, smiling and sounding in a way that seemed insincere, as if she did not believe me fully.

I knew that I was telling the truth, but I needed my *actions* to help me. I forced myself to have patience and try my best to prove myself via actions.

However, as I will soon expound upon, I felt that whenever I did such things, it went unnoticed. It is like doing heroic acts when everyone else is looking away.

Continuing on, she said in the STEP survey that building teacher-to-student social interactions was one of my difficulties, but the overpowering evidence that I presented in this book proved otherwise. In my BST semester, I would spend my lunchtime tutoring students, to which they asked me to be their teacher afterward. On my own volition in both semesters, I would take the initiative to help students while observing other teachers. And once again, several dozen students say hi to me nearly every single day, in school and out.

It dawned on me that while everything was going on, the Mentor Teacher was nowhere near, so she could not have possibly known that I have already been building such social interactions since my BST semester. However, it would have been a long-winded, stuttering cacophony if I decided to defend myself at this point.

Furthermore, the teacher kept repeating to me to take caution about moving a certain student a number of times. I ran into him at lunchtime, and I began to apologize if I inadvertently made him uncomfortable. I was just ensuring that everybody had a partner to work with. He smiled, saying that it was totally fine, thinking that it was thoughtful that I spoke to him about it. Bearing what the teacher said in mind, though, I was cautious throughout the rest of my student teaching experience, keeping communications with the student to ensure that he is comfortable in the classroom.

Some areas (for instance, creating assessments, monitoring students, using more Educational Technology, and such), sure, I still needed to work on those things. However, facial expressions are hard for us with Autism. It is difficult to try new things before fully accomplishing the essentials.

If I could do it all over again, I would have somehow made myself understand *all* the expectations at the beginning instead of hearing it later from the teacher with an upset tone.

Apparently, the teacher also kept seeing things that I did not see. I simply missed a lot of them. Now, since it was made clearer to me by the teacher, I was determined to try harder.

Also included in her list of my difficulties was me taking tips from her and the other teachers. All throughout my BST semester, I had not only taken observational notes of her and all the other teachers, but I have personally interviewed them with my own questions that I was curious about. Furthermore, I implemented such advice in all my lessons and at Royal Rangers while I taught Discovery. This is not even mentioning all the other instructional strategies that I picked up for over a decade, including all the ones I picked up since I started taking Education courses at Vanguard.

One day, I implemented one of her tips. I sent the students off for a couple of moments to solve something independently. I walked around and observed two students using two different strategies, arriving at the same answer. When I reconvened everybody, I asked one to share his strategy and the other to share hers. (This was to prove to the teacher that when I walk around, I am not just going through the motions like she assumed. I was always checking students' work to gauge their understanding. I did not always say anything. I wanted to, but oftentimes, the students had the correct solutions. Other times, I did not always have time to formulate a succinct response, since it would require processing in my mind. Plus, I did not want to put students on the spot if my teachable-moment idea had the possibility of embarrassing them. I will admit that there were times in my student teaching experience when I displayed student's responses and had them explain each step. Unfortunately, in those rare moments, another student caught a mistake from their classmate that I did not yet see somehow . . . in front of everybody. To this day, there never seemed to be hard feelings, but I was quite apologetic.)

After that lesson, the teacher did not say anything about me implementing her tip; I had to bring it up to her. She proceeded to tell me things I did incorrectly, which, of course, is the constructive criticism that I needed to hear. However, at this part of the semester, her tone told me that I could raise every student's grade to an A+, yet I felt it would go unnoticed. It was stressful when she told me that I must do certain things when I already knew it. Sometimes, in addition to knowing it, I had been doing it all along, but she did not notice.

Furthermore, she implied in the STEP that I was hardly present in the meetings. Not only did I inquire when they were and had written it down in the planner beforehand, but I began attending meetings earlier that month, attending two of them by the time she had written this survey. Furthermore, as an eager student teacher wanting to dive in the deep end, I attended meetings in August, as well as helped out incoming seventh and eighth graders.

She said that I was just scratching the surface of being a teacher. She wrote that I do not fully understand what it takes to be a teacher, when in fact, I did, in my heart and mind. I agree that it takes a growth mindset, but her wording told me that she thinks I hardly have one. All I have been using in this journey was my knowledge that I will be *learning* through it.

I, of course, had a growth mindset.

I had no idea what was going on, but I knew that I was going to prove once and for all that I *was* serious about student teaching and wanting to be a teacher, even if it was the very last thing I ever do.

―48―

PROVING MY WORTH AND SINCERITY

Not letting any of the comments stop me, I went on an unstoppable, valorous mission to prove that I indeed knew and had what it takes to *be* a teacher. I was set on proving that I indeed took the advice of my Mentor Teacher, her colleagues, and what I learned at Vanguard.

Unit 4 was starting on October 26. It was all about functions. I had a week and a half to prepare for it. One morning, during first period, after getting the iPad and projector ready, as well as getting the desks straightened out and looking organized, I took pictures of every page of the unit from the Teacher's Edition. That way, I could use them as a reference while preparing the lessons *at home*.

I started by calendarizing the unit, mixing what the workbook outlined and how the teacher usually does it. In it, I included periodic spots where I would make review quizzes on Kahoot! and/or Quizizz, thereby making the teacher exceedingly impressed that I can, indeed, figure out EdTech. I planned out when the mid-unit and post-unit assessments would be.

I began going through lesson 1, followed by 2, 3, and 4. This time, despite what the teacher told me in September, I was going to make worksheets and show her that I could come up with great ones. By October 20, I emailed her my tentative calendar, seeking her professional wisdom on it, and four worksheets for the first four lessons. She seemed unequivocally amazed and began praising me a bit, as this was something she thought was unattainable for me.

Within the next three days, after speaking with her and getting her input, I emailed her an updated schedule with minor edits, along with the answer keys to the first three worksheets. I sent worksheets for lessons 5 and 6 along with my three-page draft for quiz 1.

Furthermore, on my own volition once again, I ensured that the iPad had all the lessons of Unit 4. For units that were not there, I took pictures of all its pages. I made certain that there were master copies, as well as blank copies for both math periods.

Being the teacher and planning, not just delivering the lessons, is something that I could unquestionably do and not just in Royal Rangers. I was trying to prove that in the first half and in my BST semester. But now, I was unstoppably endeavoring to prove it at all costs! With everything that I submitted to her, there were tweaks and fixes that I had to make.

From that moment until early November, I continued producing worksheet after worksheet, upon going over each lesson in its entirety in the workbook. Upon the teacher's approval of the worksheets, I made answer keys, emailed them to her, and made all the copies to hand out to the students. Simultaneously, I continued teaching lessons, setting my classroom expectations, and getting my work done for Vanguard.

I wanted to prove to the teacher that I can set and *maintain* expectations. On the first day of Unit 4, in both second and third period, I reiterated that I would like them to come in more quietly and to automatically open their workbook up to the lesson. I told them that they have Nutrition, lunch, before school, and after school to talk about other stuff. I reminded them of where in the classroom to turn in late work and where they can find worksheets that they missed when they were absent. I asked them to stay with me during the lesson in lieu of jumping ahead to do the homework, summary annotations, or other activities in the workbook, which was common in the honors classes. I told them that I would say when it was time to pack up. I showed them where in the workbook they could find the learning targets for each lesson. That way, they can do a quick self-assessment. I reminded them that they have my email to ask any math or class-related questions.

If it was not any clearer to the teacher, then nothing would ever work. Sure, I admit that the teacher saw things that I did not catch, but I indeed worked hard to minimize such clumsy mistakes on my part.

Before *and* during Unit 4, I indeed asked students to turn back to the right page and to quiet down, yet the teacher did not always seem to notice those things. She interjected a few ideas for me to try next time, which I kept in mind and sometimes implemented. By my admission, however, a couple of her ideas simply confused me, and I had other things on my mind that I had to do for each lesson, thereby causing me to resort to my go-to pedagogical strategies.

Nevertheless, I was not stopping, and I truly felt that I was on the right track. Until Halloween.

-49-
My Favorite Lesson I Ever Taught

Before I explain what happened on October 31, I want to take a brief moment to talk about my favorite lesson.

It was October 27, and it was the second lesson of the unit, about function notation, such as f(x) ("f of x") and real-life applications of using such notation. The last activity was titled "Birthdays." *My specialty!*

There were two rules and their tables. The first one took a name as an input and the person's birthday as an output. Their example was Abraham Lincoln; when he is the input, February 12 is the output. The second one took a date as an input and somebody who has that birthday as an output.

(The first one was a function, whereas the second one was not.). Both tables had three entries left. *I thought I'd have a little fun!* Since it was October 27, I thought it would be fair to put "Theodore Roosevelt" as the next input.

"May I make a suggestion?" I told the class. "Let's put Theodore Roosevelt for the input. When Theodore Roosevelt is the input, October 27 would be the output." I had written it down on the iPad for them to copy. "Now I'll give you one guess as to why I chose Theodore Roosevelt."

After a moment of silence and a guess, the students realized that it was his birthday that day.

"Correct, because today is his birthday; he was born on this day in 1858."

"Okay, can somebody give me the name of any president?"

"Barack Obama," one of them said.

"Okay, when Obama is the input, August 4 is the output. Okay, another one?"

This continued until the entries were filled.

"Did you just go and memorize them all?" one of the students asked.

"Uh, yeah," I said and smiled, pretending that it was a normal feat to conquer.

Now on to the second rule.

"Okay, let me just randomly choose . . . um, [this date]. Is this anybody's birthday?"

The student whose birthday was that date smiled and raised his hand.

I said, "All right, when [this date] is the input, [that name] would be the output."

I did this for all three entries, each of which got increasing amounts of laughter among all the students.

After answering the few questions that followed, we discussed why the second rule was not a function. "The first rule is a function because everybody is born once, but the second rule is not. The world currently has 7.98 billion people, last I checked, so there are probably millions of people who were born on . . ."

I proceeded to list out a whole bunch of random dates, when, in actuality, the dates were in the order of the students seated all across the front row and around the side. I must have recited eleven or twelve birthdates back-to-back without pausing in between. Some of their eyes lit up, giving me looks of amazement.

After I was done with the lesson, one of the students smiled and told me, "That was a really impressive lesson."

The student who asked if I memorized the presidents whispered to me, "Do you have an eidetic memory?"

"No, I don't." I explained, "I find patterns in dates and numbers, making it easier for me to retain."

This immediately became my favorite and most-enjoyed lesson. And then third period had to happen the way it did, and I still lose sleep over it to this day.

I have no idea what happened, but I got tongued-tied and forgetful of a couple of their birthdates, insofar as stuttering. Again, I am my biggest critic, so I do not think anybody noticed. A few moments earlier, I also made the mistake of calling out a birthdate to which two students raised their hands. I kicked myself because I knew they shared the same birthday. I was trying to be as randomized as I could.

Still, some students from both periods remember that particular lesson to this day.

~50~

No Matter What I Say . . .
No Matter What I Do

I continued to drill myself, seven days a week.

I painstakingly made worksheets and quizzes. Upon approval, I made answer keys and emailed them to the teacher.

I taught all the lessons, scrupulously implementing as many instructional strategies as possible from the Mentor Teacher that I could, in order to prove that I do listen to her. I searched and found my own resources when appropriate.

I maintained classroom expectations and was actively present during the assessments more than ever. I made myself more aware and attentive to raised hands, forgoing the simple mistakes I made in the past. In this manner, I could start grading or doing workbook checks while being able to see raised hands more clearly. On that note, I felt that I was greatly improving the skill of taking questions during assessments; it became less daunting.

I continued to volunteer with after-school tutoring twice a week. At the same time, my Tuesdays, Wednesday, and Thursdays were often fourteen-hour days, along with church on Sundays.

Yes, I admit that it was still a ton of work. I continued to grade mountains of quizzes as well as hundreds of TRFs for AVID automatically. Sometimes, I stayed after the teacher left, finishing until the last bell rang. One time, I graded over sixty assessments by hand, each of which had four pages. In the end, however, it was not *work*. It was passion that drove me. Besides, it was rewarding for me to see how much the students understood the math that I was teaching them. That is what made it worth it.

I continued to observe classes, which led me to come up with something original, hoping that it would encourage many. I was observing my former Language Arts teacher in the classroom next door. A student who was just disciplined returned to his seat, lamenting that, according to him, he would not attend college and would never be successful.

Before the bell rang, students were lining up by the door.

I told him, "You can be successful if you *choose* to. It does take determination and perseverance, but *you can* do whatever you set your heart to do, and that includes going to college. But again, it's *your* choice. I definitely would not be where I am today if I didn't persevere when I was younger."

Suddenly, out of the blue, a few things happened all at once.

On Halloween morning, I arrived at Ensign, set everything up, and started to plan the lessons from the workbook.

Already, I dedicated several days of planning for Unit 4. I had meticulously created, discussed, and made copies of just under a dozen worksheets, followed by answer keys. Likewise with the quizzes. I already made the first quiz, and I completed creating the second one early the next morning around 3:00 a.m. By Halloween day, I had completed planning two-thirds of the unit (the first twelve of eighteen lessons).

In the classroom, after turning everything on and straightening out the desks, I always asked the teacher if additional copies needed to be made of anything, or if I could enter anything in the gradebook. I ensured that I automatically graded the TRFs from AVID, which was twice a week. Only after all of that, if I had time, would I open up the workbook and plan lessons. I continued to teach every lesson the best I could. I was actively involved during the quizzes like never before. I did the grading of workbook checks and quizzes.

I was unstoppable and was set to complete the entire unit, while showing through my actions that I had "being the teacher" down pat with all the privileges I was given. I assertively took many initiatives of getting things accomplished for the benefit of the teacher and our class. I was set on attending every pertinent meeting I could at Ensign, so much so that the act of asking was what nearly got me in hot water on that Halloween day.

"Um, do I need to come tomorrow?" I asked the teacher, expecting a quick yes-or-no answer. I was about to walk out the door and observe a seventh-grade math class for seventh period.

She looked at me, shocked, her mouth hanging open. Having jolted, she responded calmly yet forcefully, "Uh, can we talk about this later?"

"Oh, sure," I said and walked out.

For clarity, there was no school the day after Halloween. However, I found out that morning that the staff still needed to come. Nobody told me that before.

Oh good, I thought. *Another opportunity to show that I do have interest in attending these sorts of things.*

After I left, on the way to observe the math class, I was riddled with a conglomeration of guilt, embarrassment, and anger. It was mostly at myself, who was I kidding. I could not believe my darn brain did what it did. I asked the teacher that question right before seventh period started. I could already tell that she was busy. She had just finished talking with a couple of students who were leaving SSR and had to go around to speak to some AVID students.

I guess I got too carried away with assertiveness, which has never been my specialty. I do not know what prompted me to ask that simple question to a busy-looking person. I knew better. Already, I was trying my hardest to prove that I *could* be a real teacher, taking in all the pedagogical advice and wisdom that I received from her.

However, readers might wonder why I chose that time to ask. Well, during most of first period, while I was planning lessons, the teacher had someplace to be. I can't remember the details, but I could not have asked any time before seventh period. Otherwise, I would have asked. Moreover, she usually left immediately at eighth period to pick up her two children at their schools. My sole opportunity came when the bell rang for SSR.

However, students came up to her to ask things for nearly the entire passing period, which, of course, takes precedence over my question. The teacher still had things to do before the bell rang, but that was when I unfortunately asked her my question. I assumed it was a simple yes-or-no answer, which was all I needed to hear.

I entered the math class that I was observing and took a seat in the back. I was hammered with guilt and the impending-doom feelings of bleak failure. As I was observing the math lesson, I decided to pull out my phone to text my Mentor Teacher simultaneously. In the text, I apologized for asking the question. Having Autism, every word is painstakingly important in texts and emails; I always proofread many times, making bits of changes. Thus, the paragraph of a text took several minutes, as I was paying attention to how the teacher was teaching at the same exact time.

I observed the rest of the lesson, after which, for eighth period, I went to another seventh-grade math class to observe. Suddenly, within minutes after the teacher's own student teacher began, I got a text from my Mentor Teacher saying that she would be in the classroom all period long. She reminded me that *that* was the time to talk to her. But again, she was not always available, so how was I supposed to know for sure? Plus, it was not excruciatingly important to ask in person, but again, I do not know what was wrong with me earlier. I could have texted or emailed her all along, but I guess I wanted to hear her answer in person.

After receiving such a text, I had to walk out. I quickly explained it to the math teacher; he was okay with it. (Later, I apologized to him with the full story, which he understood). I was worried because I had just asked if I could be there, and then I immediately had to leave. Thank God he was understanding.

Nevertheless, I was severely nervous. I did not want to set foot in her classroom for fear of what I would hear. After a few minutes, I shyly, yet boldly, walked in. I waited a moment for her to finish a conversation with another teacher.

"All right. Peace out," the other teacher said and walked out the door.

"Bye," my Mentor Teacher called out in one breath and said in the next, "Okay, so this is the time, Matthew, when you're in eighth period and you can talk to me. And then you start talking to me, and you can see I'm *clearly* busy, right?"

"Yeah, and I was kicking myself right afterward. I always do things like that at the most inopportune time."

"Like a *horrible* time. My only response can be like, 'I can't do this right now.' It's like you kind of put me in a bad position, where I have to almost be like . . ." she thought for a second. "I don't want to make you feel bad in front of people. I've been here. I'm waiting. I'm going to have to leave to pick up my daughter, but tomorrow *is* a school day, you know? And waiting until right now to ask me this is, again like, you should be planning ahead like, 'Where am I going tomorrow?' Not, 'Do I have to come?' If you want to be a teacher, you come every day."

"Yeah," I said, nodding. But again, in my defense, nobody ever told me in my life that teachers come on November 1 (or the school day following Halloween) until that morning.

"And then," she continued, "if you're observing teachers, please don't have your phone out, because I've gotten multiple comments that you've been on your phone when you're observing."

"Okay," I acknowledged. However, I only recall having my phone out (during class hours) when I was texting an apology note in the previous hour. If I have looked down at my phone, then I admit that I am enslaved to the habit of checking my notifications for five to ten seconds. I would only do that during dry parts, like when students are doing independent work, and I cannot do anything for a minute.

"I can't have you out observing if I can't trust you on these things because it comes back on me. You're putting me in a lot of bad positions."

"Oh, I apologize for that."

"Okay. You have to understand that this is a place of work. We all come here and take our jobs seriously."

I irrefutably agreed with this since I always had that mindset with a lifetime of having the passion to be a teacher.

She continued. "I know you're texting *me* in his class. *Why* are you texting *me*?"

"I felt I need to apologize."

"No! You need to be here when eighth period started, so that you can sit down and say, 'I'm sorry' face-to-face. You don't apologize on a text. You come back and you fix it, and you ask your question. Like, what am I supposed to say? I'm not spending ten minutes on a text, because there's a *whole* thing for tomorrow. You don't have to come because I can't make it, so I don't care. But it's at CDM for math teachers about data and all the stuff they're doing. But can you *please* help me conduct yourself in a professional manner."

"Yes," I boldly announced.

"I told you that this is ultimately a job interview every day. Obviously, you *wouldn't* get the job," she said, pounding the sentence like a sledgehammer. "Maybe you should leave after fourth period. *Campus!* No more observing because it's too much coming back on me."

"I guess I didn't realize all of this. Teachers were not coming to me. I wonder why. I didn't know that there were things going on you," I felt bad.

"*Everything* comes back on me, Matthew. Everything. No one knows you. Why would they come to you?"

"They have my school email."

"We don't communicate that way. We go to someone and say, 'Your student teacher, whom you're supposed to be teaching, is doing this, this, this, and that.' I'm just letting you know that I hear a lot, and it *all* comes back on me. I'd appreciate it if you just say, 'I'm sorry. You're right,' instead of coming up with excuses. Other teachers are looking around like, 'Oh, I thought it was a kid and it was a teacher.' Nobody wants anyone to observe them and be on their phone. How would you feel? Just be aware of what you're doing and how it looks. So yeah, I won't be here tomorrow. There is something. It is a school day, but you don't need to go because I'm not going to be here. It's at CDM and I don't even know if you can get a ride. And it's a half-day over here at Ensign."

There was an inauspicious silence.

"There's a lot of reforming I'll do for the latter month and a half," I said, even though I already underwent hyper-determination, which I previously elucidated in microscopic detail. "Come November—"

"Yeah," she said, cutting me off. "*I'm* going to be taking over after Thanksgiving, for sure. Like, after Thanksgiving, *I'm* fully going to be taking back over."

My heart dropped right then and there, as it confirmed my preconceived suspicions that I held for quite a while.

I simply confirmed it.

This is why I labored so intently and methodically to prove that I am, in fact, a person dedicated to becoming a teacher. No matter what I said. No matter what I did.

"So I'll see you on Wednesday," I said.

"Okay," she replied. "Anything else?"

"No. You've answered all my questions earlier, so."

"Well, not really, but yeah," she said, not believing me. "Okay, thank you. Bye."

"Bye."

I walked out of there feeling that that was it. I have no more purpose. My life is going to . . . never mind. I felt like I was just in the interrogation room, with law enforcement hounding me on accusations that required the full story.

The full story is that I *have* been dedicated to teaching since the very beginning of the program. In fact, for twenty years. The past couple of weeks, I set out to prove it more than ever. I do try to maintain professionalism as a person holding the position of a teacher. Every time I was in a classroom or volunteering to tutor after school, I did nothing but ensure that students understood the math, to which students and staff alike appreciated me for it.

I admit and assume responsibility for all of my clumsy, absentminded mistakes, such as briefly having a phone out while observing. I only recall texting once, which was earlier that day for reasons that I already conveyed. Ninety-nine percent of the time, I had been devotedly following along and taking down notes of things I observed, such as instructional strategies and methods of teaching a math concept, including asking teachers if I could step in and help, of which they were very appreciative.

Also, my Autistic brain cannot function as the common neurotypical. A lot of stuff that I do (stuff that is relayed to my Mentor Teacher) is the result of my brain. The purpose of this book is to prove that Autistics *can* become teachers if they want to, but all of their neurotypical colleagues must understand our brains. Everybody's different, but we could usually be absentminded where habits automatically become second nature, such as checking notifications for ten seconds during dry parts where there is nothing to observe.

In addition to that, we usually need a minute to think, regroup, remember, and/or reword. This simply requires a small amount of patience, but I, for one, can do it. And if *I* can do it, so can others, despite a "disability."

Next in my telling of the full story, I categorically disagree with my Mentor Teacher's statement, "No one knows you."

Let me tell you, I have built a rapport with nearly every single teacher and office staff within all my months of student teaching. We would smile and say hi to each other. Sometimes we had conversations. They were always okay (and more than that, *happy*) to let me observe their classes, answer any of my questions, and allow me to walk around and help their students.

At least one of them wanted me to give her input on how she was teaching in relation to all the other things I observed from other teachers. Some of the teachers whom I subbed for in the spring would smile and tell me that their students really enjoyed having me as their sub. Moreover, several teachers and office staff even remember me from when I was a student there and tell me how proud they are of me.

As for her comment about teachers and other faculty doing a double take on whether I was a student or an adult (according to her), I will say that there were a *couple* of times when I walked into a math class to observe. I usually sat down at the back and remained there quietly. At some point, a student would turn around, look at me, and whisper something like, "Did you just transfer to this class?" or "Are you a new student?"

Anyway, after leaving the classroom, I walked inside the office and ascended the staircase, not knowing where I was going.

"Hello, sir," said the security personnel with a smile.

As soon as I got to the top, I ran into one of the counselors who was happy to see me, asking me how my day went and if I had any plans for Halloween. I implied that I was great, but in reality, my mind was spinning. Shortly after, she left, and I stayed in the lounge. Thinking. I started calling into question my sanity. *Was all of that just in my imagination? Was I really invited into all of these classrooms? Were all those smiles from teachers and other staff legitimate?*

I started having delusions, metaphorically speaking. A confederate (or several confederates) throughout Ensign were shrouded behind a smile, I thought, pretending to be on my side. For my Mentor Teacher to be accurate about what she said, there *had* to be some people who really had a form of strong disapproval, but for some reason, they were keeping it from me. In my mind, I began going through *all* of the teachers I observed, feeling my heart drop at each one at the possibility that they merely tolerated me this whole time.

I knew I had to inquire about this myself. I knew my Mentor Teacher was not going to answer me. I was still perplexed as to why those people did not come to me themselves! If there were teachers, admin, or whoever questioning my behavior (or *whatever* it was), and since I knew pretty much *all* of them, despite what my Mentor Teacher claimed, then why the heck did they not come to me? Or at least email me?

Nobody told me I was doing *anything* wrong. I admit that briefly taking out my phone during dry, quiet parts was probably not the wisest choice, even if it was only for ten seconds or less. However, I knew I would never get sleep again unless I asked around.

Therefore, after eight silent minutes of contemplating in the lounge, I decided to go back downstairs. I stood in the hallway next to the principal's office. As I took a few moments to reformulate what I wanted to say, as is common for us Autistics, I nearly lost it. I took a deep breath and brushed it off. A couple of steps closer. I felt the tears starting to water my eyes more.

I deeply moaned in my mind and took a step back, brushing it off again. *Seriously, brain?* I was frustrated with how my mind operates in moments like these.

I took a second to ensure that I was ready to ask concisely without displaying my entire panoply of stuttering. And for sure without breaking down like I did on October 12. Being a teacher meant my entire life to me. I felt that after all my work and after all my proof, it was going unnoticed. I was drowning in the Mariana Trench at this point. I felt as if I were just about to get a dishonorable discharge from the military in spite of everything else.

"You're not like the other teachers because you bring magic into the classroom and are more engaging," one of the Enhanced Math students told me while tutoring in the library, patting me on the shoulder with a huge, wide smile. Additionally, he asked me to sub for one of his teachers sometime.

Multiple faculty members appreciated my heart of volunteerism when it came to after-school tutoring or helping students throughout the day. Something was up! I had no clue what it was, but I was going to find out!

I shyly stepped right underneath the threshold of the principal's office. A few awkward seconds passed. I lightly knocked on the open door.

"Oh, hey. How's it going?" she said with a big, reassuring smile.

"Very good," I resorted to a go-to answer, even though it was not reflective of how I was really feeling at the moment. I was still nervous and did not want to say out of the blue that I felt emotional.

"What's up?"

With great timidity, I said, "I was just curious really quick, is there anything you'd like to talk to me about?"

"Uh, about what? No."

I concisely opened up the thoughts in my brain, expressing the stress of what was going on.

"Oh. Um, nothing from me. I only heard great things. My observations of you are that you're very involved and work really great with the kids and all of that."

After conversing for a few more seconds, the principal reaffirmed, "I don't know, but I've only observed really good things, Matthew."

"That's really reassuring, and I'm just trying my best to make a good impression, while also being a help and an encouragement."

"Yeah."

"Put smiles on faces."

"You do that. You do that," she said, nodding. She said that she would follow up with my Mentor Teacher about it. She also said that we are always learning and growing.

"Yeah, having a growth mindset," I said and smiled.

"That's absolutely right. You're doing a fabulous job, so I know we'll get there, whatever it is."

"Thank you. I appreciate it."

"You're welcome. Have a good day. Happy Halloween."

I walked out the side door toward the front of the office and into the door next to the library, which took me back up to the lounge. I was relieved but was still not content in my heart. Ascending that staircase, I ran into one of the science teachers who was descending.

"Coming to chess club this week?" he asked, smiling.

"I'll try. I would really like to," I responded.

"All right. Well, we'll see you there."

This further showed me that I was indeed in good standing with another teacher. I observed his seventh-grade science classes multiple times, taking pages of notes, and asking questions. He imparted a lot of pedagogical wisdom like my Mentor Teacher, as did *tons* of teachers at that school, frankly.

Once again, I nervously paused for about five minutes, but I mustered up the courage to talk to an administrative intern whom I knew.

"Hi, Matthew," she said.

"Hello."

"What's up?"

"Do you have a minute?"

"Sure."

"Or less?"

"Yeah."

Once again, I asked how I was doing as a student teacher on campus and if there was any concern that I should be aware of.

"Uh, no. I mean I think it's been very helpful that you've been doing tutoring, and I haven't gotten any kind of negative feedback on that, so yeah. I think everything is great."

After a couple of moments, we concluded our conversation.

Walking down the hallway, I ran into one of the two Assistant Principals.

We said hi and passed each other. I kicked myself for being so nervous. I wanted to eventually talk to both Assistant Principals, and I just allowed one of my chances to walk by. However, when she walked back to her office a moment later, I gave myself the courage to ask if she had a minute and if I was on the right track.

"I see you out helping and you're always visible, so that's a good thing."

"I always love helping."

"We always appreciate the extra eyes."

All of these words were reassuring to me like you would not believe. I was beginning to fear that I was making faculty nervous for being out during the morning, Nutrition, lunch, and after school, as I volunteered to supervise around the campus. That is partly how I have built a rapport with several other students and staff, ever since spring. That is why I believed that if they had a problem with me, then they would come up to me directly. Something that gave me reassurance was that sometimes, *they* smile and say hi to me *first*, not the other way around.

(Still, I did not find out who was talking with my Mentor Teacher regarding me and my performance. I was raised to speak and apologize directly to others, thereby making amends and knowing exactly what to do in the future. Thus, on Wednesday morning before school, I continued to talk with faculty, keeping it general and not adding specifics. The security guard pretty much said what one of the Assistant Principals told me. The seventh-grade math teacher whom I observed that Halloween day told me that I was doing great. However, he asked me not to take my phone out again while observing or helping. He said that a few students asked him why I got to have the phone out and not them. I surmise that, once again, I looked like a student sitting back there.)

Back on Halloween, after I left Ensign and got a ride home, I walked over to my local Juice It Up! to get one of my most-favorite drinks. When I was just down the street from where I live, I felt vibrations. It was the Credential Analyst/Student Teaching coordinator at Vanguard calling me. Right after I walked inside my room to put my stuff down, I received a text from the director. They both wanted to check in with me and meet in person that day. Earlier that day, the coordinator had sent me an email. I had twenty minutes to arrive by the time I received it.

I explained to the director that it was too short of a notice. We planned for me to come the following day, but after assessing the work I had, I determined that I could manage to come that day. They were still available, so I rushed over there.

"Hey, Matthew. Come on back," the director said. "Thanks for coming on short notice."

We walked to his office.

"Did you move offices?" I asked.

"I did."

I took a seat at the round table. Seated beside me was the coordinator.

The director took his seat and thanked me again for coming.

"And you're off tomorrow?" he asked.

"Yeah."

"School closed?"

"Yeah, for the students."

"Okay, like a faculty day or something?"

"Yeah, and I asked the teacher, and she said that I don't have to attend that."

The coordinator notified the director that NMUSD always did that the day after Halloween. I said that that is how it was when I was a student.

"So um, Matthew," the director commenced the discussion, "we wanted to circle back on some of the things we've talked about. We're getting close. Tomorrow is November 1. We wanted to see from your perspective how things are going and talk about the timeline for the rest of the semester. And things to work on and pay attention to in order to finish strong. Let's just start with a little word of prayer and ask for God's blessing on our time together and on your continuing work, okay?"

After the prayer, the director said, "Let me just start with kind of a general question. How are you feeling about things at this point? We had that meeting a few weeks ago now. How do you feel like things have been going since then?"

"*Chaotic*," I admitted before one second had passed since being asked that question.

"Chaotic?" he repeated. "Talk a little about that."

"Well, I feel like I'm doing better. A *lot*. But sometimes I, I guess honestly, was thinking about calling another meeting. Honestly," I stuttered all the way through. "It's kind of bit hard to express this right now, but, um, sometimes there are things where I'm not exactly sure what, uh, the Mentor Teacher, *exactly* wants. And sometimes I feel that if she says something or doesn't say something, I'm not exactly sure what to do, and I'm always nervous to go up to her and ask, because I'm not sure what her reception of it would be. I say this because sometimes she's very busy and other times she's not.

"I try to do things that . . . are . . . okay to do? Or try to do things, kind of in a way that might . . . *placate* her, in a sense?" I struggled to find the right words. "And, um, I'm trying my best and sometimes I'm hearing it out on the other side, such as clumsy mistakes I made, inadvertently. And I just don't want to anger her or anything like that, so sometimes, I just basically keep silent and just . . . hope for the best? And such? Other than that, I think things are going well because I'm coming up with the worksheets way in advance. I'm communicating with her, and we're piecing together worksheets and quizzes with her input. And then I go home and refine it and send it back to her. My recent lessons, she mostly praised me, saying that I'm doing much better in the teaching. Just try to jazz it up a bit. Make it a *little bit* more fun."

"That's good. So, the communication has been challenging, it sounds like."

"Uh, in a way. It's something I'm trying to develop on professionally and in life in general."

The director asked how the co-teaching had been, to which I responded that it was going okay.

"Matthew, how do you respond when she chimes in?" the coordinator asked. "How does that make you feel?"

Not telling everything that I already wrote earlier, I said, "Well, I just let her talk. I'm like, 'Okay, this is something I need to know for the future, some additional things I must've not said.' And I take that, and I'll know for the future to teach what she says."

"When you do your assessments with your lessons, what has been the results in terms of students being able to do things you want them to do?" the director asked. "I know that students are at different places, but give me an overall assessment on how students are doing with the lessons."

"I usually get a lot of thumbs up during my informal assessments. Students are usually honest with a thumbs down or thumbs in the middle. I give time to have them ask any questions so I can help them understand, which happened in the past."

"So, you're giving them a self-assessment opportunity that then gives you information on what needs to be addressed."

"Yeah, I either need to back up and ask them, 'What can I help you with in understanding?' or if I'm ready, move on."

"What about a formal assessment? Take your TPA for example. You gave them a formal assessment. What were the results?"

"I saw a lot of students understanding parts of it. And then there were common errors that I addressed in a re-teach lesson. So, I ended up doing a re-teach on just the graphing part. They seemed to do well from there, based on the subsequent assessment."

"Okay, good. So you saw progress from the first formal assessment to the next formal assessment."

"Yeah."

"Um . . .I think you continue to be on a really *strong* track in terms of the teaching. Your actual instructional and responding abilities are strong. As we noted last time, the challenges have been more of the communication, and 'being the teacher' kind of thing, and the interaction with the Mentor Teacher."

"Yeah, I've been emailing her most often now, but it's more like, 'Here are the worksheets that I came up with. Here are the keys.' Some of those times, I have a general question."

"And has she responded to those questions?"

"Uh, responded *verbally* the next morning."

"I understand."

"Sometimes, it's in the late morning or early afternoon, but I know she gets them but doesn't usually respond back unless it's pressing."

After a few minutes, we segued into talking about the messages that the teacher has been getting. I expressed my utter confusion regarding why teachers and administrators never came to me if I needed correction. On the contrary, *all* of them were nice to me, waved, smiled, and talked to me. They knew who I was. Additionally, some of the comments I received after school that day with the administrators seemed to validate all of that. I questioned why I was just now hearing about it.

"Well, part of it is," the director said, "the authority structure in a student-teaching situation is that the Mentor Teacher is your authority. Others could have spoken to you, but *they're* trying to make that authority structure clear. Instead of twenty people telling you what to do, it's *one* person telling you what to do, and that's your Mentor Teacher."

For the next length of time, we discussed effective communication skills and relating my student teaching experience to all my years as a commander in Royal Rangers. We discussed how to be flexible and adapt to other people's communication style.

The coordinator then said, "And another thing, if you are having issues with your senior commander, would you go to *his* boss to solve the communication problem you two may have?"

"You mean like, go to the pastor?"

"Pastor or anybody? Or would you write a letter up in Springfield?"

I was puzzled.

"The correct answer is *no*," the director said after a couple of seconds.

"Oh, I was thinking this was a trick question," I said, after which we all began laughing.

"What do you think that does to your relationship with your senior commander?" the coordinator asked.

"That would probably make us lose trust, and as he always said, he always wants to build *trust* with people, very emphatically."

"So, when you went to other admin and other teachers afterward, what do you think that did?"

"Um . . ." I could not speak for seconds. My entire innermost being dropped. The only possible conclusion as to the rationale behind her question is that just prior to the meeting, my Mentor Teacher communicated with them on what I did after I was done talking with her that day, which was asking around the office on how I was doing, or if there needs to be correction. I did not believe that what I was doing was wrong because I had an amicable rapport with all of them. Some of them enjoyed asking me how I was doing in school, anything I did over the weekend, or what plans I had for the upcoming weekend.

Again, I was starting to feel like a lost cause that day, a person most teachers and admin tolerated this entire time. Were they hiding behind smiles? Moreover, I had been working *extra* hard on Unit 4, which started immediately after the whirlwind of getting through the TPA, just to prove that I *could* do it.

I honestly never thought that the fact of me asking others, whom I knew very well, would be told to my Mentor Teacher, much less that quick! I, as a person who felt like he failed life, was tremendously concerned and needed answers. Based on how the teacher was talking to me in eighth period, there was absolutely no talking to her. Anything I would say, she would cut me off, not wanting to hear it. In fact, I did mention my concerns, but she assumed that I was coming up with excuses or trying to garner sympathy. I honestly discerned the care that she had in her voice, but still.

Communications is one of the biggest issues among us who have Autism.

"When I went to other admin?" I broke the silence, wanting to confirm my suspicion of how they knew.

"Mhm. When you went around your direct authority. What do you think was the perception that she felt?" the coordinator asked.

"I had not thought about that."

"And that's what we're wanting you to do, to have those moments where you are like, 'Oh. I see how that can damage our relationship and communications.' It's learning how to be a good faculty member, so that you're a team player. You're not always usurping your immediate authority. Your Mentor Teacher *is* your authority at Ensign. And *she* has authority, but they're not yours right now. Just your Mentor Teacher is."

The director added, "That's such a great point that she is making, but of course, if somebody was doing something immoral or dangerous, you're obviously going to talk to a higher up, but that's one out of a thousand situations. And the other 999 cases, you want to talk to them directly."

The director then segued into the timeline. I pulled out my AST log and handed it over to the coordinator.

"Okay, so you have 300 hours right now," the coordinator said. "And you have 239.5 in your BST. So we need about sixty more hours. Your Mentor Teacher said something about finishing before Thanksgiving on the eighteenth. And I think she talked to you about that today? That she's going to take over teaching?"

"Very briefly and all of a sudden. I was just hearing my professor say that it was December 15, and I already planned until December."

"And this is where we need to adjust. And you have to be willing to adjust at this point in time. And we're going to see that you *can* adjust because you're meeting the criteria that we need. We know that you turned in the TPA Cycle 2 early; we know that we're going to get the results back by the twenty-third at 10:59 p.m. We know that you turned in two out of four formal lessons that are required."

"And let me just add here," the director said, chiming in, "the email that your professor sent out is correct—that single-subject student teachers will go all the way to the end of the semester. So that's correct. In this case, it is a specific request from your Mentor Teacher. She *wants* to take the class back, so we're responding to her request."

"She explicitly gave me that information today," I said, resigning to my fate. At this point, I knew that I was going to pass the semester. We were confident that I passed the TPA. The coordinator said that she would be absolutely shocked if I did not pass it, which boosted some hope.

However, there was no hope to return to Ensign to student teach. This is in spite of all the incredibly immense amount of work I did in the recent weeks leading to this point, proving everything to her. She simply did not see or notice *all* that I was doing just to prove everything, as well as taking the initiative and doing things automatically.

At this nanosecond in time, I knew that I could have saved the entire world from obliterating disaster, and it would go unnoticed. What I mean in that hyperbole is that I could have raise the grades of every single student in America, and I still would not be asked to student teach her class again.

However, there is nothing I could do but to just continue to listen. I chose not to fight it.

(When I briefly brought up this entire enigma to one of my professors in class, she completely dropped her countenance and said, "I heard about your situation with your Mentor Teacher. I'm so sorry that happened to you.")

"So, the beauty of it is, you're in a place in terms of your hours where you can finish by November 18," the director said in a reassuring tone.

We later talked about my modified timeline of due dates, which was summarized in the email that I got the next day. My Clinical Practice will irrefutably end on November 18th. I need to get my third formal observation done by November 4th and my fourth and final one by November 18th. In lieu of my Mentor Teacher filling out the final STEP survey, the director said that he was going to do that. My Lead University Supervisor and I will fill out our parts, as was the protocol anyway.

I could not believe that it was going to end like this, but I was exceedingly grateful that I still had the chance to just barely pull through and finish successfully.

They talked about post-student teaching life and that substitute teaching, which I planned to do, would be of great benefit for me, getting more classroom experience. We began talking about my next two formal observations. The director and coordinator asked how I felt and if it seemed obtainable for me. I said yes. I had already been considering those lesson plans, and they knew that that was my strength.

The director told me, due to how quickly things needed to go, that he could do a formal observation if the supervisor could not make it.

As we were concluding our meeting, which lasted just under an hour, the coordinator reiterated that she follows me on YouTube and had enjoyed watching my entire journey. She also enjoyed hearing how transparent I have been during challenges, as well as going through the CSETs and TPA. She enjoyed my adventures in substituting and how at some places, I am reliving memories from when I was a child or teenager.

I love making these videos, but I personally hope that those teaching updates will encourage aspiring teachers.

After the meeting, I communicated with my Lead University Supervisor and planned the next two formal observations, the first one being that Thursday and the second being the following Monday. That was when I began thinking how special it would be if the director, who had been like a mentor to me since 2021, could witness an actual lesson of mine in action.

I called him on Wednesday to invite him to my final lesson as a student teacher, which was the date of my fourth formal observation. We arranged it so that he would come at third period, at the same time as my Lead University Supervisor.

"I would love that. That'd be great, Matthew," he said. "Thanks for letting me know. I'm looking forward to it."

─51─
FACING THE MUSIC

By the middle of the next afternoon, November 1, I felt panicked. I feared returning to Ensign the next morning with all of my innermost being. I wrote a lengthy email to the coordinator, explaining that I was frightened about what to expect. I told her that I was not exaggerating when I answered the director's first question, when I instantly responded, "Chaotic," without blinking or thinking twice about it. I had been contemplating all my clumsy mistakes and what my Mentor Teacher had said to me. I was questioning if she was fully on my side, not at all, or somewhere in between, despite the coordinator saying that she is also on "Team Matthew" the day before.

At the same time, I was feeling bad about all the heartache and frustration that I have been causing her. I wrote that she might be assuming that I am a defiant person who won't take instructions, but the truth is that I am a slow processor who is prone to mistakes as I learn. I could not always do things as fast as she expected. I cannot hear something and be expected to remember it after two seconds without writing it down on paper first. Then I get accused of not listening.

At times, when I tried to defend myself, my mind, and Autism, she cuts me off with the assumption that I am trying to gain sympathy over the CalTPA. All I was doing was just explaining all the work that I had been doing and how I had to time manage with everything else. Nevertheless, it is true that I cannot carry a huge load. I was *explaining* why I could not perform as well or as quickly as she wanted. I was not trying to gain sympathy. I can do a ton of things with little use or benefit, or I can take my time on a few things and change the world.

I simply summed it up by hypothesizing that there is a lack of complete understanding about my brain and how I am wired. As I inferred earlier in this book, if I could have done it all over again, I would have expressed this right at the beginning, somehow. I was still coming to terms that I still had limitations due to Autism, despite how old I am. However, I did not feel like I had to explain much of anything. The teacher of the first semester seemed quite different than the teacher of the second semester. I am certain that she was understanding the entire time, but at the beginning, she seemed more supportive, encouraging, motivating, and easier to go up to and ask questions. For whatever reason, I felt it harder and harder and harder to even ask a question. At the same time, whenever I asked anything, she answered, but not always happily.

I think what was hard was asking questions that I should have known the answer to. A common trait of Autism is that we *need* to ask confirmatory questions just to make sure we understand correctly, even if that means asking the same thing over and over again. I later made a YouTube and TikTok video talking about this in 2023.

Nevertheless, as I expressed in the email to the coordinator, I am deeply blessed to have had her as my Mentor Teacher because her wisdom, patience, and care are unparalleled. I was just trying my best to get my points across in understandable ways. I guess in the process, I must have sounded ignorant or in some cases, defiant.

I came forward with what I did, that I went around the office to talk to the admin, asking them how I was doing or if I needed correction. I wanted to apologize to whomever an apology was due. That is why I was terrified. I thought that I was going to hear of it from the teacher the next morning during first period.

That was the gist of my near 250-worded email. She responded by advising me to remember a Bible verse that she quoted. She recommended that I let the teacher know that it is my desire to do my best for the remaining few weeks, as well as reaffirming how much I do, indeed, appreciate her.

The next morning arrived. I woke up at an odd hour of the night. It was raining and pouring. I could not go back to sleep for the life of me. I decided to get up for the day and do a lot of homework for class. Then I arrived at Ensign. The office staff greeted me, as usual, happy to see me. I signed myself in and went upstairs to make a bunch of copies for class. I was quite vigilant with a lot of worries.

While there, one of the seventh-grade math teachers walked in to make copies on the other copier. I asked, in general, without details, what his observations of me have been as a student teacher.

"I mean, the only thing I've seen, like tutoring in the library, you have positive interactions with the kids, but I think you want to have more of an authoritative presence. Be loud at times. I haven't seen you in the classroom to give you feedback on that, but in the library, you've gotten involved, talked with the kids, and helped them on stuff. It's positive."

I appreciated his comments and agreed that I will need to work on such a presence. Royal Rangers had not been a problem nowadays, but in a public school, it was a different dynamic. Before the teacher left, I told him that I have benefitted from observing him, his student teacher, and other teachers. He was happy to hear that.

A while later, I exited the copy room and crossed the lounge. Just then, my Mentor Teacher walked through the door I was about to exit.

My countenance lit up. "Hi!" I exclaimed as my initial reaction.

To my total surprise, she smiled when she saw me too.

I was not holding back my tongue and blurted out, "I just want to say really quick, I appreciate everything and in these last three and a half weeks, I'm going to try my best. A hundred percent."

"Yeah. Try not to talk to anyone in the office."

"I know."

"That was *really* a poor choice."

"I found that out afterward. A person at Vanguard told me *after* the fact."

"Now *everyone* is talking to me. *Everyone* is wondering why you came to do that. It's really odd. I'm just going to let you go. When you're being observed, you'll teach. You could finish this week out, and otherwise, I'll teach. And we'll just finish. You'll finish your hours by observing, okay?"

"Okay."

"It's too much. You're causing problems at *my* work. And I did you a favor by letting you student teach with me. You kind of messed it up."

"Clumsy mistakes. I'm absentminded."

"Yeah, but it comes off on me."

"I'm absentminded. I didn't think about the repercussions of that."

"Yeah, you want to try to think before you act."

"I just wanted to apologize myself to people. I didn't know it was going to—"

"*Don't* go to anyone else. Just talk to me. You're here and *I* am your boss here, right?"

"I found that out."

"So if you have questions, you can ask me, but otherwise, you don't need to go ask *my* boss, right? That makes *no* sense, because *she* has signed off that it's okay for me to have you here. She can easily say, 'It's not okay.' And that's why we're ending it early. It's just not working. It's just too many things where you're just not following instructions. You don't take my advice. And everyone tells you to take my advice, but you *still* don't! And you had to have a meeting, so, we'll finish off the next few weeks. We'll figure out what two lessons you'll teach."

"Tomorrow and Monday."

"Okay. So, Monday will probably be the last teaching day."

"The last lesson."

"Yeah."

"All right. And what about today? I planned on today."

"You can teach today. Yeah, you can do this week and Monday, okay?"

"Okay, this will be the antepenultimate lesson then," I said, knowing that there is a quiz on Friday.

"Yeah, it kind of makes sense for this scenario. Then I don't have to be giving advice that you won't follow and get me in all this trouble at my own job. Not trouble, because everyone knows it's not me. It's just *more* work for me. I don't have time."

"And I do own up to my clumsiness, so they should be complaining to me and correcting me."

"No, they shouldn't. It's not their job. *I* signed up for this. It's *my* job. That's what you don't get. *No one* should be talking to you besides me. And *you* don't need to be talking to anyone. This is what you're not understanding. When you're a student teacher, your Mentor Teacher *is* the person you report to. *That* is the person who does your observations, right?"

"Right."

"That's the person. Not all the other staff members of this school. They don't have anything to do, right? They don't know what's going on. They might give me feedback, like this is what happened. Whatever. But it's not up to them; it's up to me. Do you understand that?"

"Yeah, I do."

"Okay, so, you don't need to be going to anyone else. And I'm honestly not going to say anything else because what I say doesn't get taken in. You're not an employee here. Nobody is coming to talk to you but me. So, if you choose not to listen to me, then that's fine, but don't go to anyone else."

"I won't go to anyone else."

"Okay. Thank you. I'll see you in a little bit."

I went to the classroom to organize everything, including my thoughts. There were so many truths but so many misconceptions in a brief period of time—misconceptions that I have already addressed in this book. I already suggested that the solution is to simply talk things out before all of this even happens. I should have explained to the Mentor Teacher my limitations when I first detected it. I have also set out to prove that I indeed took her advice on many things, predominately teaching strategies and being the teacher.

A moment later, she walked in the door.

"Okay, so do you kind of understand now? Or do you have more questions?" she continued as she walked toward her desk.

As I tried to respond to her (saying that I *do* understand her), she immediately cut me off, saying, "Do you understand the predicament you put me in?"

"Yeah."

"And you have kind of not given yourself a good name to all the admin at this point. If you ever try to go above me to them, they're like, 'No way.' Do you understand that?"

"Yes."

"That's how that looked to everyone. And they're like, 'What in the world was that?' because that's *not* cool after all I've done for you. So, I don't know what you were trying to do in that situation, but again, whatever it was, it was not a good choice."

"I know that now," I said, feeling like my world just collapsed. Like the past chapter's title conveyed, there was nothing I could say or do to prove that I am utterly handcuffed to the limitations of Autism. That is what it came down to. I am like the way I am solely because of Autism. I implemented her advice a lot of times, some of which she did not notice. I worked extra hard and even stayed up past midnight at times just to ensure that Unit 4 would be the *best* that she had ever seen in her life.

Moreover, the only interactions I have had with admin was them telling me that they are proud of what I have done and are thankful for all my volunteerism, which I cited evidence of.

Additionally, the students' assessments and responses tell me that they are understanding and retaining nearly all of what I am teaching them. This really does not bear repeating, but outside the class, students seem to accept me for who I am, and they like waving and saying hi to me. In both semesters, there has never once been an outburst, fight, or sign of disrespect toward me, my teaching, or my Autism. Some students talked to me about my Autism, eager to know more.

I simply had no idea what was going on. It was no different than feeling like you are living in a way that is glaringly different from reality, as if I were mentally insane.

The way my Mentor Teacher has been explaining things seemed different than what I have seen, as if the faculty that *I* talked to and that *I* engaged with were figments of my imagination, as if they were ghosts or not real. A lot of what she said were things that I utterly did not see and on the contrary, were undetectable.

Nevertheless, after seconds of silence, the teacher continued, "It's just like, I don't have anything left to give you. I've given you the whole year. And I don't think you—"

"You've given me a lot of good wisdom that I will retain forever."

"Yeah, hopefully. *I'm* the person who gave you this opportunity, right?"

As I was saying, "Yeah, and I sure appreciated that," she talked over me and said, "Because no one else at Ensign would have done that. Did you know that? *No one!*"

"Yeah," I said, knowing very well that two other math teachers currently have student teachers, one of whom is from Vanguard. However, it was no use defending myself, so I just let her talk and I listened. I exhaustively did *everything* I physically and mentally could to prove how most of the things she said were wrong and that some of the little mistakes were caused by Autism. I am truthful when I say that I own up to those mistakes, however. Still, some of the things that she seemed to insinuate were foreign to me.

"Okay, but then—" she started.

"I have a lot of appreciation."

"Yeah, you show it in a very funky way."

"And to [this person], too." I was referring to a friend at Mesa Church. She used to teach science there at Ensign when I was a student, but I never had her since I never took a science class. She worked for Vanguard as one

324

of the supervisors for student teachers. She was currently a volunteer for Brave Hearts, which is the sister organization of Royal Rangers, so I saw her almost every week, filling her in on how student teaching had been going.

"Well, she was the one who came to my house when I already said no. Just so you know, it's like *everyone* else said no, and so did I. But then I said, 'Fine. Okay, I will. I'll give him the opportunity.' And it's like, you keep messing with me after all that I've done. It's very frustrating."

"Again, I apologize. It's lesson learned."

"Mhm."

I slowly turned around and walked back to the table. "Other than that, I've given you the other worksheets and the quiz I made a couple of days ago and a couple of keys."

She did not say much of anything. Probably a quiet "Okay."

I went on to teach what I believed was a flawless lesson.

I was not sure where she was getting *all* of her information. The last thing I ever wanted since January 3 was to be a burden. In fact, that is my life's story, as God is my witness. Whether in her classroom or observing *all* the other classrooms, I had not been anything but quiet and respectful, other than that one time, texting her. On the contrary, teachers said it was fine to help students during practice time. "Come by anytime," one science teacher always said.

I completely and lifelessly felt like a person who was misunderstood, not believed, underestimated, and—at the worst—falsely accused.

—52—
MY FINAL LESSON
NOVEMBER 7, 2022

My final lesson ever as a student teacher was Unit 4, Lesson 7, which was all about finding the Average Rate of Change based on their graphs. I did, in fact, plan up to Lesson 12, but me teaching those other lessons was now not going to happen.

One thing that my Mentor Teacher always encouraged me to do was use EdTech, such as a Kahoot! or Quizizz. As I already put in the calendar, I was going to do that a couple of times during review days. However, since my final lesson came before that, I decided to just do one.

Three days before the lesson, I familiarized myself with Quizizz.com, got an account, and effortlessly made my first one. I was going to use it as one of my formative assessments for the lesson plan and collect the data for my calculations thereafter. The quiz had conceptual true-and-false questions, had students calculate the Average Rate of Change over given intervals of a given graph, had them determine which interval had the greater rate, and which one had the lesser.

I had a worksheet of the entire thing as a backup, just in case technology, which usually was not my friend, went haywire. I practiced my quiz myself to ensure that it was accurate and went smoothly.

I emailed the link to my Mentor Teacher, telling her, "Surprise!"

She said it was a great idea and that we would get it set up the following Monday when I arrived. Afterward, she could export the data for me.

Since this lesson meant a lot to me, I rehearsed it a number of times over.

November 7 arrived. That morning, I was reflecting on February 1, 2022, the date of my first lesson. I was reflecting on all that went on from then until now. I considered how much I had improved in teaching and pedagogy, and how much I had learned.

"Good morning," I said as I entered the classroom.

"Good morning," my Mentor Teacher returned the greeting. "How are you?"

"Sentimental."

"Last day!"

"Last *lesson* . . . but, *excited.*"

We both began discussing what I would be doing from here until my actual last day, in order to complete the six hundred clinical hours. We determined that I would help out in various skills classes throughout the day, helping those who need extra math support, which I was more than willing to do. She also said that she and her two AVID classes would love to have me help with tutorials twice a week, just like I had been doing since spring. (I will say now that I later calculated that I should arrive at six hundred hours on Wednesday, November 16. At that point, we agreed that that would be my final day.)

"Okay. And then do you want to observe periods two and three? Or do you want to help?"

"Can I think about it?"

"Yeah. I'll be the one who will sign off, because I'm, obviously, your Mentor Teacher, so don't go to anybody else. Okay?"

"Okay."

"Because they don't know the whole deal. I just have to keep track and make sure where you are. So, I'll figure that out with one of the administrators."

"Perfect. I'm willing to help seventh graders and eighth graders with different teachers who are doing skills."

Suddenly, my Mentor Teacher segued into discussing Quizizz. She told me that she was having a problem accessing the quiz and that it would require an upgrade. For the next length of time, we tried to figure out what to do. We decided that I would sign in using my Google account.

First, I was wary about signing into Google on another device, even if it was, in fact, safe and secure. Second, I did not store my exact password in my long-term memory. Nonetheless, I was trying to access my own Google password on my phone. Having a slow phone did not help.

In the interim, I went to make copies of the backup worksheet and my self-assessment rubric that I would hand out. I eventually succeeded and found my password. When I arrived, as fate would have it, the door was closed and locked, but the security personnel soon unlocked it for me.

My heart was beating fast and hard because, if I can admit, I was proud of my first quiz on Quizizz and frankly, I was also trying to prove to the teacher that it was of no effort to me. Admittedly, I did get sidetracked, especially in Unit 2 with the CalTPA. With the load of work for both the TPA and Vanguard, I did not put gamification and game-based learning as my priority. I wanted to get the unit, up until the mid-unit assessment, planned out first. Then I would look into making a quiz on Kahoot! or Quizizz.

Once I got back to the classroom, I signed into Google on her laptop, did the verification on my phone, and got it ready. I was relieved but was glad to have a backup just in case, feeling thankful that I had the foresight. I was super appreciative of the teacher's help and guidance since without it, I am sure it would not have worked.

"I *love* how you waited till your final lesson to do a Quizizz," the teacher kept saying a couple of times with a hint of sarcasm.

Yeah, I get it, I said to myself. I was not really sore over it. If I had done the entire unit like I initially planned, I would have made a *couple* of these. Again, I did not do it in Unit 2 for the reasons I stated above.

Within ten minutes before second period began, I asked the teacher if I could deliver a formal good-bye to both classes after my lesson, as I had dreamed (and at times, *dreaded*) to do. She said it would be okay.

A minute before the bell rang, I went over to the door. I just stood there, reflecting. It was going to be my last day doing this as their student teacher.

The bell rang. Students flooded out of their first period classrooms and came into their second.

Second period came and went, and it went well. Still, it was not as perfect as I would like, but for third period, I modified accordingly. Again, I am my biggest critic, so I may have been melodramatic inside.

The bell rang to signify the conclusion of second period.

My Lead University Supervisor arrived and took her seat up at the front.

I quickly went to the office for something and saw from afar the director of Vanguard signing in at the front. I felt overjoyed knowing that both of them were there.

As I was waiting for third period to begin, a student walked in and asked, "Mr. Kenslow, are you going to be here all year?"

"Um, I'll let you know at the end of class."

"Okay."

A moment later, the director walked in and greeted me.

I delivered my entire lesson, and I believe that it went perfectly. In both periods, the quiz on Quizizz worked well. It was a good thing I made backup copies anyway, since a couple of students did not have working Chromebooks that morning.

Here is what I said at the end of both periods:

> *I have a special announcement. It's been very wonderful being your student teacher since August 22. And from August 22 to now, you guys have been very great to me. You guys have been very patient with me. You understood that I was making some of my mistakes in the beginning because I'm learning how to teach. I'm learning how to teach effectively. I just want to thank you for that.*
>
> *What you just saw was my final lesson as a student teacher. And today is my final day here. And I'm not going to go away immediately. I'm going to finish my hours elsewhere on campus, but I just wanted to take this moment to thank you. I want to thank one of the greatest Mentor Teachers on earth, as well as the faculty of Vanguard University, who has a strong commitment to us, who help trained us to be the teachers we are today.*
>
> *Thank you so much.*

In both periods, students applauded. In second period, I remembered to add that it had been my dream to be a teacher for twenty years, and I will do whatever I can to become a teacher one day.

While I was speaking, all eyes were glued on me. In second period, one student quickly looked up at me with a surprised countenance. I noticed other students giving me smiles of congratulations. The director seated at the front table with the supervisor had a huge smile that told me he was very proud of all my accomplishments.

"Congrats," one third-period student whispered as I walked by.

"Congratulations," the person seated next to him (who was a former Royal Ranger at my outpost) said.

Just then, the first student reached inside his backpack. "You deserve a gift." He gave me a small bag of Skittles. "I hope you like Skittles."

In both periods, I left a melancholy tone because students were sad that I was about to leave sooner than what I had told them. When I defined the classroom expectations at the beginning of the unit, I implied that I would be teaching them until the middle of December, when Unit 4 would be finished.

Students called out after leaving, "Thank you, Mr. Kenslow!" "Thank you for teaching me," and "Thank you for all the help." Throughout the day, I would ask a few of them about how I taught and if I improved since August. They all said that I was really good, which was quite reassuring to me. They told me that they learned a lot and enjoyed my teaching style.

While it was still the passing period between third and fourth, I was standing by the door and a student rushed up to me. "I can't believe I'll never see you again."

"Well, I'll still be on campus," I said.

"Are you going to tutor still?"

"Yeah, I'm going to tutor probably until next week."

"Where are you going?" a second student nearby asked.

"Today was my final lesson, so . . ."

"Where are you going?"

"Well, I'll probably sub around, but I'll still be here for a bit."

"Sub for [this teacher's] class, period 2," the first student said.

Soon, my supervisor and I went up to the lounge for the final time to discuss the lesson. After talking over a couple of parts, she said, "There were *so* many good things in this, Matthew. There were so many good things. Um, my recommendation last time was that you color-code things. And I think that really helped too, especially during this lesson."

We continued to dissect the lesson for a while. For the self-assessments, she said that she saw a lot of thumbs up, implying thorough understanding. "It's a great group of kids," she said. "Your 'Thank you' to your students and your Mentor Teacher was really well said. And you can tell that it was heartfelt, so I think that was really good. And I think the kids appreciated it. I really do."

Toward the end of our conversation, she added, "You have a great career ahead of you."

Later that day, I started helping a skills class during seventh period, helping one of them in eighth-grade math. (The next day, he entered seventh period, saw me, and said, "Can you help me in math?" to which I smiled and said that I would be glad to.)

I also interviewed a seventh-grade math teacher and an eighth-grade math teacher, both of whom I not only observed but helped their students. They were happy to answer my questions. The interview was part of an "Alternate Classroom Observation" assignment for one of my classes at Vanguard. Both of them, along with everyone else I told, were exceedingly happy and congratulatory to hear of the milestone of my final lesson.

When I got home, I posted throughout social media the following:

> With great sentimentality and bittersweetness, I just taught my final lesson of student teaching. Some students were sad, but they all applauded after I delivered my "farewell address" (if you will), where I thanked them (the students), my Mentor Teacher, and Vanguard University. They were wonderful sets of classes. I told them that I'm not leaving right away. I'm going to be helping out in various Skills classes throughout each day until the middle or end of next week, until I reach six hundred clinical-practice hours. Plus, I will for sure substitute until June, so I'll probably be coming back to Ensign here and there.
>
> One of the students gifted me with a bag of Skittles and many said, "Thank you, Mr. Kenslow," and "Congratulations!" I am very thankful that one of my professors (and mentor) got to witness my final lesson and see me teach in action, along with my supervisor from VUSC for my final formal observation. I am excited for this next chapter in my life and getting to substitute around again; also, to be a volunteer speaker and juggler to all the eighteen thousand plus students of NMUSD (and beyond) . . .

Like the teacher, I kept all the details under wraps from 99 percent of everyone. I simply said upon being asked by students, staff, and Vanguard classmates, "I just got my hours and lessons done a bit early." Inside, I wished to have continued until mid-December.

That Wednesday, after class, I went up to my professor to inquire about something in SEL. Afterward, she asked me, "Did the director talk to you about the final lesson you did?"

"No, he had to leave, but we plan to debrief later."

"Well, he said it was the best lesson he's ever seen," she said and smiled.

That gave me hope and reassurance. It took communicating back and forth, but the director and I were both free in the afternoon of November 14.

I knocked on the door to the director's office.

"Come on in, Matthew!" he said, smiling. "How're you doing?"

"Hello. Very good." I went to take a seat at the table.

"I'm just signing this off and then I'll be with you."

We started discussing what it had been like going to skills classes throughout the day. I said that I was thankful.

"Well, I *really, really* enjoyed your lesson. I thought that was just a fantastic lesson," he said.

We discussed how I thought it went, as well as the debrief with my supervisor afterward.

"You know what really impressed me is that they were 100 percent on task, which is really hard to do," the director recalled, marveling. "You had a class full of, I think there were thirty-two students in there, and they were *all* on task the whole time. That's amazing."

We later talked about the reward system with the tickets that my Mentor Teacher used and how I employed it at Royal Rangers.

"Well, she seemed to be really excited about the Quizizz. How'd you feel about that?"

"Um, proud. Not only did I make it, but it actually worked." I smiled.

"They were very into it."

We continued to talk more about the lesson for the next fifteen minutes, before segueing into the status of the TPA, my immediate plans after Wednesday, and finishing up the semester.

Afterward, I ran into the Credential Analyst/Student Teaching coordinator, who was in her office. She said that the director was really impressed with my final lesson. We briefly talked about the next steps and that she would come into one of my classes soon to give more directions on what is next.

~53~

My Final Days of Student Teaching

The morning after the day of my final lesson, I entered a history teacher's classroom whose first period was Skills. From then until the sixteenth, eighth-grade students (usually four of them) got in a group. I stood by the whiteboard and tutored them in math, bringing in all of the instructional strategies that I learned, observed, and implemented.

The classes for the rest of the day usually had me do one-on-one math help. Sometimes it got very boring as I just sat there, since either nobody needed math help, or they just completed math. One of the teachers I helped was my former R.S.P. teacher from when I was a student. Additionally, I continued to help with tutorials in AVID, as well as after-school tutoring in the library.

My Mentor Teacher told me that she immediately started hearing a lot of positive reports about me. As it got closer to the sixteenth, she received a whole pile of thank-you cards for me from students. They were very thorough; some of them had amazing art drawings for me. A couple of the students handed cards to me in person. The former Royal Ranger drew a big Royal Rangers emblem on his card. Another came up to me and gave me a bag of Skittles taped to a Bucheron chocolate bar.

Students had written that I was one of their favorite teachers at Ensign, enjoying every second that I taught, were glad that I made the class fun, and were happy that I engaged with them. They congratulated me for receiving a teaching credential, admired my passion for teaching and education, told me that I made a difference in their lives, and wished me good luck in my teaching career.

One wrote that she was very nervous entering Enhanced Math, but when I got up in front of everybody and taught, most of her stress vanished. She added that I made math fun, better, and easier for her, adding that she was not kidding. She went on to write that I got her through the hardest part, which was starting. She thanked me repeatedly.

Students appreciated my kindness, as well as my patience and understanding for when somebody does not yet understand. They admired that I took the time to ensure that students understood every lesson and that I explained the homework when others could not comprehend it. A couple said that I would be greatly missed by all.

One added that she wished success for my writing career and that I will write about my experiences, which is exactly what I am doing now, authoring this book, which I hope is encouraging and enjoyed by all.

A few expressed happiness that I remembered their birthdays and found it neat that I could remember the birthdays of all the students. One expressed the hope that I will get a million YouTube subscribers one day. Another expressed gladness that I taught them, saying that they were sad to see an "educated and talented student teacher leave."

All of these letters did not go unnoticed. They brought me as much comfort as the letters I received throughout my BST semester. It was especially reaffirming to me that I did an excellent job.

Even though my Mentor Teacher could not see *all* that I did and the impact that students said I left, I at least know that the *students'* lives were changed because of me, which is much more important in my heart.

Reading how much confidence they have now is the reason I want to be a teacher. My hope is that *every* student will receive the motivation to learn, thereby succeeding in life.

It is categorically my joy and pleasure to do my part in the mathematics department. And just to say too, I could not have done it without my Mentor Teacher.

As it was nearing the sixteenth, students from all across the campus were asking me if it was my last day soon. Throughout the days, students would come up to me to talk about that.

The day before my final day, during lunchtime, one student fell on his knees and pretended to cry.

The librarian was also very sad because I had been a great help during after-school tutoring. She told me to be sure I come back.

November 16 arrived. It was the final time walking to Ensign from my drop-off location. On this day, I made my rounds throughout the office and school to say my good-byes, including the front office personnel, the principal, assistant principals, counselors, security, and tons of the teachers I observed and helped. All of them expressed sadness that I was leaving, but at the same time, they were very proud.

It was bittersweet. Hundreds of fun memories—big and small—were made, from motivating entire classes of students in math to the time when a little bird flew into our room during AVID.

Word continued to get around among the students. In about half of the classrooms that I went to throughout the day and during Nutrition, students asked about me. "Mr. Kenslow, is it your last day today?" they would ask. A few students either followed after me or walked up to me to say good-bye.

I would usually answer, "Well, I'll probably be back to sub." Students and staff also asked me what I would be doing next.

When I walked into my Mentor Teacher's classroom, her eyes lit up. She gave me a hug and a stack of cards, including one from her, in which she thanked me for the effort I put in. She told me to let her know if I needed anything. She appreciated all my help and my priceless heart in helping the students, amid the arduousness of this journey.

As one of my professors kept telling us, this is *not* an easy journey.

I honestly will never forget how much care she had to at least give me the opportunity. I gave her a big card expressing this, writing up on top that this letter would be imbued with understatements. I said that I truly listened, learned, and benefitted from her wisdom. I sincerely endeavored in the undertaking of student teaching to the absolute best of my capabilities.

I thanked her for her patience and the time (albeit shortened) that she gave me. I thanked her for what trust and confidence she had in me, in spite of the simplest of mistakes. I acknowledge that those are the times I learn the greatest and that I have a growth mindset.

I will certainly not forget her, all the other staff, and all the students, this year and the last. The teacher also gave me some hope, saying that if ever I cannot find a sub job, I could come to volunteer.

Again, she heard praise from the skills teachers, and I can come back to help them too.

During eighth period, I went upstairs where I ran into a counselor, a vice principal, and the on-campus safety officer.

"Hi, Matthew. What's up?" the counselor said.

"I just wanted to say, that's it."

"Oh, you're going." She gave me a hug. "We're going to miss you."

"Bigger and brighter things now," the on-campus safety officer said, smiling.

"Yeah, what's next?" the counselor said.

"Substituting. From here to June 9. And in about a month, I will have an exit interview at Vanguard, and they'll recommend me for a full math credential."

"Yay!" They clapped. "Good for you."

"Oh my gosh, you're a huge success," the counselor said, smiling. "I'm so proud of you. That's awesome. You've done an amazing job."

I expressed that I would miss my student teaching days but was excited for the future.

"Now you already have a feel for the school, so you know what you're doing," said the counselor.

"Yeah. I mean, maybe I'll be led to teach here. I don't know. I still need to apply."

"Okay, we hope you do. We will miss you."

"Thanks, Matthew," the assistant principal said. "Take care. Good luck."

After saying our good-byes, I walked through the lounge and said good-bye to the administrative intern. "Thanks for all your help," she said.

Afterward, I walked over to a seventh-grade science teacher I had observed many times. His student teacher was there, who was my classmate at Vanguard.

"Well, Matthew, best wishes," the teacher said. "If you're ever on campus for chess club, come on over. It was always great when you were here and being a pair of eyes, helping with the kids. Congratulations. What about the TPA?"

"I submitted it. November 23 is my fate, I guess."

"Yeah, Matthew submitted like two or three weeks ago," the student teacher said.

"Well, it would be great to have you back," the teacher said once I expressed interest in working at Ensign. "You were a student here, right?"

"Right."

"And a student teacher here, so it'd be fun to be back. Well, so long, Matthew. Best wishes."

"All right, thank you. I appreciate it."

"I'll see you tonight," the student teacher said, since we had class on Wednesday nights.

"Yeah, see you tonight."

I circled around the campus and entered an eighth-grade math class, seeing if I could help for the latter half hour. The teacher was happy for me to help since it was a practice day. A couple of students there continued to say good-bye to me.

After the bell rang and school was over, I told the teacher that it was a bittersweet day today.

"Congratulations. That's a lot of work. Do you feel that your experience here was worthwhile?"

"Absolutely. I learned from the ups, and I learned from the downs. A growth mindset."

"You kind of learn more from the downs, right? Just keep your head up."

She proceeded to give me more pedagogical wisdom, such as classroom management. She concluded by saying that she was there if I needed anything.

I walked over and announced the news to my former prealgebra teacher from seventh grade. She wished me all the best. She thanked me for all the help and told me to keep in touch. She said that she would keep me in mind if she ever needed a sub. I told her that I was going to write this book.

As I was walking toward the office to sign myself out, I hear, all of a sudden, "Mr. Kenslow!"

I turned around and saw two students sprinting toward me from all the way across the hall. They heard it was my last day. and wanted to say good-bye. One of them asked if he could get a picture with me.

"See you later," one of them said afterward. "Come sub!"

"I will."

I walked inside the library where there was a big Thanksgiving potluck for the staff. I said both my thanks and good-byes to a lot of them. They congratulated me, hoping that I would do well in my future.

"Keep us posted," one of them said.

Around this day and on this day, I also expressed to a couple of other math teachers that if they needed a substitute who can actually teach math, then please keep me in mind. I also reopened my request to volunteer as a speaker and juggler in an all-school assembly. The principal said that she would relay the message to the current ASB director who puts on such assemblies.

Even a couple of the crossing guards seemed sad and talked to me about this part of my journey.

In total, I completed 602 and a half clinical hours of student teaching.

–54–
Back to Subbing

While I said good-bye as a student teacher, I began authoring the next chapter of my life: substitute teaching.

For sure, I figured that there would be jobs available for Thursday, November 17. There was not.

All semester long, I had been getting phone calls (I always felt or heard the vibrations), even while teaching a lesson. I thought, *If my phone has been ringing off the hook nearly every day, then why would they stop now?*

Oh well.

My *now-former* Mentor Teacher asked me if I could come back and sub for her that Friday, the eighteenth, teaching Lesson 12 about piecewise functions. By serendipity, that was the last lesson that I planned out before being told that I was not even going to continue past lesson seven. I accepted.

As anybody would imagine, the students were surprised to see me when I opened the door to the classroom. All day, students and staff said, "I thought you left."

"I left, but now I'm back, subbing for my now-former Mentor Teacher."

Everybody was happy to see me back. As an incentive for good behavior, I brought some juggling for the end of each period. I saw a stack of TRFs and decided to grade them, surprising the teacher. It felt like old times again, even though it had only been a matter of days.

I was also excited to make my teaching updates again for YouTube, specifically about substitute teaching at various schools.

My next stop was Whittier Elementary School for fourth grade, the following Monday. After being at Ensign for nearly three months, it was great to be branching out again. It was the first time I was over at Whittier Elementary.

The night before, I emailed the teacher, who forwarded me the sub notes. Apparently, they were getting ready for their trip to San Juan Capistrano, just like when I was in fourth grade. I showed pictures of various missions, per the request of the teacher, and mixed in some of my own pictures of us being at San Juan Capistrano from circa 2005.

It was great subbing elementary again because I got to bring all of my magic tricks and my juggling. There was one trick where some students fell on the floor in disbelief. (As always, I say it is not real magic, but rather the skills of illusion that I kept practicing throughout my life.)

The students were very nice and helped explain classroom procedure to me. However, just like the past academic year, it never ceases, but students always ask me how tall I am.

"Six foot two and three-quarters . . .about." As always in those sorts of moments, I jumped up to touch the ceiling.

At the end of the day, I got to meet the Assistant Principal and told her about my willingness to speak and juggle at an assembly, voluntarily. She took down my name and information to give to the principal.

The next day, I was at Newport Heights Elementary, subbing sixth grade. The classroom was not my main sixth grade classroom, but I spent several hours in there, back when I was in sixth grade myself. As I was walking over to the playground, having morning duty over there, I overheard several students, near and far, whispering among themselves things like, "It's the YouTube guy" or "It's the juggler." Throughout the day, many students called out to me saying that they like my YouTube videos. A lot of them remembered me from substituting during the past academic year. Others remembered me from juggling for them when they were in first grade.

At the end of the day, one of the teachers saw me and asked, "Hey, did you survive today?"

"Uh, no! I'm a ghost." I smiled. "Have a good Thanksgiving."

We laughed at my joke, and I said that it was honestly a great day. Kind of loud at times, but overall, it was good.

It brought me peace to be substituting these two days, especially teaching some math lessons. After this day was the start of Thanksgiving break, knowing that the result of my CalTPA Cycle 2 was coming.

$-55-$
MY FATE OF THE CALTPA CYCLE 2 AND FINISHING THE CREDENTIAL PROGRAM

The night before Thanksgiving, I received the email with the subject line, "CalTPA Results."

My heart started beating quickly, but I was expecting the email. I previously determined that I would open it *on* Thanksgiving Day. I had high confidence in it insofar as not worrying about ruining my Thanksgiving. Still, I had always been tough on myself.

On Thanksgiving, I got ready and began to record myself for the YouTube video. After talking, I opened the email, followed by the official PDF of the results. There were nine rubrics, each of which had a score to them, one through five.

I quickly read the scores off with increasing excitement in my voice.

Then I saw that my total score was twenty-nine, thereby passing! I passed Cycle 2, and the requirements for the TPA for Single-Subject Mathematics were met!

"What a present on Thanksgiving!" I said, followed by thanking everyone who had supported me: family, friends, Vanguard University, and Ensign. Being at the end of my YouTube video, I encouraged other aspiring teachings in the midst of their TPA cycles, present and future. I now know and fully understand what it is like being in their shoes, but I encouraged them to stick with it and to try their best to fulfill the passions that they have.

I excitedly told the news to my family and sent out emails to certain people at Vanguard and my Mentor Teacher. Every single one of them was happy to hear the news, and they were proud of me.

A couple of people, including the director at Vanguard and my former third-grade teacher, I called to tell them directly in lieu of a text or email. I talked to them the following day.

"I thought I'd share what I'm thankful for this Thanksgiving. I am thankful to say that I can say, 'I passed *both* cycles of the CalTPA.'"

By this time, I had submitted all of my lessons for class, as well as the two Alternate Classroom Observation papers.

By mid-December, I completed and turned in my Professional Portfolio website that I started in 2021 and my UbD unit that I created for class. I got drafts of my resume and cover letter for when it is time to apply for a teaching career, as well as a couple of letters of recommendation from the director and my supervisor. One of my former teachers also offered to write a letter for me.

The final STEP surveys were being completed by me, the director, and the supervisor. Both the director and supervisor scored me with fives (the highest points) for the TPEs asked, saying high remarks about me. Both stated that I have strong mastery in the content knowledge of math.

The supervisor added that I was taking her advice from our post-conferences and applying them. She saw that I adequately broke the content down for the students. She noticed that students see how much I care.

The director noted that I have designed and produced "engaging, conceptually rich and practical lessons . . . that keep students focused and on task." He added that I impart my passion for math and have "deep care" for all students.

All three of us also met together via Zoom to additionally discuss the Individual Development Plan (IDP), which is a required document to fill out and sign. The point of it was to establish my TPE strengths and weaknesses. Goals were discussed and set up. After I signed it, the supervisor signed it too, followed by the director in place of my Mentor Teacher, for reasons described in this book. This document is to be taken with me when I am inducted in a teaching position.

On December 12, I picked up the IDP with all three signatures, walked down the hall to my professor's office, and had my exit interview. She was also the fourth signature. In such an interview, she puts us candidates "through the wringer," giving us a mock interview and coaching. It was quite beneficial. She was continually impressed with all of my work.

As I was leaving, I heard, "Hey, Matthew?!"

It was the Credential Analyst/Student Teaching coordinator, calling out from her office. She and I planned to have our AST Preliminary Credential

Advising meeting the following day, but she figured that since I was there, we would get it over with. I was thankful.

We discussed the entire checklist for receiving a credential that I began in 2021. This time, I had everything pretty much checked off. I gave her authorization to go inside my CTC account to recommend me for a credential.

"You have three emails to look for," she told me. "The first will say that the application for recommendation was received. You'll have to go on and pay the fee. The second one will confirm your payment. The third one will say that your credential has been issued. Sometimes it takes a few weeks and other times, it's much shorter."

I acknowledged that I understood.

"Well, you know now that we didn't lie when we said in the beginning that this is a rigorous program."

I cannot refute that. It is indeed extraordinarily rigorous. She congratulated me on all of my hard work. I was relieved that I could enjoy Christmas; it was a weight off my shoulders. I was done! I received all three emails, the last of which came to me on January 6, 2023.

January 6 was the day in my life when I was officially issued a Preliminary Single Subject Teaching Credential in Mathematics, authorizing me to teach math anywhere from twelfth grade and below, as well as classes for adults. It was surreal, as this was one of the hugest hurdles in becoming a teacher.

Back on November 27, 2022, I officially started writing this book to describe all it took to go through these hurdles as a person with Autism. I had been primarily hoping that this book would motivate aspiring teachers to persevere. Having a disability should never make a person quit. Since the beginning, my goal has been to encourage the whole world that everybody *can* do whatever they set their heart and mind to do, despite a disability.

I will say, I kept passionately typing and typing as much as my other book, not to mention my trilogy that I began in 2013. In fact, for a few weeks, particularly during Christmas and New Year's break, I would be awake half or *all* the night, every night, typing this book (not to mention what I got done during the day).

On May 10, 2023, Vanguard's Graduate Education Department hosted their annual Teacher Education Advisory Council (TEAC) Banquet. This big, momentous, cordial event was where we were officially declared "teachers," versus "student teachers." We had *officially* completed the Teaching Credential Program.

I ran into past classmates and professors there, including a couple of professors I had not met in person yet, since a couple of the courses were on Zoom. A lot of Mentor Teachers and University Supervisors attended as well.

A month later I was interviewed for Vanguard's *Graduate Education Department's Podcast*, "Education for Love and Wisdom," hosted by the director. I was on episode 1 of season 2, which premiered on September 11, 2023.

–56–
BEGINNING THE MASTER'S PROGRAM

Toward the end of the credential program, a couple of people from the Graduate Program in Education (a professor of the Master's program and the department's Program Coordinator) came in and talked with us about the Master's program. They told us about the trek through the Master's Program and that we had two routes to choose from: a two-semester route or a three-semester route. The three-semester route was to start in January and last until May 2024.

I expressed my interest in starting immediately, but I had to discuss things with the Program Coordinator first, which I did on December 14 right after subbing fifth grade at Paularino Elementary. That meeting further solidified my decision, and he later enrolled me in the classes.

Three days after receiving a math credential, I was back in class at Vanguard University for a master's degree, traveling in the three-semester route. My first class was in the same room where I took the unit-design course in the previous semester. Now, I was taking a curriculum-design course. The class typically lasted for three and a half hours, one evening per week for eight weeks.

On this first day, I became a research partner with another student. Throughout the semester, research partners discussed things together during class and did a project at the end. We looked into curriculum critiquing, unpacking the standards, neuroscience, and more. I critiqued the McGraw Hill Illustrative Mathematics curriculum that I used throughout student teaching.

Required was another UbD Unit, but a more thorough one, culminating with a presentation at the end. In my credential program, I chose Unit 4 of the McGraw Hill curriculum. For this class, I chose Unit 6. Here is where I had to unpack the standards, produce my enduring understanding and essential questions, create a performance assessment with its corresponding transfer goals, create a rubric, calendarize the unit, and plan any seven of the lessons in detail.

I (relatively quickly) breezed through most of that, impressing my professor, since it was fresh in my mind.

After the presentation, the professor said, "I can really tell how passionate you are in your field."

Eight students were in the class. One of them was a classmate of mine back in the fall of 2021. He is now a math teacher teaching at Costa Mesa High School, utilizing the same McGraw Hill curriculum that I student taught out of. I asked him to keep me in mind if he ever needed a substitute.

Another classmate was an English teacher at Newport Harbor High School. I told him that I went there as a student. One day, I subbed for a chemistry teacher. Throughout the day, I would go around the several buildings to say hello to my former teachers. I found his class and thought I would say hi to him. Later, he told us in class that he got confused when he saw me. "Is it time for class at Vanguard now?" he questioned himself.

I always thought it would be fascinating if I got to sub for the couple of classmates who were teachers in NMUSD, and then one day it happened! I got to sub for that English teacher. Two of the three classes that day were filled with freshman, so most of them were really happy to see me, remembering me from Ensign. I would not have subbed English otherwise, but I could not resist.

In March, my professor emailed me saying that I was going to receive a 100 percent in that class, telling me that I should be very proud of my work.

The other class was Current Issues in Education, which was quite . . . *interesting.* We explored several theories and philosophies of education, looking at epistemology (theory of knowledge), metaphysics (philosophy of reality), axiology (philosophical study of value), and other things I had never heard of.

We explored several chapters of current issues in the education world, writing about both sides of the argument, and choosing which one aligned with our educational philosophy. Additionally, we delivered a couple of presentations.

We also began our research by creating an Annotated Bibliography. In the beginning, we had to produce independent variables to lead to our dependent variable. What intervention do we want (the independent variable) to help each student in academic achievement and disposition (the dependent variable)? I chose to focus on game-based learning, authoring a three chapter action research proposal based on a quasi-experimental design that fall.

All in all, it is a *ton* of work! Each class had a few books to read, of which we had selected chapters to write about. Each paper to write was usually a few pages long. The Annotated Bibliography required fifteen sources, and each source required a couple of pages to write about.

As a person with Autism, reading is a struggle, which I elucidated in my first book. I was able to find a digital version. That way, I could listen to it and follow along, which was incredibly helpful to me and my success. Using digital copies was something that I started doing years prior.

About a month and a half in, I was still dealing with a *lot* of work. I was not even a full-time teacher yet, but rather substituting almost every day. On top of that, I still had Royal Rangers on Tuesday nights, youth at Lighthouse on Wednesday nights, band rehearsal almost every Thursday night and early Sunday mornings, and worship on late Sunday mornings.

Simultaneously, I keep up with my daily posts all across social media to encourage the world and arrange opportunities to speak. I knew that this semester was just the beginning. One of my professors showed me what I called a "book" that I would have to write for my research. I had one "book" to write per semester for the next two semesters. On top of that, there were extensive summer research assignments, including multiple books to read and papers to write.

With all of that said, I divulged with a lot of faculty members, family, friends, friends on Facebook, and all of my classmates in the curriculum-design course that I was considering taking an additional year to substitute. In this manner, I can have more focus on all the research and writing.

After class on the evening when I gave my thoughts, the classmate who taught at Newport Harbor told me, "I believe you'd be making a wise decision if you take a year to sub." He then began to whisper, "It was *grueling* with all that I had to do *and* be a teacher at the same time." He was one of the classmates who was almost finished with the program.

I soon solidified my choice, believing it to be the wisest. In this manner, I will probably come out of the program knowing and benefiting more. This also came by accepting my limitations to Autism but not allowing it to stop me from my end goal.

~57~

ADVENTURES IN SUBSTITUTE TEACHING

There are *so many* adventures in substitute teaching that I cannot fit all of them inside this book, unfortunately. I therefore chose some special highlights in my journey to write about within these concluding chapters. If you would like to watch my adventures, I have a subseries in my YouTube playlist "Journey to Becoming a Teacher." The subseries is named "Adventures in Substitute Teaching," of which I have produced over 35 episodes so far (and counting, as of publishing this book).

On November 28, I was back at Whittier Elementary, subbing third grade. It was one of the best and most respectful classes that I have ever subbed for to date. The students were very motivated to learn. One of them recognized me; she was the younger sister of one of the AVID students at Ensign.

There was a moment that I counted as victorious, to an extent. As a person with Autism, I cannot read well, especially aloud, unless, of course, I am *very* familiar with what I am reading. Sometimes I find the audio on YouTube for students to listen to. On this day, I could not. Thus, I pre-read the chapter while the students were out playing. As I was reading out loud to the students, it was almost flawless. I kept hearing soft chatter while I read, however, but I soon realized that students practice reading *with* the teacher, which I thought was a neat strategy. (Throughout the remainder of the school year, I periodically had to read aloud from a book, but I kept improving in this skill.)

That night, I accepted a position to substitute a math class at TeWinkle Middle School. It would be the first time subbing there. I was ecstatic and emailed the teacher saying that I had just completed student teaching math. However, he was actually teaching Technology and Design/Modeling electives this year. I still felt up to the challenge and got several envelopes ready for one of my magic tricks.

Throughout the day subbing at TeWinkle, here and there, students took me up on my offer to help in math. However, each period was a loquacious bunch. A couple of the periods did not earn the magic trick, consequently. Other periods ran out of time, so I gave a little juggling act instead.

One of the students was so impressed by the tricks that he asked to film me during lunch. I told him that he had to ask the principal. The principal was all right with it as long as he got my permission. He recorded me doing a few magic tricks and was eager to show his family. He told me that day, "You're my second favorite sub."

Also at lunch, a student wanted a picture with me, knowing that I am a YouTuber.

This day had a "first" for me. It was the first time I subbed where there was an assembly.

During Nutrition, as I was walking back to the classroom, I suddenly hear, "Kenslow!"

I looked up, wondering who would know me. It was a student from first period, so I thought, thankfully, *Okay, good. I must've made some form of an impact, being the first time at this school.*

To my surprise, some students pointed me out as the person who juggled at Rea Elementary in the past. (I continued to substitute at TeWinkle a few times throughout this school year. The students got more and more excited to have me as their sub each time. One time, students walked in before first period to say hi for a few moments. Another time, a student gifted me with a drawing he had made for me.)

Afterward, I went over to Ensign because one of the math teachers requested that I sub for her that Thursday and Friday. I walked in and she explained everything that I would be teaching to her eighth graders and honors seventh graders. I felt so honored to do this.

Walking back to the parking lot where my ride was, a couple of eighth graders saw me.

One of them said, "Mr. Kenslow! I thought you left. I didn't get to say 'Good-bye.'" He was another person I used to mentor at Royal Rangers before COVID.

I said that I did, but that I am coming back later that week.

The other asked, "Can I get a picture with you?"

"If you want," I said. "I was just subbing at TeWinkle, and a student there asked for the same thing."

"You're popular," the former Royal Ranger said.

I returned to Ensign on December 1. Periods one and three were the eighth-grade math classes and on these two days, I taught on systems of linear equations. Period two was her prep period and on the first day, there was an evacuation drill during that time.

While walking out there, I ran into a teacher who taught the skills class during seventh period, wherein I tutored students during the end of my student teaching. "Hey, Mr. Kenslow," she said. "All my students are saying, 'We miss Mr. Kenslow and all of his math tutoring.'"

That was quite reassuring to me. Later, one student walked by and said that his friend was deeply sad that I left.

The last three periods were Enhanced Math for seventh graders. The first day, I got to teach a McGraw Hill lesson about equations, graphs, and real-life context. It really brought me back to my Mentor Teacher's classroom. On the second day, it was just independent reviewing. All the students appreciated my teaching and tricks.

On day two, an eighth-grade student raised his hand in the middle of my teaching, asking, "Can you teach here every day?" Some of the Enhanced Math students said that they wanted me to teach them when they got to eighth grade.

The next Monday was the first of two times I got to sub at Corona del Mar Middle and High School during this academic year.

After signing in, I entered a history classroom to say hi to my former World History and Geography teacher from Ensign. He marveled at the picture of he and I from fifteen years prior, noting that he did not have black hair anymore.

Throughout the day subbing a French class, I got to help a little bit of math and even Chemistry. I always try to play music as students walk in. Being December, I could finally play the great Christmas songs, which is partly what I live for every year. This continued from here until Christmas break.

A few people recognized me. One used to be a student at Ensign for whom I had subbed. Another was in the youth group at Lighthouse where I interned. And another said, "You're one of my favorite YouTubers. Can I get a photo with you?"

Later that week, I was subbing a fourth-grade class at Newport Heights Elementary. It was one of the best fourth-grade classes I ever subbed for, quiet and respectful. As I was teaching the math lesson, the students were dead silent and on task. They were fully participating, and it brought me back to my student teaching days. Afterward, I taught them math shortcuts. I later said to the teacher that I would not be surprised if any of them would end up in Enhanced Mathematics. In fact, one of them had an older brother whom I student taught.

During my lunch break, I went to juggle for two first-grade classes who were gathered in one classroom. My former third-grade teacher was not there at that time, but his student teacher (my now-former classmate) was in charge. Another person who was my classmate was there too.

I was so excited to be a substitute here, as well as a volunteer. That is my daily motivation, putting joy and smiles on people's faces, helping them out in their academics, and motivating them to succeed in life.

The next day, I went to Davis Magnet School for the first time. This school emphasizes STEM. Several years prior, a lot of the Discovery Rangers attended this school. On this day, I was subbing sixth grade. I ran into two students who were currently Discovery Rangers at my outpost. I also ran into another student teacher who used to be a classmate of mine.

Once again, students were diligent, silent during the math quiz, respectful, and baffled by the magic tricks and juggling at the end. I also taught them math shortcuts. There was an aide there throughout the day for a student. She was the aide to a person I went to school with back at Newport Heights. Small world. She helped with the reading portion since there was not an audiobook.

I was very glad to be there, for I had been very impressed by this remarkable school for quite a while. I had been following it on Twitter for several years up to this point. It was recognized as a National Blue Ribbon School in 2021. Unfortunately, I could not meet the principal after all these years, but I told the assistant principal about myself and my willingness to volunteer as a speaker, motivator, and juggler. In fact, in almost every school I subbed at, I got to meet and speak with the principal about what I am willing to do at my expense.

While I am still waiting, I, in the meantime, take advantage of my juggling performance at the end of the day. I emphasize my juggling analogy about not giving up, even if things drop in life.

For the rest of the academic year, I always wanted to return to Davis Magnet. Strangely enough, unlike any other school across the district, I actually accepted five positions ahead of time within the course of a month. Before each day arrived, each assignment was cancelled, one by one.

Speaking about a small world, the next Monday, I subbed sixth grade at Mariners Elementary. I ran into the same assistant principal from Davis. We were both astonished to see each other, causing both of us to do a double take. Furthermore, the P.E. teacher is the father of a student from Ensign (whom I student taught Enhanced Math in my BST Semester) and his twin brother (whom I helped out in AVID). Later, in 2023, I subbed for his daughter at that school, who was in third grade.

The day after that was nostalgically special. I accepted a sixth-grade substitute position at Paularino Elementary School, the school that I attended from kindergarten to second grade. I relived a plethora of memories, which I expressed in a sentimental video that I made, including a myriad of pictures and home videos from back in the day.

The classroom I subbed in was at the same part of the campus where the old building was, in which I spent first and second grade. I told the office personnel and students about it, showing them a couple of pictures from back in the day. As I was walking the students diagonally to the multipurpose room for lunch, I could not help but reflect on how twenty years prior, that was the same itinerary in which my teacher led us.

Afterward, I walked by my kindergarten classroom that is still there. A person thought it was neat that I was a student in that classroom but notified me that it is now a state preschool. The day was surreal to say the least.

However, I had a humorous start. Being the first time subbing there, I probably did not realize the bell schedule, if there was a warning bell or not, or exactly where the students line up at. Suddenly, I got this instinctive feeling inside. I rushed out of the classroom and around the portables. Standing there was the last class to be picked up. *My class!*

They all began cheering because I remembered to pick them up. I was very apologetic. They were not waiting out there for a long time, just to say. I thought the bell I heard was a five-minute warning bell.

Later, the McGraw Hill math lesson about surface area and volume went well and, as in many cases, brought me back to student teaching, since the students were respectful and actively engaged. Afterward, I was having fun helping students in their independent practice, so much so that I actually lost track of time. Suddenly, students realized that lunch was starting.

One of the students in this class knew that I was an author, speaking of which, I mentioned Paularino five times in my first book. This day was definitely one for the books but was nearly reversed the next day. (Sort of.)

When I got home, there was a position available to sub fifth grade at Paularino. As I was considering, I quickly read the note. It said that if this particular person runs out, then call the office immediately. That was my first red flag, but I decided to accept the position anyway.

That evening was the Royal Rangers Christmas party. I was not intending to juggle for every single person, but I happened to have accidentally brought my big juggling supplies, so I figured, *Why not?*

The next morning, December 14, 2022, I relived some more memories, which I told on YouTube. Speaking about YouTube, as I was walking toward the office, one student kept looking at me, already having heard about me, eventually asking, "Are you really a YouTuber?"

"Yes." I smiled right before entering the office to sign in.

This time, at the start of school, I knew to go outside *when* the bell rang. No warning bell. The day previous, it was easy to locate my class since it was the only class standing out there, but now, there were tons of classes. I did not know which one was the fifth-grade class I was subbing for.

I asked a student who looked to be in fifth grade who his teacher was. When it was not the teacher I was subbing for, I asked him where I could find the class. That was when he started to laugh nervously, "Oh no." Covering his face with one hand, he proceeded to point in the direction with the other hand, nonverbally telling me where to go.

"Uh, thank you," I said and smiled, knowing that I was given my next red flag.

I introduced myself to the class and endeavored to get them in line as straight and silent as possible. When we got inside the classroom, it took a little while for some of the students to stop dancing and to start listening. Some students had their desks isolated across the room, a couple of which were placed on the other side of a room divider.

I told them that I attended this school for three years one score ago, and that I had many incentives throughout the day if they showed good behavior.

At one point, the intercom went on and announced a lockdown drill. I happened to have known about the drill for a day at this point, since the sub binder contained all the dates for drills.

Enter the nightmare. (I say that loosely because I am sure that the students are kind in heart and simply need extra discipline).

Some of the students could not stop talking or yelling out. One was dancing on a table, and another had a chair (or some piece of furniture) over his head, running around the room. I kept calmly telling them that they must remain silent, but it only lasted two or three seconds.

After quite a long while, I thought I heard light knocks. I peeked out the blinds and noticed doors opened. I was in a quandary. I then noticed a person walking over, and the next thing I heard, somebody was unlocking our classroom door from the outside. They got the class to line up and walk out.

Gobsmacked, I told them that I never heard the announcement saying to evacuate. We walked outside in a line. Every student and staff were staring at us. Let me tell you, I felt that this was a walk of shame!

One of the ladies asked me how many students I had. I could not remember what happened one minute ago, much less the census of the class, but I gave an estimate based on the best of my memory. Let us just say that we eventually figured it out.

I held up the green sign and the principal dismissed everybody. After walking back to our classrooms and while I tried to talk with them, in walked the principal.

And let us just say that she got the entire class—the class that had just been hollering and jumping up and down—to be dead silent. She gave them a long, much-needed-to-be-heard lecture, as well as a revocation of their recess. Instead of playing outside, they had to write a paper based on what happened and what *should* have happened. We were the last class out in the field, and she had to hold everyone out there until we came. She was appalled that they treated me, a "guest teacher," in this manner and that they were so loud, that I could not even hear the all-call to evacuate.

Shortly thereafter, during recess, I felt this sensation enveloping me. *I belong here today!* Not all students were misbehaving. On the contrary, quite a few were respectful and even helped me out. However, the students who were not behaving well, I believe they were kind in heart but just needed more discipline and encouragement. They were not necessarily rude to me in terms of being hurtful or hateful. I believe in the potential of *all* those students, including the misbehaving ones. Therefore, I worked extra hard.

"Listen, guys," I said before a big math lesson on rounding numbers. "I'm giving you three warnings, after which I cannot show you this magic trick. And listen, guys. I *believe* in you! I *believe* that you can do this. I *know* you can do this. Just discipline yourself and try the hardest that you can possibly do."

I delivered the math lesson, having so much joy inside. This was an opportunity for me to take such a class for one day and put some light into it. (I am not saying that the teacher does not do that, but I counted this as an opportunity to be an additional source of motivation and optimism.)

I only gave two warnings, but we got through all of it. During many parts, they were completely silent. I had to give extra support to a couple of them, reminding them to exercise self-discipline, which quickly prompted them to apologize and comply. Everybody, including the misbehaving students, wanted to see the trick, which was converting three pieces of rope (six ends) into one long piece of rope (two ends).

At lunchtime, I formally introduced myself to the principal, telling her how the day had been so far. I told her that I believe the students are good in heart, not totally being rude or mean. They were mostly silent during the math lesson since I offered an incentive. I was thankful that I accepted the position.

The principal thought that that was admirable of me, telling me that this class "is the hardest, most challenging class in the entire school." A couple of moments later, she welcomed me to Paularino.

"This is probably my three-hundredth time here," I responded, unsure of the exact number, which was probably a couple hundred more than that.

She gave me a peculiar look before I told her that I was a student there for three years, showing her some old photos on my phone. She was fascinated by how the school used to look back in the day as I was describing it to her.

"Well, welcome *back*," she said, smiling.

"Thanks. By the way, do you by any chance have like ten or fifteen seconds?" I asked shyly, before introducing myself as an author and sharing my eagerness to *volunteer* doing an all-school assembly someday soon.

"Sure, I'll keep you in mind as the year goes on," she said.

By the end of the day, the fifth-grade students worked hard and earned the juggling performance at the end. This time, I really, *really* emphasized my juggling analogy about not giving up. I believe that they got the message.

I was very proud of the class. Not 100 percent perfect, but much better than that morning. They, including some of the misbehaving ones, thought that I was an excellent teacher. One expressed complete sadness that the day was over and that I would no longer be his sub, pretending to cry. A student also gifted me a holographic ruler.

This was also the first time I was asked if I could be referred to as "Mr. K." (For months after this day, including the next day, students started asking me the same thing. I also began telling students that it is Ken-*slow*. Not Ken-*fast*, but Ken-*slow*. Ironically, I used to be one of the fastest runners.)

When I subbed at Paularino in the future, their teacher told me, "They're all asking me to take a day off so that you can sub for them again."

The next day, I was subbing at California Elementary for the first time. Students and staff alike remembered me from juggling back on June 9, happy to see me again. I immediately ran into another substitute whom I met at Ensign as I was nearing the end of my student teaching days.

As I was setting up and getting prepared to sub for the fourth-grade class, listening to old-time, classic Christmas music, in walked three students.

"Uh, you're the sub?" one of them asked while the other two were trying to outdance each other.

"Yes."

"Well, just to let you know, this class is really loud and crazy."

Oh boy, I thought as I smiled and replied, "Uh, thanks for the warning."

"Yeah, and they walk on the ceiling and everything."

"Thanks for the warning. What are the two boys' names standing behind you?"

She told me and those were the two students I had just read about in the sub notes, telling me to watch out for them. All three of them left.

I did it yesterday; I will do it again today. I took a deep breath.

I soon picked up the students and walked them to class. I stood before them at the front of the classroom with the thought that it might be another challenge. I was armed with all my SEL strategies.

I began speaking. *The students were dead silent.* Respectful. Listening. Even during the post-unit math assessment, they were mostly silent and raising their hands to ask questions.

Sure, it got rambunctious a couple of times, but overall, they were good. By fortuity, while I was juggling at the end, giving my juggling analogy, a person from the nurse's office was there. I later found out that she was extremely inspired by my message. I told her that I spoke and performed at a small assembly there in June. I was wanting to talk with the principal about me coming back to do an assembly for the entire school. I later emailed the principal and she agreed to help set that up someday. Likewise with the principal of the nearby TeWinkle Middle School.

Earlier, during recess, a student ran up to me, saying that I subbed for her brother at TeWinkle. She also said that she watched my YouTube video about it.

The next week was a nightmare in terms of trying to find a job. On Monday, I texted my former Mentor Teacher asking if I could come and volunteer in the skills classes. After communicating back and forth, she said, "Come on in!"

Enthusiastic, I went over to Ensign and began helping with the skills classes. In third period, I went over to the seventh-grade science teacher's classroom. His student teacher (my former classmate) was there. Later, the teacher came in and absolutely marveled at the fact that I was volunteering my entire time to help students, due to not getting a sub position.

Teachers and students alike were happy to see me back, extraordinarily thankful for my help and willingness. In some of the classes, I got to help students with homework or with studying for an assessment, but in other classes, I just sat there bored to death. Still, it was the passion to help students that drove me. I spoke with all the teachers to confirm that I have an open door. That way, I did not always have to text my former Mentor Teacher.

I returned to Ensign for the next two days since there were no sub jobs available for me. However, that Tuesday, the students in first period did not need any help. This was because they just took the quiz that I helped them study for. I went to the library since there was nowhere else to go. I asked the librarian, who was very happy to see me again, if there was still after-school tutoring. She said that there was but asked me if I wanted to help organize books in the meantime.

"Sure," I said.

For the next few periods, not only did I help organize hundreds of books, but I learned parts of the Dewey Decimal System. In second and fourth period, an English class came in, so I checked in returned books and checked out new books. Many were happy to see me but were probably wondering why a math teacher became a librarian.

The latter half of the day was all math, including after-school tutoring. During seventh period, as I was helping the student who always wanted my help, the teacher got a phone call.

"Mr. Kenslow," she said. "I'm sorry to interrupt, but you are asked to go upstairs to the lounge. Two boys need math help."

To the lounge I went. It felt neat that a person in the office knew that I was on campus, found out which room I was in during that period, and knew that I would probably be the best person to help those students in math. One of those students, just to say, remembered me from Rea Elementary.

The next day, I saw a student whom I taught math for as a sub in the past. He asked me, "When will you sub for my math teacher again?"

Later in March 2023, I got to teach another math lesson for my former Mentor Teacher's class. It was the final lesson of Unit 6. In fact, I observed the teacher teach that same lesson fifty-three weeks prior to the day.

All the office staff were happy to see me back.

"Oh, Matthew's on campus," said a seventh-grade science teacher that morning.

When I told one of the security personnel that I was teaching another math lesson, he said, "Right up your alley."

Suddenly, the storage space was used up on the teacher's iPad, insofar as not being able to write anymore. It was a good thing that I caught that before second period began. I went up and made copies to use under the document cam. Sure enough, after starting to teach second period, the iPad would not allow me to write anymore, so I switched to the document cam.

As I opened the door to both math classes, all the students were both surprised and happy to see me again teaching another lesson. It was the same with the AVID classes and all the other students throughout the day who saw me.

It was phenomenal getting to teach another math lesson. I told them that they will have fun in Unit 7 about Quadratic Equations and ultimately using the famous Quadratic Formula.

Throughout this entire academic year of subbing, there have been several students who complimented me. Some said that I was a good teacher and others enjoyed all my magic tricks. I believe that all my rewards gave students a boost of motivation to do good and learn, as each class worked together as a team. I had been asked by elementary school students if I could be their math teacher once they reach middle school. Several teachers, principals (and other administrators) throughout the district were always happy to see me walk in.

On a couple of days, I served two half-days consecutively. The first time, it was at the same school. The second time, it was at two different schools. Some days, I got to serenade students on the piano. Once, I was subbing elementary music at Newport Heights Elementary, doing live musical chairs, so to speak.

I have had a number of "duh" moments and blunders while subbing too, many of which are told sparsely throughout my subseries on YouTube. For instance, at a few schools, I could not find the classroom, sometimes walking around in freezing-cold weather. Another time, at Kaiser Elementary, I could not find my students after recess. Suddenly, I heard, "Over here! Over here!" and there they were in a line far away, waving me over.

Out of the blue, I sometimes received a surprise card or drawing from students. Once, I was subbing sixth grade at Killybrooke for the second time out of three subbing for this particular class. When I arrived, the teacher told me that her students were so happy to hear that I was coming back. Later, one of those students handed me a folded piece of paper, saying that I was the best sub ever. Nearly thirty students signed their name on it.

Something to note about this set of students, however, is that it could be a challenging one, which I was told. Upon hearing the positive reception from students after the first time I subbed that class, the teacher requested me back twice. Students have been nice, silent during tests, and engaged with the material.

One of the student's parents ran the PTA/ELAC Instagram page for Killybrooke. I was thanked "for bringing some extra joy to their day when it could otherwise be extra stressful not having their normal teacher." The daughter enjoyed the day and was impressed with my tricks and juggling.

After the third time subbing that class, the school's Instagram page told me that I am "so wonderful with them" and that I am "an inspiration to students AND STAFF!"

—58—

TWO REMARKABLY INCREDIBLE ENCOUNTERS WITH THE BOARD PRESIDENT

On January 26, I subbed at Adams Elementary for the first time. It was not my first time being there. My former fifth-grade teacher became the principal there, and I visited him a couple of times. He had since moved to Harbor View Elementary in Newport Beach. (I later subbed Elementary Science twice at Harbor View and saw him both times.)

I was subbing sixth grade on this day. Most of the students knew my former fifth-grade teacher. A lot of great things occurred, but while I was teaching the math lesson (my specialty) in the middle of the day, I heard one or two students say, "It's the principal."

Two ladies walked in the classroom. *Pressure's on*, I thought. I waved and smiled. I continued to teach, but almost as if I were being scrutinized, which I knew was unlikely. After a couple of moments that seemed like several minutes, both ladies smiled and left.

During lunch, I walked to the office to find out if anything was happening that I needed to be aware of, but the principal was in a meeting. After I got back to the classroom, the phone rang. It was the principal. She told me that the new board president of NMUSD was checking out the school.

I was gobsmacked. I did not know that the board president had changed. (The last one, I substituted for all of her children at Newport Heights and Ensign; one of them, I student taught Enhanced Mathematics.)

"Nothing was going on. She was just observing different classrooms," the principal told me.

"Oh, okay."

"But I wanted to let you know that I was very impressed with your math lesson."

"Oh yeah." My entire day felt brighter.

"Yes. I liked what I saw of it, but especially when you were getting one of the quiet boys to speak and participate."

"It's my pleasure."

"Well, welcome to Adams Elementary, and thank you for being here!"

A couple of students in that class needed additional support to stay focused. I recognized that right away. Therefore, when this particular boy kept mumbling, I called on him and asked what the next step would be, redirecting him to stay focused. That was when the principal and board president were in the room.

Whenever I sub around and get to teach (especially a math lesson), I pull out everything I learned and implemented while student teaching, including the informal assessment of asking students to show me a thumbs up, middle, or down before moving on.

During lunchtime, one of the aides (who was also present in the classroom) said to me, "I really liked your math lesson."

"Well, after six hundred and two point five hours of student teaching Enhanced Mathematics, I love teaching math lessons."

After school, as I was returning the key, one of the office ladies said, "Thank you so much for helping us today. The principal wanted me to let you know that she was really happy with you and that hopefully we will be seeing you again. Can you write down your name, and we'll give it to the office manager?"

"Okay." I wrote down my information. "Is she still around?"

"She's in an IEP meeting for the next hour. She wanted to let you know that she was really happy with the care you showed to everyone in the class. She was really glad that you were able to help a student."

I felt very joyous inside.

A couple of moments later, I met the assistant principal, officially. He happened to know my former fifth-grade teacher and alternates between Adams and Harbor View as an assistant principal. Small world.

"Do you have a card that I could give the principal and tell him that you were here?" he asked.

The only card I had was the one for my book.

After talking about my former teacher for a couple of minutes, we began talking about my book. The assistant principal asked me if I was part of a training, because he said that he had seen my book somewhere. After a few moments thinking aloud, we pinpointed the HALO Benefit. He said that he would relay the message to the principal and my former fifth-grade teacher about my willingness to volunteer at an all-school assembly, similar to what he had seen at the HALO Benefit.

(The next time I subbed at Adams, the principal and I discussed it, and she said that she would bring it up to the leadership meeting that was going to be conducted the following day. Also, as I was leaving that same day, one of the other office ladies leaned forward, looked me in the eyes, and said, "Please come back. Keep your eyes open.")

The very next day, on January 27, I subbed at Eastbluff Elementary for the first time for fourth grade. After lunch, there was virtually nothing I could do, due to P.E. and science.

By lunch and after P.E., every person in that class was chanting out loud, "Best sub! Best sub!" over and over again. They enjoyed the magic and juggling tricks so much.

They were a great class, as well as troopers, I would say. There were four short quizzes back-to-back for the first hour after flag deck (one math, one reading, and two vocabulary quizzes). The only rambunctiously hectic moment was pulling out the bonus ball in a jar. All the others had their class number on it. Upon being pulled, they all got up and did a chair-train conga-line.

During lunch, I went inside the central part of the building where a few teachers were eating. I expressed desire to help if needed, especially in math, since I had only ten minutes with the students after lunch and nothing else to do.

They suggested that I help the teacher grade those quizzes, which I ultimately did (most of them). However, one of the fifth-grade teachers remembered a boy struggling with ratios and long division. She thought that I could explain it better than she could. Thus, while my class was in P.E., I tutored that fifth grader with his math in that central room.

The moment I was done, in walked the principal with the new board president whom I saw the day prior!

"Boy, you really get around, don't you?" the board president said, smiling.

"Yes, indeed. And this is my first time subbing here too."

While I continued to talk with the president, the principal talked with the boy I was tutoring. "That was a very great math lesson you did yesterday. The principal over there told me that you got a boy to talk, and he never talks."

At that point, the principal of Eastbluff looked up at me and said, "I was just talking with this boy you were just helping, and he told me that you really helped him a lot."

Later on, I returned to that fifth-grade teacher to give back her math paper. She told me that her student understands a lot more math now and that he was greatly helped by me.

"It is my joy and my pleasure," I replied and smiled. I later got to sub for her class, and I was told that the teacher was happy to see that I accepted the position.

Previously, I ran into that principal in her office to introduce myself. She said that she would take a look at my book and see if I could volunteer in an assembly someday.

After school, another person (who was probably a PTA member) told me, "You're really good at this. I walked in a couple of times, and everybody was really silent."

Again, there were patches within the seven hours where it got noisy, but overall, they were very nice. At the end, several of them were begging me, "Can you please, *please* come back and sub for us? You're the best sub."

When I later met the teacher, she said that all her students talked about me when she returned, asking when she will need a sub again.

I shared the stories from these two remarkable days with family, friends, and professors in the Grad Ed Department at Vanguard. The director shared it around the department and asked me if he could share it with an education council, believing that my story would encourage them.

–59–

FINALLY (PART 2)

On Wednesday, February 1, I received an email from the Special Education representative of Chaparral Elementary School in Capistrano Unified. The school was having their annual Ability Awareness Day on February 7. She apologized for the short notice but was wondering if I could be a guest speaker throughout the day.

She heard about me because of a form I submitted in 2020. A person from CUSD reached out to me on Facebook with information on signing up to do assemblies. Thanks a lot to COVID, unfortunately, nobody was having such assemblies. Nearly three years later, she found my information in a binder, and, out of the blue, I received her email.

Enthusiastically, I replied saying that I would be happy to attend, requesting further information and explaining exactly what I do. She replied with the schedule that I would be following. I soon confirmed that I would be there.

On February 7, I arrived at Chaparral Elementary in Ladera Ranch around eight o'clock. The entire school was surrounded by signs about Ability Awareness, kindness, quotes, and such.

I was introduced to a few people and was stationed in the library. Up until the night before, I thought that I was going from classroom to classroom, but apparently, there were stations throughout the school. The principal walked by, saw me, and introduced herself, happy that I was there.

As I was waiting, several students of the lower grades were silently walking in line to the main assembly. A lot of them saw me and started to smile and wave. I smiled and waved back. As they were returning, they saw me practicing my juggling and were amazed.

From just before nine until just past two, I spoke and juggled for *sixteen* classes. Each class came one at a time, so I delivered the same message sixteen times. Each grade level had four classes, and I juggled for four grade levels. The first set was fifth grade, followed by second, followed by an hour lunch break, followed by third, and concluding with the fourth.

All the students, teachers, the librarian, the PTA, and others were super appreciative of me, kind, listening, and respectful. Once I began talking, everybody was totally silent and eager to hear what I had to say.

"Hello, everybody. My name is Matthew Kenslow. Thank you so much for having me," I said as I started each rotation. "For the next ten minutes, I will hopefully be an encouragement to you guys, as well as an entertainer," I directed attention to my juggling supplies and water bottles for my science demo analogy on the side. "But first, I ask that you take a few moments to hear what I have to say."

I talked about who I am as a person with Autism, the pros and the cons, my personal definition of Autism, and poured out all of my encouragements, including my "Be Number One" encouragement. I delivered my analogies about not giving up and not bottling things up inside, as well as my stance on inclusion and encouragement to be a friend to everybody, thereby making them feel included. I also briefly interjected my math shortcuts and presidential knowledge.

I never allowed Autism to beat me down, as it can easily do to many people. Autism is like an enhancer plugged into our brain, enhancing our perception in life. Living with this burdensome weight on my shoulders is hard, but I have toughed it out and am still bearing through it victoriously. We are not any different from anybody else; it is merely how our minds work. We are all unique and have purpose. I believe that Autism has given me a different lens with which to view the world and that it is really a different ability to live life. I feel thankful for the ability to captivate an audience with entertainment, all while giving them an important message about disability awareness and acceptance.

Summarizing about this day, lest I go on and on, seems to be filled with understatements on how truly phenomenal and special this day had been. At the end, I asked one of the coordinators how many students I had spoken to. She estimated 425.

Before leaving, the aforementioned representative was writing out a check for what I did. I said that when I filled out the form, I offered to do it all at no charge, but she quickly said, "You were worth every penny! You were a hit!"

After talking some more, she said that she will cycle my name around the district for more opportunities. When I got home, I emailed the person who first reached out to me in 2020 and told her all about it. That night, while teaching Royal Rangers, she called and left a message. She said that she heard what "a wonderful, amazing job" I did that day and that *everybody* was quite thankful for me. She said that she will continue to share my information too.

This has been my dream come true! Everybody, again, was extraordinarily nice. Yet, no matter where I go (even in another district), students ask how tall I am. The representative later described me as "educational, informative, and impactful," and said that I "truly changed lives that day."

Three days prior was the HALO Benefit at Costa Mesa High School. By fortuity, I ran into a trustee of the NMUSD school board, the one who emailed me in August, inviting me to come to a board meeting and introduce myself to all the members. She introduced me to a couple of her friends; they all enjoyed my HALO performance. I talked to her about my zeal to volunteer at assemblies at every school.

Later, she forwarded me an email from the Harbor Council PTA, whom she contacted. They said that the message was very timely. They were about to provide their PTA presidents with information in March; she said that she will definitely share my information with the leadership.

Furthermore, there is a Royal Ranger at my outpost who was currently in sixth grade, attending College Park Elementary in Irvine Unified. After a Royal Rangers meeting one night, he had me write down my contact information to give to the principal, in hopes that I could come juggle and speak about my Autism. Shortly after, the principal emailed me, and we started discussing an opportunity for me to come on by.

The big day was April 27, 2023. I juggled and spoke for an estimated six hundred students within three assemblies (twenty to thirty minutes each), broken down by sets of grade levels. By coincidence, the street name that College Park was on is Chaparral Drive, and my preschool in NMUSD was named College Park. They told me that they get calls from NMUSD parents by mistake all the time.

"You should start charging for your assemblies," the principal said to me afterward while handing me a jar filled with a few gifts of appreciation. After each of the three assemblies, she told the students to discuss what they learned upon returning to class. One of the psychologists told me that I almost brought one of the adults present to tears who was inspired by my message.

The principal and school psychologists began to circulate my name throughout IUSD and beyond. The mother of that Royal Ranger boy who helped make this a reality told me that the principal sent an email to everyone, describing me as an "angel" who came on campus.

When I returned home that day, I received an email from the principal of Greentree Elementary (IUSD), requesting me to do an assembly during the following school year. Later, a person from Meadow Park Elementary (IUSD) reached out to me via Instagram, wanting me to do an assembly over there too, which occurred later on September 7, when I did four assemblies for approximately 600 students total, Pre-K to sixth grade.

I was so appreciative of these opportunities and the fact that I can help change lives. Nevertheless, I knew that I still had to do my part in circulating my name across the county, since I believe that I will eventually be in every school of OCDE doing these assemblies (not to mention private schools, churches, et cetera).

I therefore emailed nearly every single council president of the Fourth Council PTA. Each council president presided over all the PTA presidents of the schools in their council.

Only one got back with me, the Garden Grove Council. I was able to speak to the PTA presidents of Garden Grove about who I am, my message, and what I had done in the past. One person invited me to the 4th District PTA Vendor Fair at the OCDE headquarters. For four and a half hours, on May 20, I was a vendor, juggling for passersby. I made connections with dozens of people from across the county. Some marveled that I was willing to do everything for free.

Moreover, Strategic Kids reached out to me via Instagram and invited me to speak and juggle at a chess tournament in Laguna Hills, which I did. One boy over there even recognized me from YouTube. I later returned to juggle at a small carnival at their facility. They said that they could help me get more opportunities for speaking and juggling throughout Orange County during the summer.

Back in January, a professor at Vanguard University found me on LinkedIn and reached out to me. We sat in her office, and I discussed what I believe my calling is. She began helping me find opportunities to volunteer as a juggler and speaker. Consequently, on April 6, I had the opportunity to do so at an Autism Awareness event at Vanguard's Needham Chapel, as well as be a panelist answering questions.

To conclude this chapter, I want to say that in the fall of 2023, I began doing many more assemblies, encouraging staff and students who were beyond words. Usually teachers say that my message is so timely and important. Sometimes they follow up with me to say how beneficial the post-assembly discussion was with their students back in their classrooms or while talking with other teachers.

After doing six assemblies for about 625 students at Ladera Ranch Elementary (CUSD), the assistant principal was exceedingly impressed with my assemblies, later noting my ability to modify what I say and do for the younger students, when I get right to the point to maintain their attention span. Soon he introduced me to the principal at Laguna Niguel Elementary (CUSD). Nearly a month later, I did three assemblies there for about four hundred students; they greatly endorsed my book. I signed three of them while there.

The Harbor Council PTA eventually got back with me. On November 6, I spoke before the entire council for twenty minutes at a meeting in the NMUSD board room. I gave them an outline of what I say and do, while bringing in my juggling, science demonstration, and new card tricks that I use as analogies as well. At the end, the council president had tears in her eyes and many PTA presidents were moved. I soon got in communication with setting up assemblies at College Park (which took place nine days later), California, Andersen, and Mariners. It was already established to do an assembly at Harbor View, as well, later that month.

One of the PTA members asked if I were willing to speak to the adults, including parents too. I said yes. Just prior to this, on November 1, I spoke to the bus drivers and monitors of NMUSD at Lincoln Elementary, being invited by my former bus driver that I had not seen in over twenty years. I also got to speak to my entire church, Lighthouse Community, for forty minutes on September 17.

This all had been a dream for years, and I believe that one of my true callings is finally coming to fruition.

-60-

What Substitute Teaching Means to Me

For me, it is my joy, passion, motivation, and pleasure to serve as a substitute teacher. Knowing that students are motivated to learn and that I am effectively getting students, especially shy students, to engage and participate in the lessons is why I want to be a teacher,. I also enjoy rewarding them with all of the incentives that I brought throughout the day.

Rarely, I get to see my former teachers. Sometimes, I subbed for elementary school teachers who taught people that I met at Ensign.

When time permits, I get to teach extra things, from math shortcuts to planespotting. At Eastbluff, when I subbed there for the first time, a student was playing with a plane model during flag deck. I told him that it was a UPS Boeing 747. Being relatively close to John Wayne Airport, tons of jets fly over, so I was pointing them out to a couple of the fourth-grade students, saying, for example, "There's a Delta Boeing 757" or "Southwest Boeing 737."

Other times, over the months, I often interjected humor that I had since elementary school.

"Mr. Kenslow, I'm done. What do I do now?"

"Uh, bust out an invisible ukelele and start jamming."

"How many paragraphs am I supposed to write?"

"Three hundred and fourteen," I joke without blinking.

"What's up, Mr. Kenslow?"

"Um, the sky? The ceiling?"

Several times, whether at the end of the day or seeing students while walking in the neighborhood, I heard, "Mr. Kenslow! You were the best sub," or "You were better than the sub I had today."

One time, I was helping a third grader in rounding numbers for ST Math while subbing at Newport Heights Elementary. It took a couple of tries, but he ultimately understood it for his game. He leaned over with a smile and said, "Thank you for helping me understand."

It is moments like those (and beyond) that warms my heart with joy. It is confirmation to me that I have the ability to motivate either one student or a whole classroom of students. It is confirmation to me that I can teach in such a way that is understandable—not just in solving skills, but that I, as a person with Autism, can effectively communicate to children and teenagers.

Furthermore, whenever I sub at the same school multiple times, several students would wave and/or call out, "Hi, Mr. Kenslow!" Some would come up to me to start a conversation. A couple of times while subbing at Newport Harbor High, I was surrounded by fifteen or twenty freshmen who remembered me from Ensign, many of whom checked to see if I still remembered their birthdays.

Additionally, several teachers and office staff are happy to see me again too. One day, approaching the office of Mariners Elementary, I overheard an office lady tell the other, "Oh, our friend's back." I am thankful to have made such a rapport.

There were times, of course, that were challenging. A few elementary and middle school classrooms were full of loquacious students. However, what always gave me a boost of motivation (soon turning into a boost of joy), was the fact that I was probably called there that day to be a source of encouragement to them, implementing what SEL strategies I know. It soon gave me feelings as if I belonged there that day.

I was subbing a math class at TeWinkle Middle School. I was teaching part of the lesson, but at least half of the students in some of the periods were extremely talkative. A couple of weeks later, on Valentine's Day, I subbed another math class there, teaching a longer lesson. That was the day when I had objects thrown at me for the first time. It happened twice. One missed my face and the other hit the back of my neck. I looked up and both students pretended to be innocent.

I talked to them for a moment, and they denied it, of course. After dealing with students treating me in a not-so-good way, one student looked at me and said, "You're so calm."

At the end of class, I did a little juggling, *really* emphasizing my analogy. What I care more about is that my message of not giving up in life gets across. I believe my message might be remembered longer if it is mixed with the entertainment of juggling.

Again, I started to feel joy and belonging in my position on days like these. I have the opportunity to make a difference (and maybe a life-changing difference) to students, emphasizing how much they have purpose and that I believe in them.

Some people hate school; some hate math. But do not give up! I revealed that I got Cs and Ds in seventh grade, but then I chose to listen to the teacher and tried my best. I got fourteen As and two Bs in eighth grade alone, not to mention As and some Bs all throughout high school. I began believing in myself. At least one student applauded at such a pep talk.

I have the mindset that if difficult stuff like that *does* happen, then this is where I belong. If stuff like that does *not* happen, and all the students behave, then it is still where I belong. I do not really have hard feelings. Ninety-nine to one hundred percent of the students are very kind at heart and simply need an extra person to bring light into their lives by being an encouragement and a person who believes in them.

None of my teachers, commanders, or pastors have ever given up on me, so how can I turn around and give up on anybody else? I simply do not have that mentality. I firmly believe that *anybody* can learn and that everybody has a reason to live here on earth.

The teacher I subbed for on Valentine's Day taught one period of Enhanced Math, and let me tell you, those students had the same assiduous disposition as the students I student taught over at Ensign. I really enjoyed it. TeWinkle is one of many schools where students say, "Hi, Mr. Kenslow," and are excited to see me again.

I also appreciate the sense of humor that a lot of students bring. One student at Paularino (whom I was not subbing for) came up to me and said, "See you tomorrow."

"Um, tomorrow's Saturday."

The student smiled as if saying, *Darn it*, thinking he stumped me.

Other students liked to tell me jokes and riddles.

Throughout subbing, I found that whenever I *had* to read, I felt that I was getting better. I still find myself tripping up on my words at times, but students have been respectful.

A lot of students throughout the district, here and there, would find out that I am an author. One time at Mariners Elementary, a student talked with me about Autism and my book during recess for about fifteen or so minutes. She said that I am really inspiring her as a person with Autism being a substitute teacher. She considered it brave of me that I chose to go out into the world with my book.

One fifth grader whom I subbed for at Kaiser is actually the son of the principal at Newport Heights Elementary. At a later date, I subbed a morning half day at Kaiser for third grade and an afternoon half day at Newport Heights for second grade. Right before I left, the principal pointed at me with eyes lit up and said, "Matthew, you subbed for my son, and he came home that day saying that you are the best sub ever. He really loved that day."

Speaking about that day, subbing at Kaiser for those fifth graders, I truly enjoyed it. It was one of my most favorite days subbing. They were highly respectful, thereby earning all the magic tricks, to which they screamed really loud afterward. Come to think about it, students seem to be getting louder and louder after the climax of the tricks these days. I also got to teach a chemistry lesson about the states of matter, physical changes, chemical changes, et cetera, something that I have been waiting to teach for a decade.

There have been days subbing at Kaiser where I am surrounded by twenty or thirty students, wanting to see a magic trick. I started worrying that admin would rush over, which happened before. Several of the students told me to sub for this teacher or for that teacher. It had gotten so that when students come to class in the morning, they get very excited when they see I am going to be their substitute. Elsewhere in the district, students begin jumping and cheering because they know who I am.

One day at Kaiser, I was walking toward the office during lunch. A teacher walked by and told me, "Everyone is raving about you. They all want you to be their sub."

This actually began happening at other schools too.

Additionally, at a couple of schools, I sometimes overheard students whom I subbed for whisper to my current students, "Oh, you have the best sub. You'll really like him."

There was another special moment at Kaiser. I was subbing a fifth-grade class for the second time. One student asked me if I could sign his copy of my book. To my surprise, he pulled it out of his backpack. With gratitude, I did, and he started showing his friends.

When I substitute at schools for the second or third time, I like introducing myself to the teachers whom I subbed for previously. Whether at California, Mariners, Killybrooke, Harbor View, or wherever, teachers told me that all the students really enjoyed me and wanted me back to sub for them. A couple of teachers requested in advance that I sub for them again, which I usually accept unless I had already committed to another sub position. One teacher, at Mariners, told me that her class saw me while they were walking in line. They pointed me out, saying that I was their favorite sub.

It is all reassuring to me in how much I am making a difference in the lives of thousands of students and faculty. It really helps me believe that I have purpose in this world, along with being a Royal Rangers commander, youth minister, and worship musician, of course. From a person who has Autism and faced a lifetime of discrimination, student and substitute teaching has changed my entire life. I feel more a sense of belonging and acceptance, especially coming out of 2021 with all the numbingly debilitating things that I had to deal with, not to mention all the other depressing things over several years.

As of the publishing of this book, I have subbed at over twenty-five schools of NMUSD out of thirty-three currently. I would like to give a quick honorable mention to the ones that I have not yet mentioned: Pomona Elementary, Victoria Elementary, Wilson Elementary, Sonora Elementary, Newport Elementary, Back Bay/Monte Vista High School, and Estancia High School. The remaining schools (which I hope to go to someday, either as a substitute or speaker/juggler) are the following: Newport Coast Elementary, Woodland Elementary, and Early College High School.

As of now, my current chapter is substituting throughout the 2023-2024 academic year as I complete my Master of Arts Degree in Education, as well as juggling and speaking, hopefully at every school (public and private) and church in this county and beyond—all as a volunteer.

In June 2023, I applied and soon started to be a math tutor at a local Mathnasium. Afterward, I hope to get a career as a middle school math teacher (*hopefully at Ensign Intermediate, if available*), starting within the next few years. Time will tell.

Substituting has been a rewarding joy. Again, I have produced several videos for YouTube and still plan to continue my series, telling several more stories and more details (past and future) than what could fit inside this book.

My hope is that this book, my videos, and all my interviews in the media will simply encourage and motivate everybody, especially those with disabilities and those who aspire to be a teacher. Anybody can do whatever they set their heart and mind to do, disability or not. If I can do it, then certainly, you can too, plus more. It takes perseverance and hard work, but the reward is great at the end.

I still have to accept my limitations with Autism, but nevertheless, I will never allow such hardships to win. They will never make me give up in doing whatever I set my heart toward, including becoming a teacher.

About the Author

MATTHEW KENSLOW has grown up with Autism Spectrum Disorder. As a result, life has been filled with adventure and struggle. Not allowing Autism to stop him, he became an author and is telling the world what it is like living with a disability, how people can be friends to them, and how everybody has a purpose despite having a disability.

Matthew has appeared on television, radio, and podcasts around the world, being featured in *Newsweek* Magazine, *Spectrum News*, ABC7 Los Angeles, and many more. Today, over a million people follow his story on social media, motivating the world to embrace the unique talents that they have to share with others, and that anybody can do whatever they set their heart and mind to do, disability or not.

Printed in the USA
CPSIA information can be obtained
at www.ICGtesting.com
CBHW051311101124
17125CB00002B/3

9 781956 365580